Puro Conjunto

COLECCIÓN CULTURA

This is the first volume in the Colección Cultura series, from CMAS Books. Intended for the general public, the series will present nonfiction books exploring the many facets of Mexican American culture.

Puro Conjunto
An Album in Words and Pictures

*Writings, Posters, and Photographs
from the
Tejano Conjunto Festival
en San Antonio,
1982–1998*

Edited by

JUAN TEJEDA

&

AVELARDO VALDEZ

CMAS Books
Center for Mexican American Studies
University of Texas at Austin

Guadalupe Cultural Arts Center
San Antonio, Texas

A CMAS BOOK

Editor: Víctor Guerra
Assistant Editor: Martha Vogel

Copyright © 2001 by the Center for Mexican American Studies, University of Texas at Austin, and the Guadalupe Cultural Arts Center, San Antonio, Texas. All rights reserved. Distributed by arrangement with University of Texas Press.

Photographs © 2001 by Al Rendón.

The publication of this book was made possible in part by a major grant from the Lila Wallace–Reader's Digest Program for Exemplary Community Arts Centers, and by additional support from the Lila Wallace–Reader's Digest Community Folklife Program through the Fund for Folk Culture and Texas Folklife Resources.

Library of Congress Cataloging-in-Publication Data

Tejano Conjunto Festival en San Antonio.
    Puro conjunto : an album in words and pictures : writings, posters, and photographs from the Tejano Conjunto Festival en San Antonio, 1982–1998 / edited by Juan Tejeda and Avelardo Valdez.
        p. cm. — (Colección cultura)
    Consists principally of essays and interviews taken from the festival program-magazine.
    Includes the Spanish transcriptions of interviews.
    Contents: Conjunto : a primer — Raíz y tradición : conjunto-music history — Instrumentos : accordion, bajo sexto, saxophone — Imágenes del festival : posters and photographs — Contexto : cultural and social aspects of conjunto — Platicando con los grandes : interviews with conjunto legends — Visiones de conjunto : personal histories, poems, and short stories.
    ISBN 0-292-78174-1 (hardcover : alk. paper)
    ISBN 0-292-78172-5 (paperback : alk. paper)
    1. Conjunto music—History and criticism. 2. Mexican Americans—Music—History and criticism. 3. Tejano Conjunto Festival en San Antonio. I. Tejeda, Juan, 1953– II. Valdez, Avelardo, 1947– III. Title. IV. Colección cultura (Austin, Tex.)
ML3481.T45 2001
781.62'68720764—dc21   00-023678

♻ ∞ This book is printed on recycled, acid-free paper that conforms to the American National Standard of permanence for printed library materials, as approved by the American National Standards Institute.

Printed and bound in the United States of America.

First edition. First impression, May 2001.

En memoria de
Valerio Longoria
1924–2000

And for all
the conjunto greats
who came before,
nuestras raíces

Contents

Acknowledgments — xi

Introduction — xiii
Juan Tejeda

PART ONE
Conjunto: A Primer

1. The Unofficial Conjunto Primer for the Uninitiated Music Lover — 3
   Carlos Guerra

PART TWO
Raíz y Tradición: Conjunto-Music History

2. The Emergence of Conjunto Music, 1935–1955 — 13
   Manuel Peña
3. From *Ranchero* to *Jaitón*: Ethnicity and Class in Texas-Mexican Music — 31
   Manuel Peña
4. Conjunto Music: The First Fifty Years — 61
   Manuel Peña
5. The Accordion on Both Sides of the Border — 71
   Carlos Jesús Gómez Flores

6. Three of the Greatest *Bajo Sexto* Players
   in the History of Conjunto   81
   Ramón Hernández, Jr.
7. Women in Conjunto Music   85
   Ramiro Burr
8. El Conjunto Bernal: Style and Legacy   97
   Max Martínez
9. The Tejano Conjunto Festival en San Antonio:
   Eight Years of Change   107
   Carmen Luévanos

PART THREE

Instrumentos: Accordion, Bajo Sexto, Saxophone

10. Accordion Menace . . . Just Say Mo'!   115
    Carlos Guerra
11. The Accordion: Passion, Emotion, Musicianship   121
    Ramiro Burr
12. An Informal History of the *Bajo Sexto*   127
    Ramón Hernández, Jr.
13. Macías: The Stradivarius of *Bajo Sextos*   131
    Ron Young
14. *El Saxofón* in Tejano and *Norteño* Music   135
    José B. Cuéllar

PART FOUR

Imágenes del Festival: Posters and Photographs

   Posters: various artists ◆ Photos: Al Rendón   157

PART FIVE

Contexto: Cultural and Social Aspects of Conjunto

15. Tejano Music as an Expression of Cultural Nationalism   191
    José R. Reyna
16. The Popular in *Conjunto Tejano* Music: Changes in
    Chicano Class and Identity   199
    Avelardo Valdez & Jeffrey A. Halley

17. La Voz del Pueblo Tejano: Conjunto Music and the
    Construction of *Tejano* Identity in Texas   211
    Cathy Ragland
18. Why Are There So Few Women Conjunto Artists?   229
    Avelardo Valdez & Jeffrey A. Halley
19. El Baile: Culture and Contradiction in Mexican
    American Dancing   241
    José E. Limón

PART SIX
**Platicando con los Grandes: Interviews with
Conjunto Legends**
*(original Spanish interviews followed
by English translations)*

20. Santiago Jiménez, Sr.   255
    Juan Tejeda
21. Valerio Longoria   279
    Max Martínez
22. Eva Ybarra   295
    Juan Tejeda
23. Bruno Villarreal   301
    Clayton T. Shorkey
24. ¡Conjunto! Estilo y Clase: Narciso Martínez,
    Valerio Longoria, Tony de la Rosa, Paulino Bernal,
    Flaco Jiménez y Esteban Jordán   315
    Juan Tejeda

PART SEVEN
**Visiones de Conjunto: Personal Histories, Poems,
and Short Stories**

25. Confessions of an Accordion Abuser   355
    Ismael Dovalina
26. An Odyssey through the Magical Land of
    Conjunto, El Movimiento Xicano, and the
    Tejano Conjunto Festival   359
    Juan Tejeda

27. Un Recuerdo a Valerio   379
    Lonnie Guerrero
28. Esteban   381
    Edén Torres
29. Steve Jordan   383
    Jerry Tumlinson
30. Conjunto at Night   385
    Frances Yturri
31. El Baile Grande   387
    José Flores Peregrino
32. Body by Fisher   389
    Joe Saldívar
33. Conjunto Memories   403
    Susana Nevárez Morton

About the Contributors   409

Index   419

Acknowledgments

We extend our *más sinceras gracias* to the following people and institutions:

The Lila Wallace–Reader's Digest Fund, the Fund for Folk Culture, and Texas Folklife Resources, for their support in the publication of this book.

José Luis Benavides and Estevan Azcona—associates of the Center for Mexican American Studies, University of Texas at Austin—for lending their expertise to the copyediting. The artist Luis Guerra, for his insights on the cover and book design. And Theresa May and David Cavazos, of University of Texas Press, for their advice at several junctures in the publication process.

The University of Texas at San Antonio's Hispanic Research Center and Center for Drug and Social Policy Research and their staff—in particular, research assistants Evelio Escamilla, Lilian Huerta, and Katherine Vela-Orozco—for their help in the preparation and review of the manuscript.

The staff of the Guadalupe Cultural Arts Center, especially David Mercado Gonzales and Rudy "Diamond" García, who since the very beginning have worked long hours producing the yearly Tejano Conjunto Festival *Tonantzin*. And the hundreds of volunteers who have given generously of their time, year after year, to help make the festival a success.

And, finally, the countless musicians, recording companies, radio stations, promoters, and fans, who have kept conjunto music alive.

Introduction

JUAN TEJEDA

The legendary conjunto accordionist Tony de la Rosa was onstage at Rosedale Park. It was Sunday, May 24, 1982, and his conjunto was the last of seventeen groups to perform that weekend at the first Tejano Conjunto Festival en San Antonio. De la Rosa had already played a couple of songs when, amid the applause and *gritos* of thousands of adoring fans who crowded onto the dance floor and around the stage, he stepped up to the microphone and spoke:

> Bueno, como ya saben que pocas veces hablamos por micrófono, pero qué bonito es estar con los profesores, y yo que fui discípulo, estar viviendo y estar en el mismo foro que ellos, como Valerio Longoria, Narciso Martínez [*applause*], don Pedro Ayala, los pioneros de la música, onda regional, don Santiago Jiménez, todos los muchachos. Estoy seguro que todos ellos se sienten tan jóvenes como yo. No le hace qué edad tengan, pero el corazón es el que manda, y es bonito, es lo más bonito. Y yo, como ellos también son conocidos por las polcas, yo también tengo algunas que ustedes vinieron a conocer y [*applause*] . . . gracias . . . también nos aceptaron con eso. Y traemos otras cositas que orita también se las vamos a tocar, pero yo no pude venir a una cosa de estas y saber que todos los demás tocaron sus polquitas, y yo no tocar las mías.[1]

That said, he adjusted the straps on his red, three-row Hohner button accordion and squeezed out the piercing first notes of "Atotonilco," one of the classic instrumental polkas that, since the 1950s, have defined his unique staccato style. *La raza* exploded with more *gritos* and applause as the bass, *bajo sexto,* and drums jumped in on cue to provide the rhythmic accompaniment to de la Rosa's accordion lead.

In front of the stage a crowd of people stood, concert-style, some tapping their feet to the driving polka beat, while several women raised their arms and moved back and forth in time with the music. Two men lifted their beers to salute de la Rosa as they yelled out their approval. Lovers held each other round waist and shoulder, swaying from side to side.

The pavilion's concrete dance floor was filled with Chicano men and women gliding and shuffling to the rhythmic one-two *compás de la polca*. Couples in cowboy hats and blue jeans twirled, spinning into and away from each other's arms. *Chucos* strutting their *tanditos* and Stacys clung tight to their *rucas* as they executed the stylized steps of *el tacuachito* and *el serruchito*. Older couples moved in harmony, holding each other in respectable, upright, stoic embraces. Children danced with their mother or father and sometimes, if they were very young, were cradled in their parent's arms. And little girls danced together joyfully, as they imitated the grown-ups on the floor. At the tables alongside the dance floor *compadres* sat, listening to the music or talking and drinking, some eating their *tacos de tripitas* and *fajitas con guacamole*. Others stood behind the tables, soaking up the suds and reveling in the music under the stars.

On this dance floor, there were no rich or poor—just a community of people enjoying the *alegría* of conjunto music as they danced, counter-clockwise, in a circle, or listened and swayed to the beat. This festival was a celebration of a music, a people, a culture. It was *la raza* claiming their identity, their rights, their public space. It was sharing. It was sacred. It was the first of many more Tejano Conjunto Festivals to come.

La Música

The music that all these people came to enjoy and celebrate—conjunto music—is one of the two principal types of music created by Texas Chicanos, or Tejanos. The other is *orquesta tejana*. Both types fall under the larger rubric of Tejano music.

Conjunto music will be defined and described in multifaceted detail in the chapters that follow, so for now just a few basic words should suffice. "Conjunto" in Spanish simply means "group," or "ensemble." For Tejanos, however, "conjunto" has come to denote a specific type of musical group, and a specific form of music that combines German, Mexican, Latin American, and U.S. influences. The lead instrument in the traditional four-piece conjunto is the button accordion. The other instruments are the *bajo sexto* (a twelve-string bass-rhythm guitar), bass guitar, and drums. Conjunto music is dance music, and currently its most popular rhythms—enjoyed on the dance floor of the Tejano Conjunto Festival and in clubs and dance halls around the nation—are the polka and the *cumbia*.

El Festival

For eighteen years, from 1980 to 1998, I had the good fortune of working as director of the Xicano Music Program for the Guadalupe Cultural Arts Center in San Antonio, Texas. In that role, I founded the Tejano Conjunto Festival en San Antonio and directed it for seventeen years, until my departure from the center. Avelardo Valdez, the other editor of this volume, also has a long history with the festival and the Guadalupe Cultural Arts Center, having served on the board in various capacities over the last twenty years, including two years as chairperson.

The Guadalupe Cultural Arts Center was established in 1980, as a nonprofit, *barrio*-based organization. It is dedicated to the preservation, promotion, and presentation of Chicano, Latino, and American Indian arts and culture. Now one of the largest and most diverse organizations of its type in the United States, it offers programs and classes in music, literature, visual arts, theater, dance, and media arts. Among the annual events and festivals produced by the center, the Tejano Conjunto Festival stands out, especially in terms of the size and scope of its activities.

Since its inception, the Tejano Conjunto Festival has played a major role in sustaining and cultivating that original genre of Chicano music known as conjunto. It has showcased the best in conjunto music, from the traditional, to the popular, to the progressive. It has honored those artists who pioneered this genre and have made key contributions to its development. And it has nurtured a deeper understanding and appreciation of Chicano music and culture. Indeed, the festival has been credited with contributing to the revitalization of conjunto's popularity that took place during the late eighties and early nineties, and with broadening its audience base, taking it beyond the *barrios* and the *pueblos* of South Texas and onto a world stage.

The Guadalupe staff achieved these results by carefully crafting the festival's program of performances, as well as by developing a range of complementary events and projects. We founded the Conjunto Music Hall of Fame, which honors the tradition bearers as well as the innovators of conjunto. We initiated classes in button accordion and *bajo sexto* that are offered to the community, along with conjunto student recitals. We established an annual poster contest, whose winning entry becomes the official poster for that year's festival. And we created a program-magazine that, in addition to the festival's schedule of events, contains essays and stories on conjunto music and interviews with conjunto artists. Since 1984, the festival program-magazine has appeared as a special annual issue of the Guadalupe Cultural Arts Center's magazine, *Tonantzin*. We also began documenting the festival in various formats—audiotape, videotape, and photographs—for historical, public-relations, and commercial purposes.

Thanks to the success of these various programs and ventures, over the years the Tejano Conjunto Festival evolved into a tradition, a mainstay of the cultural life of the city of San Antonio, which became known as the Capital of Conjunto Music. The festival, which began as a three-day event in 1982, grew to seven days by 1992, tapering slightly to six days thereafter. Some years saw special theme nights such as "Women in Conjunto Music," "Conjunto Meets Cajun/Zydeco," "Conjunto in Film and Video," "Raíces Mexicanas," and "New Directions in Conjunto Music." Between 1982 and 1998, thirty-two individuals were inducted into the Conjunto Music Hall of Fame, and more than one thousand students enrolled in the accordion and *bajo sexto* classes. Over 150 different bands performed at the festival, with many returning for repeat performances. They included all the legendary local and Texas groups as well as conjuntos from elsewhere in the Southwest, from the Midwest, and from Mexico—and even one, Los Gatos, from Japan. And every year thousands of people flocked to the festival from all over Texas and the United States, with international visitors arriving from Mexico, France, Italy, Japan, Germany, Australia, Brazil, and other countries.[2]

El Libro

Like the Tejano Conjunto Festival, this book, *Puro Conjunto, An Album in Words and Pictures*,[3] celebrates conjunto music. Exploring the music from a wide variety of vantage points, it provides a panoramic portrait of this vital popular art form. It offers seventeen years' worth of writings on conjunto and a special commemorative portfolio of posters and photographs.

Prior to the festival's inception, only a handful of writers had taken up the subject of conjunto music, and consequently very little had been published on it. Even today, other than the present volume there are only three books dealing extensively or substantially with conjunto.[4] This collection should thus serve as a valuable resource for students of Chicano music and culture.

All the writings in the collection originally appeared in the festival's *Tonantzin* in the years 1982 through 1998. There are thirty-three pieces, diverse in genre. They include scholarly essays, popular accounts, interviews, personal histories, poetry, and short stories. Twenty-four authors are represented, among them some of the most renowned Tejano-music scholars and journalists. Most of the articles were commissioned specifically for *Tonantzin*. Few have been published elsewhere.

The book has been organized thematically rather than chronologically (according to the years in which the articles were published). It is important, however, to keep in mind when these pieces first appeared, because they contain specific temporal references—to the conjunto festival, to certain individuals, some of whom have since died, and to occasions and places. For this reason, the year of publication is included on the title page of each chapter.

Because the writings were previously published, they underwent only minimal editing for this book.[5] The titles of a few articles were altered slightly, primarily for concision.

The portfolio contains color reproductions of seventeen Tejano Conjunto Festival posters along with twenty-two black-and-white festival photographs. The photos are all by native *sanantoniano* Al Rendón, who has photographed the festival throughout much of its history. The posters, representing the first seventeen years of the festival, are the official posters for each year, selected by means of a juried contest. Three artists won the contest twice, so there are fourteen artists represented here. They are a widely diverse group, especially in terms of art background and style, and include commercial artists and both self-taught and academically trained fine artists.

THE SEVEN PARTS

Part One. Part 1, which consists of one article, provides a basic introduction to conjunto music. In this "primer," the San Antonio columnist Carlos Guerra describes the beginnings of conjunto in the late nineteenth and early twentieth centuries among poor *mexicanos* in rural South Texas. He also discusses the subsequent development of this highly danceable form of music, giving special emphasis to the instrumentation of the traditional, four-piece conjunto ensemble.

Part Two. The eight articles in part 2 explore conjunto history from a variety of perspectives. Manuel Peña, the foremost scholar of Tejano music, contributes three essays. In the first one, he discusses the emergence of conjunto music among the working-class Texas-Mexican people during the 1920s and 1930s. Peña traces the stylistic development and maturation of this music through the 1960s, examining the contributions of such influential performers as Narciso Martínez, Santiago Jiménez, Sr., and Paulino Bernal. He focuses on the sociosymbolic significance of conjunto music for working-class Texas-Mexicans in relation to both Anglo domination and the emerging Mexican American middle class.

Peña's second article examines the relationship between conjunto and *orquesta tejana* during the period 1935–1965. Peña demonstrates how both forms, in a "remarkable accident of history," came into their own at the same time. He also explores the dynamics that sustain these twin forms, considering them in terms of working class versus middle class, ethnic resistance versus cultural assimilation, *ranchero* versus *jaitón*.

In his third essay, Peña surveys the first fifty years (1936–1986) of conjunto music, recapitulating the significant contributions of the key figures in the genre. He concludes that since the late sixties conjunto music has maintained a conservative, stable course without any major innovations. And that in spite of commercialization and the onslaught of "pop" music, conjunto music "continues to provide the *tejano* working class not only with a satisfying vehicle for esthetic expression, but also with a powerful source of self-identity and cultural reaffirmation."

Part 2 continues with the Mexican writer Carlos Gómez Flores, who takes a look at the historical development of *música norteña* (conjunto's cousin, the accordion-based music of northern Mexico) and *conjunto tejano*. He offers a comparison of accordion styles on both sides of the border and quotes from interviews with such *norteño* notables as Juan Torres, the accordionist from Los Tremendos Gavilanes, and Javier Ríos, from Los Invasores de Nuevo León.

The next four articles in part 2 address an assortment of conjunto-history topics. The music writer Ramón Hernández goes in search of three of the best *bajo sexto* players in the history of conjunto music: Santiago Almeida, Reynaldo Barrera, and Eloy Bernal. The article by Ramiro Burr, music writer with the *San Antonio Express-News,* provides an overview of women in conjunto music beginning with Lydia Mendoza, Carmen y Laura, and Chelo Silva, and ending with Chavela, Lupita Rodela, Eva Ybarra, and Laura Canales. Burr briefly explores the reasons for the scarcity of women in conjunto music. In the following article, the San Antonio novelist Max Martínez traces the development of one of the greatest conjuntos in the history of Tejano music: El Conjunto Bernal. The last article in part 2—by Carmen Luévanos, a graduate student at the time—poses the provocative question, Did the Tejano Conjunto Festival start out as a celebration for Chicano people and end up being for the tourists?

Part Three. Part 3 focuses on the two principal instruments in the conjunto ensemble—accordion and *bajo sexto*—and also on the saxophone, which has played a peripheral albeit interesting and increasingly important role in the modern, progressive-style conjunto.

In the section's first article, Carlos Guerra informs us that the accordion was invented by Friedrich Buschmann in 1822 in Berlin, and then apparently reinvented the following year by Cyril Demian in Vienna. Guerra goes on to trace the accordion's evolution and discuss some of the different types in existence. Ramiro Burr follows with a look at the accordion and its importance in the world-music scene. He also examines its growing presence in U.S. popular music. What explains the accordion's recent comeback? he asks.

For him the answer is simple: in the age of high tech, it's an acoustic instrument that produces earthy sounds and makes the kind of "real" music that people are craving.

The *bajo sexto* is the subject of the next two articles. Ramón Hernández provides us with a brief account of the origins of this twelve-string, bass-rhythm guitar, and also discusses its tuning. In addition, he explores the *bajo sexto*'s uniqueness and its incorporation into the conjunto ensemble as the principal companion instrument to the accordion. The article by Ron Young, a music journalist and songwriter, focuses on Martín Macías, master craftsman and specialist in handmade *bajo sextos* and guitars, and the legacy that he left his sons Alberto and Luis.

Part 3 ends with a groundbreaking essay by José Cuéllar, a San Francisco–based scholar, activist, and musician. His article chronicles the introduction and development of the saxophone in the kin traditions of Tejano and *norteño* music. He examines the life and music of various saxophonists on both sides of the border, contrasting their distinctive styles of playing. Cuéllar concludes that the saxophone has become integral to the sound of contemporary *norteño* and Tejano groups.

Part Four. Part 4, the portfolio of posters and photographs, serves as a centerpiece, and visual counterpoint. Most of the photographs depict major conjunto figures—such as Narciso Martínez, Valerio Longoria, Tony de la Rosa, Esteban Jordán, and Eva Ybarra—performing live at the Tejano Conjunto Festival. Other photos capture different aspects of the festival, such as Lydia Mendoza accepting her Conjunto Music Hall of Fame award, Flaco Jiménez signing an autograph for a fan, and a couple dancing in the *chuco serrucho* style. All the photographs were shot at the festival except for three: Valerio Longoria's accordion class at the Harlandale Civic Center, Toby Torres's *bajo sexto* class at Toby's Custom Recording Studio, and Santiago Jiménez, Jr., performing at a student recital at the Guadalupe Theater.

The posters' colorful images represent conjunto music and the Tejano Conjunto Festival in ways that words could never do. The poster from 1983, for example, depicts a typical restaurant "table-top-scape" complete with salt and pepper shakers, *pico de gallo* and *salsa* dispensers, and a cold glass of beer. Above the table is an old-style jukebox selector listing songs by conjunto artists. You can almost hear the music as it pulsates from the small speakers. The poster from 1985 portrays the conjunto pioneer Don Santiago Jiménez, Sr., playing his two-row button accordion as he looms like a saint over the San Antonio skyline. In contrast, the central figure in the 1988 poster is a Chicano man who plays a double-sided accordion. Sporting a golden *guayabera* and dark gray pants, he also has chicken feet! He is the devil that is said to appear at *bailes* all over South Texas.[6] All of these posters are classics. They eloquently convey the spirit and texture of conjunto music and the culture that gave birth to it.

Part Five. Part 5 addresses the cultural and social aspects of conjunto. In the first article the scholar José Reyna explores Tejano music as a major source of cultural identity and pride for Tejanos—which in turn, he argues, explains the music's survival and growth. In the following article, the sociologists Avelardo Valdez and Jeffrey Halley demonstrate that the increased popularity of conjunto during the 1980s—and of Tejano music, in general—is linked to changes in Chicano class formation and cultural identity. The authors describe how different "scenes" such as clubs and festivals attract people from different social classes. Chicano music is a hybrid, just like the Chicano people. Thus it expresses a reconciliation of diversity and class distinctions that affirms ethnic identity. The ethnomusicologist Cathy Ragland also explores the complex relationship between Tejano music and social identity. In addition, her article offers an analysis of how this music must compete as a commodity in the popular-music industry.

In the next article, Avelardo Valdez and Jeffrey Halley apply their critical perspective to the question of why there are so few women in conjunto music. Is this scarcity due to the *machismo* of the Chicano culture? they ask. Or does it reflect relations in general between men and women in the music world and in the larger culture? Valdez and Halley contend that it involves a combination of both factors. Part 5 concludes with an essay by the noted anthropologist José Limón, who takes us on an ethnographic excursion in search of that devil figure—*güero*, good looking, and debonair—who has been spotted at Chicano dance halls throughout South Texas.

Part Six. In part 6, "Platicando con los Grandes: Interviews with Conjunto Legends," we hear from the musicians themselves. The first four chapters contain one-of-a-kind interviews with Santiago Jiménez, Sr., Valerio Longoria, Eva Ybarra, and Bruno Villarreal that provide valuable insights into the lives and music of these important conjunto accordionists and tradition bearers. The last chapter in part 6, "¡Conjunto! Estilo y Clase," presents edited interviews with six major accordionists: Narciso Martínez, Valerio Longoria (again), Tony de la Rosa, Paulino Bernal, Flaco Jiménez, and Esteban Jordán. In this set of interviews, the goal was to have these conjunto artists talk about their views on style: whether they felt that distinctive styles had developed within conjunto, what characterized these styles, and who the major stylists were. All of the interviews are presented in the original Spanish and followed by English translations, done specifically for this book.[7]

Part Seven. Part 7, which ends the book, consists of two personal histories, five poems, and two short stories, in that order. In the opening essay, Ismael Dovalina traces his affinity for conjunto music, recounting how he came to take accordion classes with Santiago Jiménez, Jr., and describing the discoveries he made as a beginning accordionist. In the second essay, I explore the path that took me from my culturally discordant childhood and adolescence in San Antonio, to my involvement in the Chicano Movement and my work with the Guadalupe Cultural Arts Center and the Tejano Conjunto Festival.

Of the five poems included in this section, two are *homenajes* to Esteban Jordán, *el mago del acordeón*. Edén Torres and Jerry Tumlinson evoke the spirit and style of Jordán and his music in their poetic tributes. Lonnie Guerrero's *canción*-style poem petitions Valerio Longoria for a job with his conjunto. Frances Yturri depicts the sultry magic of conjunto music on a hot summer night. And José Flores Peregrino takes us to "El Baile Grande," where one can see, hear, and feel the musicians, the music, and the dancers as they unite in the celebratory ritual of the big dance.

Part 7 concludes with two short stories. Joe Saldívar's "Body by Fisher" is a classic tale of *barrio* life set in the West Side of San Antonio. Excitement and tension mount as a special group of *camaradas* prepare to attend a wedding dance, where Mingo Saldívar y sus Tremendos Cuatro Espadas will be playing.[8] Finally, Susana Nevárez Morton's "Conjunto Memories" tells the story of a teenage girl who asks her mother to show her how to dance. Her mother complies by teaching her how to dance to conjunto music. In the process, the daughter learns not only about her heritage, her mother, and herself, but also about the father she had never known.

As Tony de la Rosa says, "el corazón es el que manda, y es bonito, es lo más bonito." Conjunto music springs from the very heart and soul of the Chicano people. We hope that this book will in some measure convey its breadth, depth, and beauty.

Notes

1. *English translation:* Well, as you already know that I rarely speak over the microphone, but it's so good to be with the teachers, and I who was a pupil, to be living and to be on the same stage with them, such as Valerio Longoria, Narciso Martínez [*applause*], Don Pedro Ayala, the pioneers of the music, the *regional* style, Don Santiago Jiménez, all the guys. I'm sure that all of them feel as young as I do. It doesn't matter how old they are, but it's the heart that rules, and that's beautiful, that's the most beautiful thing. And I, like they too are known for their polkas, I also have some that you have come to know and [*applause*] . . . thank you . . . you also accepted us for that. And we've got a few other little things that we're going to play for you right now, but I couldn't come to one of these things and know that everyone else played their polkas, and I not play my own.

2. My essay in this book, "An Odyssey through the Magical Land of Conjunto, El Movimiento Xicano, and the Tejano Conjunto Festival" (chapter 26), provides an account of the founding of the Guadalupe Cultural Arts Center as well as a more detailed history and personal impressions of the Tejano Conjunto Festival. Another article in this book, Carmen Luévanos's "The Tejano Conjunto Festival en San Antonio: Eight Years of Change" (chapter 9), includes a review of the early development of the festival.

3. The book, whose full title is *Puro Conjunto, An Album in Words and Pictures: Writings, Posters, and Photographs from the Tejano Conjunto Festival en San Antonio, 1982–1998*, is a collaborative publication of the Guadalupe Cultural Arts Center and the Center for Mexican American Studies of the University of Texas at Austin. It is the first joint project of its type for both centers. For the Center for Mexican American Studies' press—CMAS Books—it also inaugurates a new series, Colección Cultura, marking a departure from strictly scholarly publications.

4. I am referring to Manuel Peña's trilogy: *The Texas-Mexican Conjunto: History of a Working-Class Music* (University of Texas Press, 1985), *The Mexican American Orquesta: Music, Culture, and the Dialectic of Conflict* (University of Texas Press, 1999), and *Música Tejana: The Cultural Economy of Artistic Transformation* (Texas A&M University Press, 1999). While *The Mexican American Orquesta* focuses primarily on the evolution of the *orquesta*, conjunto music plays a pivotal role in Peña's analysis. I should also mention the reference work by Ramiro Burr: *The Billboard Guide to Tejano and Regional Mexican Music* (Billboard Books, 1999).

5. The reader might notice, for example, that a word such as "Tejano" is treated as an English word in some articles and as a Spanish word, *tejano*, in others. This was done to allow each article to retain its original style.

6. José Limón investigates this *diablo* phenomenon in his essay in this book (chapter 19). The poster and the essay coincidentally both appeared in connection with the same festival. Limón's essay had already been accepted for publication in the 1988 festival *Tonantzin* when this poster by Douglas Jasso was selected, by a jury that at the time was not aware of Limón's submission.

7. It should be noted that the interviewees' statements were transcribed verbatim, so as to faithfully represent their actual speech, including regional expressions and pronunciations. Sometimes, rendering pronunciation accurately required the use of unconventional spelling. Deserving special mention in this regard is the case of the word *ahí*, which in South Texas and Mexico is often pronounced like the English "I" rather than "ah-*ee*." Following Américo Paredes's usage in his ethnographic transcriptions, this pronunciation has been rendered as *ahi*, without the accent.

8. It is interesting to know that Joe Saldívar is writing from experience here. Mingo is his brother.

Puro Conjunto

PART ONE

Conjunto
A Primer

1

The Unofficial Conjunto Primer for the Uninitiated Music Lover

✧

CARLOS GUERRA

1989

It is a music as original as any the United States has ever produced, and, not yet a century old, it has a following substantial enough to support hundreds of full-time musicians, a complete record industry, and a growing number of radio stations. Still, conjunto music, with an occasional exception, remains a secret to all but the people it emerged from, the same people who support it today.

Suddenly, though, conjunto music is being discovered by vast numbers of people. The better-known musicians are drawing big crowds in major European venues and Chicano record distributors are getting large orders from several countries in Europe and from Japan.

What's going on?

It's simple. Hollywood, Nashville, and even the Smithsonian have discovered it and spread the word. Many Americans are finding that "Lady of Spain" isn't the only melody accordions can produce. They've discovered that the squeeze box is the source of wondrous sounds, played in rhythms which—like the accordion itself—they always thought were corny. Furthermore, they are finding that unlike so much of the new music of today, which is digital and computer-generated, this is a music richly expressive and infectious.

This primer is the Tejano Conjunto Festival's welcome for new fans. We hope new conjunto lovers will find the beauty of this treasure.

It is a happy and boisterous music made primarily for dancing. Spanish lyrics revolve around German accordion sounds to pulsating rhythms provided by modern basses and drums. *El conjunto* emerged from the same meld of *mexicanos* and German immigrants who co-existed in southern Texas in the early twentieth century.

It remains today largely the music of *los mexicanos,* but there is more than the mixing of cultural influences that makes it different. Conjunto music originated as the music of the lower class in a time and in a society that allowed for little upward mobility and even less mixing of its social classes. And it has remained just that, with no apologies.

Origins

Texas in the late nineteenth century was rough and inhospitable. Mexicans remained culturally separate, because, unlike with the non-*mexicanos,* there existed well-developed social institutions that supported their *mexicanismo*. Contact with Mexico was frequent since Mexico was geographically closer and friendlier to them than was the United States.

Mexico, like most of the Western world, was swept by a wave of popular music, essentially salon music, or *música de baile,* that included polkas from Germany and Poland, waltzes of the famous Austrian composers, redowas and schottisches, occasional quadrilles, and even minuets. These forms were easily absorbed by the already musically inclined Mexican culture and the process of Mexicanizing them began immediately. The *huapango* (Huasteca in origin) and the *canción ranchera* were modified into the hodgepodge of this *música de baile*.

The turn-of-the-century Mexican society had a rigid two-class system. *Mexicanos* were either *gente decente* or *gente pobre* (decent people or poor folk) and most were *gente pobre*. Mexico's popular music at the turn of the century was usually made by *orquestas típicas,* which were ensembles of strings, horns, and voices. There were many of these local groups in Mexico, and Texas too.

The accordion, introduced into Mexican culture by the Germans around the last half of the nineteenth century, had a significant and lasting impact. The poor rural Tejanos took to it quickly since it could mimic several instruments simultaneously and it was cheaper to pay one *acordeonista* than an *orquesta*. The diatonic accordion had the capacity to produce both melody and bass parts, and the tuning and button arrangements are such that when two adjacent buttons are played together, they usually produce a third interval, the basic harmony of Mexican vocals.

The accordion was first played solo or with a *tambora de rancho,* apparently some sort of homemade drum. Other instruments—violins, various woodwinds, and guitars—were occasionally teamed with the accordion, but the classic match was yet to come.

The conjunto was born when the *bajo sexto* was added for rhythmic bass-guitar accompaniment. This reed-and-string duet arrangement quickly became the popular music form for dances, a basic entertainment form of the lower class. Tejano *orquestas típicas* continued to be popular, but they remained the preferred music of the *gente decente* (or "*los* high society," as they were then called) and the conjunto became the choice of the poor folk.

Development

The pairing of the solo *acordeón* and the *bajo sexto* at the turn of the century created a core sound of conjunto which still exists today. The bass fiddle was introduced soon after, and there were early experiments with saxophones. The invention of the gramophone created a group of consumers hungry for records of their own music. Conjunto filled that need.

The first conjunto recordings were made by the major record companies, and the recording and distribution continued until World War II, when shortages of needed materials brought the industry to a standstill. After the war, the majors dropped conjunto music and moved their recording operations to Mexico. This left a large market unserved.

Chicano entrepreneurs jumped into the business, recording in living rooms and garages and pressing their own records in small numbers. The Chicano record industry developed with limited resources and remains geared for small runs even today. Forced by economic factors to keep costs down, these recording companies developed low-cost methods of producing their products. Often, this meant one-take recording sessions and doing without the most sophisticated recording technology. Success was difficult for those indigenous record producers. They were selling to only a part of the market, *mexicanos,* and they were among the poorest people of the country.

If on the one hand this resulted in recordings of relatively inferior technical quality, on the other hand it also encouraged the recording of music in great variety and production in small quantities. Now, few mainstream recording artists can claim more than a handful of albums. For the older conjuntos, however, twenty LPs is not an unusual number, and some have so many singles in their discographies that they have lost count. Several have over a hundred albums to their credit.

The music developed social institutions as well. The *bailes*, originally festive events, eventually spawned the commercial *bailes grandes* that charged admission at the gate. Other entertainment forms, especially nightclubs, remained underdeveloped in Texas until liquor by the drink was legalized. Like country and western, conjunto music developed a substantial culture around large dances and dance halls.

After World War II, conjunto music came into its own. Fortunately, many legal barriers of segregation were relaxed for Mexican Americans. Nevertheless, separate Anglo, Black, and Mexican societies continued to be a reality. The returning Mexican American soldiers set off an important population shift of *mexicanos* to the cities. This urbanization crowded large numbers of rural people in strange and often hostile environments. Conjunto became a unifying force that provided familiarity in the new urban area. By the fifties the popularity of conjunto music was so great that even some *orquestas* began including accordionists in their lineups.

Now being played in large halls instead of intimate surroundings, conjunto adjusted accordingly. Drums and electric basses replaced the stand-up bass in the standard conjunto and P.A. systems replaced *el puro pulmón* (sheer lung power). And there were other developments, as well. The drums settled and slowed the tempo of the music, making it possible for accordionists to concentrate on the more complex finger work which today distinguishes conjunto music. Returning soldiers brought with them influences they'd absorbed from their contact with mainstream America. The new U.S. dance styles crept into the *bailes*.

Polkas, *chotís*, *redovas*, and *huapangos* continued to be played, but the polka began to evolve away from its Germanic origins and into the distinctly Chicano product we have today. The essentially European dance-floor stylings of the past were replaced by a smoother, gliding dance form, *el tacuachito*.

El tacuachito has now become very localized, and touring musicians play to local preferences of tempo (*el compás*), to suit the local dance styles. A purer form of *el tacuachito* is still found among many of the older dancers of the Rio Grande Valley. Smooth, gliding, and very stylized dancing is found in the areas around Alice, Robstown, and Corpus Christi, and rhythms other than polkas are quite popular. San Antonio styles often include stylized side movements sometimes called *el serruchito* (the saw). West Texas *bailadores* move more rigidly, with stiffer movements, or *el tiezo* (stiff). The Lubbock area prefers a fast, racing style with a quicker tempo, *bien corridón* (very rushed). Dancers are admired for their natural fluidity, and it is an expression which is often as entertaining for the spectator as for the participant.

The Basic Conjunto

The basic conjunto is now an ensemble of accordion, *bajo sexto,* bass, and drums. Perhaps in recognition of its diverse origins, the conjunto world seems to encourage diversity and growth. The basic quartets are traditional, but many conjuntos also include a wide variety of added elements, from saxes to synthesizers.

ACCORDION

The accordion is the lead melody instrument. The accordion of today is a modified version of the first one, invented in 1822 in Germany. Of the three basic types of accordions, diatonic, piano, and chromatic, most *acordeonistas* prefer the diatonic, which, like a harmonica, produces one note when the bellows are pulled and another when they are closed. The treble or melody is on the right side, the bass is on the left, and the notes are produced by forcing air through multiple reeds.

Diatonic accordions vary widely, but conjunto players usually prefer the three-row Vienna-style accordions, usually German made, though some opt for the more expensive Italian brands of diatonic accordions, the piano accordions, or the full five-row chromatic accordions. Vienna-style accordions, also called Italian-style, have one to three rows of treble buttons on the right side, each row being a major scale, and four to ten bass buttons on the left. Since diatonic accordions are limited to major and minor scales with no chromatic variations, they come in various key combinations, the most popular being F-B-E and G-C-F.

Many players retune and occasionally rearrange the reeds, and some remove the bass reeds, which have been all but abandoned by conjunto players who concentrate on the intricate *pasadas,* or runs, on the treble side.

BAJO SEXTO

The *bajo sexto* is the other key element of the conjunto sound. This often underrated twelve-string, guitarlike instrument adds a bass-rhythm and melodic counterplay to the accordion. The *bajo* is tuned an octave below the standard guitar except for the last two strings, which are tuned up a half step. Many of the *bajo sextos* used nationally and in Mexico are made in San Antonio by the Macías family.

Originally acoustic, the *bajo* is now usually amplified. New developments include the *bajo quinto,* which is a ten-string version of the *bajo sexto,* and the replacement of the *bajo sexto* with a standard six-string guitar or, sometimes, the standard twelve-string guitar.

BASS

The electric bass was added to the conjunto in the fifties, giving the conjunto a solid bass line. Previously, some conjuntos used a contrabass, or stand-up bass, but the advent of amplification brought this logical progression. The electric bass is now considered a part of the standard ensemble.

DRUMS

The first accordionists, according to some accounts, often played with a *tambora de rancho,* though there is some question as to what exactly these drums were. But the drum disappeared when the accordion was teamed with the *bajo sexto* and didn't reappear in the conjunto until the late forties and early fifties.

When drums were added to conjuntos in the fifties, they were only used in performances. They were left off recordings because producers considered them too crude and noisy. At first people ridiculed their introduction, but eventually the standard trap set became another basic element.

The Music

People tend to generalize conjunto music as being *música de acordeón,* polka music, *regional, ranchera,* or the like. These generalizations often have just enough truth to make them credible, but each excludes far more than it includes.

Certainly, *la polca* is a big part of the rhythmic underpinnings of conjunto music, but it is far from all of it. Since the beginning, conjuntos have also played waltzes, schottisches, *redovas,* and *huapangos.* The *canción ranchera,* which is now a polka with vocals, has become part of the repertoire, along with the conjunto-ized *boleros, tangos, chachachás,* rock, blues, country, and *cumbias.* The list is still growing.

Creativity and originality are important in the conjunto tradition. A different sound, a different arrangement, a different rhythm, a different anything is expected of each conjunto.

Those who are attending the festival for the first time can expect the very same thing as those who have seen all the performers before. Expect to be surprised!

Note

This article first appeared in the *Tonantzin* program for the Seventh Annual Tejano Conjunto Festival en San Antonio, 1988. The 1989 festival *Tonantzin* carried a revised version, under the title "The Unofficial Conjunto Primer for the Uninitiated Music Lover, Revised." It is the revised version that is reprinted here. —EDITORS

PART TWO

Raíz y Tradición

Conjunto-Music History

2
The Emergence of Conjunto Music, 1935-1955

✧

MANUEL PEÑA
1982

The emergence, in the years between 1935 and 1955, of a highly popular style of Texas-Mexican music known as "conjunto" poses interesting questions for ethnomusicologists. These questions hold significance for other social scientists as well, because, as the ethnomusicologist John Blacking (1974) has suggested, the interpretation of musical activity can serve as a key to understanding other aspects of social organization. Thus, in tracing the development of modern conjunto music from its embryonic appearance in Narciso Martínez's first commercial recording in 1936 to its full-blown stylization by such artists as Paulino Bernal in the mid 1950s, we might well ask two questions.[1] The first is musicological: How can we describe the style of conjunto music? The second question is ethnomusicological: Given that the accordion and the other instruments used in conjunto music have been extant along both sides of the border for at least a hundred years, why did a distinctive, durable, and highly identifiable style of music not reach fruition until after World War II?

It is my purpose in this article to attempt preliminary answers to these questions. I have worked out the ideas presented here on the basis of about a year of ethnomusicological research into this music, as well as some twenty years of performing and hearing it. I should note that the style is sometimes identified with *norteño* music (a form common throughout northern Mexico). However, most *tejanos* prefer the label "conjunto." What differences do exist between northern Mexican and *tejano* accordion music are quite subtle. For example, until recently the saxophone was more commonly identified with Mexican *norteño* groups. I feel, however, that the changes in conjunto music I will be describing (including the first use of the saxophone in a conjunto group) were generally wrought by *tejano* musicians and only then emulated by their Mexican counterparts. In any case, the distinction blurs considerably when we learn that some important Mexican groups, such as Los Alegres de Terán, have set up permanent residence in the United States.

I would also note that the research on which this essay is based has actually focused on a comparative analysis of conjunto music and what is commonly known among Chicanos as *orquesta tejana* music (or simply *orquesta*), another popular style. Together the two forms comprise *música tejana*. I will restrict my comments here to conjunto music, although some references to *orquesta* will be necessary.

The Evolution of Conjunto Style

There are two explanations of how the accordion, the instrument fundamental to conjunto style, was first introduced to the border area. The first posits that European settlers, especially Germans, first brought it to the attention of Chicanos, who quickly adopted it for their use; the other, held by some of the older accordionists such as Pedro Ayala, that it came from Mexico, specifically Monterrey. Neither theory has been conclusively proven, to my knowledge.

In either case, we know that the accordion as a solo instrument was popular by at least the 1890s, particularly among the predominantly poor, rural Mexicans on both sides of the Texas border. An article in the *San Antonio Express* of 1897 mentions an "accordion artist who wends his way through the chaparral." And my own father, who was born in 1895 in the border village of Salineño, Texas, has described for me some of the *bailes de jacal* (usually patio weddings) of the turn of the century, which featured accordion soloists accompanied by what was known as a *tambora de rancho* (ranch drum). Narciso Martínez and Pedro Ayala, two popular accordionists who started their musical careers in the 1920s, corroborate this information. According to them, the one-row button accordion was commonly used in those days at dances, either as a solo instrument or in combination with the *tambora de rancho*. This latter instrument, incidentally, was evidently fashioned out of native (i.e., not store-bought) materials—including its skin of *cuero de chivo* (goat skin), the wooden mallets used to play it, and even the body of the drum itself. Only occasionally were the guitar, *bajo sexto,* or a violin used to accompany the accordion. Thus it is clear that, by the 1890s at least, the accordion had become so popular among the working classes that it had begun to replace other types of music (such as *orquesta típica*) as the *marco musical* (musical frame) for weddings, *bailes de regalos,* and other domestic celebrations.

Certainly, as a solo instrument much in demand from those early days up until the 1920s, the accordion must have undergone some common stylization by musicians of the same sociocultural background. Narciso Martínez, Pedro Ayala, Santiago Jiménez, and other accordionists of the 1930s were undoubtedly heirs to this stylization. But the variability of the early accordion ensemble, such as it was, would probably ensure not only that this earlier music differed from modern conjunto, but that a well-defined style, using certain instruments in certain prescribed combinations, was unlikely to develop. We may thus posit, as the date of the emergence of a definable conjunto style of music, the year 1936—when Narciso Martínez recorded his first polka, "La chicharronera," for commercial distribution. This is, however, a more or less arbitrary date; Chris Strachwitz (1974a) claims Martínez had commercial precursors, notably Bruno Villarreal and Lolo Cavazos, either or both of whom recorded as early as 1931.

To be sure, Martínez was not the sole exponent of the music in its early days. Less popular musicians, such as San Antonio's Santiago Jiménez, contributed their talents as well. A recording by Lolo Cavazos from 1939 comes remarkably close, in its articulation, to the style of the next generation of musicians, who launched the mature phase of the music. I will have more to say about the musicians who were important in shaping conjunto style later. For now I merely wish to emphasize that it was in the 1930s that this incipient style, featuring at first only the two-row accordion and *bajo sexto* (and occasionally the guitar), began to take hold in the area from the Rio Grande to San Antonio. And it was with Narciso Martínez, whose popularity exceeded that of all other conjunto musicians in the 1930s and 1940s, that the style took off.

Since the 1930s, and especially since the early 1950s, when musicians like Martínez began to tour as far away as California and Chicago, conjunto music has gained currency over wide areas of the

United States (and Mexico). The diffusion of the style seems to have coincided with the migration patterns of Texan and *norteño* Mexican workers, who, quite naturally, took their music with them wherever they traveled. Many such individuals, as we know, have migrated, particularly to California and the Midwest, and their cultural impact on the Chicanos of these regions has undoubtedly been significant. However, studies of such intracultural assimilation are almost nonexistent. I can only cite, from personal experience, the fact that by the 1960s both *orquesta* and conjunto music were firmly established in the music-and-dance tradition of central California.

Chris Strachwitz (1974b) has called Narciso Martínez the "father" of conjunto music. The label is apt, I believe. He was the most popular musician of the 1930s and of the better part of the 1940s. He was an innovator; according to Pedro Ayala, who started his career at the same time, Martínez strongly influenced those who followed him. Martínez, like most conjunto musicians before and after him, came from a rural working-class background. Now in his sixties, he was born in Reynosa, Tamaulipas, Mexico, across the river from the Rio Grande Valley, and was brought over to the United States as a small child. Having received almost no formal education, Martínez started his professional career in 1927. By 1935 he had graduated from the antiquated one-row button accordion to the new two-row model. His professional opportunity came when Bluebird, a recording subsidiary of RCA that was developing regional talent in Texas, brought him to San Antonio, liked his music, and put him on commercial recordings.

Martínez's first record, "La chicharronera" (flip side: "El tronconal"), was released in 1936. An instant success, "La chicharronera" set the stage for the emergence of a definable and enduring conjunto musical style. The recording itself shows that style in its embryonic form. It paired up Martínez on accordion with Santiago Almeida on *bajo sexto;* the two instruments have since become staples in the conjunto. Martínez's technique is especially noteworthy with respect to the style's subsequent development. Like the accordionists who followed him until the late 1940s, Martínez played with a fluid legato which connected all the notes within a phrase. The polka, which became by far the most popular dancing tune, was played at a brisk 120 to 130 beats per minute. The sixteenth-note patterns common in the polkas of Martínez and his contemporaries made the phrases seem to run into each other in rapid succession. The overall articulation sounded rushed, as Martínez himself pointed out to me in a recent interview. The phrases run into and trip over each other. The *bajo sexto,* serving as both harmony and bass line, tended to emphasize the bass notes over the upbeat strum.

Santiago Jiménez was only slightly less popular than Martínez in the 1930s and 1940s. A native of San Antonio, Jiménez started his career in the early 1930s. Like Martínez, he grew up in the relative poverty of the proletarian Mexican worker. Despite their popularity, neither of these two early musicians was ever able to rely exclusively on his music for economic support. Both had to turn to other occupations traditionally available at that time to Mexicans in the United States. Jiménez spent a good part of his working life as a public-school janitor, while Martínez alternated between truck driving and working in the fields. Pedro Ayala and other early conjunto musicians faced the same hardships. Professionalism, in the sense of sole economic reliance on music, was not to become a reality until the next generation of musicians arrived on the scene.

Jiménez recorded his first selections in 1936: two polkas, "Dices pescao" and "La Luisita," with the Decca label. The fluidity of his articulation probably indicates Martínez's influence, although it also reflects the prevailing conception of what the accordion should sound like. Jiménez did make one important contribution to the then-emerging conjunto style: he was the first to incorporate the contrabass, generally known as a *tololoche.* No one else did so until after 1948.

The commercial distribution of the music of Santiago Jiménez, Narciso Martínez, and other popular conjunto musicians of the 1930s undoubtedly had much to do with the course of the music's stylization. Many other conjunto musicians (such as Lolo Cavazos) also recorded for major labels, whose financial backing added impetus to the music's popularity.

One may argue, as some have with respect to the mass distribution of U.S. pop music and other commodities, that such commercial dissemination of conjunto music "froze" conjunto style into a more or less common form. Particularly after World War II when, as one informant told José Limón (1978), the popularity of public ballroom dancing increased dramatically, competition among conjunto musicians was keen. Each group strived to please not only its audiences but the local recording companies which had replaced the large labels after the war. This competition probably tended to restrict the range of stylistic innovation, although we must keep in mind that the style had been changing gradually since the 1930s—and changed dramatically after 1948. However, I do not feel that commercialization can adequately account for either conjunto music's strong stylization or its overwhelming appeal to Texas-Mexican proletarian workers. On the contrary (and major-label support notwithstanding), conjunto music came of age at precisely the time that conditions seemed least favorable for its development, as I will explain below. Moreover, other types of musical groups, such as *orquestas típicas* and singing duos with assorted accompaniments, recorded both in Texas and California, and greater Mexican music in a wide variety of styles, were as popular then as now among Mexicans in the United States. Yet of all these possible musical influences, only the accordion style introduced by Martínez and Jiménez was incorporated into the fully evolved and eminently popular conjunto style of music, whose mature expression began to take form in the late 1940s.

In the meantime the popularity of Narciso Martínez, in particular, soared. He earned the epithet El Huracán del Valle, as a sort of recognition (or advertisement) that he was a trailblazer. Santiago Jiménez was never quite as influential as Martínez, perhaps because, unlike Martínez, who toured extensively throughout the Southwest, he rarely ventured outside San Antonio. Both Martínez and Jiménez recorded prolifically, usually dance music—the ubiquitous polka as well as such universal favorites as *redovas* and schottisches. They and other conjunto musicians also recorded the *norteño* variety of the Mexican *huapango* and a brisker version of the *redova* called the *vals alto*. Then, as now, when we speak of *tejano* music we must include the dance. The two elements, music and dance, form one symbolic structure.

Elements of the *redova* (which Texas Mexicans also called *vals bajito*) and *vals alto* were incorporated into the modern conjunto (and *orquesta*) version of the *vals,* or *canción ranchera*. The *canción ranchera* first appeared as such in recordings of the late 1940s. Played in the 3/4 time of the *vals,* in a slow 6/8 time, or in the 2/4 polka meter, these songs (often the lament of an abandoned lover) enjoy wide popularity today through their performance by both conjuntos and *orquestas tejanas*. No other genre, however, brought Martínez, Jiménez, and their colleagues of the 1930s and 1940s more acclaim than the polka, whose distinctive performance in even the early recordings adumbrated the fully "Chicano-ized" (if I may use the term) polka.

Consequently, and not surprisingly, the polka and its variations (such as the later addition of *ranchera* song lyrics) emerged by the early 1950s as the quintessential expression of Chicano music and dance. As I mentioned, of all other genres prevalent in the conjunto's early days only the adaptation of the *redova* and *vals alto* to the *canción ranchera* has remained popular. The durability of the polka and *ranchera* is, I feel, related to the whole push of conjunto music, during its twenty years or so of development, toward a common stylistic denominator. And this push, as I will propose below, was in turn linked to the high levels of social interaction and integration among a class of people, the proletarian workers. To this group conjunto musicians were intimately tied, both socioculturally and economically.

Pedro Ayala, a contemporary of Martínez and Jiménez and also from the Rio Grande Valley, started his musical career at the same time as Martínez. He made his recording debut rather late, however—in 1948, only shortly before a number of younger musicians such as Valerio Longoria, Tony de la Rosa, and Daniel Garcés propelled conjunto music into the next level of development. Yet Ayala's style in 1948 clearly presaged the changes which were about to transform the conjunto sound into its modern expression. Whereas the accordion technique of Martínez and Jiménez tended to be fluid and the phrasing and articulation blurred by their extreme legato, Ayala's first recordings evince a marcato quality carried further in the deliberate staccato of de la Rosa and those who followed him. In addition, Ayala, together with bandleader and saxophonist Eugenio Gutiérrez, was probably the first to attempt the important union between the conjunto and *orquesta* styles. The two recorded the polka "El naranjal" in 1948; quite possibly this was one of the first times the alto saxophone was incorporated into the conjunto style of music. Shortly thereafter, however, Martínez and the "father" of the modern *orquesta tejana* style, Beto Villa, went a step further. They incorporated the accordion into the *orquesta*, recording, among other selections, "Rosita vals" and (surprisingly) the American tune "San Antonio Rose."

After 1948 the final, mature phase of conjunto music took shape rather rapidly, as a younger generation of musicians emerged. Among the most influential of these was Tony de la Rosa, from Corpus

Christi. He was possibly the first (although this honor might belong to Valerio Longoria) to record with the instrumental ensemble that has since become thoroughly traditional—the three-row accordion, the *bajo sexto* (amplified by an electric pickup), the electric bass guitar, and the standard dance-band drum set. De la Rosa and Longoria, who performed in the Corpus Christi–San Antonio area, were caught up in what in retrospect were significant changes that were taking place not only in the music but in the whole music-and-dance tradition. These changes seem minor, yet they were important to the style's direction and for its relationship to the contemporary social scene. What de la Rosa and others did was to slow down the tempo of the polka from the earlier accordionists' brisk 120 to 130 beats per minute to 100 to 110 beats—or less.

These slower speeds made it easier to play the accordion with a more deliberate, choppy, staccato technique (or else the adoption of the staccato technique forced the tempo to slow down). Additionally—as can be heard, for instance, in a de la Rosa recording of the "Flamingo Polka" from the early 1950s—a wholly novel but soon characteristic prominence was given to the drums. Lastly, as the electric bass took over the bass line, the *bajo sexto* developed a characteristic emphasis on the upbeat accompaniment strum of the polka that has endured to this day.

The overall effect of these changes, particularly of the slowed-down, staccato style of articulation on the accordion, was to set off rather sharply the new, revised conjunto style of de la Rosa and others from the older style of Martínez and his contemporaries. The links were there, of course (Tony de la Rosa always declared that his teachers were Martínez and the other early players), but with the new additions and changes conjunto music could finally be said to have come of age. By the early 1950s the new style had completely caught on, and thereafter it became a kind of ideal, almost normative, conjunto sound. The final change was the deliberate grafting of the new style to a new dance style that, according to Narciso Martínez, had made its appearance in San Antonio in the late 1940s.

This new dance, *el tacuachito* (the possum), quickly became popular all over Texas among working-class people, whose support had been vital to the development of conjunto music. The name of this dance identified it metaphorically with the native by associating its gliding movements with another popular native inhabitant—the possum. By the early 1950s the new dance had become a standard feature of the traditional Saturday-night Chicano dance. Young working-class Chicanos, many of whom had also adopted the characteristic style of the *pachuco* (Vaseline-groomed ducktail, baggy slacks with ankle-tight cuffs, shellacked double-soled shoes, etc.), added their own peculiar movements to the basic dance form. As a member of a migrant farmworking family who "tagged along" as my two older brothers regularly attended Saturday-night dances, I witnessed many of these dances during the 1950s in cities and towns from McAllen in the Rio Grande Valley, to Lubbock in the Texas Panhandle.

Within this special Saturday-night dance setting, young men and women came to meet each other, to break the monotony of the daily grind in the cotton fields. In dancing *el tacuachito* they stamped their own interpretation on a durable Chicano esthetic reality. Older people did not usually attend these dances—not because they did not like the music but because it was understood that young people went there to meet potential mates. (Many young women were escorted by watchful mothers.) At other types of dances, such as the frequent weddings, young and old participated alike. And, whether one attended dances or not, conjunto music was always available over the airwaves; Spanish-language radio stations were common enough even then. In this way, then, conjunto music proliferated and came to pervade the daily life of the Chicano working class.

One last exponent of conjunto music deserves mention. Paulino Bernal is recognized as one of the best accordion players of all time. His group took conjunto as far as it was to go until recently, when younger musicians such as Óscar Hernández and Esteban Jordán began to revitalize the style. Besides refining the style by perfecting the staccato and exploiting the high register (indeed, the whole range) of the accordion, Bernal's group generally raised the conjunto sound to a new level of sophistication. Bernal achieved this step by adopting (possibly the first conjunto musician to do so) the vastly more flexible *acordeón cromático*. This chromatic, four- or five-row button accordion obviously facilitated key changes and more complex harmonization. Bernal also had much to do with integrating *ranchero* song texts into the conjunto style (not previously a common practice—although in the late 1940s Narciso Martínez provided instrumental backing for various groups, and Los Alegres de Terán, a Mexican conjunto which featured a vocal duo, had begun its rise to fame). The Bernal group's renditions of *canciones rancheras,* both in polka and *vals* meters, are, by common consensus among Chicano musicians, some of the best in the conjunto repertoire. The group's phenomenal success since the mid 1950s (which Bernal later parlayed into his own recording company) clearly supports this peer appraisal.

Organized in Kingsville, Texas, in 1952, El Conjunto Bernal began introducing its own material shortly after de la Rosa had broken new ground with his innovations. The polka "La Capirucha," which features a marvelously fast sixteenth-note staccato effect, and the *vals ranchero* "Mi único camino," which incorporated three-part sung harmonies into conjunto for possibly the first time, are some of Bernal's earliest performances and reflect the changes he wrought. These changes included the rapid staccato patterns and the three-part harmony, as well as a similarly staccato style of singing, more complex chord progressions, crisp drumming (with well-placed double rolls for more effective breaks), and a heavily emphasized upbeat strum on the *bajo sexto.* Immensely popular and highly influential, Bernal's style could easily be said to represent the apex of the Chicano-ized, *pachuco*-ized *tacuachito* polka.

By the mid 1950s, then, conjunto music had evolved into a highly identifiable musical structure—particularly with respect to the polka, which was by far the most prevalent genre. It is worth noting that after World War II the primary occupation of the best professional and semiprofessional conjunto musicians was to play for dances of all kinds—weddings, *cumpleaños,* anniversaries, *jamaicas,* and so forth. After 1948, a rapidly increasing public-ballroom commercialization of the music allowed the most popular musicians to turn fully professional. Many were busy the year round touring all over the Southwest and beyond, parlaying the popularity of their records into dollars by their appearances at large public dances throughout the Southwest. By the early 1950s, Narciso Martínez, Tony de la Rosa, and others had made touring a common practice for conjunto musicians. Given the music's immense popularity in this commercial context and the economic livelihood it now afforded, it is not surprising that it, and especially the polka, its quintessential genre, should have been subjected to such elaboration and stylization. Conjunto musicians strove both to bring fresh variety to their music and to maintain a valued tradition.

Since the mid 1950s, however, and until recently, only minor changes were made in conjunto style. An alto saxophone often alternated with the accordion between the melody line and the so-called *segunda* (a line usually parallel to and a third below the melody)—but usually in Mexican *norteño* music rather than in conjuntos. Moreover, this combination was not really new, since Pedro Ayala and Narciso Martínez had combined their talents with saxophonists Eugenio Gutiérrez and Beto Villa, respectively, in the 1940s. In the 1960s and 1970s, as conjunto and *orquesta* converged with each other (for reasons which I can only touch upon briefly in this paper), the former did develop a more complex system of chordal progressions. Particularly as the Mexican *bolero,* with its more demanding harmonies, gained increasing popularity, modernized conjuntos like that of Bernal began to substitute the more harmonically flexible guitar for the *bajo sexto*. By this time also, in recognition of the electronic age and the requirements of large ballrooms, amplification systems had been added. One consequence had been the permanent substitution of the electric bass for the old *tololoche* (contrabass). Additionally, after the mid 1950s the instrumental polka gradually gave way to the sung *ranchera,* which was superimposed over the polka rhythm. The accordion thus functioned less as a solo instrument and more as a counterpart to the singing. But by and large the general style had evolved by the mid 1950s and remained rather static thereafter, while its sister style, *orquesta tejana,* oscillated between it and other domains of music.

Since the mid 1970s, however, conjunto groups such as those of Esteban Jordán, Óscar Hernández, and Roberto Pulido have begun to revitalize the style. Pulido has achieved a remarkable synthesis between conjunto and *orquesta,* successfully integrating two alto saxophones into the ensemble to create a blended sound. Jordán's innovations have been wide-ranging; he has incorporated elements from such disparate styles as hard rock, blues, and jazz into the more traditional conjunto sound. Óscar Hernández, who once played with Bernal, has probably replaced him as the best technical virtuoso; his style evinces clean, rhythmically (and harmonically) complex lines. El Conjunto Bernal, which Paulino has quit because of religious convictions, has achieved modest innovations. However, it is too early to assess the impact these explorations will have on the direction of conjunto music, other than to note the style's revitalization and its definite convergence with *la orquesta tejana*.

An Ethnomusicological Interpretation

Now that I have described in a summary fashion the historical development of conjunto style, I would like to address myself briefly to the question of the style's timely appearance. Because conjunto music and *orquesta tejana* have evolved in a dialectic with each other, and because the limitations of this essay do not allow for a full explication, I must necessarily abbreviate my comments on this question. Briefly, then, I propose that conjunto music has historically represented the response of the Texas-Mexican proletarian worker to the antagonism, not only of an Anglo America which threatened from outside an ethnic boundary (cf. Barth 1969), but of the emerging Chicano middle class. This latter group, whose growth was spurred by the Second World War, openly considered the poor and/or unacculturated Mexican an impediment to Mexican Americans' upward mobility in U.S. society. They felt the proletarian workers clung unreasonably to Mexican values, weighing themselves down with what Edward Murguía has called "excessive cultural baggage" (1975: 3), and thus hindering all Chicanos' chances for acceptance in U.S. life.

The Second World War—and even the decades before, for there had always been an incipient, if small, middle class—had ushered in an era of increased opportunities as well as increased sociopolitical awareness on the part of Chicanos, an era that saw the number of middle-class Chicanos gradually rise (Grebler et al. 1970: 302 ff.). These Chicanos, a number of whom had been involved in the war, developed egalitarian ideals and a desire to be like other U.S. citizens—in short, to assimilate into U.S. society and gain a share of the affluence that surrounded them. These were the Chicanos who formed the backbone of a new and increasingly Americanized, or Anglicized, group which began to aspire for new cultural symbols to express its newfound identity (cf. Gómez-Quiñones 1979: 63). It was at this point, in the late 1940s, that modern *orquesta* music emerged among and for the middle class, partly as a result of that search for new cultural symbols. Not surprisingly, to these people conjunto music, like so many other aspects of Texas-Mexican culture, smacked of *lo ranchero,* that is, the rustic and backward, or *lo arrabalero* (from the outskirts, low-class)—in short, of the lower-class proletarian society from which they were trying to dissociate.

Dismay and antagonism can be discerned in some of the language then (and I suspect even now) in use among upwardly mobile, assimilative Chicanos: "they" (that is, the lower, less-acculturated class) were *el peladaje, la plebe, la gente corriente, gente ranchera, animal de uña, gente arrabalera,* and any number of more or less pejorative terms. "We," on the other hand, were *gente de razón, gente de roce social, gente decente,* and other genteel expressions. Not surprisingly, the differences ascribed in language carried over into the realm of music evaluation. While both groups of Chicanos inherited a culturally deep tradition of music and dance, the two musics, conjunto and *orquesta,* seemed to articulate the divergence in values and ideologies that the linguistic terms indicated. The musics were, to borrow Richard Bauman's (1972) terminology, expressions of differential identities. Narciso Martínez stated his understanding of this differential identity very succinctly: "la orquesta es pa' 'high society'" (*orquesta* is for high society); "el conjunto era pa' la gente ranchera, era música ranchera" (conjunto was for rural folk, it was rural music). (However, I would add that conjunto music appealed just as much to the poor urban worker.)

Let me cite a case of differential identity expressed in music. In Weslaco, Texas, in the mid and late 1950s, Saturday-night dances were commonly held in the town plaza. They featured conjunto musicians, such as Rubén Vela and others, who were then popular among the laboring class. These open-air dances naturally attracted large crowds of *pachuquillos* and other lower-class types, so that the dances evinced a distinctive working-class ethos. On more than one occasion I recall hearing Chicanos whom everyone would consider *de buenas familias,* that is, of middle-class orientation, make disapproving remarks such as "Qué indecente se ven" (How vulgar they look) about the dancers they observed. This association of conjunto music with the supposedly coarse lower class is not an isolated case. While I was playing one time in an *orquesta* for a predominantly middle-class audience in Fresno, California, an annoyed woman complained to me that the band was becoming too *ranchera,* and thus sounding too much like the conjuntos which played in the "low-class *cantinas*" in West Fresno. She had made the association because she felt we were playing too much *música corrida* (i.e., songs in polka tempo conjunto-style). And recently an informant in Corpus Christi, the wife of a deceased *orquesta* leader who had been prominent in the 1940s and 1950s, told me about the kinds of people who had gone to her husband's dances. "A los bailes de mi esposo iba pura gente buena" (Only high-quality people attended my husband's dances), she said—as opposed to the vulgar types who supported conjunto music.

Narciso Martínez clearly understood the split musical consciousness of Chicano society. He deprecates his music, recalling how ashamed he was to play in front of the great Luis Arcaraz from Mexico. "Esas eran orquestas," he says, "no mugrero" (Those were *real* bands). It was his own music that was *mugrero* compared to the power and brilliance of such a band. And, as he said, he wouldn't dare venture into the big cities of Texas and California for head-to-head confrontations with *orquestas* without reinforcing his *débil* (weak) accordion with a pair of saxophones. "Iba bien peltrechado con dos saxofones" (I was well reinforced with two saxophones), he said, to give his music a little class. In a mood of self-abasement he added, "La acordeón siempre disminuye para la orquesta" (It's true that the accordion doesn't measure up to the *orquesta*). Why is this so? Because the accordion is *ranchera* music, for the common people, and no match for the *orquesta*, which is the music of the high-powered "high society" people of the city. Still, on another occasion Martínez talked proudly of the power of his own music. He recalled an instance when *la gente* spurned a "high society," tuxedo-clad band playing across the street to flock into the place where he was playing. And another time some people in Fort Worth had complained to Luis Arcaraz, "No toque usted, no toque usted; que toque Chicho [Narciso]" (Don't you play, don't you play; let Chicho play). "Don't blame me," Martínez said in his broken English, implying that his own music, after all, had more appeal.

The two musics, then, communicated different class ideologies (and values). Class consciousness was the crucial differentiating factor. *Orquesta* music catered to the middle class; the lower class favored conjunto music overwhelmingly. The exclusivity was mutual (though not total—recall that accordionists Ayala and Martínez recorded with *orquesta* leaders Gutiérrez and Villa).

In sum, the accelerating changes that occurred in the postwar years split the different segments of Chicano society—or, more likely, intensified nascent differences which had merely been arrested by the Mexican's confrontation with the dominant Anglo American society. And the challenge of the Americanized Chicano middle class to the fundamental values of the relatively unacculturated working class, I believe, spurred on the rapid evolution of conjunto music.

Viewed in this light, the changes that Tony de la Rosa and others introduced in the late 1940s and early 1950s take on added significance. These shifts in tempo, articulation, and so on symbolized the reactions that were taking place socially. In other words, the musical developments transcended the universe of musical discourse and interacted with developments occurring at the level of social discourse. Or, like language and social life (see Hymes 1972), music and social life relate on many levels. The changes de la Rosa, Bernal, and others wrought in conjunto style reflected the maturation of a musical esthetics which objectified the traditional proletarian ideals being challenged at that time by the Americanized Chicano middle class. This esthetics culminated in the emergence, simultaneously with the musical changes, of the new dance style *el tacuachito*. Clearly, changes in the new social structure were being transformed into changes in the musical (and dance) structures. The move toward assimilation by some segments of Chicano society was countered by a corresponding move by the proletariat to strengthen its cultural position. And the music-and-dance innovations symbolically articulated this move.

Concluding Remarks

The cleavage between the Chicano working class and the more assimilated middle class has never been as sharp as my analysis might at first seem to indicate. The potent Anglo American hegemony has kept the differentiation of Chicano society from becoming absolute. Indeed, a synchronic ethnography of Chicano music (even of a narrowly defined Texas-Mexican music) reveals multilayered structures of signification (to borrow from Geertz [1973]) which transcend class differences. For one thing, *orquesta* music has, since the 1960s, been increasingly appropriated by the less assimilated, proletarian workers. Or, to put it in the vernacular, *orquesta* has had to go *ranchero* to survive. Thus, in many ways, *orquesta* and conjunto are what we might call paired styles, which have interacted and influenced each other from the beginning. The musicians, at least, have always been aware of the provenance of the two musics and of the intricate relationships, both musical and social, which exist between them. Narciso Martínez, again, phrased it very well when he said,

"La orquesta es pa' 'high society,' pero ya orita 'ta muy concentrada en la polca, porque es lo que les deja . . . es lo que les acarrea la gente—la polca, el movimiento, la cumbia—todo eso" (The *orquesta* is for "high society," but these days it concentrates on the polka, because that is what lets . . . that is what draws the people—the polka, the rhythm, the *cumbia*—all of those). That is, *orquesta* and conjunto both tend toward the same musical denominator, and consequently come close to being a common musical expression.

On another front, both U.S. and Mexican musics have exerted powerful influences on conjunto. This influence, however, has been felt more strongly by the *orquestas,* which have tended to reflect Mexican, U.S., and the more conservative conjunto styles in turn. *Orquesta* expresses the cultural duality (cf. Marks 1974) of Chicano society: it functions as a kind of symbolic style-switching, somewhat analogous to Blom and Gumperz's concept of metaphorical switching (1972), allowing Chicanos access to both Mexican and U.S. sociomusical systems. The outspoken *orquesta* leader Little Joe has perceptively interpreted this dual access as demonstrating the "flexibility" of Chicanos.

In sum, then, the symbolic structure(s) of conjunto and *orquesta* reflect the state of flux in which Chicano society is maintained, owing to the push and pull across the ethnic boundary (Barth 1969), or the play of what Jansen (1965) calls the esoteric-exoteric factor. This factor may be described as the element which maintains the differences in the sense of ethnicity and of class that the various segments of Chicano society describe to themselves and others. And that esoteric-exoteric factor itself operates on the principles of cultural confrontation and accommodation (cf. Barth 1969; Bateson 1972), or what Paredes (1976) has described more specifically as the intercultural conflict between Chicanos and Anglos. It is against this backdrop that conjunto and *orquesta* have played out their dialectic.

Finally, I would repeat that the surprising fact is not so much that conjunto music became popular so rapidly as that it did so under conditions which seemingly should have militated against its progression. These conditions include the U.S. tendency to pressure "outsiders" into some sort of public conformity and the desire of self-described "middle class" Chicanos to identify themselves with the public U.S. culture from which that conformity emanates. I mentioned earlier that commercialization could not adequately, let alone totally, explain conjunto music's phenomenal success—especially as the major recording labels withdrew their support after World War II. One might ask how commercialization could succeed in the face of a hostile Chicano middle class and a dominant American culture—which, in the words of Luis Valdez (1972), threatened to overwhelm us with its discarded *chingaderas:* its used cars, plastic flowers, and TV sets. Yet the music has endured and continues to thrive, even as it is undergoing revitalization.

Perhaps, as Pedro Ayala once told me, "El día que a la gente le toquen otra música, no se les paran ni las moscas" (The day they play a different music for the people, not even the flies will stop in).

Note

1. In the original article, 1935 was given as the year of Martínez's first recording. The author's subsequent research led him to revise the year to 1936. We have changed it in this article accordingly.   —EDITORS

References

Barth, Fredrik. 1969. *Ethnic Groups and Boundaries.* Boston: Little, Brown.
Bateson, Gregory. 1972. "Culture Contact and Schismogenesis." In *Steps to an Ecology of Mind: Collected Essays in Anthropology, Psychiatry, Evolution, and Epistemology.* San Francisco: Chandler Publishing.
Bauman, Richard. 1972. "Differential Identity and the Social Base of Folklore." In *Toward New Perspectives in Folklore,* edited by Américo Paredes and Richard Bauman. Austin: University of Texas Press.
Blacking, John. 1974. "Ethnomusicology as a Key Subject in the Social Sciences." In *In Memoriam: Antonio Jorge Dias* (no ed.). Lisbon: Instituto de Alta Cultura.
Blom, Jan-Petter, and John J. Gumperz. 1972. "Social Meaning in Linguistic Structures: Code-Switching in Norway." In *Directions in Sociolinguistics: The Ethnography of Communication,* edited by John J. Gumperz and Dell Hymes. New York: Holt, Rinehart, and Winston.
Geertz, Clifford. 1973. *The Interpretation of Cultures: Selected Essays.* New York: Basic Books.
Gómez-Quinones, Juan. 1979. "Toward a Concept of Culture." In *Modern Chicano Writers: A Collection of Critical Essays,* edited by Joseph Sommers and Tomás Ybarra-Frausto. Englewood Cliffs, N.J.: Prentice-Hall.
Grebler, Leo, Joan W. Moore, and Ralph C. Guzmán. 1970. *The Mexican-American People: The Nation's Second Largest Minority.* New York: Free Press.

Hymes, Dell. 1972. "Editorial Introduction to Language in Society." *Language in Society* 1: 1–14.
Jansen, William H. 1965. "The Esoteric-Exoteric Factor in Folklore." In *The Study of Folklore,* edited by Alan Dundes. Englewood Cliffs, N.J.: Prentice-Hall.
Limón, José E. 1978. "Agringado Joking in Texas-Mexican Society." In *New Directions in Chicano Scholarship,* edited by Ricardo Romo and Raymund Paredes. La Jolla: Chicano Studies Program, University of California, San Diego.
Marks, Morton. 1974. "Uncovering Ritual Structures in Afro-American Music." In *Religious Movements in Contemporary America,* edited by Irving I. Zaretsky and Mark P. Leone. Princeton, N.J.: Princeton University Press.
Murguía, Edward. 1975. *Assimilation, Colonialism, and the Mexican-American People.* Austin: Center for Mexican American Studies, University of Texas at Austin.
Paredes, Américo. 1976. *A Texas-Mexican* Cancionero: *Folksongs of the Lower Border.* Urbana: University of Illinois Press.
Strachwitz, Chris. 1974a. Jacket notes for *Texas-Mexican Border Music.* Vol. 4 (no. 9006). El Cerrito, Calif.: Folklyric Records.
———. 1974b. Jacket notes for *Texas-Mexican Border Music.* Vol. 10 (no. 9017). El Cerrito, Calif.: Folklyric Records.
Valdez, Luis. 1972. "Introduction: La Plebe." In *Aztlán: An Anthology of Mexican-American Literature,* edited by Luis Valdez and Stan Steiner. New York: Vintage Books.

3

From Ranchero to Jaitón
Ethnicity and Class in Texas-Mexican Music
(Two Styles in the Form of a Pair)

✧

MANUEL PEÑA
1983

This article presents an interpretive summary of certain musical developments among Texas Mexicans, or *tejanos*. It is the result of several years of fieldwork research related to two popular musical styles that were forged by *tejano* musicians during and after World War II. The styles are known as *orquesta tejana*, or simply *orquesta*, and *norteño*. Among *tejanos* the latter is more commonly referred to as *conjunto*, and that is the label I will be using here. I should point out from the outset that each style, though symbiotically related to the other, actually merits its own study. Nonetheless, the intricate relationship between the two types of music presents an intriguing challenge to students of musical culture in particular, and to social scientists in general. It is in response to that challenge that this interpretive outline is offered here.

I shall focus mainly on the period 1935–1965, with particular emphasis on the postwar decade. Additionally, my primary interest is to explain the dynamics that sustained the conjunto-*orquesta* relationship, particularly the series of contrasts the two musics came to articulate and, indeed, embody: working class versus middle class, cultural assimilation versus ethnic resistance, continuity versus change, and folk versus "sophisticated." Moreover, underlying these contrasts, or oppositions, was what I propose to be the key factor operating in the emergence of both conjunto and *orquesta*—namely, the shift in *tejano* society from a Mexicanized, rural, folk, and proletarian group to a class-differentiated, urban, and increasingly Americanized and literate population. Needless to say, the complications arising out of such a shift involved considerable conflict, so that the contrasts I have listed are best analyzed within the framework of a conflictual schema, as opposed to a "functional," or consensual one (cf. Abercrombie, Hill, and Turner 1980).

In an earlier essay (Peña 1981) devoted mainly to conjunto, I noted two questions that are raised in considering the emergence of this popular style among Texas Mexicans. Since these questions (and their answers) impinge directly on the emergence of *orquesta* as well, they are worth recalling here. The first question had to do with the problem of describing musically the evolution of conjunto—with describing the stylistic elements involved. The second dealt with the social and cultural significance of the music—that is, the timing of the style's appearance and development, and, specifically, why a well-defined style should emerge among this particular group of people at this precise moment in their history (1935–1965). These questions hold as well for *orquesta,* since in a doubly remarkable accident of history, at the very same time that conjunto music was establishing itself as a formidable artistic expression, *orquesta tejana* was likewise coming into its own.

Thus, keeping in mind the contrasts I mentioned, I want to propose two hypotheses on the dynamic relationship between *orquesta* and conjunto, as a first attempt at answering the questions I have posed. I will then devote the remainder of the essay, first, to a descriptive account of the two musics and their most important exponents, and, second, to an explanation of the two hypotheses. First, I propose that at one level—call it historical—the two musics unfolded within a framework of emerging class differences and conflict among Texas Mexicans, and that as such they have signified an intrinsic class dialectic working itself out within *tejano* society. My second hypothesis is linked to the first, but builds on a more synchronic base, as it were. That is, it posits *orquesta* and conjunto as symbolic projections of a Texas-Mexican social structure that was solid enough to survive both the disruptive effects of interethnic contact with Anglo American society and the fragmentation introduced by class differences. To put it another way, from a synchronic (structural) perspective the two styles should be considered dual expressions of a unitary musico-symbolic whole that emerged out of the conflict between an ethnic *tejano* culture and a dominant, often hostile Anglo American social order.

Before proceeding with the discussion of Texas-Mexican music, I want to sketch out a definition of style—one that hopefully captures both formal and cultural features. If we grant to music (and musical style in particular) the status of a cultural system, we may then ascribe to it the following properties: It is a repeatedly employed combination of sounds produced by vocal, instrumental, and/or other means, arranged into recognizable patterns, and situated within specific social contexts, wherein the style will acquire varying degrees of symbolic significance. The last point is especially critical for a culture-sensitive conception of style, because only when we recognize the symbolic dimension can we account for normative rules of composition and performance, as well as evaluative criteria. As these rules accrue upon a given style, they gain a determinative role in the acceptance or rejection of modifications that innovative artists may introduce. Lastly, once a musical style attains the status of a tradition, it may associate with and reinforce other crucial behavior patterns upon which the continuity of a culture hangs.

One other observation on style that bears on the thrust of this study should be noted. Although I have seen few ethnomusicological studies that focus on the question of the dynamics involved in style formation, at least one sociologist of music has addressed the need for an approach that makes "intelligible for us why a certain style may have emerged in the social and cultural structure of a given period, and thus clarify the sociological prerequisites and conditions involved" (Serauky, quoted in Etzkorn 1973: 9). And an art historian has advanced a theory that I find highly suggestive for interpreting the emergence of the two *tejano* styles in question here. Thus, James Ackerman proposes that the creative impulse out of which new styles spring may be thought of as "a class of related solutions to a problem—or responses to a problem" (1962: 228). Applying Ackerman's theory to our case, I propose that the changes wrought by World War II and its aftermath posed a challenge to Texas-Mexican society that demanded solutions to a number of problems. Artistic expression offered one solution, and, as we shall see, stylistic developments in conjunto and *orquesta* suggest themselves as specific examples.

Distinguishable stylistic elements coalesced first around the accordion ensemble that Texas Mexicans forged between 1935 and 1965. The *orquesta tejana,* whose instrumentation was a simplified version of the U.S. dance band, began to acquire its unique qualities after the war. Groping for direction at first, both conjunto and *orquesta* had gained coherent and expressive forms by the mid 1950s. By this time each ensemble had gravitated toward its respective social context: conjunto toward the mass of proletarian workers, *orquesta* toward a small but growing and influential middle class.

Nonetheless, despite their social and musical differences, and in line with the hypotheses I set forth earlier, the two ensembles, as well as their musical styles, are best described as tending to diverge at the level of class consciousness but to converge at the level of ethnic consciousness. Moreover, the tendency to converge, both stylistically and socially, was much stronger after the mid 1960s, a result of the closer alignment (for reasons I shall explore later) of *orquesta* with the musical preferences of the working class. In the decade immediately following the war, however, the tension between convergence and divergence was much more pronounced, a state of affairs that, needless to say, reflected the inevitable contradictions that Texas-Mexican society faced as a consequence of the contrasts I mentioned earlier, especially the contrast between cultural assimilation and ethnic resistance. I will discuss these contradictions later; now I would like to turn to the historical development of the two musics.

Conjunto: Una Música Vernácula, del Pueblo (A Folk Music, of the People)

The lead instrument in the modern conjunto is, of course, the button accordion—ordinarily the diatonic, three-row model, though until World War II, the two-row and one-row models were the rule. I have discussed elsewhere the accordion's early history. Here it will suffice to say that from its beginnings in northern Mexico and Texas (sometime around 1860), the instrument was shunned by genteel society, but not by the mass of proletarian workers, among whom it quickly gained widespread acceptance. It was often played solo in weddings and other domestic celebrations, though by the late nineteenth century it had begun to be paired with the Mexican *bajo sexto* (a large, twelve-string guitar), and sometimes with a native folk drum known as a *tambora de rancho* (ranch drum), to create a unique though rudimentary *norteño* ensemble. By the 1920s this ensemble had virtually replaced other instrumental groupings in the musical celebrations of the working class.

In the evolution of the modern conjunto, certain men stand out as especially creative artists. I want to present short sketches of their lives and contributions, so that we may obtain a glimpse of the human context in which the ensemble and its style unfolded. I should stress, however, that the development of conjunto music was, in every sense of the concept, a folk phenomenon. It was, as one *orquesta* musician said, *una música vernácula, del pueblo* (a folk music, of the people). Without exception, its contributors had two characteristics in common: they were mostly of an illiterate background, and they belonged to the proletarian class. In short, they belonged to a folk society with features not unlike those described by Robert Redfield. But, unlike Redfield's "ideal" folk society, which existed in a world unto itself, the *tejanos*' participation in an expanding U.S. political economy had contributed for some time to the erosion of many elements of their traditional culture. Lastly, in recognizing the collective nature of conjunto music, we should be aware that many anonymous musicians were actively involved in the creation of the emergent style. However, I simply cannot hope to account for the contributions that these nameless artists undoubtedly made.

We thus begin with the man who has been called the "father" of the modern conjunto—the accordionist who eclipsed all others in popularity in the early days of the music. Narciso Martínez—"El Huracán del Valle," as he was called—was born in 1911, in Matamoros, across the border from Brownsville, although he was raised in Texas. Like all other conjunto musicians, Martínez received little formal education, and he spent most of his working life in the agricultural fields, augmenting his income by playing the accordion. Here I should add that, although he recorded prolifically for Bluebird (RCA), and later for Ideal and other small *tejano* labels, Martínez attained neither wealth nor "stardom" of the kind people associate with mass-market music celebrities. This was because, not only did conjunto music develop in a folk, working-class context, but, despite the undeniable profits that RCA and other companies reaped from their investment in *tejano* music, for the early performers no market existed that would sustain them economically. It was not until a more extensive commercialization of conjunto music got under way in the late 1940s—aided by the proliferation of large, public paid-admission dances—that at least the most popular conjunto musicians were able to rely solely on their performances for economic support.

Martínez began his musical career in 1927; he produced his first recording in 1936. As most musicians with whom I had contact observed, Martínez's prominence in conjunto music stems from one primary accomplishment: he was the first *tejano* to successfully exploit the capabilities of the treble (right-hand) side of the accordion. In so doing, he initiated a radical departure from the earlier style that the Mexicans had inherited from the Germans: he virtually neglected the left-hand, bass-accompaniment elements, leaving the rhythmic and chordal accompaniment to his capable *bajo sexto* partner, Santiago Almeida.

The net result of Martínez's experimentation was a brighter, more "treble" sound, and a technique that facilitated a more rapid and staccato execution, two developments that sharply distinguished the new *tejano* sound from that of the earlier Germanic style. Martínez's innovation took hold so completely that few accordionists after him bothered to acquire more than a rudimentary familiarity with the accordion's left side. In sum, Martínez's influence was so great that Pedro Ayala, a contemporary, once told me, "After Narciso, what could the rest of us do except play like he did?"

Although Martínez was not the first *tejano* accordionist to record commercially (Bruno Villarreal was first, in 1928), his entrance into the commercial field made it possible for the emergent conjunto to consolidate its strength within the *tejano* working class, finally supplanting other sundry instrumental combinations that had survived from an earlier period. However, as I mentioned, Martínez was neither the first nor the sole propagator of conjunto music.

There were, in fact, a number of lesser-known figures who provided him with musical material and ideas. Among these were José Rodríguez and Lolo Cavazos, the latter an inventive musician who stands out in a retrospective assessment. By the late 1930s he already evinced a technical facility that foreshadowed the style of postwar musicians, those who began their professional careers with the small *tejano* labels that sprang up after the war, when the major labels abandoned their regional operations in favor of a mass Latin American market.

Two other contemporaries of Martínez deserve recognition—Santiago Jiménez, "El Flaco" (the Skinny One), from San Antonio, and Pedro Ayala, who, like Martínez, was born across the border but raised in South Texas. Jiménez was born in 1913, and, like other conjunto musicians, he descended from poor agriculturalist families.

Jiménez occupies a special position in the evolution of the modern conjunto by virtue of his introduction of the contrabass, or *tololoche,* into the ensemble. He did this in 1936, on his very first recording. Now, the contrabass had been a fairly common instrument among *tejanos,* even in the makeshift ensembles that were the rule among the working class, but to the best of my knowledge it had never been used with the accordion—at least not in any systematic fashion. In fact, until the postwar phase of conjunto's evolution only Jiménez continued to utilize it with any regularity. Others, meanwhile, continued to prefer the newly standardized accordion–*bajo sexto* combination.

Ayala merits our attention because, though he did not begin to record until 1947, he clearly belongs to the older generation, having been born in 1911. By 1947, however, his style displayed a strong similarity to that of the younger generation of musicians, so that it is logical to place him in an intermediate position between the first and second phases in the development of conjunto music. Interestingly, it was Ayala who popularized the use of the *tololoche* in the recording studio. After his example most accordionists included the instrument as a matter of course in their recordings. However, for the public paid-admission dances that became such an important context for the dissemination of conjunto music after the war, the accordion and *bajo sexto* continued to be the preferred combination, until the drums gained wide usage in the early 1950s. But the principal reason for the contrabass's restricted use seems to have been the sheer scarcity of players. Since the demise in the early 1930s of the once-popular string *orquestas,* there were evidently few proficient *tololoche* players.

Meanwhile, with Pedro Ayala's entry into the recording market, the last of the first generation of accordionists had made his mark. Thereafter, the evolution of the conjunto style was in the hands of a new crop of musicians, those who appeared on the scene after World War II.

Appropriately enough, the first of the postwar musicians to transcend the musical ideas of Narciso Martínez's generation was accordionist Valerio Longoria, a veteran of the war. Born in Kenedy, south of San Antonio, Longoria began playing for "nickels" in 1931. He was a mere seven years old at the time. He broke into the recording business in 1947, with Corona, a tiny label from San Antonio, though his most creative period began with his association with

Ideal Records, a larger label operating out of Alice, Texas. That was in 1950. Nonetheless, from the outset of his recording career, Longoria established the first of several precedents: utilizing his talents as a singer, he became the first conjunto musician to incorporate the Mexican *canción,* a vocal genre, into his repertory. He did this by simply superimposing the lyrics of the *canción* over the polka (and sometimes over the waltz), which in the conjunto tradition had previously existed as an instrumental category.

Of course, the *canción* had long occupied a central position in Texas-Mexican folk music, but prior to Longoria's precedent conjuntos had seldom included vocal music, restricting themselves exclusively to instrumental performance. (The reasons for this restriction had to do with social conventions. A combination of instrumental and vocal music was associated in the public mind with the disreputable atmosphere of the *cantina.* Thus, in order to avoid giving the wrong impression, "decent"—that is to say, domestic—celebrations such as weddings strictly precluded conjuntos from performing vocal pieces. The social upheaval ushered in by World War II changed all that.) Incidentally, besides polkas—which comprised fully two thirds of the repertories—early conjuntos also performed the *huapango tamaulipeco,* the redowa, schottische, waltz, and a few other genres the *tejanos* had inherited from the salon tradition of the nineteenth century.

In any case, once Longoria had succeeded in combining the polka and the *canción* (with the label *ranchera* often added on), other conjuntos quickly followed suit. I should point out, however, that for the time being neither Longoria nor any other conjunto singers deviated from the long-standing practice of duet singing, done mostly in parallel thirds. Ultimately, with the successful union of *canción* and polka, the instrumental version became less and less prominent, so that by the early 1960s conjuntos included it mainly to display the skills of the exceptional accordionists or to give the singers a break during dance performances.

Longoria also holds one other distinction. He was the first conjunto musician to perform the Mexican *bolero,* a genre that added a totally new dimension to the accordion ensemble. Long associated with a genteel tradition, the *bolero,* with its greater demands on singing finesse and rhythmic and harmonic execution, had previously remained beyond the capabilities of conjunto musicians. I suggest that Longoria's successful integration of the *bolero,* and his working-class constituency's acceptance, signaled both the readiness of modern conjuntos to upgrade their musical status vis-à-vis that of the *orquestas,* and the desire of the working class to demonstrate its capacity to appreciate the music of the *jaitones* ("high toned" people, i.e., the middle class)—provided, of course, that it be performed for them by conjuntos.

Longoria's final and perhaps most important contribution to the unfolding conjunto style was his enlistment of the modern danceband drum set. Again, the drums had been in use by *orquestas* for some time, but conjuntos had avoided them, because, as Pedro Ayala once told me, they were considered "too noisy" for the accordion and *bajo sexto*. Longoria's experiment soon caught on, however, and with this accretion the modern conjunto's evolution was almost complete. By the early 1950s the ensemble was nearly in place, except that the contrabass was still confined to the recording studio. However, in the mid 1950s, in response to the shift toward complete amplification of the music—a significant development in itself—the electric bass not only replaced the *tololoche* in the studio, but also became a regular member in the now-complete four-man ensemble: accordion, *bajo sexto,* drums, and electric bass.

While Longoria may justifiably be considered one of conjunto music's most innovative artists, he did not, ironically, enjoy the kind of lasting public recognition that he perhaps deserved. This may be explained in part by the fact that he was away from Texas—naturally, conjunto's stronghold—for twenty years beginning in 1959, and, as he admitted, "Me fui muriendo" (I began to fade). But it also has to do with the considerable popularity of one of Longoria's contemporaries, a popularity that overshadowed the former's undeniable accomplishments. I refer to Tony de la Rosa, whose name is well known to this day. Born in the settlement of Sarita, the onetime farmworker was clearly influenced by Valerio Longoria. In fact, what de la Rosa did was to follow in Longoria's footsteps long enough to acquire a reputation of his own. But once he had done that, he was able to stamp his own unmistakable mark on the innovations Longoria had wrought, thereby installing himself as the premier accordionist for the better part of the 1950s. After 1955 it was Tony de la Rosa's style, more than any other, that set the standard by which other conjuntos were judged.

De la Rosa's career was launched obscurely enough. He began playing for backyard weddings in 1941, when he was ten, and at sixteen he decided to strike out on his own, moving to nearby Kingsville, where he played in *cantinas.* "Anduve mucho tiempo con el acordeón por un lado," he once told me, "y el cajón de *shine* por el otro" (I spent a long time with my accordion on one side and the shoeshine box on the other). Eventually, however, he came to the attention of Armando Marroquín of Ideal Records, and he began in 1950 to turn out the first of the polkas for which he became so well known. At first these featured only the accordion and *bajo sexto*—sometimes the contrabass—but by the middle of the decade the drums had become a regular member in the Conjunto de la Rosa. By this time, too, de la Rosa was able to rely solely on his music for economic support, as he crisscrossed the state of Texas in pursuit of what one *orquesta* leader called the taco circuit—large public dances that attracted thousands of itinerant farmworkers who followed the seasonal cotton crop.

This brings us, finally, to the last major exponent of conjunto music during its formative years—Paulino Bernal. El Conjunto Bernal is recognized, even by less-than-enthusiastic *orquesta* musicians, as "the greatest of all time," as one of them judged it. This view is generally shared because most musicians agree that El Conjunto Bernal took the newly developed ensemble and exploited every one of its stylistic elements to the limits of public acceptance—all the while adding some important new ones of its own. El Conjunto Bernal's achievements clearly owe much to the virtuosity Bernal developed on the accordion. Patterning his style after that of de la Rosa, he was soon able to exceed the latter in technique and inventiveness, in time succeeding in commanding the total range of the accordion as no one had done before.

Bernal was born in Kingsville, Texas, in 1939. Like all his predecessors, he was raised in the unremitting poverty of the *tejano* worker. In his youth he worked in the fields to help his divorced mother support the family of six. From early on Bernal and his brother Eloy exhibited unusual musical talent, and by 1952 the brothers had organized El Conjunto Bernal, featuring Paulino on the accordion, Eloy on *bajo sexto,* and a friend, Adán Lomas, on drums. Before long the group drew the attention of the enterprising Armando Marroquín, who brought them in for their first recording in 1954. Bernal's talents (and those of Eloy) began to pay off almost immediately. The brash, gutsy style of Paulino's accordion and the sentimental *rancheras* they sang captured the enthusiasm of the *tejano* working class. As the group's popularity began to rise, the Bernals' days in the fields were numbered. After 1955 they turned exclusively to public-dance appearances for their financial support.

But El Conjunto Bernal did not surpass all others on the strength of Paulino's talents alone. Rather, it did so because it was able to attract the best musicians available at the time. For example, Bernal's own brother Eloy is to this day still recognized as the finest *bajo sexto* player in the history of conjunto. Moreover, beginning in the early 1960s Bernal recruited some of the best drummers available, including the versatile Armando Peña, whose experience ranged from jazz to *tropical* (a catchword for styles derived from the Afro Caribbean). Additionally, the singers that gravitated toward El Conjunto Bernal as it gained prestige were some of the most capable in the *canción ranchera* style, men like Rubén Pérez, who joined the group in 1958, Gerardo Reyes (later famous as a *mariachi* singer), and the inimitable tenor, the late Manuel Solís. Last, and perhaps most far-reaching of all, was Bernal's decision in 1964 to enlist the talents of the gifted young accordionist Óscar Hernández. The first (and one of the few) conjunto accordionists to adopt the vastly more flexible five-row, chromatic accordion, Hernández induced Bernal to do likewise, and for the next two years the two were regularly featured on dual-accordion arrangements that have never been duplicated and that others now recognize as "classic."

Given the relatively high quality of musicians Bernal had assembled, it was inevitable that the group would begin to experiment and expand the limits of the conjunto style, while at the same time it tested the musical tolerance of its working-class public. Thus, in addition to the dual accordions, El Conjunto Bernal also introduced the three-part harmonies long popular in the Mexican vocal-trio tradition; it expanded the conjunto repertory by adding *música tropical—cumbias,* cha-cha-chas, and the like; it raised the level of harmonic and rhythmic complexity generally (though it seldom abandoned the basic *ranchero* sound); finally, it even borrowed ideas from U.S. rock music. As Bernal put it, "We wanted to branch out, to include some good music and draw in other kinds of people" (besides the bottom-rung workers).

Sometimes, however, El Conjunto Bernal's experiments failed. Despite the group's immense prestige, people did reject what they felt were serious violations to the basic conjunto style and repertory that had been fashioned by earlier artists and that by the 1960s had become such an integral part of working-class life. However, Bernal was acutely aware of the group's core constituency, and he quickly learned how to balance the demands of his audience with the creative urges of his musicians. Not surprisingly, El Conjunto Bernal remained unchallenged in popularity for the better part of the 1960s.

Since the innovation of El Conjunto Bernal, conjunto music has remained virtually static, especially with respect to its most unique and characteristic genre: the *canción ranchera* in polka tempo. In fact, considerable retrenchment took place after the decline of El Conjunto Bernal in the early 1970s, when Bernal abandoned the group in favor of the ministry. At this time the field was left to other groups more in line with the pre-Bernal style—groups like the durable Tony de la Rosa's and newer ones like Los Relámpagos del Norte, Ramón Ayala y los Bravos del Norte, and others.

The question, of course, is why this happened—why conjunto music suddenly turned conservative. My own interpretation is based on sociocultural considerations—that is, on the crucial connection between music as a cultural phenomenon and its social context. However, I will postpone the question of conjunto's resistance to further change—indeed, to its emergence in the first place—for later. Here I want only to reiterate that the cultural strategies of a class, transposed to the esthetic realm, were the driving force in the rise to prominence of this unique style among *tejanos*. Now I shall turn to *orquesta* and trace briefly its own emergence vis-à-vis conjunto.

Orquesta Music: Squeezed between Ranchero and High Class

Let me emphasize first that *orquesta* music did not burst spontaneously upon *tejanos* at the outbreak of World War II. On the contrary, both wind and string *orquestas*—albeit few in number—had existed in Texas-Mexican society since the nineteenth century. However, it is impossible for me to render any account of those *orquestas* here. I can only say that the few fully organized *orquestas* that did exist, especially prior to 1930, were under the patronage of a small group of merchants and professionals that were to be found in Texas-Mexican society since the previous century. On the other hand, among the preponderant mass of impoverished *tejano* workers, makeshift ensembles were the rule. These ensembles were assembled for diverse celebrations on an ad hoc basis, and could range from as few as two, to as many as eight, depending on the availability of musicians and often-scarce instruments.

The modern *orquesta tejana,* modeled after the U.S. dance band, began to appear with increasing frequency around 1930. It grew out of the early ad hoc ensemble, which now began to acquire better and more permanent organization. As indicated by the large numbers of U.S. pieces to be found in their repertories, it is apparent that the new *orquestas* articulated through music the strategies of a nascent group of upwardly mobile Texas Mexicans who wanted to distance themselves from the mass of proletarian workers, while at the same time desiring to imitate the lifestyle of the U.S. middle class. By the early 1930s several well-established *orquestas* operated in cities like San Antonio, Corpus Christi, Kingsville, and in the Rio Grande Valley.

It was in the early 1930s—1932, to be exact—that Beto Villa, Narciso Martínez's counterpart in the modern *orquesta tejana,* began his professional career. Since his name became synonymous with *orquesta* music in Texas, and since he became such an influential man, I would like to devote some space here to discuss his music and his career.

Villa was born in 1915, but unlike Narciso Martínez and the other early accordionists, he was fortunate enough to remain in school until he was seventeen. This is a critical fact about Villa's life, because his educational accomplishments were the exception, rather than the rule, for the Mexicans of his time, and also because Villa's musical experience in high school had a profound influence on the direction his musical career would later take. One more point about Villa's early life should be noted, and that is the fact that he was able to stay in school as long as he did because of his family's economic stability. His father was a prosperous tailor, as well as a musician of some note, having learned his art in Monterrey, a city in northern Mexico that until recently enjoyed special prestige among *tejanos* as a center of musical culture.

It is interesting that the first group Villa organized was known as the Sonny Boys. Although the members were all young, Mexican high-school students, the band emulated the style of the U.S. swing bands then in fashion—Benny Goodman, the Dorsey Brothers, and others. It is important to note, too, however, that Villa was also exposed to Mexican music, having played with his father's group, as well as others active in the Falfurrias-Kingsville area, where Villa was born and raised. Through these bands the young saxophonist had become familiar with Mexican and other Latino styles and genres.

Villa's opportunity to enter the commercial recording market came in 1946, at almost the same time that the first Chicano recording companies appeared on the scene. Indeed, Ideal Records, for a time the most active of these early companies, owed much of its initial success to the popularity of Villa's own music. Yet Villa's commercial debut was inauspicious at best. For one thing, by 1946 the "father" of modern *orquesta tejana* seems to have postponed his pursuit of a U.S. musical ideal. Instead, Villa opted for the folk, *ranchero* sound then associated with conjunto music. That is, he restricted himself to the polkas and waltzes that had dominated traditional *tejano* music since the late nineteenth century. More than that, however, the "*ranchero*-ization" of Villa's music convinces me that he fully realized that only by adopting a *ranchero* style was he likely to reach a wide audience. But this is not surprising, since in 1946 at least three fourths of the Mexicans in Texas were working-class people who subscribed overwhelmingly to the *ranchero* music that conjuntos and the Mexican *mariachi* had so thoroughly popularized.

In any case, when Villa approached Ideal Records, Paco Betancourt, Marroquín's business partner, did not immediately accept him, because he felt the band was not "professional" enough. It was a minimal *orquesta,* consisting of alto saxophone, trumpet, contrabass, and drums. Consonant with its *ranchero* orientation, the group featured simple melodies, with unsophisticated harmonies. Indeed, it was the generally unpolished sound of the *orquesta* that prompted Betancourt to object. In the end, however, Villa prevailed, and, at his own expense, Ideal released two 78-rpm sides: "Por qué te ríes vals" and "Las delicias polca." According to Marroquín, here is what happened: "So then the record came out—Boy! About a month after Betancourt started distributing it, he called me and said, 'Say, tell him to record some more.' They were asking for it in bunches. It was like a conjunto; it wasn't even an *orquesta* yet . . . There were only five or six . . . real small, *ranchero*-like" (my translation).

With this first recording, Villa's position in Texas-Mexican music was assured; but Marroquín's statement on the group's similarity to the conjunto is provocative, because it confirms the link between *orquesta* and conjunto, a link made possible by the *ranchero* sound that all conjuntos shared and that many *orquestas,* including that of Beto Villa, were beginning to incorporate into their repertories. This brings up an important point: I propose that it was the *ranchero* sound complex that served as the common denominator that linked the two ensembles, although in other critical features they of course differed sharply, both in style and social acceptance. We may thus be certain that Villa never lost sight of the *ranchero*, ethnic origins of his music. This is clearly demonstrated, for example, in his willingness to collaborate with none other than Narciso Martínez on a number of recordings. Especially fruitful was their collective effort on the tune "Rosita vals," an immensely popular recording whose success Ideal was never able to duplicate.

Yet it soon became obvious that, despite his successes with El Huracán, Villa was hardly interested in becoming permanently associated with conjunto music. In fact, by 1949 he had decided on a drastic change. First, he weeded out the folk musicians—those who had no formal training—from his fledgling *orquesta*. Second, he began to de-emphasize the *ranchero* sound (though he did not abandon it altogether) in favor of more cosmopolitan styles that would amalgamate U.S., Mexican, and more generalized Latino genres. In short, Villa was ready to return to his first love—the big U.S. band sound, though he aimed to retain a Latin flavor as well—including the indispensable *ranchero* style. But above all, I believe that Villa was striving for a combination of styles that would mediate the contradictions between the ethnic nature of his audience, which was inescapably tied to the *ranchero* roots that conjunto epitomized, and the class aspirations of that same audience—aspirations that aimed at cutting all links with conjunto music and the "low-class" life it symbolized.

Since the term *ranchero* keeps coming up, perhaps it is time for me to offer a few explanatory remarks about it, and see what light its symbolic significance might shed on the subject under discussion. To grasp how the concept of *lo ranchero* finds significance in *tejano* (as well as Mexican) culture, we need, first, to understand that Mexican society has traditionally been folk and agrarian, and only in recent times has it moved forward with modernization. Second, since the latter part of the nineteenth century, the ideology of romantic nationalism has been endemic among Mexicans, manifesting itself in numerous facets of national life. Particularly germane for this discussion is the heavy commercialization since the 1930s of some of the symbols of that nationalism, as capitalists began to convert them into profitable mass commodities, principally through music and film. It was, in fact, in the 1930s that the *ranchero* label was first attached to the Mexican *canción* as part of the larger effort by commercial promoters to capitalize on the ideology of romantic nationalism, or *mexicanismo*.

Now, the symbols I refer to belong to the vast collective consciousness that is Mexico's cultural heritage, symbols that have been selectively chosen for exaltation as representative of the glory of Mexico's history and culture. They find expression through diverse channels of communication, though nowadays the mass media predominates. As expressions of the ideology of romantic nationalism, these symbols have served to crystallize a number of concepts in the popular consciousness. For example, the uniqueness of the Mexican religious experience finds expression in the symbol of the Virgin of Guadalupe, and the grandeur of Mexico's indigenous past is embodied in the familiar Aztec warrior. But two symbols that encompass the concept of *lo ranchero* are especially applicable here: the arrogant manliness (*machismo*) of the Mexican as represented by the *charro,* and the humble but perseverant spirit of the Mexican as expressed in the figure of the *campesino,* or peasant.

These last two have been singled out for intensive exploitation in both music and film (often simultaneously) since the 1930s. More than any others, the twin symbols of the *charro* and *campesino* have imparted to the concept of *lo ranchero* its visual substance. The one's dauntless *machismo* and penchant for action coexists with the other's stoicism and humility, which border on inertia and diffidence. But this juxtaposition creates tension, as the two symbols—representing opposite qualities—pull in different directions. In fact, they threaten the integrity of the concept itself. But this is precisely what Victor Turner has suggested about "root metaphors," which our symbols clearly are. Attached to concepts that are "linked analogically to the basic problems of an epoch," they are subject to great ambiguity and even contradiction. Such is the case with *lo ranchero* and its symbols, especially among Mexicans in the United States, where the contradictions are painfully apparent.

On this side of the border the ambiguities attached to *lo ranchero* are compounded by the pressures for assimilation and conformity. For example, to espouse *lo ranchero,* as many Chicanos do through their advocacy of *música ranchera,* is to overvalue their Mexican "roots": to ennoble the culture of agrarian life, which is presumed unspoiled by the pretensions of social snobbery. Yet this mystified vision can quickly turn into disillusion when jarred by the reality of modern life, especially in the United States, where the Mexican *campesino* (the sleeping man with the wide-brimmed *sombrero*) is a symbol of inertia and laziness. Thus, to the "progressive" Mexican, the negative side of *lo ranchero* is never completely hidden. It lies ready to spring into consciousness and convert nostalgia into rejection, for the romanticized *rancho* also happens to harbor the *arrancherado*—the low-class, coarse, excessively Mexicanized peon who cannot possibly appreciate the subtleties of modern, civilized life. There is an apt folkloric expression that captures the acculturated Mexican American's indignation: *México, recoge a tu gente*. An appeal is made in this well-worn refrain for Mexico to reclaim its vagabonds, who are an embarrassment to us all.

Yet despite the paradox, if there is one encompassing musical symbol among Texas Mexicans, it is that conveyed by *música ranchera* (as is true among Mexicans generally, for that matter). *Música ranchera* is an interstylistic sound that compresses a wide range of feelings and attitudes into a single esthetic moment. People immediately recognize *ranchera* music, whether it be interpreted by a conjunto, *orquesta*, or any other group, although it is true that some types of ensembles are considered more "naturally" *ranchero* than others—for example the conjunto and the *mariachi*. But inevitably, the music stirs vaguely defined but deeply experienced feelings of *mexicanismo*—or, in other words, ethnic, romantic nationalism.

Thus, *ranchera* music has always been an integral part of the Texas-Mexican musical consciousness, even among the upwardly mobile urbanites. That fact was never lost on Beto Villa and other *orquestas tejanas*. Consequently a *ranchero* style has been cultivated by all but the most Americanized (i.e., culturally assimilated) *orquestas*. As one *orquesta* musician put it, "I think we have always included *rancheras* because it goes back to our ancestors and the type of music they liked and we listened to when we were little." And, as the astute Armando Marroquín observed in discussing Beto Villa's popularity, "What helped Beto Villa was the fact that he had everything—*ranchero* and 'high class'" (my translation).

Yet the negative side of *lo ranchero* was not lost on *orquestas* either, and it helps to explain why *orquesta* musicians were so caught up in what one of them called *lo moderno*—the modern, which we should interpret as a code phrase for the assimilation of middle-class elements, not only from the U.S. swing bands, but also from similarly situated *orquestas* in Mexico. However, *orquesta tejana* was also powerfully affected by developments in conjunto music, and it was never able to free itself completely from the latter's influence. Indeed, one of the problems we face in analyzing *orquesta* as a cultural expression is its extreme stylistic fluctuations—its many faces, as it were. For to a far greater extent than any of the other music that influenced it, *orquesta tejana* has never been a one-dimensional musical expression. Marroquín's comments on Beto Villa's oscillation between *ranchero* and "high class" should make it clear that, unlike conjunto, which adhered to a strongly homogeneous style, *orquesta* encompassed a broad spectrum of styles, only one of which, properly speaking, stamped the *tejano* label on it.

Thus, many *orquestas* attempted to amalgamate a number of disparate types of music, including those associated with U.S. dance bands (e.g., fox-trots, swings, etc.), Mexican and Latin American dance bands (*boleros, danzones, mambos,* etc.), and, of course, the *ranchero* regional style of the conjunto. Within this spectrum of styles and genres there were some *orquestas*—particularly the most culturally assimilated and middle-class oriented—that emphasized the cosmopolitan styles, while others encroached more on the regional style of the conjuntos. The most popular ones were those that, like Beto Villa's, succeeded in accommodating both the sophisticated, or "high class," and the *ranchero*.

Given the social and cultural dynamics that spurred the emergence of *orquesta* (and conjunto), it should not surprise us that of all the genres Villa integrated into the *orquesta tejana,* it was the polka—the very same genre that established conjunto's identity—that provided the framework for the one style that made the ensemble unique. It was natural, then, for Villa to turn to the polka, already rooted in the Texas-Mexican tradition, and use it as the vehicle to launch his career—and that of *orquesta tejana*. Not especially surprising either is the fact that, despite its efforts at distancing itself socially from conjunto music and its clientele, *orquesta* music should in the end be forced to align itself more and more with its sister style.

Meanwhile, Villa's success encouraged a spate of imitators, though some pursued a more cosmopolitan approach than others. They played, in the words of working-class *tejanos, música más jaitona* (more high-toned music). Among the more *jaitón orquestas* was that of Balde González, the blind pianist from Victoria, Texas. A highly acclaimed performer in the early 1950s, González, much more than Villa, attempted to project a smooth, cosmopolitan sound, one that blended U.S. fox-trots with romantic Mexican *boleros* employing relatively complex harmonies. In fact, a measure of González's cultural assimilation of U.S. musical ideas (tempered, nonetheless, by the limitations of his ethnic background) was his habit of adapting Mexican vocals to U.S. rhythms, especially the fox-trot.

A more *ranchero* path was taken by González's most popular successor in the rapidly expanding *orquesta* music market. I am speaking of Isidro López, from Corpus Christi. Born in 1933, López learned to play alto saxophone and clarinet in high school, as many other *orquesta* musicians did. In the meantime he was gaining experience by playing with various local *orquestas*. A significant development in López's life was his association with Narciso Martínez. For a time in the early 1950s he accompanied El Huracán on some of his tours around the state. This experience convinced López (as he pointed out to me) that at bottom there has never been much difference between *orquesta* and conjunto. However, López also played for Balde González shortly before he organized his own *orquesta* (in 1955), and that association did leave its influence on his subsequent style.

In any case, although Isidro López clearly belongs in the *orquesta* tradition, he was acutely aware that the future of *orquesta tejana* music lay with the traditional working class, and its strong affiliation with the *norteño* variety of Mexican culture. Thus, although he did incorporate a variety of styles, López nevertheless leaned heavily toward the *ranchero* sound—one that he claims combined elements from both conjunto and mariachi. He labeled it "texachi," López's own neologism, derived from the terms "Texas" and *mariachi*. The synthesis worked. Adapting the *canción ranchera* to the idiosyncrasies of the *orquesta*, López surpassed all his competitors in public appeal from the mid 1950s until 1965, when two new *orquestas* entered the picture: Little Joe (Hernández) and the Latinaires, and Sunny (Ozuna) and the Sunliners. In a retrospective assessment it is clear that Isidro López was the man most responsible for setting in motion the final shift of *orquesta* music toward that of conjunto.

However, that shift did not proceed in an uninterrupted sweep—an indication of the conflicting currents that determined the course of *orquesta* music. Thus, Little Joe, who most personifies the next phase of *orquesta* music, and Sunny Ozuna, who also ranks among the leading personalities, began their careers in pursuit of a share of the exploding rock-and-roll market of the late 1950s. This was a time when, according to one *orquesta* musician, "Mexican wasn't in"—when many young musicians shunned not only conjunto but the music of a Beto Villa and an Isidro López as well. They preferred, instead, to emulate a Bill Haley or a Fats Domino. Little Joe and Sunny Ozuna were no exceptions.

Clearly, what was taking place among the Mexicans in Texas was the inexorable drift toward cultural assimilation. The post-Depression babies—the first generation of Mexicans to enjoy a measurable upgrading in their education—were responding to the pressures of that assimilation, even if the barriers that effectively kept them from complete integration into U.S. society (i.e., through primary associations) remained firmly in place. With cultural assimilation came a desire to emulate the lifestyles of American mass society. What Arthur Rubel observed about upwardly mobile *tejanos* in South Texas who had fought in World War II and Korea certainly applied to many in the post-Depression generation. These *tejanos,* too, aspired "toward life goals which included social equality with Anglos" (Rubel 1966: 11). They felt entitled to "clean" occupations, "high school and college education, and possession of such other status markers as automobiles, refrigerators, television sets"—in short, to the amenities of middle-class citizenship. Lastly, among the symbols that signified upward mobility was music—specifically music that approximated the ideal of mainstream U.S. life.

Thus—to discuss his rise to prominence first—Little Joe's first recording was a rock tune with the title of "Safari." This was followed by a number of sporadic efforts throughout Little Joe's career (and that of his brother, Johnny), to break into the Top 40 pop-music charts. That proved to be an impossible task—as it has always been for most musicians, even non-Chicano ones—and by 1965, perhaps discouraged by his failure, Little Joe finally decided to try his fortune in the *tejano* music circuit. He signed on with Zarape Records, a small label from Dallas, which produced an album entitled *Amor Bonito* in 1965. It was a phenomenal success, catapulting Little Joe and the Latinaires into the forefront of *orquesta tejana* music. As trumpet player Tony Guerrero, who later was to become a mainstay in Little Joe's *orquesta,* put it, "I was in California when I heard about this new band out of Texas that was called Little Joe and the Latinaires, and a promoter told me, 'These guys are kicking Isidro López's ass all over the place.'"

Of the utmost significance, however, was the style Little Joe and the Latinaires had fashioned: it was thoroughly *ranchero*. Clearly, *Amor Bonito* signaled Little Joe's newfound interest in *tejano* music, but it also marked the revival of *ranchero* music among the younger generation. In short, Little Joe's new style symbolized the final step in the "*ranchero*-ization" of *orquesta* music. Thereafter, despite *orquestas*' conspicuous forays into non-*ranchero* music (e.g., the always-popular Mexican *bolero*), the staple genre, now played in what became the typical *tejano* style, was the *canción ranchera*. This was, of course, the very same *canción,* set to the tempo di polca (and sometimes waltz) that had earlier become the hallmark of the conjunto style. After 1965, then, with the exception of a few local, "high toned" *orquestas,* the convergence of *orquesta* and conjunto was all but an accomplished fact.

Sunny Ozuna deserves our attention because, first, for a fleeting instant, in 1963, the former carhop did manage to break into the Top 40 charts with a rhythm-and-blues tune titled "Talk to Me." It was, however, a short-lived glory, as Ozuna quickly faded from the pop-music scene. Second, although Ozuna soon discovered—as Little Joe had done—that his only real alternative was to pursue a career in the *orquesta tejana* field, to this day, as his manager once revealed to me, Sunny and the Sunliners have always tried to "cater to a more middle-class crowd"—that is, to those *tejanos* who think of themselves as being a cut above the common workers. Like many other *orquestas* before him, Ozuna has done this by consciously maintaining some sort of balance between *ranchero* and "high class" (to recall Marroquín's statements about Beto Villa). Ozuna has been successful: like Little Joe, he has maintained a visible presence in *tejano* music since the mid 1960s.

As the comments of Ozuna's manager indicate—and as I have hopefully made clear—there have been two discernible (and contradicting) trends in *orquesta tejana* music since its inception. One is obviously *ranchero* and heavily influenced by the conjunto style. The other is difficult to classify neatly, since it has always aimed at amalgamating a number of disparate styles. We may, however, label it collectively (as I have done) as sophisticated, cosmopolitan, or modern. Or, we may follow the native, working-class usage and call it "high class" or *jaitón*. In either case, some *orquestas* have not hesitated to shift back and forth between *ranchero* and *jaitón*. Moreover, the consensus among musicians is that the distinguishing characteristic between *ranchero* and non-*ranchero* is harmonic complexity and, to a lesser extent, genre selection.

For example, a *canción* set in tempo di polca and arranged with relatively simple harmony—say, a I–IV–V–I chord progression—is unequivocally *ranchera,* especially if, as is often the case, certain pre-established, formulaic licks are employed (e.g., a recurring dotted-eighth-, sixteenth-note pattern). On the other hand, the same *canción* may be substantially transformed by making more extensive use of harmony—for example, adding altered chords, alternating keys, introducing syncopation, et cetera. The resulting sound would then be considered sophisticated, rather than *ranchero,* depending on the degree of complexity introduced. In sum, the more harmonic and rhythmic complexity introduced, the more sophisticated the style is judged to be. Conversely, the less complex the harmony and rhythm, the more a piece falls in the *ranchero* category.

Within the broad spectrum of styles that define the tradition, some *orquestas* have chosen to pursue a more exclusively *ranchero* style. The first of these was undoubtedly Isidro López, followed by the *orquestas* of Agustín Ramírez, Freddie Martínez, and Joe Bravo, to name three of the most popular to this day. On the other hand, *orquestas* such as Sunny and the Sunliners, Latin Breed, and Jimmy Edward (Treviño) have opted generally for less *ranchero* modes—those that incorporate more diverse genres, such as the *bolero,* rhythm and blues, and a host of others derived from Afro Caribbean traditions. At the same time, even when making utilization of the *canción ranchera*—either in waltz or polka tempos—the latter groups are easily distinguishable from the former by their use of the "sophisticated" elements I listed above. Lastly, I should point out that there are still a number of localized *orquestas* that specialize in cosmopolitan, or *jaitón,* music. They cater exclusively to the *tejano* middle class. Significantly, none of these *orquestas* enjoy commercial recording exposure—proof that the principal target of the *tejano* recording industry is the still-preponderant working class.

One more point needs to be brought out in connection with the stylistic variation within *orquestas tejanas*. Since the mid 1960s, when the tradition committed itself to a working-class orientation, it has had to limit its range of musical expression, insofar as it has become sensitive to the dictates of its new constituency, not to mention its economic survival. This means that experimentally minded *orquestas* must thread a thin needle, indeed. For if they exceed the stylistic limits imposed on them by the working class, then they threaten to dissolve the slender threads that link them to *tejano* musical culture. This they cannot afford to do, since, as one *orquesta* musician put it, "We can't afford to experiment too much anymore. *Orquesta*'s crowd is getting smaller and smaller. We're squeezed in between the conjunto and American music." Indeed, some conjunto musicians, sensitive to the competition *orquestas* offer, have predicted, with more than a trace of satisfaction, the imminent demise of *orquesta tejana.*

Nonetheless, these predictions notwithstanding, and despite the "squeeze" imposed by social restrictions, *orquesta* music is anything but dead. On the contrary, while it has faced some adverse times, it has continued to hold its own through the years. For example, the mid 1970s witnessed a major resurgence and a burst of innovation that has been unrivaled before or after. In fact, it probably is not too soon to label the 1970s as the "golden age" of *orquesta tejana* music. Beginning with a 1973 album by Little Joe y la Familia (the Latinaires renamed), titled *Para la Gente,* an active new phase was ushered in. A score of productions by other *orquestas* followed, each attempting to match La Familia's rather daring experiments, which included the addition of violins, four-part harmonies, and a constant assault on the basic polka beat of the *canción ranchera*. The experiments worked commercially, partly, I think, because in the midst of the experimentation, the basic *ranchero* sound was preserved. But they worked, too, because the *orquestas* gained substantial support among the younger generation of high-school and college students who were at this time re-examining their whole ethnic identity as a result of the Chicano Movement, and who were ripe for artistic expressions that would reflect their newfound pride in things Chicano. Much more than conjuntos (which perhaps smacked too much of the cotton sack), *orquesta* fulfilled their expectations admirably.

Since about 1978, *orquesta* music has witnessed considerable stylistic retrenchment, as well as a decline—though not a demise—in its popularity. But, as one *orquesta* musician put it, "Conjunto music has its epochs, we have ours. We'll come back." Rechristened *la onda chicana* (the Chicano wave), it seems to be enjoying a mild resurgence of late, thanks largely to the efforts of the indefatigable Little Joe Hernández.

An Interpretive Summary

Now that I have traced the evolution of conjunto and *orquesta,* I would like to add a few comments on the social and cultural variables that were present at the inception of these two styles, and the possible relationship between these and the emergence of the two styles.

First, as a number of researchers have observed, *tejano* society experienced important—if not dramatic—socioeconomic changes during World War II. Indeed, the war ought surely to be considered a threshold for Texas-Mexican society. This was a period when the process of urbanization was greatly accelerated, when the native-born for the first time outnumbered the immigrants, and when *tejanos* began to be absorbed into the U.S. political economy in occupations that offered some upward mobility. In addition, thousands of young men fought in the war, and they returned to civilian society with a new sense of purpose that contributed to the redefinition of citizenship, not only for them, but for many other Mexican Americans as well. In sum, these *tejanos* demanded—with some success—equal treatment in housing, education, employment, and so forth. But the success had its ramifications for the structure of *tejano* society: among other things, homogeneity of class gave way to differentiation and its attendant distinctions in status (e.g., "clean" versus "dirty" occupations). In short, World War II changed the face of *tejano* society forever, presenting it with a set of challenges it had never before faced.

Perhaps the most far-reaching consequence of the changed nature of Texas-Mexican society was the increasing disparity in cultural assimilation between the middle and working class, a disparity that was reflected in the rift that developed between the two classes. For example, even the old ethnic solidarity was called into question by upwardly mobile *tejanos* who were caught up in the assimilation of Anglo American middle-class ideology. It is important to remember, however, that despite the internal changes in *tejano* society that emerged during World War II, the formidable ethnic boundary that separated *tejano* and Anglo remained, posing a nearly insurmountable obstacle against the total (structural, marital) assimilation of *tejanos* into Anglo American society.

It was against this backdrop of internal socioeconomic differentiation and external ethnic segregation that *orquesta* and conjunto were cast. Here it is worth recalling James Ackerman's comments on style formation as a response to the challenges of an age. These remarks are eminently applicable to the emergence of conjunto and *orquesta*. For what *tejano* society witnessed was a fundamental shake-up of its infrastructural composition, along with a high degree of social upheaval. It is my contention that this social upheaval could not be negotiated without profound cultural dislocation. This dislocation, expressible in terms of cultural uncertainty and conflict, necessitated solutions. This is where conjunto and *orquesta* fulfilled their design: they were cultural solutions to infrastructurally generated problems.

In the case of conjunto we can explain its emergence in this way: in the face of an unsympathetic middle class that saw the working class as an impediment to the acceptance of Mexicans in U.S. society because of its presumed "backwardness," the less-acculturated working class felt obligated to respond in kind and to elaborate cultural strategies in its defense. These strategies were intended to define and at the same time legitimize working-class existence and cultural sovereignty. Thus, if upwardly mobile *tejanos* cast aspersion on the working-class lifestyles, then the latter countered with its own criticisms. Middle-class-oriented people were considered *agringados* (*gringo*-ized Mexicans), or, worse, *agabachados*—an even more acerbic epithet for Mexicans who were seen by traditional (usually) working-class people as snobs who pretended to be what they were not. Worse, in so doing they not only demeaned themselves, but also committed the contemptible act of denying their true cultural heritage, their Mexicanness.

Thus, working-class *tejanos,* convinced that only they and their kind were true Mexicans, clung ever more obdurately to their culture. "Soy puro mexicano" (I am pure Mexican!) was a popular Mexican phrase that working-class *tejanos* certainly subscribed to. Rightly or wrongly, the working class saw itself as the defender of a beleaguered Mexican heritage and its traditions. Never mind that many of those traditions were then being seriously undermined by Anglo American ideology, or that many were also in the process of rapid change. To the *tejano* proletarians they were immutable and imparted continuity to their threatened system of values.

It was out of this clash between change and continuity, between cultural assimilation and ethnic resistance, and between middle-class and working-class ideology that conjunto music derived its cultural energy and symbolic power. By balancing innovation with tradition—changing certain musical features while retaining others—conjunto music, as a symbolic expression, negotiated through esthetic means the conflicts and uncertainties that its constituency was experiencing in the social and economic sphere. In sum, the creation of this unique artistic expression was a symbolic solution to the conflicts I have outlined.

A similar case can be made for *orquesta*. Just as the stylistic maturation of conjunto signified a working-class response to the challenges posed against it by the changing conditions of its existence, so did *orquesta* likewise correspond to the Texas-Mexican middle class's search for an appropriate expressive (artistic) response to its own emergence as an ideological bloc in *tejano* society. On the one hand, *orquesta*—at least in its formative stages, up until 1960—was clearly an alternative mode of artistic expression to conjunto. That much was made abundantly clear by the musicians and others I had contact with during my research. The comments of Moy and Delia Pineda, two veteran *orquesta* musicians, sum up the relationship between *orquesta* and the middle class—even today, when conjunto and *orquesta* are so much closer in form and substance. The following is an excerpt from a conversation I had with them:

> *Peña:* Do conjuntos and *orquestas* cater to the same people?
> *M. Pineda:* No, they're both different . . . *la gente que le gusta la orquesta* [people who like *orquesta*], they like something a little more sophisticated.
> *Peña:* Well, do you think class might have something to do with it?
> *M. Pineda:* There you go . . . yes, definitely.

The words of Carlos González, another *orquesta* musician, are instructive. He said, "I have always considered conjunto a vernacular music, of the folk; *orquesta* is more modern, more sophisticated" (my translation). Two implications are deducible from this statement: first, *orquesta* has surely signified the middle class's desire for "modernization," which we should interpret as cultural assimilation, or Americanization. Second, implicit in the ideology of assimilation is a decision to distance oneself as much as possible from the working class and its cultural expressions. This of course explains the scorn for working-class lifestyles, including many middle-class people's strong condemnation of conjunto as "low class," *cantina* music.

Yet the unavoidable reality of interethnic conflict and the subordination of *tejanos* generally—especially before the civil-rights gains of the 1960s—made middle-class status for Texas Mexicans a rather precarious proposition. Quite simply, upwardly mobile *tejanos* were caught on the horns of a dilemma. On the one hand they aspired to be American, though Anglo society did not welcome them into its midst. On the other hand, a retreat to the cultural position of the traditional proletarian class was out of the question, because the middle class's ideology—which was shaped, paradoxically, by Anglo American middle-class institutions such as the schools—clashed at many points with the ethnic culture of traditional *tejano* society. The middle class's position can be summed up succinctly: socially and culturally they lived in a state of contradiction.

Musically, this state of contradiction was mediated—and reflected—by *orquesta*'s extreme variations in style. For the sake of analysis, these variations may be reduced conceptually to simple bimusicality, with U.S. styles on one side and Latin ones on the other. Moreover, the bimusicality was an extension of middle-class *tejanos*' increasing biculturalism, a biculturalism that straddled the interethnic boundary between Mexican and Anglo life experiences. Beyond bimusicality there was also pervasive bilingualism and ambiguous attitudes toward family, religion, and folklore—all a commentary on the contradictory position of the middle class. (Ambiguity crept into working-class life as well, but with far less unsettling results.) In short, the upwardly mobile *tejanos* were caught in a bicultural bind that promoted considerable social stress. I suggest that the stylistic flip-flopping *orquestas* engaged in—their struggle to mediate the differences between the Mexican and traditional versus the U.S. and "modern"—was a stark reflection of that stress.

In summary, *orquesta* music represented a symbolic response on the part of the middle class to the challenge of socioeconomic differentiation and the pressures of cultural assimilation. As I have pointed out, this challenge was fraught with contradictions that were reflected in the music itself. Given these contradictions, middle-class *tejanos* responded with what was probably the only alternative available to them. Thus, preaching assimilation, but frustrated in their attempts to gain the Anglo's acceptance, they sabotaged their own ideology by reverting to ethnic resistance. The musico-symbolic dimensions of this contradiction were beautifully illustrated for me by Moy Pineda. Speaking of certain "elite" dances he played for, Pineda commented that "they want to show off by getting a big orchestra, and they have their daughters presented to society.... It's supposed to be very exclusive.... They want that big band, and we got those fancy tuxedos, but the music—the first hour we do, man, special arrangements—and nobody's dancing. But after about an hour—I take off with 'Los laureles,' 'El abandonado' [*ranchera* tunes]—*¡Ching!* Everybody gets on the dance floor.... When they start drinking they go back to the roots."

In such ways the middle-class *tejano* attempted to validate his existence—by embracing selected aspects of U.S. culture, while out of necessity retaining many of his antecedent symbols. Pineda's statements attest that he was—and remains—bicultural, but not so much by choice as by default. And, in this betwixt-and-between position that the middle class has often found itself, *orquesta* music has played its unique role, by negotiating the contradiction between a frustrated assimilation on the one hand and a persistent ethnic allegiance on the other.

Postscript: Two Styles in the Form of a Pair

As I have pointed out, since the 1960s *orquesta* and conjunto have been on a strongly convergent course. Among the reasons that can be cited, the surrender of upwardly mobile *tejanos* to the attraction of U.S. popular culture stands out as one of the most salient. But others can be adduced: these include the prevalence throughout the Southwest of a highly commercialized, so-called *música moderna*, which is international in scope and which has cut into *orquesta*'s clientele; and the further accommodation between Anglo and Texas-Mexican societies, an accommodation that has enabled them to minimize at least the worst effects of interethnic conflict. This has made it easier for upwardly mobile *tejanos* to embrace U.S. middle-class culture, including its musical products. Moreover, in my estimation the mitigation of conflict, especially its attendant prejudice and discrimination against *tejanos*, has been accompanied by a corresponding decline in the symbolic power of both conjunto and *orquesta*, although the former retains strong proletarian support. With this decline has come a paucity of innovation, especially in conjunto music, but this may be a reminder that, as Ackerman contended, new styles flourish best in the face of new challenges.

And so, in the case of conjunto, once the original conflict between proletarians and their middle-class antagonists was mediated musically—that is, once conjunto music was seen as consummated—further modifications came to a halt. In short, as an esthetically satisfying expression, reflective of working-class sentiments, conjunto music was considered "perfected" by its practitioners. Thus, new accretions—such as the introduction of the piano accordion, for example, were seen as superfluous or detracting from the singular beauty of the music. Much the same can be said of *orquesta,* which by the late 1960s had settled into a common stylistic denominator with conjunto, insofar as it had turned increasingly to the *canción ranchera* for its sustenance. However, please recall that *orquesta* did undergo a renewed efflorescence in the 1970s, which, as I pointed out, was fueled by the emergence of the Chicano Power movement.

In a current assessment of the two musics one easily notes the similarity between *orquesta* and conjunto, though obvious differences exist: for example, a wind ensemble can never sound like an accordion. Moreover, some of the more "modern" *orquestas*—for example, that of Jimmy Edward—have maintained a dialogue with other types of music, including U.S. rock and even country, as well as Afro Caribbean. By doing so, these *orquestas* have kept open new horizons at the other end of the *orquesta* spectrum. On the other hand, groups like that of Roberto Pulido y los Clásicos have managed to achieve a credible synthesis by combining two saxophones with the accordion, thereby creating a hybrid sound.

Thus, by the late 1970s it was possible for U.S. journalists to lump conjunto and *orquesta* into one rubric, that of *música tejana.* This classification was basically correct. Today the similarities between the two musics are readily acknowledged by most performers in either tradition. As Narciso Martínez perceptively observed when I asked him about the present state of conjunto and *orquesta,* "Ahorita está muy cerquita una cosa de la otra" (Right now one thing is pretty close to the other). It is also recognized in an offhand, tacit way, by the people themselves, who often refer to the two styles as *música tejana.* That is why it is possible to speak of conjunto and *orquesta* as twin forms, or—to paraphrase Eric Satie—two styles in the form of a pair.

References

Abercrombie, Nicholas, Stephen Hill, and Bryan S. Turner. 1980. *The Dominant Ideology Thesis*. London: George Allen & Unwin.

Ackerman, James. 1962. "A Theory of Style." *The Journal of Aesthetics and Art Criticism* 20: 227–237.

Etzkorn, K. Peter, ed. 1973. *Music and Society: The Later Writings of Paul Honigsheim*. New York: John Wiley & Sons.

Peña, Manuel. 1981. "The Emergence of Conjunto Music, 1935–1955." In *"And Other Neighborly Names": Social Process and Cultural Image in Texas Folklore,* edited by Richard Bauman and Roger D. Abrahams. Austin: University of Texas Press. [Chapter 2 in this volume.]

Rubel, Arthur. 1966. *Across the Tracks: Mexican Americans in a Texas City*. Austin: University of Texas Press.

4

Conjunto Music
The First Fifty Years

✧

MANUEL PEÑA

1986

The year 1986 marks the fiftieth anniversary since Narciso Martínez, considered the "father" of the modern *tejano* conjunto, made his first commercial recording. It seems only fitting that on this the fifth anniversary of the Tejano Conjunto Festival en San Antonio we should take stock of where this venerable style of accordion music has been and what its future may be.

The pioneers of the conjunto should perhaps be recognized at the outset for the contributions they made early on to a fledgling style of music that unbeknownst to them would one day rise to become one of the most powerful regional styles among Mexicans anywhere. Many of these pioneers, these *músicos de ayer,* as Don Chicho Martínez referred to them, are now dead. But among the first accordionists to popularize the music commercially through records, one name stands out—that of Bruno Villarreal, "El Azote del Valle." Now completely blind and long ago forgotten, Villarreal was nonetheless the first *tejano* accordionist to record commercially. This was in 1928, a good eight years before Martínez made his debut. Many were to follow in El Azote's footsteps.

Other early contenders who deserve mention are Lolo Cavazos (now deceased), who in his best recordings displayed a technique that is reminiscent of that of *la nueva generación* (the new generation), that group of artists who made their impact in the years following World War II. Jesús Casiano, "El Gallito," should also be remembered, as should José Rodríguez, who early on had considerable influence on El Huracán del Valle himself, Don Narciso Martínez.

In fact, Don Narciso remembers the lively rivalry he and José Rodríguez had once carried on. He recalled the time Rodríguez was playing at one of the notorious *bailes de negocio,* as *cantina* dances were called before World War II, when Don Chicho dropped in to see what his rival was about. "Estaba tocando José cuando yo llegué," he said. "Al rato me divisó. 'Ah,' dijo, 'ya me fregó. Ya me robó cuatro o cinco piezas.'"

"He was right," continued Don Chicho. "I had snatched them from him. I was recording by then. He was recording too, but he had not sold."

In such less-than-cooperative ways, then, did the early musicians apparently jockey for position in the initial stages of the modern conjunto's development amidst the atmosphere of competition that U.S. recording companies like Columbia and Victor encouraged. Friendships and rivalries coexisted. Speaking of another accordionist, Pedro Ayala, Martínez commented, "Se hizo amigo mío—bueno. En aquel tiempo no me miraba bien, que digamos, porque asina es la vida." On the other hand, Ayala himself recalled that a *compadre* of his, reportedly an excellent accordionist who had been offered an opportunity to record for Victor, recommended Ayala instead. Furthermore, he even gave Ayala one of his polkas to record. Unfortunately, the talent scout sent by the company did not like Ayala's playing, and he had to wait another ten years before his chance arrived.

Meanwhile, farther north in San Antonio, another memorable figure was building a name for himself—the late Don Santiago Jiménez, known as El Flaco. Don Santiago was well known for his polkas, of which "Viva Seguín" and "La Piedrera" are the best remembered. He was also the first accordionist to incorporate the *tololoche,* or contrabass, into the fledgling *norteño* ensemble. It was not until the postwar period that others followed his lead in this important innovation.

But beyond a doubt the best-known and most creative of the early conjunto accordionists was El Huracán del Valle, Narciso Martínez. Martínez's fame is fully deserved. From the beginning of his commercial career he more than anyone else was responsible for creating a unique *tejano* style, especially in the polka, which among *tejanos* became the foremost genre for dancing. In brief, what Don Chicho did was to move completely away from the earlier Germanic style of playing of his contemporaries, almost totally de-emphasizing the left-hand buttons on the accordion and concentrating on the "treble," melodic end. The effect was a strikingly novel sound that was much choppier than that of other early accordionists.

In short, El Huracán established a new precedent in accordion music while building a base for a lasting new *norteño* style. However, Martínez's experimentation worked thanks to a new relationship that was evolving among *tejano* musicians between the accordion and an instrument of Mexican origins—the twelve-string bass guitar known as the *bajo sexto*. Some excellent *bajo sexto* players were active by the time Martínez began his career, and in his case the instrument was played with great virtuosity by his talented partner, Santiago Almeida. The duo of Martínez and Almeida, then, was heavily responsible for launching the modern conjunto on its way. It remained for the musicians of *la nueva generación* to bring the rapidly evolving style to full maturity.

La nueva generación—that group of young musicians who made their mark on conjunto music between the years 1947 and 1965—includes a number of outstanding musicians, accordionists in particular. Among the best-remembered groups is Los Tres Reyes from San Antonio, which recorded one of the all-time favorites in conjunto music—"Los pizcadores," a song that captured the spirit of the *tejano* cotton pickers with great fidelity.

Rubén Vela, Los Donneños, Arturo Niño, and guitarist Lorenzo Caballero deserve mention, as each one of these individuals and groups contributed in one fashion or another to the unfolding style. Mention should also be made of two groups which were not actually of *tejano* origin but which nonetheless exerted great influence on the conjunto tradition. These are the internationally known Alegres de Terán and Los Relámpagos del Norte, which in the 1970s was reorganized by accordionist Ramón Ayala under the name of Los Bravos del Norte.

All of the above-mentioned groups played an important role in solidifying the popularity of conjunto music among the *tejano* folk—that mass of proletarian workers who made up the bulk of the agricultural labor force in the state of Texas until the mid 1960s. By the 1950s, in fact, the conjunto had become synonymous with the *tejano* workers, at the same time that "homegrown" artists had succeeded in forging a style that had an unmistakable *tejano* flavor strengthened by a uniquely *tejano* polka dance that emerged in San Antonio in the late 1940s—*el tacuachito*.

But undoubtedly, of all the postwar conjunto musicians who made a lasting impact on the style, three names stand out above the rest: accordionists Valerio Longoria, Tony de la Rosa, and Paulino Bernal. The first was Valerio Longoria. According to the gifted accordionist Óscar Hernández, it was Longoria who started *una nueva onda,* striking out in new directions when he began to record commercially in the late 1940s. A musician with many accomplishments to his credit, Longoria was the one who first popularized the *canción ranchera* within the conjunto tradition. This was a notable feat since up to this time conjuntos had seldom performed *canciones,* relying on instrumental genres for their repertoire—in particular the polka, redowa, schottische, and *huapango.*

Longoria was apparently responsible also for introducing the popular Mexican *bolero* to the conjunto repertory. The *bolero* had of course long been a staple in the repertories of *orquestas* and vocal trios, but among conjuntos it had been avoided because it was too associated in the minds of the workers with *jaitón* (high tone) versions played by the *orquestas.*

Longoria's most important contribution, however, was his enlistment of the drums, sometime in the late 1940s or early 1950s. Again, the drums had been in extensive use in the *orquestas,* but conjuntos had shunned their use, principally because, according to accordionist Don Pedro Ayala, they were considered "too noisy." "Tapaban el acordeón y el bajo sexto," was Don Pedro's assessment. By the mid 1950s, however, thanks to the introduction of amplification (a significant step in itself), the drums had become a permanent member of the modern conjunto.

Accordionist Tony de la Rosa, from Sarita, Texas, is another of the most influential musicians of the *nueva generación.* Still well known to this day, de la Rosa was best known in his early days for his superb polkas, the best of which were recorded in the 1950s. Featuring a slowed-downed tempo and hard staccato playing, de la Rosa's polkas quickly became a standard by which others were measured, especially since they were considered perfect for *el tacuachito.* By the mid 1950s, de la Rosa's fortunes had risen so much that he was in great demand throughout the Lone Star State, in what one *orquesta* leader called the "taco circuit"—large public dances that attracted thousands of cotton pickers who followed the seasonal harvest from the Rio Grande Valley to the plains of Lubbock.

Lastly, there is the accordionist Paulino Bernal and El Conjunto Bernal, frequently hailed by fellow musicians as "the greatest of all time." El Conjunto Bernal is credited with several important innovations, including the introduction of three-part singing in the style of the Mexican trios and the use of the chromatic accordion. In fact, in the mid 1960s El Conjunto Bernal boasted two such accordions, played by Paulino himself and a young and talented Óscar Hernández. The Bernal-Hernández tandem combined to record such memorable classics as "Idalia Polka," selections that in their deft combination of complexity and *alegría* have never been matched. In sum, El Conjunto Bernal's greatest distinction lies in its ability to take the traditional elements of the conjunto and raise them to a level of excellence no other group has duplicated. Surrounding himself with the finest conjunto musicians available (including Eloy Bernal, possibly the finest *bajo sexto* player in conjunto history), Bernal created a highly popular sound that was based on a unique blend of the traditional and the innovative. The result was a group that, as Tony Guerrero of Tortilla Factory once observed, "was the greatest, and the only one of its kind."

Since the 1970s, when El Conjunto Bernal turned to Christian music, it can unequivocally be said that conjunto music has achieved maturity as a musical style, and that, moreover, it has reached the limits of its evolution. In fact, since the late 1960s no fundamental innovations have been introduced as conjunto musicians have relied more and more on reworking the familiar ground tilled by Longoria, de la Rosa, El Conjunto Bernal, and others. True, a few new combinations have been tried from time to time—for example, Roberto Pulido's use of the alto saxophone and the substitution of the electric organ or even the synthesizer for the accordion. However, such experiments have not violated the basic style worked out in the 1950s and '60s. Indeed, the traditional four-instrument ensemble, featuring the three-row button accordion, the *bajo sexto* (or sometimes the electric guitar), the bass, and drums, has remained the cornerstone of conjunto music.

Why conjunto music has become so conservative since the 1960s is a question worth exploring. The answer lies in the fact that despite the radical transformation that took place in the 1950s, conjunto was the product of an essentially conservative, tradition-oriented *tejano* working class. The creators of the style, as well as its supporters, were members of a society that subscribed to long-standing beliefs and values based on a strongly homogeneous *norteño* variety of Mexican culture. However, in the period after the Second World War, this culture was under great pressure to change, as the Texas Mexicans emerged out of their prewar isolation into the economic mainstream of U.S. society. The change did not take place without conflict and dislocation. Indeed, it was out of the *tejanos*' attempts to negotiate rapid socioeconomic change and its attendant cultural upheaval that the modern conjunto was forged. Thus, despite the rapid development that the music underwent at the hands of the *nueva generación,* conjunto was nonetheless part of the ongoing effort by the *tejano* working class to reaffirm its cultural position, especially in the face of challenges posed by upwardly mobile segments of *tejano* society who were attempting to remake that society in their own newly Americanized image. In short, the development of the modern conjunto was wholly consistent with working-class ideology, which aimed at maintaining traditional *tejano* culture in the face of a newly transformed world.

To reiterate the point: the conjunto did change dramatically in the post–World War II years, but it never lost its basic character, a character in which were embedded the elements of the music as it had existed since its early days. That is why even the members of *la nueva generación,* such as Paulino Bernal, acknowledge that the music has a long lineage, one that extends as far back as the era of Narciso Martínez and his contemporaries. That is also why, despite the dramatic changes, conjunto never lost touch with its constituents: the changes in the music actually corresponded with and helped smooth out the changes the *tejanos* themselves were experiencing at the socioeconomic level.

The most critical stage of change was effected by the mid 1960s, when *tejanos* had been fully incorporated into the postwar political economy—a few in a newly acquired middle-class status, the vast majority in proletarian occupations, especially in agriculture. By this time *tejano* culture, which had been shaken to its very moorings, had begun to redefine itself. Conjunto music, in its new stylistic transformation, played a part in this redefinition, particularly insofar as the working class was concerned. By this time the conjunto had become an inseparable symbol of working-class *tejano* life, as opposed to other symbols that other sectors of *tejano* society had appropriated for themselves—for example, the modern *orquesta tejana* exemplified by such figures as Balde González.

The 1960s, then, provided the requisite climate for the end to any further changes in the conjunto. It was a time for people to take stock of where they had been—socially, economically, and politically—and what must be done to restore a cultural equilibrium. The changes that had occurred had been nothing short of phenomenal—conjunto music itself was a testimonial to that fact—and the time had come to reaffirm the integrity and continuity of working-class *tejano* culture. It was, in short, a time for conservatism. For the conjunto, the limits of change had been reached. Hereafter conjunto musicians would have to content themselves with reworking the stylistic and repertorial base laid out by *la nueva generación* in the 1950s and '60s.

The 1970s and '80s have thus witnessed little movement. This has of course met with the wholehearted approval of conjunto supporters, who are clearly satisfied for the historical moment with letting conjunto mark time, as it were. This is understandable, if we keep in mind the essentially conservative nature, culturally speaking, of the society that nurtured the music from its inception. In this respect it is well to recall that conjunto music remains to this day a basically folk expression. It is, as one veteran *orquesta* musician put it, "una música vernácula, del pueblo."

As such, and despite commercialization, conjunto music has never been subjected to the degree of trivialization that mass (pop) music (e.g., "Top 40" music) has endured. Nor is it driven by the dynamic of novelty and change that the market imposes on pop music. That is, unlike individual pop-music styles and, especially, tunes, which tend to be ephemeral and quickly forgotten in favor of "new, improved" products, conjunto music has maintained a remarkable continuity. It simply refuses to go away. Its style has for the last thirty years retained a steadfast identity, and even individual melodies are often incorporated into an ongoing tradition.

In a sense, then, conjunto is antithetical to pop music. The latter demands constant turnover, conjunto demands permanence. Pop-music styles have shallow cultural roots (that's why they come and go), conjunto's roots are deeply entangled in *tejano* culture. Conjunto is a "key" symbol in *tejano* culture and, like all key symbols, it exists at the core of a culture. Pop music, on the other hand, is a different sort of expression. Its existence is rooted in commodity production, and, like all commodities, it is driven by the logic of consumption. Once consumed it is discarded; the market creates an insatiable appetite for new products. Hence, it cannot take root in culture because market competition chokes off its cultural lifeblood. Historically, the conjunto has resisted being transformed into a commodity. Thus to this day it remains an organic symbol of *tejano* working-class culture.

Of course, it can be argued that there are drawbacks to the conjunto's strong ties to bedrock *tejano* culture and to its resistance to further change. Highly creative musicians—performers like Steve Jordan, for example—may find their creativity stifled. "No one wants to explore anymore," was Jordan's terse assessment of the music today. Worse, since the music has not totally escaped the consequences of commercialization (it is at one and the same time a folk expression and a commercial product), a constant tension exists between permanence and novelty. On the one hand, as a folk expression with roots that extend into a well-defined past, conjunto defies easy change. On the other hand, as an increasingly commercialized product, it is subject to at least some of the pressures that mass markets exert: It needs constantly to be "improved," repackaged, and otherwise kept competitively up-to-date. This it has refused to do for the most part in the last twenty years—hence the perception in some quarters that it has become sterile and worn out.

Nonetheless, it is the contention of some art theorists—and I would agree with them—that artistic expressions that occupy a central position within a people's culture (as conjunto undeniably does within *tejano* culture) do not change in response to the whims of "fashion" or commercial pressure. Only significant social, political, and economic upheaval can bring that change about. Of course, it was just such upheaval that brought about the great changes in conjunto music. Moreover, it is axiomatic that once the upheaval is overcome, artistic expression settles into a period of stability and conservatism. Again, such has been the case with conjunto music, much to the disappointment of adventuresome artists like Steve Jordan and others.

To sum up: conjunto music at present maintains a stable course. No major innovations have been seen in the past twenty years. Moreover, it is unlikely that any changes will occur until another period of social turmoil overtakes *tejano* society—or until conjunto makes the complete transition from organic folk symbol to mass-market commodity. In either case, we may witness changes of such magnitude that the conjunto as we know it will disappear altogether. In the meantime, despite some erosion caused by other types of music that commercial interests relentlessly promote among the Texas Mexicans (e.g., *música moderna* of the Julio Iglesias type), conjunto music still reigns supreme in working-class celebrations large and small, public and private.

Thus, from Austin to Laredo, from Lubbock to San Antonio, this unique (if embattled) musical style continues to provide the *tejano* working class not only with a satisfying vehicle for esthetic expression, but also with a powerful source of self-identity and cultural reaffirmation.

5

The Accordion on Both Sides of the Border

✧

CARLOS JESÚS GÓMEZ FLORES

1997

Humans, as economic beings, transcend their daily struggle through their survival. It is important to note that since the Spanish Conquest, those who inhabited what once was Desert America—a geographic region that includes the Mexican states of Nuevo León, Coahuila, and Tamaulipas, and the state of Texas in the United States—had similar productive tasks, basing their economy on agriculture and livestock.

Communities celebrated the end of the harvest, the coming of the rains, and, naturally, their patron saints. Each celebration was accompanied by music, music inspired by European rhythms but which, once Americanized, took on new dimensions.

For a long time stringed instruments marked time in the melodies of this region's rural plains. Some of these melodies have resisted the passage of time and remain as a heritage of our history, in the category of traditional music. The European influence was fundamental, then, to the population that began to mix racially and that later, through this nascent identity, would detonate the struggle for its independence from colonialism. But at the same time, there also arose traditions and customs that were integrated with people's work, because the capacity to dream and to hope is intimately bound to humans, no matter the circumstance. Thus, at their parties, weddings, and general celebrations they began to play redowas, polkas, mazurkas, *huapangos,* and waltzes: musical rhythms that later generated musical styles and ways of dancing. The unassuming musicians who lived in these lands before the Río Bravo became the boundary between Mexico and the land of the "star-spangled banner" had everything in common: surnames, behavior, customs, and music.

It is clear that these economic beings experienced emotions and sentiments, the same as those they conveyed by playing instruments like the accordion—which will be the focus of this article.

From the Borderland

Mexico lost an important part of its territory to the United States in a process that began in 1847 and ended, by treaty, in 1848. North of the dividing river, Mexico left a nation's most precious resource: its people. This population did not stop thinking with a Mexicanist attitude. In reality, the border was not an actual border, given that, in the second half of the nineteenth century and in the first decades of the twentieth century, families crossed from one country to another without needing special permits or passports. During the period of the Mexican Revolution thousands of people came to the United States in search of safety, and, although many of them returned after the war was over, some settled in areas which once had been exclusively for Mexico's citizens.

What happened, then, in the Mexican-origin communities located in Texas? No doubt they began to resent the economic and ideological influence of foreign schemes. And in the face of having to share their ancient territory with Polish, German, and Anglo-Saxon people, they began to create elements of cultural resistance, thus giving rise to the valiant Chicano community.

The folklorization of the music, then, began to take on different tones after the geographic border became more restrictive. At that point, the Mexicans south of the Río Bravo and the Mexicans north of that river launched distinctive processes in the development of their music.

Over on This Side (Mexico)

Early attempts to analyze the origin of *norteño* music clashed with a reality that we still endure: an almost nonexistent literature on the subject, and a great many myths about the origins of this manifestation of popular culture. Oral information tells us that in the Salinas Valley (Mina, Hidalgo, El Carmen, Abasolo, Ciénega de Flores, and Salinas Victoria) in Nuevo León, it was the custom at the beginning of the twentieth century for accordion music to be played at weddings. But before the appearance of the button accordion, whose sound is central to *norteño* music, there were other ensemble instruments that acquired a forceful presence in the region: the *bandolón* (large mandolin), tenor banjo and mandolin banjo, bass drum, six-string guitar, seven-string guitar, transverse flute, clarinet, alto saxophone, stand-up bass, *bajo sexto,* and even *pianola* and harp. (The *pianola* is a small upright piano with a three-octave range.)

If we subdivide the northeastern region of Mexico by musical traditions, we can intuit, given the empirical evidence, that there are three distinct regions: the region of the high plains, including the area south of the eastern Sierra Madre, which has a Huastecan influence; the region of the eastern Sierra Madre; and the region of the Gulf plains.

In the region of the high plains, which encompasses part of Nuevo León, Coahuila, San Luis Potosí, Jalisco, and Durango, music is made with percussion, wind, and string instruments. Examples are the *sones, huapangos,* and Huastecan dance songs, in which the harp appears, and, of course, the music of drums and clarinet in the area of San Carlos, Tamaulipas, and in Linares, Nuevo León.

In the region of the Sierra Madre, wind and string instruments are typical. Suffice it to mention the famous group Los Montañeses del Álamo, who are originally from Santiago, Nuevo León. Their music forms part of the dance tradition in the northern state of Durango.

In the Gulf plains region the predominant music is based on the accordion and the *bajo sexto*. In the central part of Nuevo León, in the very towns of Marín and General Zuazua, there were musical groups consisting of the violin and accordion—for example, the group Los Diositos. They were the original composers of the song "El chubasco," which much later was popularized by Carlos y José. But without a doubt the richest daily use of the accordion occurs in the towns of China, General Bravo, Los Ramones, and, naturally, General Terán, in Nuevo León, as well as the cities of Reynosa, Río Bravo, Matamoros, and Nuevo Laredo, in the border region of Tamaulipas.

Over on this side (Mexico), the process of folklorization has preserved its roots—that is, the forms of interpretation and the discursive content of song lyrics. Yet it must be emphasized that among the geographical regions there is an interplay of talent, as much among singers as among songwriters and composers. For this reason it is not surprising that there are songs sung with different accompaniments, including songs originally accompanied by guitars that later were accompanied by the accordion and *bajo sexto*.

Groups like Los Alegres de Terán were pioneers in the massive promotion of *norteño* music. They opened avenues that today are traversed by groups such as Bronco, Los Tigres del Norte, and even Límite.

To the North of the Río Bravo

In Texas, the process of folklorization assumed a unique form. Regardless of the path which brought the accordion to the Rio Grande Valley of Texas and to the cities of San Antonio, Brownsville, and Corpus Christi, a historical event is self-evident: the great migratory movements which occurred in the formation of the United States. In the case of the area in question, there were German, Polish, and Czech immigrants. Some of these groups were present prior to the new dividing line. The style of accordion playing was influenced by this segment of the population, which, without a doubt, possessed a more classical style of playing. The two-row button accordion, known since the second half of the nineteenth century, accompanied rural people in their routine tasks because it was easily transported. Also, it offered a rich combination of chords and melody line, produced by the vibration of a jet of air (caused by opening and closing the bellows) over flexible metal flaps. The accordion acquired its residence papers in the United States among Mexican-origin workers, who later added the saxophone and, little by little, other instruments such as the guitar, electric bass, and drums.

In Texas there appeared marvelous accordionists such as Narciso Martínez, whose nickname was El Huracán del Valle. He recorded *huapangos* like "El tecolote" and others in 1937 and 1938. Other well-known accordionists are Lalo García, Juan López, Pedro Ayala, Pablo Elizondo, Mario Montes, Rubén Vela, Ángel Flores, Tony de la Rosa, and, from the Conjunto Bernal, Óscar Hernández. All of them are of Mexican descent.

Commercialization

The music began to reach huge numbers of people through radio. To do so, musical groups (duos, trios, and ensembles) began airing radio programs supported by the incipient record industry. It was evident that the music could be commercial. Thus, from 1926 to 1932, one could hear songs like "Señorita cantinera," by Juan Gaytán and Timoteo Cantú; "Vive feliz," by Daniel Ramírez and Santiago E.; "Delgadina," by Lydia Mendoza y Familia; "Sierra mojada," "Yo fui el primero," and "Paloma mensajera," by Pedro Rocha and Lupe Martínez; and "Esos enamorados" (first and second parts), "García y Zamarripa," and "Morena de ojos negros," by Alfonso and Martín Chavarría. Among other songs recorded between 1930 and 1948 were "La mariguana," written by E. Vigil y Robles and recorded by the Trío Garnica Ascencio, which was formed by the sisters Julia, Blanca, and Ofelia; the traditional songs "Federico el pelao" and "Aborrezco la vida," by Lydia and Leonora Mendoza; "La guía," with Leonora Mendoza on guitar, María Mendoza on mandolin, and vocals by Juanita and Manuel Mendoza; "Los pachucos," written by R. Rodríguez and E. Carranza and recorded by Juanita and María Mendoza; "Suerte ingrata," a traditional song sung by Carmen y Laura, with Narciso Martínez playing the accordion; "Qué rayos," by Jesús (Chucho) Monje; "Río Grande," by María Padilla; "El norteño," by Acuña y Leal; and songs sung by the sisters Margarita and María Padilla, who were accompanied by the group Los Costeños.

The accordion began to take center stage through the success of Los Alegres de Terán with tunes like "Los madrugadores," which had been previously recorded in the late 1920s by Chicho y Chencho, accompanied by guitar. In 1953, after recording two unsuccessful LPs, Los Alegres de Terán recorded "Carta jugada," with the brilliant accordion work of the unforgettable Eugenio Ábrego—and from then on, there was no stopping them. In the countryside, it is said that the song was so popular that "even the dogs were singing it in every neighborhood."

I believe that the commercialization of the music on both sides of the border has significantly increased the desire for popular music in which the accordion is the instrument breathing life into the songs.

Some songs have become virtual regional hymns, forming an essential part of the *norteño* folkloric dance movement. Such are those composed and played by Antonio Tanguma Guajardo. Tanguma, who was born January 26, 1903, in China, Nuevo León, was justly known as the King of the Accordion. The discography of this musical genius includes almost fifty LPs. Among some of his most famous songs are "El Cerro de la Silla," "De China a Bravo," "La

Evangelina," "El naranjo," and "María de Jesús." The festive music of Don Antonio Tanguma was later choreographed by the great ballet scholar José Daniel Andrade, in the style that is known in folkloric dance terms as that of the central region of Nuevo León.

Norteño Musicians' Views on the Accordion and Its Players: Footnotes

Although there is historical evidence regarding the appearance of the accordion, information about its development, styles, and techniques of playing is not widely known. What is known is that it was invented by the Viennese Cyril Demian, who on May 6, 1829, patented the accordion. Different models of the instrument were later built in Italy, Austria, Germany, France, and Russia. The prototype had a single row of buttons. Later, between 1835 and 1890, accordions with two rows of buttons were constructed. This type was introduced into Texas and the border states of northeastern Mexico in the second half of the nineteenth century.

It is very interesting to hear the views of some interpreters of *norteño* music regarding how the accordion came to Desert America. Julián Garza Arredondo—who was born in Los Ramones, Nuevo León, and is the singer and composer of the duo Luis y Julián and the composer of such songs as "Las tres tumbas," "Pistoleros famosos," and "La venganza de María"—comments that at the beginning of the twentieth century the accordion arrived in the town of General Terán and, consequently, *norteño* music was born. Regarding the best accordionists, both past and present, Arredondo states, "Each one is good in his style. The most *norteño* are Eugenio Ábrego [of Los Alegres de Terán], Lupe Tijerina [of Los Cadetes de Linares], Carlos Tierranegra [of Carlos y José], and Juan Torres. They all play 100 percent *norteño* music. Of the Tejanos, Rubén Naranjo, Narciso Martínez, and Lalo García [are the best]. The best of all time was Lupe Tijerina. The Tejano conjunto accordionists have a style that is happy and pleasing. The accordion should be played with the bass [buttons] because it comes with them. There are some who don't use them and remove them."

Juan Villarreal, the accordionist for the group Los Cachorros de Juan Villarreal, who was born in Reynosa and still resides there, comments that the accordion came from Europe via the port of Matamoros. From there it traveled to Reynosa and Nuevo Laredo, and also to San Antonio, Brownsville, and Corpus Christi. He also states that the accordion is the centerpiece of *norteño* and Tejano conjunto music. About the accordionists he says, "I began learning to play the *redovas, huapangos,* and waltzes," which were his specialty, "while with Narciso Martínez. He and people like Juan López and Pedro Ayala played in a very complicated way because it was a two-row button accordion. Now we have the three-row [accordion], and we no longer move the accordion as much. Before, it was in and out, just to play a note. Long ago, it was a two-row accordion and those players came out with some things . . . that we struggled to find. Today we find them a lot easier."

Regarding the styles, Juan Villarreal states, "None of us wants to be left behind. Tejano conjunto music is more studied than ours, which is more rural, more open. It's played faster. As far as I'm concerned, all the styles are better, even though Óscar Hernández, who lives in McAllen on Jackson Street, is the best. The music he made twenty-five years ago, while with the Conjunto Bernal, is what's being heard today. Their music was of such high quality that we're still learning from it."

The extroverted and colorful accordionist Juan Torres—a former member of Los Tremendos Gavilanes and, more recently, of Los Dos Rancheros, who is given to self-praise but is widely recognized as a musical virtuoso—says that "the older *norteño* music is better than that of today. There are no more musicians like Tanguma. I copied him. Back then there were good accordionists such as Lalo García, Pablo Elizondo, Rubén Vela, Tony de la Rosa, and Ángel Flores. Our music went in that direction. At the present time, *norteño* music is evolving. It seems to be *norteño,* but it isn't *norteño* because it's *cumbia*. These new conjunto groups, who think they're great, they don't know how to play, they don't know what I used to play."

The composer and accordionist Mencho Martínez comments that *norteño* music began in General Terán. For him, the more-talented accordionists have been Eugenio Ábrego, Mario Montes of the group Los Donneños, Lalo García, Ramón Ayala, Lupe Tijerina, and Javier Ríos. "The *norteño* makes his own music," he states with pride.

"As I understand it, the first accordion was brought over from Texas," says Javier Ríos, the accordionist for Los Invasores de Nuevo León, who is originally from Ramones, Nuevo León. He adds, "Nuevo León is the cradle of *norteño* music, although there are good accordionists both here and over there, like Eugenio Ábrego and Narciso Martínez. But, without belittling anybody, Tejano conjunto music will never compare with *norteño.*"

It would be very important to undertake fieldwork on the folklorization of *norteño* music and the contributions of its musicians in this area. In northeastern Mexico alone there are more than three thousand regional music groups registered with unions, and aside from these there are many others as well. Other points of view to consider are those of *norteño* music promoters and radio programmers, because they have lived so close to the phenomenon of the rise of *norteño* music. Many of this music genre's originators are still alive, and their songs are still being promoted on the radio. Here it is sufficient to mention that on the radio station XETKR, its programmer, Don Anselmo Hernández, manages a catalog of "golden hits." This catalog contains close to one hundred polkas, *huapangos, redovas,* and schottisches—for example, "California," by Cornelio Reyna y su Conjunto; "Ciudad Victoria," by Los Montañeses del Álamo; "Robstown," by Lalo García y su Conjunto; "Zapateando en Burgos," by Juan Torres with his awesome accordion; "El chanclazo," by José Ángel Reyes y los Norteños de China; "La presumida," by Los Tamborileros de Linares; "María," by Los Gorriones del Topo Chico; "La cápsula," by Los Broncos de Reynosa; "Las perlitas," by Los Donneños; "Las capitanas," by Rogelio Gutiérrez y su Conjunto; "Tampico hermoso," by Tony de la Rosa; "De China a Bravo," by Carlos y José; "Arriba Torreón," by Rafael Silva y su Conjunto; "El palomo y el gorrión," by Juan Colorado; "La chicharronera," by Narciso Martínez; "La escopeta," by Los Hermanos Prado; "El ponchón," by Juan López; "El oso negro," by Rubén Vela; and "Evangelina," by Los Madrugadores.

"The Norteño Style Is Performed by the Fingers but Is Played with the Heart"

Without a doubt, traditional music is a reflection of the role of human beings in the productive process, but the way it is interpreted has to do with their emotional sensibilities, and with their need for transcendence.

After the establishment of the geographical border, which divided people within the same population of origin, foreign influences north of the Río Bravo enriched the accordion technique, making it more sophisticated there. Meanwhile, to the south, the people continue to live under the same sociocultural conditions. Just as people in Texas have a certain way of forming phrases when they talk and sing, so in northeastern Mexico is there a form of speaking and singing.

The accordion of *norteño* music has a different accent, because it is rooted in different sentiments. There are Tejano accordionists of considerable ability who have the opportunity to record using the latest technology. Although they have the same ethnic and linguistic roots as the *norteños,* their performance is less passionate. The *norteño* style is stronger, and has more presence. Although less harmonious and less exquisite, it still has the interpretive force of an established tradition that is jealously preserved by its masters, who are still living and who, through their heirs, hope to preserve it. Perhaps the *norteño* accordion style is simpler and more staccato, but it is played to the beat of the heart. The hands that play it express the emotional charge conveyed by cerebral energy: it is a matter of sentiment.

Will the Music Border Disappear?

At the present time, the possibility that Tejano conjunto and *norteño* music will reach a point of confluence, such that their styles become unified, seems remote. It would be like beginning to speak the same musical language.

But at the beginning of the nineteenth century, how could someone have imagined the birth of radio? And that this circumstance would allow, in the specific case of Desert America, for Tejano accordion-based music to be heard daily in northeastern Mexico, and for *norteño* accordion-based music to be heard in Texas? Yet during the twentieth century we have witnessed the influence of border *norteño* music on Tejano conjunto music, from the end of the 1920s to the end of the 1970s, and the growing influence of Tejano conjunto music on *norteño* music since the 1980s.

My hypothesis, which I must prove, is that the ever-increasing mass diffusion of music by radio will cause the technology used by Tejano conjunto groups in producing their music to be adopted by *norteño* groups, until the two styles become one. Perhaps the lyrics will continue to have a different focus, but not even popular music can escape the impact of economic globalization.

To put it another way, we can say that if the geographical border does remain, the musical border will disappear, and surviving all this will be the magical sound of the accordion.

Note

This article originally appeared in Spanish, under the title "El acordeón: Cuestión de sentimientos." It was translated into English for this volume by Max Martínez. —EDITORS

6

Three of the Greatest Bajo Sexto Players in the History of Conjunto

✧

RAMÓN HERNÁNDEZ, JR.

1986

In thinking about who we were going to induct this year into the Conjunto Music Hall of Fame, we decided that this would be the year that we honored those great bajo sexto *players who made a name for themselves in the formative years of conjunto music. The* bajo sexto, *after all, is now the primary companion instrument to the accordion in the conjunto ensemble. We consulted various knowledgeable people in the conjunto field and asked them who they thought were the three most important* bajo sexto *players in the history of conjunto music. Invariably, the names of Santiago Almeida, Reynaldo Barrera, and Eloy Bernal kept popping up. Santiago Almeida, for firmly establishing the* bajo sexto *as one of the principal instruments within the conjunto ensemble; Reynaldo Barrera, for his exceptional playing; and Eloy Bernal, for being considered one of the greatest* bajo sexto *players to ever play the instrument.*

We asked local Tejano-music writer Ramón Hernández to research these three individuals and see what he could come up with. However, information on Santiago Almeida and Reynaldo Barrera was difficult to obtain, and because of time constraints we decided to postpone the induction of the bajo sexto *players into the Conjunto Music Hall of Fame until next year so that we could research them a little better. In the meantime, we are publishing this preliminary article by Mr. Hernández, anyway. Our search, or should we say re-search, continues.* —J.T.

Santiago Almeida, Reynaldo Barrera, and Eloy Bernal are three conjunto-music pioneers who made a name for themselves long before *música tejana,* or the *onda chicana,* as we know it today, existed. They achieved recognition for their virtuosity on the *bajo sexto* during the time when conjuntos were made up of only three musicians, using the bare essentials—before the addition of synthesizers, other electrical instruments, and special effects.

"Conjuntos then were the accordion, guitar, and *bajo sexto,*" Narciso Martínez, a 1982 Conjunto Music Hall of Fame inductee, said. "Of course at that time there was no electricity. We played under the light of kerosene lamps. Electrical instruments weren't available until 1948, but most people could not afford them so our music, which we only knew as *regional,* did not start to change until 1949. That's when people started calling it *música tejana,*" Martínez said. "Conjunto music then, however, had the same rhythm. The accordion carried the melody while the guitar and *bajo sexto* took care of the harmony," the seventy-four-year-old accordionist explained.

Santiago Almeida was one of his friends. Together they recorded fifty-eight singles between 1935 and 1938. "Last thing I heard about Santiago, who is about my age, is that he was living in Washington State and was very ill. I wonder how he's doing now," the San Benito resident said.

Neither Beto Villa, Armando Marroquín, Paulino Bernal, Eloy Bernal, nor anyone else I have talked to knows about his condition or whereabouts.

Reynaldo Barrera, a blind musician with whom Martínez recorded in the fifties, is another conjunto pioneer, whose life unfortunately ended when he was killed in a car crash in Robstown while en route to a performance in Corpus Christi on August 17, 1957. He was thirty-nine years old.

His daughter Elvaray Silvas, who was born twenty-two days after his death, said the *bajo sexto* player was not born blind. "He was born normal. What I am told happened is that when he was five weeks old his eyes started getting a watery discharge. My grandmother, then fourteen, unknowingly took him to a fake doctor who gave him very strong medication, which burned his vision." Irma

Salas, another daughter, added, "But there were days that he could see shadows. He could see a little bit."

Barrera, born in La Reforma, Texas, on April 16, 1918, made his home base on a ranch called La Parrita in the area of Concepcion and grew up throughout the state, later settling in Bishop. As a small boy he learned to play the accordion, piano, guitar, violin, steel guitar, harmonica, saxophone, and *bajo sexto*. When he was a teenager, he toured with a "hillbilly band" in West Texas, long before he joined any conjunto, Evelia, his wife, said. His big break came in 1937 when, as a pianist, he toured with La Carpa Monsiváis circus, where he was discovered by Beto Villa. The rest is history.

Other names he played with were Isidro López and Tony de la Rosa. By 1950, he had mastered every instrument except the saxophone (because of poor lungs resulting from a bout with pneumonia). Although his son Jesús once played guitar with Los Muchachos and still has the guitar that belonged to his dad, no one followed in his footsteps.

Eloy Bernal was born in Orange Grove, Texas, on March 11, 1937. "It wasn't the first instrument I learned," he said about the *bajo sexto*. "When I was about eight years old, I learned to play guitar, and Paulino, my brother, the accordion. Later, I bought a *bajo sexto* in Reynosa and, by the time I was thirteen, I was already recording on Armando Marroquín's Discos Ideal. Who influenced me was the enthusiasm of two *bajistas:* Amadeo Flores and Lupe López."

Originally, it was Los Hermanitos Bernal, then they added Adán Lomas on drums, Rubén Sáenz on upright bass, and a singer, Rubén Pérez. "Although I had recorded with Carmen y Laura, Gaitán y Cantú, Los Hermanos Ayala, Tony de la Rosa, and then–child singer Beatriz Llamas, we did not record anything as El Conjunto Bernal until 1954, when we made 'Mujer casada' *de* Daniel Garcés," he said.

In 1960, there was trouble in Laos and Bernal volunteered to join the Army, where he served in Hawaii and Okinawa. Once he fulfilled his military obligation, Eloy rejoined the band, and they enjoyed a peak between 1962 and 1967. During this period, Pérez left and was replaced by Manuel Solís.

"Later, Juan Sifuentes and I started co-writing and doing different arrangements—that's when we started doing more vocals," Bernal said. "In 1967, Óscar Hernández took Paulino's place when he left to spread the word of the Lord and I kept the group going. However, I was unhappy. It was before Christmas, 1967, that I screamed out to God to show me the truth. I had good record sales; I had tried all things the world had to offer," Bernal recalled. "Christmas came, then we played Corpus on the twenty-ninth, Lubbock the thirtieth, and Corpus again on New Year's Eve. Then we had a family reunion during which Paulino preached the gospel—it was then that God took the blindfold off my eyes. I realized I could be saved from drugs, or a highway accident, so I decided not to record anymore."

Bernal said that now God has let him rejoin Paulino, another brother, Luis, and his nephew Ernesto to reform and to glorify Christ through music. "It's still the same music, same rhythm, same style, but a different message, stating Christ is the answer," Bernal explained.

The Bernal family is currently on a fifty-day tour of California.

7

Women in Conjunto Music

✦

RAMIRO BURR

1991

Conjunto music, that button accordion–based music of South Texas and northern Mexico, originated as the popular music of the Texas-Mexican working class in the early twentieth century. Given the prevailing conditions in that earlier age, it's not surprising there have been so few women in the genre. And like the history of conjunto, which began to unfold when various social, cultural, political, and musical influences coalesced almost sixty years ago, the role of and contributions by women in this regional, folk-based music were not chronicled or noted with any precise detail. This story is not meant to be a definitive work on the contributions by women in conjunto music. Rather, it is simply an exploratory look at the developmental history of women in this uniquely southwestern folk genre. And because of scarce documentation on the subject, most of the information was gathered from the oral accounts of interview subjects. —J.T.

Conjunto, with its accordion-fueled polka songs, has always been widely considered simple, but happy, dancing music. This despite a lyrical content which often focused on the *campesinos*' experiences of romance and passion, loss and desolation, struggle and survival. But the harsh lifestyle and the need to relax and have fun through music and dancing was not limited to men. Women also shared the pain and suffering, the joy and the celebration. The same primitive, many times oppressive, conditions that shaped conjunto music in its infancy affected both men and women: low pay; little or no respect (the music was slighted for its rural base and considered more appropriate for the uneducated masses); one-sided recording contracts which often meant as little as ten dollars for each album recorded in crude studios, with no royalties; and the music's image as strictly *cantina* (saloon) music. While most of the best-known pioneers and proponents in conjunto have been men, women have been an important part of the genre as singers, songwriters, and instrumentalists.

In the early 1900s, the most common form of popular Mexican music in the Southwest usually featured a singer accompanied by a guitar. This was dictated by simple economics and the lack of mass-produced, affordable instruments.

Eventually, says veteran San Antonio producer and retailer Salomé Gutiérrez, the groups featured two guitars and, at some point, an accordion, most likely the early, single-row model. "Back then, the arrangement was usually having one singer who played at *carpas*, or tents," Gutiérrez said. "Entertainment at these *carpas* also featured clowns and magicians. Conjuntos were seen more in *cantinas* and nightclubs. The old theaters, like the Guadalupe and the Alameda, were usually used for big-name artists from Mexico who would put on a show, as opposed to a dance."

Musicians in conjuntos and *mariachi* groups were also called *taloneros*, said Gutiérrez. "*Taloneros* meant people who hustled on their feet, who went from restaurant to restaurant and *cantina* to *cantina*, asking the patrons, 'Can I sing you a song, or play you a song?' They would usually get twenty-five to fifty cents a song." The modern version of these can still be seen in area restaurants like Mi Tierra and La Margarita in the forms of *tríos, mariachis,* and an occasional accordion-*bajo* duo.

In the sixty-plus years of conjunto's development, outside of the relatively few "superstar" conjuntos, the situation has not dramatically improved economically for the musicians in general—men or women. The prevailing attitude that *cantinas,* one of the few places where conjunto could be heard, were no place for "decent women" certainly did nothing to help the female gender in the genre. It's not surprising, then, that the few early women in Mexican music in the Southwest tended to be singers, who usually ventured into the more widely accepted forms of *rancheras, boleros,* and *música romántica.*

The First Women

Perhaps the first woman to enjoy widespread popularity in the Southwest was Lydia Mendoza. Born on May 13, 1916, in Houston, but raised in Monterrey, Mexico, Mendoza began singing at the age of twelve in the Rio Grande Valley (she had returned to Texas at the age of ten). She was taught the guitar by her mother. In 1928, Mendoza and her father, mother, and sister formed El Cuarteto Carta Blanca and recorded their first productions on the Okeh label. The Mendozas played in barbershops and restaurants throughout the Valley. Shortly afterward, the family moved to Detroit, where they found a ready audience of Mexican American farm and factory workers who had migrated north for jobs. When the depression hit in 1929, the family was forced to return to Texas. They settled in San Antonio in the 1930s, where they would perform at the legendary Plaza de Zacate, or Haymarket Square, in the evenings.

"I always liked music, ever since I was a little girl," said Mendoza recently. "My mother played the guitar, and she showed me how to play it, too. So I sang and played the guitar." Mendoza was still a teenager when a local radio announcer discovered her. She was soon contracted to play her twelve-string guitar and sing on a nightly Spanish program, *La Voz Latina*. Her repertoire included *rancheras, boleros, corridos,* and a few polkas. As for composers: "I liked them all, from Agustín Lara and José Alfredo Jiménez, to Miguel Aceves Mejía, Cuco Sánchez, and Pedro Infante," she said. "I got to meet many of them too."

After winning a Pearl Beer singing competition on the radio, Mendoza was signed to a recording contract by the now-defunct Bluebird Records. In 1934, Mendoza recorded her first big hit, "Mal hombre," which led the family to performances in clubs, theaters, and church halls throughout Texas. Part of Mendoza's wide appeal was her music and lyrics, which spoke to the daily concerns of backbreaking migrant labor, economic hardships, and discrimination.

By the early 1940s, Mendoza had recorded more than two hundred songs. With the outbreak of World War II, the recording industry essentially stopped for six years. But soon afterward, Mendoza resumed her recording and touring career. In the 1950s, Mendoza started recording albums with the Orquesta Falcón and Beto Villa y su Orquesta. Later she went into the studio with conjunto greats

Narciso Martínez and Valerio Longoria: "It was the record companies' idea," Mendoza recalled. "Ideal [in Alice] and Falcón [in McAllen] all saw what I was doing in my career and so they suggested my recording with conjuntos." Mendoza doesn't recall the exact number but estimates she produced almost a dozen records each with Martínez and Longoria. She also recorded with the legendary Tony de la Rosa.

If there was any discrimination or slanted attitudes against conjunto music at the time, Mendoza wasn't aware of it: "To me, it was all the same, whether it was *boleros, rancheras*, or conjunto I was singing," she said. "It was exciting music just the same."

During the 1980s, Mendoza recorded more than sixty songs for Gutiérrez's DLB record label, on occasion accompanied by conjunto musicians like Eddie (Lalo) Torres and El Conjunto de Bennie Medina. Today, Mendoza, seventy-four, is retired, the result of a stroke in 1988 which left her partially paralyzed. Through the years, she won numerous awards and honors, including a National Heritage Fellowship from the National Endowment for the Arts, and induction into the Tejano Music Hall of Fame in 1984 and the Texas Women Hall of Fame.

In San Antonio, Rosita Fernández was on a parallel course with Mendoza, making a name for herself in the Alamo City. Like Mendoza she started her career young, making her singing debut with Trío San Miguel in the late 1920s. In 1931, she recorded "Chaparrita pretenciosa," on the Bluebird record label. She later teamed up with Laura of the female duo Carmen y Laura, to form Rosita y Laura. Fernández was also a featured vocalist with the Eduardo Martínez Orchestra and Trío los Conquistadores. As a vocalist, Fernández was not into conjunto music, since her style lent itself more to the romantic *boleros* and *rancheras*. But Fernández did record several 45s with the Beto Villa Orchestra, which included an accordionist, in the early 1940s. Eventually Fernández earned the nickname San Antonio's First Lady of Song, and in her fifty-plus-year career she has sung for a dozen United States and Mexican presidents.

During the 1940s, Carmen (Marroquín) y Laura (Cantú), of Alice, emerged as one of the top female duos in the Southwest. Their first big recording was "Se me fue el amor," on the Four Star label. They also teamed up with Juan Gaytán and Reymundo Treviño and were among the first *tejanas* to include blues, swing, beguines, and foxtrots in their repertoire, which also included polkas, *rancheras*, and *cumbias.* "They were one of the few women duos who crossed frontiers into Mexico, into Monterrey, that were popular," said Gutiérrez. The duo later recorded for the Ideal record label, which was founded by Carmen's husband, Armando Marroquín, in 1947. That same label also recorded the first works by Tejano-music pioneers Beto Villa and Isidro López.

In the 1950s, Corpus Christi produced one of the biggest names in Tejano conjunto music: Chelo Silva. Silva began her career recording *boleros* and *rancheras* for the Falcón record label, but eventually produced albums for RCA and Columbia. Her music was also popular in Mexico. Her biggest hits included "Cheque en blanco" and "Como un perro."

Silva is remembered as being one of the most successful female singers in the genre, according to Gutiérrez: "There have been several women in the early 1900s that performed Mexican *ranchera* or conjunto music," Gutiérrez said. "But most reached only local or regional success. Silva was one of a half dozen that not only landed a recording contract with a multinational label, but also toured extensively."

Silva died on April 2, 1988, of cancer.

The Sixties

Sometime after the 1940s, duets became one of the most popular forms of music, particularly male-female duets. The conjunto duo of Irene y Fidel made their mark in the 1960s. Originally from Monterrey, the duo moved to San Antonio in 1965, where they began recording for the DLB label. Known for their stylized *románticas* and *rancheras,* Irene y Fidel scored big with "Puño de tierra," written by Carlos Corrales, and "Piedras Negras." In 1985, Irene suffered a stroke and the duo was forced to retire.

The same time period saw other groups like Las Hermanas Góngora, of Corpus Christi, and Las Hermanas Degollado. These duos were unable to get recording contracts and achieved only limited touring success.

In the early 1960s, another name came into prominence: Beatriz Llamas. Llamas sang mostly *rancheras* but she also recorded conjunto music with Eddie Torres. Her hits included "Donde empieza la noche," "Tres amores," "Ya te fueron con el chisme," and "La paloma del norte." She was known locally and regionally, but toured as far away as Phoenix and Colorado. During her peak, from 1965 to 1975, she also recorded on the Discos Bernal and Sombrero labels. She retired in the early 1980s, but recently recorded an album with Los Dos Gilbertos.

Alice, Texas, also produced another important female singer in the 1960s—Linda Escobar. Born in 1957, Escobar began singing at six. Raised in an impoverished setting, Escobar was stricken with polio when she was less than a year old. Her father, Eligio, who was bedridden after a traffic accident, influenced her when he began his musical career. She got her opportunity at a festival in Alice, singing "La bola negra," which she would later record into a hit. At the festival, a KROB DJ in Robstown asked her father to bring Linda over to sing live on the radio. That led to Linda's first contract with Ideal Records, which produced "La huerfanita" and "La bola negra."

Linda and her father then began touring the Southwest with Los Guadalupanos de Joey López. She later recorded for the Bego and Bernal labels. In 1965, Linda recorded perhaps her biggest hit, "Frijolitos pintos," for Cometa Records, which earned her a gold record. She also recorded with conjunto legend Tony de la Rosa under his label in the late 1970s and produced a duet with Al "Chato" Chavarría from El Grupo Mayo titled "Looking for Love." She formed her own group, Zamen, in 1980 and recorded under the Supremo label. Recently she recorded on the Dina label with Los Hermanos Cadena. Since then, Escobar has recorded and toured the Southwest and Mexico. Through the years she received various honors, including Conjunto Female Vocalist of the Year at the West Texas Awards in Lubbock in 1987.

A female member of the famous de la Rosa family also ventured into conjunto music in the mid 1960s—Eva de la Rosa, sister of legendary accordionist Tony. Eva, now living in Kingsville, did not play the accordion but sang lead vocals with her brother Adán, during a stint together as Adán y Eva y su Conjunto. They were also known as Los Hermanos de la Rosa. She toured with her brother and recorded two albums on the Freddie label. In 1978 she started her own group, Eva de la Rosa y su Conjunto, and recorded two cassettes for the Canasta label. Inactive since 1981, Eva said she is working to regroup her band: "I expect us to be together again sometime in late summer but I can't say exactly when," she said.

In San Antonio, a local group known as Dueto Carta Blanca de George y Mague (Orozco) began to gain prominence in the mid 1960s.

The pair met and married here but moved to Los Angeles, where they lived for seven years. George played the bass and sang while Mague sang lead vocals. After returning, they performed on Jimmy Flores's program on the then-new radio station KEDA-AM. Recording impresario Joey López heard the duo and soon after, George y Mague were backed up on tour by the Guadalupanos. Their first recordings in 1966 were on López's Comet label. In their twenty-seven-year recording career the pair produced several local hits including "El chubasco," "Morena, la causa fuistes," and "Paloma, ¿qué rumbo llevas?" They also toured Europe performing for U.S. troops in Germany and Italy. The duo also recorded for TH-Rodven Records and the local labels of DLB and Toby Torres.

California Connection

While Texas has produced most of the important vocalists and instrumentalists in conjunto music, California produced what can be described as perhaps the first successful female accordionist—Chavela (Isabel Salaiza). Known as La Dama del Acordeón, Chavela also sings and heads her own group, Grupo Express. Born in Fresno, Chavela inherited her love of music from her family. She started playing the accordion at the age of nine, when she helped form Las Incomparable Hermanas Ortiz, which included her mother on *bajo sexto,* her father on electric bass, and her sister on drums. This family lineup was something of an oddity in conjunto music. "I got the accordion as a gift from my mother," Chavela said recently. "I got it as sort of a practical idea, since my sisters played drums and guitar and another sister played bass." Did she ever consider any other instrument? "I played a little guitar, but I got into the accordion. It was a little hard at first but I got the hang of it."

From the beginning in 1964, the group, Las Incomparable Hermanas Ortiz, performed in nightclubs and community events, disbanding in 1968. In 1976, Chavela joined Brown Express as accordionist and vocalist. She formed her own group in 1980. She remained true to her distinctive style of *norteño* conjunto music, while also playing ballads and *tropical.* Her 1987 album, *El Rey del Barrio,* on the Discos Fama label of Los Angeles, earned a Grammy nomination.

Chavela said she didn't encounter any negative feedback as a woman in conjunto until she started her own group: "Some promoters felt uneasy that a woman could handle bookings and the business end of things," she said. "There's still some of that today, but not as much." She also never gave much thought to her being one of the very few women playing accordion: "I really didn't think of it as any advantage. I was more concerned with just keeping recording and staying in the market." Her advice for any aspiring female accordionist? "I would say if she liked it, to keep going. It's like anything, if you like something, you can succeed at almost anything if you just keep at it." Chavela has produced fifteen albums for various labels, including Profono and Fonovisa, and has toured extensively in the United States and northern Mexico. She is married to Eduardo Hernández of Los Tigres del Norte.

The Eighties

In the last decades several female-led conjuntos began attracting regional acclaim.

Besides the stigma of playing in a "man's domain," Lupita Rodela had to overcome another major hurdle. Blind at birth, Rodela learned to play by the feel of her fingers and by listening. Rodela said she learned the instrument when an uncle let her have an old beat-up accordion when she was a toddler. "He helped me a little, but mostly I learned by myself, listening to records," she said. She said she picked the accordion over other instruments because of its complexity: "I liked complicated instruments. To me, the accordion is something that provides a lot of different sounds. And it's an instrument that makes me use my head a lot."

Grammy winner and noted accordionist Flaco Jiménez also helped out Rodela early in her career, and not just in technique: "He gave me encouragement," Rodela said. "He told me there would be problems and obstacles but not to get discouraged." Now forty-two, Rodela fronts her band, El Conjunto de Lupita Rodela, performing at area nightclubs, dance halls, weddings, and debuts. Her last record was on the Toby Torres label.

Rodela said she was aware of the stigma of conjunto music years ago but said it didn't faze her: "I realized back then I had to fight it," she said. "I thought, someday this music will pick up, I don't know where or when. But I tried to work as hard as I could. I really owe a lot to Flaco for his support."

Considered by many to be the best female accordionist ever, Eva Ybarra, from San Antonio, started playing the instrument at the age of four, learning from her brother Pedro, who had his own group. (Pete Ybarra, who plays the accordion for Emilio Navaira, is her nephew.) "I learned mostly by listening to records, which wasn't easy," Ybarra said. Now forty-six, Ybarra has been fronting her own group, Eva Ybarra y Sistema, for almost eleven years. She has also played with other groups, including Jet Martínez and Sunny Ozuna. "There aren't very many women accordionists, but still Eva has to be one of the best female players in the country," said Chris Strachwitz, of Arhoolie Records. Ybarra names Manuel Guerrero, Aldo Rizardi, and Óscar Hernández among her influences. Her last single was titled "Yo soy tu palomita," and she is currently recording her next album at Zaz Studios on the West Side. "It'll be called *Danny, el Juguetón,* after my nephew," she said. She expects to have it put on her own label—Accordion Discs—by early summer. Both Ybarra and Rodela recorded on small, independent regional labels, but, like most conjuntos, neither has enjoyed a particularly lucrative career.

La Onda

In what is known mostly as Tejano music, or *la onda chicana,* several women have also carved out their own recording careers, including Laura Canales, Patsy Torres, Cathy Chávez, Shelly Lares, Janie C. Ramírez, Laura Reyes, Linda V., Jeanne Le Grand, Sunny, and Selena Quintanilla. Many of these women have achieved notable success in that genre, which is sort of a modern, urban cousin to conjunto. Several may have had an occasional accordionist in their band or recorded a few conjunto songs.

But perhaps only one has remained true to the authenticity of conjunto. That is, kept an accordion player in the lineup and consistently played a repertoire of the traditionally polka-based conjunto music. That would be singer Laura Canales, a native of Kingsville. Canales is recognized widely as the Reina de la Onda Tejana (Queen of Tejano Music). She rose to the top of the music industry during the early to mid 1980s. She holds the record for winning the most female-vocalist and female-entertainer honors (and consecutively) at the Tejano Music Awards. After breaking up with her longtime group Encanto in 1986, Canales had a few tenuous starts with several bands. In 1989, Capitol/EMI Latin signed her up, giving her career a much-needed boost. Her first two LPs for the label have met with success, but, more importantly, she has included the accordion-fueled polka sound in her repertoire.

"The polka sound, and conjunto music, has always been a big part of what we call Tejano music," Canales said. "To me, it's the music people like to dance to."

Why So Few?

There is no agreement on why there have been so few women in conjunto music. Adrián Treviño, archivist at the University of New Mexico and owner of the largest record collection of music of the Southwest, said the "tomboy attitudes" may have been one factor: "I don't think it was so much that the men were chauvinistic," he said. "It's just from a practical standpoint, women were not going to be traveling with a group of men on the road, unless they were married to them. So often we had women who were either the lead singer–owners or accordionists, both of which were always the center of attention in bands. But to ward off derogatory remarks or come-ons by the males, a 'protective guard' was usually in place around the women," he said. "You know, an older brother, husband, or close friend. In any case, they had to be big," Treviño speculated, "to discourage any kind of problems."

Treviño doesn't see an increase in the number of women in the genre in the future: "The same problems that have been affecting the groups in the past will continue," he said. "Attitudes, low pay."

Albert Dávila, general manager for radio station KEDA-AM, thinks stereotypes of conjunto have discouraged a lot of women: "I think some people have preconceived ideas that it [conjunto] is a male-type, barroom, beer-drinking music, which I don't agree with. Low pay is probably a factor, but it's the image it has had, as mostly a blue-collar, *cantina* thing that probably has hurt it the most."

Many officials think that conjunto in general has not been attracting a large-enough audience through the years, particularly the youth, to generate significant revenues for recordings and bookings. Yet it survives and, judging by the proliferation of conjuntos throughout South Texas and the continued popularity of the accordion, one could say it has even thrived. Each year there have been a smattering of new faces in the genre, but not enough, in Dávila's opinion, to really provide a boost to the industry. As for the future, Dávila is a little sanguine: "I think it [conjunto] is a large untapped market for women. The problems with attitudes and stereotypes will always be around, but I think the women will get past that."

Laura Canales believes female-led bands will continue to include the accordion in their instrumentation, just like male-led groups: "If it's hot, like the accordion is right now, bands will include whatever it is," she said.

Lupita Rodela says she doesn't know what the future holds for female players but has this advice: "My advice to anyone—male or female—is that they really have to love this music if they want to get into it. Too many young people have got discouraged when they find out there's not a lot of money to be made."

8
El Conjunto Bernal
Style and Legacy

✧

MAX MARTÍNEZ

1990

El Conjunto Bernal was one of the most innovative and accomplished conjuntos of all time, and, by general agreement, one of the greatest of them all. Under the leadership of Paulino Bernal, it gained such dominance in conjunto music that its influence continues today, after more than twenty years. The reverence in which El Conjunto Bernal is still held has little to do with nostalgia. El Conjunto Bernal is distinguished by the sheer brilliance of its musicianship. In fact, much of the experimentation and innovation that they brought to conjunto music remains unsurpassed today.

Conjunto music has an easily traceable history. The diatonic accordion was introduced into the rural areas of northern Mexico and South Texas at the turn of the century. It quickly displaced the violin as the principal instrument used for the *bailes, jamaicas,* and other festive gatherings of *mexicanos*. Within a generation or two, it became the signature instrument of a new cultural element among *mexicanos:* conjunto music.

In the near century of its existence, conjunto has undergone various musical developments. From 1928, when Bruno Villarreal made the first conjunto-music recording, through the end of World War II, the dominant figures were Narciso Martínez, Santiago Jiménez, and Pedro Ayala. The music of these dance-hall and radio personalities was relatively simple, largely instrumental, and intended primarily to keep people dancing.

From 1945 to 1955, Valerio Longoria and Tony de la Rosa emerged as the major figures. It was their music which comprises the transitional phase to the modern conjunto. They standardized the basic conjunto instruments (accordion, *bajo sexto,* bass, and drums) and shifted the repertoire from largely danceable instrumentals to a greater variety of tunes, including vocals, to which the audience could dance.

Valerio Longoria was perhaps the most innovative of the two. Undaunted by the limited musical range of the button accordion, with its inability to produce the full musical scale, Longoria experimented with retuning until he could play notes previously unheard in conjunto music. He is also credited with creating his own style, which was radically different from that of his predecessors, and with expanding the conjunto-music repertoire by introducing the *bolero,* the soft romantic ballad of the Caribbean with strong Afro Cuban rhythms.

Tony de la Rosa can be credited with creating a new way of playing the accordion. He slowed the bass tempo while at the same time he increased the fingering of the keyboard, producing a sharp staccato sound. Occasionally, he would jerk the bellows to produce a banshee screech to punctuate a riff. De la Rosa's new sound, wild and energetic, which allowed for a graceful turn on the dance floor, was quite a contrast to the predictable and exhausting rhythms of the earlier conjuntos. Tony de la Rosa's music proved to be irresistible with the public, and he enjoyed immense popularity during the fifties and beyond.

As Manuel Peña notes in his authoritative work on conjunto music, the end of World War II signaled important social changes among *la raza.* While the conjuntos of old remained popular, the new breed of musicians, among whom Valerio Longoria and Tony de la Rosa were in the forefront, brought to *mexicanos* a new musical sound to match the changes occurring in their lives.

Paulino Bernal was born in 1939 in the Rio Grande Valley. At an early age, his parents separated. Paulino's mother moved the family of six to Kingsville. Despite the poverty and hardship, the Bernal family did not sink into despair. It was always possible to brighten a bleak existence with a song.

One day, a man happened along who had a guitar he would sell. Paulino's mother bought it for her children. Paulino instantly began to exploit his innate musical talent, picking out tunes, doggedly forcing himself to learn the mysteries it could yield, to the gleeful approval of his family. Paulino learned to play the guitar well enough to join up with an old accordion player who plied the bars around Kingsville, playing for nickels and dimes. The accordion, with its giddy, elongated sound, fascinated Paulino. Paulino determined to play the accordion, borrowing it as often as the old man would lend it.

A friend of Paulino's received an accordion, but it was Paulino who got the most use out of it. He practiced constantly, improving his playing until he could perform in front of an audience. Meantime, Paulino's brother Eloy had received a *bajo sexto* from their father, and he began to accompany Paulino.

Not long after elementary school, Paulino and Eloy left school to help support the family. They worked in the fields, picking the seasonal crops during the week. On weekends, however, they performed as Los Hermanitos Bernal wherever they could find bookings. It was in 1952, and, by this time, Adán Lomas had joined the brothers on drums.

Los Hermanitos Bernal were good enough to establish themselves among a loyal if local following. They were also good enough to be noticed by the relatively small conjunto recording industry. Their big break came in 1954, when Armando Marroquín, of Ideal Records, recorded El Conjunto Bernal. The first recording did little more than reprise the standard sound of conjunto music, but with a slight difference. That first record, as Paulino later recalled, consisted of a *bolero* on one side and a version of "Mujer paseada" on the other. What made the Bernals' version of "Mujer paseada" so successful was its instrumental variation. The public was accustomed to the song in a soothing, formal waltz time. El Conjunto Bernal burst forth with a faster, more upbeat polka rhythm perfectly suited for an exuberant dancing crowd.

As Paulino was to say many years later, their initial success came from remaining solidly within the expectations of a conjunto audience while incorporating slight, but nonetheless important, variations. It was taking the old and familiar and making it sound fresh and new. It should be noted that their youthful and neat appearance, along with the maturity of their playing, contributed significantly to their instant popularity. They became so successful, in fact, that in 1955, at the age of sixteen, Paulino Bernal became a full-time professional musician.

⋄◆⋄

The creative spirit is essentially restless and normally dissatisfied with existing realities. The creative urge always seeks ways to explore known possibilities and to find in them a deeper and richer expression.

In the early sixties, despite the Conjunto Bernal's ever-increasing recognition and success, Paulino was restless and dissatisfied with the music itself. From the time that he became a professional musician, Paulino had virtually exhausted the received wisdom of his forebears in conjunto music. He was still in his twenties, anxious to strike out in new directions, to put, as it were, his personal stamp on the music. There was, however, the substantial popularity of El Conjunto Bernal to consider. How would the public respond to the music? As Manuel Peña cogently argues in his book, the conjunto audience is essentially conservative in its musical tastes. This means that any experimentation and innovation must remain within firmly implanted expectations.

Early in his career, Paulino Bernal received some advice from a fellow accordionist. The advice encouraged him to find a way to set the Conjunto Bernal apart, to produce so distinctive a sound that they would become easily and immediately identifiable. All of the great traditional conjunto musicians were easily recognizable simply by the particular style of the music they played.

Paulino began by thoroughly re-examining the elements which comprise conjunto music. Of the three major elements, the first and most important is the accordion itself. The second element consists of the coordination of the remaining instruments into a closely knit ensemble. The third element rests with the vocals. Put together, these elements make for a seamless conjunto.

The accordion is the instrument without which there would not be a conjunto. Not only does the accordion give to conjunto music its distinctive sound, it is the solar brilliance around which everything else revolves. In most cases, the "style" of a conjunto is basically the technique and idiosyncrasy of the accordionist. A reasonably good accordion player alone is enough to sustain a conjunto.

All along, Paulino had been exploring the limits of the diatonic accordion, which is capable only of a truncated musical scale. Paulino says that by constantly exploring and experimenting, he was able to play the entire scale on the accordion, something which the three-row button accordions are not supposed to do. Bernal's mastery of the accordion alone would have been enough to gain for him a permanent place among conjunto greats.

The remaining instruments in a conjunto, with rare exception, are drums, *bajo sexto,* and electric bass. How well these instruments are coordinated to mesh with and complement the lead of the accordion is what distinguishes one conjunto from another. Each of the musicians Paulino employed to fill out the ensemble displayed as much mastery over their instruments as he did on the accordion. In fact, the willingness of the musicians to match his search for excellence produced a much more consciously sophisticated sound.

The vocals further contribute to the formation of a distinctive conjunto sound. A good singer with a clearly identifiable voice, coupled with an astute selection of songs, can create a conjunto's personality in the public mind.

◇◆◇

Sometime between 1963 and 1964, Paulino Bernal added a second accordion player, Óscar Hernández, to the group. Two accordions were unusual in a conjunto. Young Hernández, who undoubtedly is one of the best conjunto accordion players ever, brought the five-row button, chromatic accordion into the conjunto.

In a recent interview, Óscar Hernández remembered that Paulino already owned a chromatic accordion at the time, but had not taken to playing it in the conjunto. Following Hernández's lead, Paulino quickly learned the larger and more musically diverse chromatic one, reserving the diatonic accordion for select numbers.

This single change, from the diatonic to the chromatic accordion, as Dr. Peña notes, represents the line of demarcation between the traditional conjunto and the modern conjunto. In many ways, it initiated the final phase in the development of the conjunto. The introduction of the chromatic accordion, Peña continues, "made possible a wide range of sonorities." This made it imperative to include in the repertoire vocals, instrumentation, and songs which were equal to the new possibilities that the instrument presented.

Since its inception, El Conjunto Bernal had relied strongly on vocal duets. Trios and quartets were popular in Mexican and American music. In the fifties—and this undoubtedly influenced El Conjunto Bernal—such groups as the Inkspots, the Kingston Trio, and the Mills Brothers were consistently on the Top 40 charts. In Mexico, crossing over into the *mexicano* community on this side of the border, were such groups as Trío los Panchos and Los Tres Reyes.

Paulino, who had already melded the conjunto's vocals into smooth, honey-toned duets, experimented with the intricate, romantic *boleros* of the Mexican trios. This was not particularly new and raw territory for the *mexicano* community, as the Mexican trios already had discernible followings. However, for purely conjunto audiences, this was indeed a departure from traditional expectations.

In combining the wider range possible with the chromatic accordion and by introducing the *trío,* along with excellent arrangements, El Conjunto Bernal highlighted what had been implicit in the music all along, namely, that it could be mature and sophisticated. The significance of this bold step in the expansion of conjunto music lies primarily in the fact that it united the working-class audience with the music of its sophisticated city counterparts.

Paulino, in his drive for a distinctive style for El Conjunto Bernal, took conjunto music itself far beyond anything which had previously existed. He distinguished himself by his personal accordion traits and he also managed to integrate the chromatic accordion into conjunto music. He introduced outstanding three-part vocalizations and innovative arrangements.

He was particularly fortunate in working with talented singers such as Rubén Pérez ("La Pulga"), Gerardo Reyes, Manuel Solís, Juan Sifuentes, and Chacha Jiménez. The singers with El Conjunto Bernal all displayed considerable vocal range and became noted for their subtle phrasing. The vocal mastery, necessary for the blossoming Bernal sound, set Bernal's singers apart from their contemporaries.

In fact, El Conjunto Bernal ended up so far in advance of their peers in conjunto music that, more than twenty years later, few have come close to matching their achievements. Musically, with the exception of Esteban Jordán, none has surpassed them.

In the quest for a proper expression of their musical abilities, El Conjunto Bernal turned as well to a wide variety of sources. According to Manuel Peña, "El Conjunto Bernal adopted many genres not normally associated with conjunto music, including *valses peruanos, mariachi sones,* and even American rock tunes."

Ironically, while their popularity remained stable, and while they had reached the pinnacle of creative expression by 1967, the supremacy of El Conjunto Bernal was coming to an end. Paulino had quit playing with the group. He had acquired a taste for business and he began to devote much of his time to managing Bego Records and to discovering new talent.

In 1973, Paulino Bernal became a born-again Christian and turned to the ministry and the pulpit. El Conjunto Bernal continued with Eloy Bernal, himself established as a very fine *bajo sexto* player and composer, and Óscar Hernández. Until 1977, when El Conjunto Bernal disbanded altogether, they were graced with a number of excellent musicians, including accordionists Ramón Treviño, Beto Salinas, and Bobby Naranjo, and vocalist Joe Ramos.

After a period of inactivity, El Conjunto Bernal was reformed as a conjunto gospel group with Paulino once again performing. It remains a part of a very successful Christian ministry established by the Reverend Bernal. Bernal performed at the Tejano Conjunto Festival in 1983, dazzling a mix of his devout religious followers and avid conjunto fans. Although the music still displays the Bernal genius and the vocals are as sophisticated as ever, the lyrics are now different.

In an interview with Juan Tejeda, Bernal admitted that his first Christian recordings met with considerable resistance at Christian radio stations. The conjunto sound was still present and this was out of the ordinary in *mexicano* gospel music. The resistance, in fact, was so stubborn that Bernal says he was moved to buy his own radio stations.

On another front, he told Tejeda, he takes conjunto music with him to all of the venues for his ministry. He is exposing Central and South Americans to conjunto music. While his chief purpose remains the Word of God, he feels that a little of the spirit of Chicanos, as it is so inextricable from conjunto music, remains behind wherever he goes.

✧◆✧

Twenty years later, the legacy and the influence of El Conjunto Bernal continues unabated. Since the seventies, Chacha Jiménez has continued the Bernal legacy with his group, Los Chachos. Óscar

Hernández and Bobby Naranjo head their respective conjuntos, each with his own style that is reminiscent of El Conjunto Bernal. Numerous other conjuntos and *orquestas* continue to incorporate Bernal's songs and style into their music, some of which include Tonka y Libre, Los Paisanos, and Roberto Pulido y los Clásicos.

Some of the more popular songs that El Conjunto Bernal left imprinted on the souls of *la raza* are "Por amor al dinero," "Idalia," "Buena suerte," "Seis años," "El vino y tú," and "Me regalo contigo."

Recently, Ramón Treviño has come out of a self-imposed retirement—although he is still a relatively young man—to form Los Chukos. Treviño includes unabashed renditions of Conjunto Bernal tunes in his performances, which, devoid of nostalgia, are pertinent reminders of the timelessness of the music.

Paulino Bernal's peers and forebears express their admiration and recognize his contribution to conjunto music. Valerio Longoria says, "Paulino Bernal, ni se diga, es un gran músico . . . otro estilo diferente, avanzadisísimo, avanzado, muy inteligente para la acordeón. Paulino desarrolló otras cosas a través del trío." (Paulino Bernal is a great musician . . . a different style, very progressive. Progressive, very gifted on the accordion. Paulino developed other things through the *trío*.)

To underscore Bernal's technical achievements, Tony de la Rosa comments, "Bernal introdució —ya había otros, pero no eran reconocidos— las tres voces. Y un estilo muy único de ellos, en acordeón, en voces, en los arreglos, señor. El compás de mi compadre Paulino Bernal, yo bailaba muy a gusto con él." (Bernal introduced the three-part harmony. Others were doing it, but they weren't known. They had a very unique style in the accordion, the vocals, the arrangements. I used to dance very comfortably to my *compadre* Paulino Bernal's beat.)

Flaco Jiménez, whose career coincides with that of El Conjunto Bernal, assesses Paulino's contributions: "Lo puchó más en sabiduría de música, en hacerlo más profesional, más progresivo. Así que creo que Paulino Bernal fue uno de los pioneros pa'l *progressive*." (He advanced it [the conjunto] more in the knowledge of music by making it more professional, more progressive. Thus, I think Paulino Bernal was one of the pioneers in progressive conjunto music.)

Finally, it seems fitting to end with Esteban Jordán. No other musician on the contemporary scene is as determined to stretch the limits of conjunto music as Jordán. He says, "El vato podía tocar toda la onda. *And then he grabbed* el tiempo que había en los tríos . . . y se hizo. *In other words,* hizo un conjunto, estableció la onda del trío dentro del conjunto. Porque traiba muy buenos elementos también —eso le ayudó mucho. Estilistas como cantantes, hacían un estilo, *overall.*" (The guy could play everything. And then he grabbed the tempo of the *tríos* . . . and it happened. In other words, he formed a conjunto, established the sound of the *trío* within the conjunto. Because he had very good elements, too—that helped him a lot. Stylists as vocalists, they created a style, overall.)

Jordán concludes, "*Paulino is good, man! Paulino is a very good man. He brought a style. From all the styles, he picked something of his own* . . . había un estilo de sangre." (The style was in his blood.)

Acknowledgment

Grateful acknowledgment of assistance in the preparation of this tribute to El Conjunto Bernal is extended to Dr. Manuel Peña for his excellent volume on conjunto music, *The Texas-Mexican Conjunto: History of a Working-Class Music,* published in Austin by University of Texas Press, 1985, and also for his article "Conjunto Music: The First Fifty Years," which appeared in the May 1986 *Tonantzin* (vol. 3, no. 3), published by the Guadalupe Cultural Arts Center [chapter 4 in this volume].

9

The Tejano Conjunto Festival en San Antonio

Eight Years of Change

✧

CARMEN LUÉVANOS
1990

Don Américo Paredes, the famous anthropologist at the University of Texas, Austin, observed in class one day that many festivals originate "by the people, for the people" and then move toward "by the people, for the tourists."

On April 29, 1982, Mayor Henry Cisneros, flanked by Juan Tejeda, the director of the Xicano Music Program at the Guadalupe Cultural Arts Center, and the late Don Santiago Jiménez, master accordionist, issued a proclamation recognizing the Tejano Conjunto Festival en San Antonio. It was the beginning of an annual festival, "by the people, for the people."

The proclamation, in part, said, "The City of San Antonio and its people recognize the significance of the artistic and cultural expression of its various ethnic groups." It goes on to say, "The style of music known as Conjunto Music . . . symbolizes a part of Chicano and Mexican life in Texas."

1982–1984: Años de Tradición

From 1982 to 1984, the festival maintained a solid and traditional conjunto-music lineup. The following is a partial list of the conjuntos participating during that period: Santiago Jiménez, Jr., Flaco Jiménez, Santiago Jiménez, Sr., Valerio Longoria, Sr., Narciso Martínez, Toby Torres, Manuel Guerrcro, Esteban Jordán, Pedro Ayala, Henry Zimmerle, Los Paisanos de Chalito Johnson, Tony de la Rosa, Johnny Degollado, Los Alegres de Terán, Rubén Naranjo y los Gamblers, Los Dos Gilbertos, Ramón Ayala y los Bravos del Norte, and Roberto Pulido y los Clásicos.

It was these traditional conjuntos that brought the crowds in to dance. Juan Tejeda, the festival's founder, says he was surprised by the turnout for that first festival. "We were overwhelmed because we got a tremendous response. A music festival dedicated completely to conjunto." Clearly, the audience from the city's West and South sides agreed that community recognition for conjunto music was long overdue.

Tejeda says, "Conjunto music has maintained a very, very solid base of support within the Chicano community and within the Mexican community. There has always been a very strong base of support that has persisted throughout the years."

It has persisted despite the musical cycle that many young Mexican Americans go through while growing up. Tejeda adds, "I think the new generations move away from conjunto music. Originally, they get it in the home, from the parents, just like they get language, the culture, and everything else. In school, they start getting into heavy conflicts about their culture, so they start steering away from conjunto music and many people have used that argument to say it's dying out. I don't think it's dying. I feel that people eventually come back to their musical roots."

In May of 1985, the Fourth Annual Tejano Conjunto Festival en San Antonio was dedicated to Don Santiago Jiménez, who died the preceding December. The official poster for the festival was drawn by Roberto Sosa. It is a portrait of Don Santiago playing his accordion over the San Antonio skyline. He is embracing the city.

The passing of Don Santiago coincides with the end of the traditional days of the Tejano Conjunto Festival and the beginning of a new direction. It moves away from a conjunto-only gathering into new musical directions with the appearance of nonconjunto groups. The move toward new musical directions has an impact on the audience, which begins to change.

1985-1989: Nuevas Direcciones

The Tejano Conjunto Festival's "New Directions in Conjunto Music" began with the inclusion of Doug Sahm, Augie Meyers, and the Westside Horns; Esteban Jordán; and Los Lobos in 1985. Since then, it has included bands like Brave Combo, Joe "King" Carrasco y las Nuevas Coronas, Test Tube Babes, and various Cajun and zydeco bands.

Variety was not the only reason for including nonconjunto bands in the "New Directions" evening. As Tejeda explains, there were also musical reasons, primarily the natural progression and common intersection of several musical styles: "The music is beginning to open up and you see the rock influences and the jazz influences within conjunto music. You see the blues and Cajun/zydeco because we're exposed to those influences. It's natural that it show up in our music."

Another reason for scheduling nonconjunto bands in a "New Directions" evening was the hook it provided in bringing in a different kind of audience. Tejeda wanted to attract a younger, nonconjunto audience in order to expose them to the festival.

"I've tried consciously to expand our audience," he says. "I've done that through our 'New Directions' night, based on the theory that I'm going to be pulling in a new audience that follows Los Lobos, and Doug Sahm. At the same time, I'm going to expose conjunto to this new audience. We're [also] bringing in Cajun/zydeco because we relate on certain levels. They use the accordion, obviously. They come from a historical development similar to conjunto. They have all these parallels. So it was a meeting of similar musical genres and different cultural traditions that are unique and distinctive and utilize the button accordion as their principal instrument."

Despite Tejeda's reasoning for including Cajun and zydeco music, in some circles it was perceived as a blatant attempt to bring in a new audience. It was also seen as an attempt to legitimize conjunto music by associating it with another type of successful ethnic music, namely Cajun music.

Criticism aside, the "New Directions" evenings pulled in people from all sides of the city, the state, the nation, and even farther away. "I was really amazed," says Tejeda, "that we pulled in people from all over the world. Little by little, the festival has gained a reputation of being a very distinctive type of festival. Where before, it was mainly San Antonio people coming to the event, now I get more people coming from outside. Most of them, however, continue to be Chicanos."

Still, Tejeda is concerned about keeping his original audience. He is also concerned with the music, although he does not feel the need to legitimize conjunto music and pull in larger audiences by having big-name stars like Willie Nelson at the festival. "I like the idea of meeting," he says. "I think it's happening very naturally. We're meeting all these other people. We're doing their music and they're doing our music. That opens it all up."

A Look at the Changes

In 1982, the festival began, as Dr. Américo Paredes puts it, as a celebration "by the people, for the people." The early program messages are clear: "lo nuestro, para nosotros." However, in eight years the festival has grown. At the close of the 1980s we see a younger, more professional and ethnically mixed audience.

So there is a dichotomy. Tejeda feels the need to maintain his traditional audiences as keenly as he feels a musician's need to evolve with the music. However, the resolution of these two conflicting forces does not have to be "either-or." Instead, it can be resolved by balancing the traditional audience's love for conjunto with the musician's need for change, by continuing along the path he has already established.

The "New Directions" night on Thursdays exposes a new and younger audience to conjunto music, whereas the traditional Friday- and Saturday-night *bailes* maintain the loyalty of the longtime audience. In the past, Sundays have been the days earmarked for surprise all-star jam sessions, such as last year's [1989] "Conjunto Meets Cajun/Zydeco" experiment.

"Conjunto has always maintained a traditional base. I feel there's going to be evolutions of the styles, there's going to be integration with other styles, but the basic core is going to remain intact," says Tejeda.

In nine years, the festival has almost completed its own evolutionary cycle. It started out as a conjunto-only celebration to bring attention and legitimacy to an often ignored form of music. It then moved away from conjunto only and began to explore all the different kinds of music that influence conjunto and that conjunto influences. It even incorporated different cultures into the festival.

Now that it is in its ninth year, the festival seems to be coming back to its roots. After three years of experimentation, it is returning to the conjunto-only lineup. Once again, it is showcasing the best within the conjunto genre, from the traditional to the popular to the progressive. However, this time *tradición* takes on a more activist role, that of promoting conjunto music, not only in San Antonio, but nationally and internationally.

The festival now has new members in the audience. There has been an emergence of Anglos, Blacks, and Chicano professionals. In recent years, Chicanos have been coming in from communities surrounding San Antonio, and farther away in the state. There are also Chicanos who come from other states in a kind of pilgrimage to San Antonio. For many of them it is the land where their parents were born, where they have roots. Also, the number of international visitors is increasing significantly. These people have joined the original festival audience. When they leave San Antonio they will take conjunto music to their faraway homes.

In turn, this will open up even more doors for conjunto music, doors that many musicians have been trying to open for years. Flaco Jiménez, one of the very few conjunto musicians who has broken the European barrier, has been touring and promoting conjunto music overseas for the past eight years. Most recently, he returned from a stint in England.

Tejeda concludes that this exposure abroad, along with a growing audience at the festival, will only serve to strengthen the popularity of conjunto music.

> People are going to start taking a little more notice. You see the beginnings of this with all the things that are happening. I think that's just going to open up. Hopefully, we'll reach the point where there will be a greater understanding of cultures, of people, of the music and that exchange.
>
> Ours is a very original type of music. It's distinctive. It's real music, a living, breathing music of our people. I feel very strongly and very positively about where we are, where we're going, and our position in the world music scene.
>
> It's our turn. You watch, it's going to happen.

The Tejano Conjunto Festival may return to its original music lineup, but conjunto music itself will never return to the status it had in 1982—primarily loved by blue-collar Chicanos. The music has developed new fans and we will continue to see them at the festival, alongside the longtime loyalists, for festivals to come.

PART THREE

Instrumentos
Accordion, Bajo Sexto, Saxophone

10
Accordion Menace...
Just Say Mo´!

✧

CARLOS GUERRA

1989

It is a simple instrument, and relatively easy to pick out a pleasant melody on.

The accordion is the central element of conjunto music and important to Cajun and zydeco music, *tangos* of Argentina, *cumbias* of Colombia, and many other regional music forms throughout the world. But to the United States, the accordion was, until recently, a joke, a corny Old World anachronism. After years of Lawrence Welk jokes, comedy bits about buxom female accordionists, and even a *Far Side* cartoon showing Saint Peter giving arriving angels harps while Satan issues accordions to his new charges, it seemed that the accordion would be laughed out of existence.

Now, the unmistakable sweet sounds are not only on both rock and country radio, MTV, and several movie soundtracks, but even on a detergent commercial. *Rolling Stone* magazine is hailing the humble accordion as the hot new instrument of 1989.

New York accordion maker Alex Carozza suddenly finds himself selling two accordions to Billy Joel between interviews with major publications. One-eyed wizard Esteban Jordán is playing in places as unlikely as a folk-music festival in North Carolina and a prestigious jazz festival in Berlin. The Jiménez brothers separately tour the United States, Europe, and even Japan. And at the tiny cluttered offices of the Tejano Conjunto Festival en San Antonio the staffers field calls from around the world about one player or another and about the festival itself.

It is ironic that in an age of rapidly developing computer music and other high-tech musical gadgetry, the United States is rediscovering the humble squeeze box. The accordion, after all, is a simple instrument which makes sounds by forcing air through sets of tuned reeds. Nothing too high-tech about that.

Reed instruments are found in most societies, dating back at least three thousand years to the Chinese *sheng*. The accordion as we know it was invented in 1822 by Friedrich Buschmann in Berlin, and apparently reinvented in 1823 by Cyril Demian in Vienna. Like the harmonica that preceded it, the "blow accordion," as accordions were first called, usually produces one set of notes when the bellows open, and another when they close. Both are diatonic, or capable of producing one or more major or minor chords fully but without chromatic variations. In other words, no sharps or flats. So, like the mouth harp, they were made in keys or key combinations.

In 1857 Matthias Hohner began manufacturing harmonicas in Germany with a single employee. With an initial production of 650 *harmoniken* the first year, by 1903 the Hohner Company was cranking out 5,000,000 a year and shipping them worldwide, employing over 1,500 artisans.

Portable, easy to play, and inexpensive, the mouth harp found a receptive world market. In fifty years the Hohner Company controlled a major part of the harmonica market. But they were stung by an apparent Dangerfield complex. "Real" musicians considered the harmonica a toy and critics were even less kind. Hohner's fiftieth anniversary catalog (1907) demonstrates the insecurity they must have felt: "Scorned by the great masters of music, the Harmonica still produces more music for its size than any other instrument known to the musical world, and at the least cost."

Perhaps they expected to gain respect for the accordion, because in 1903 Matthias Hohner's company built the world's first real accordion factory. Taking the harmonica and replacing the lung action with bellows and the mouth action with buttons and stops was a logical evolution. Accordions were already being made by artisans in Germany, Austria, Italy, France, Russia, and even the United States. But since they were usually made one at a time, they were often of inconsistent quality. Some were outstanding in their craftsmanship, but others were quite cheaply made. Mass manufacturing changed the music world.

Like their harmonicas, Hohner accordions were well made, yet inexpensive. The world responded as with the harmonica. In four years, production went from 8,000 to 150,000 accordions a year, and a second factory had to be built to meet the demand. Manufacturing both the German and Vienna (also called Italian) styles of diatonic accordions, Hohner introduced a chromatic accordion in 1907.

Piano accordions, concertinas, and various other varieties were available in different places as well. But it was the inexpensive diatonics that had greater impact. They were, in a sense, the synthesizers of the postindustrial revolution because they could mimic several instruments without the cost of several musicians. In a world without radio, television, or records, entertainment relied heavily on music performance.

In turn-of-the-century Western society, the music of the day was salon music, usually performed by strings, horns, and vocals in various combinations. Music was often elitist, because, for the less-privileged classes, the cost of a single accordionist as opposed to an orchestra meant having music or not. While accordions had been available for some time, Hohner's impact was in making a lot of them and in making them considerably cheaper.

For the Tejanos of the border area it was revolutionary. Like the rest of the Western world, the economics of the *orquesta típica* kept music limited to those who could afford it. The accordion—especially the inexpensive Vienna-style diatonic—was perfect for the poorer Tejanos. Sturdy and cheap, it was musically perfect for the Mexican tastes, too. Diatonic accordions have one to three rows of buttons, each playing two octaves of a minor chord. Each button plays two notes, and each note is produced by two reeds, one vibrating at a standard pitch and the other slightly sharp. Ry Cooder, an early trendsetter in the American rediscovery of the accordion, says, "The dissonance produces a vibrato effect that gives the button accordion its unique sweetness and delicacy. Two adjacent buttons played together almost always produce a pleasant third interval, which is the basic harmony of all Mexican singing."

Between the two main types of diatonic accordions manufactured initially, German and Vienna, the difference is significant. The German type has two to four reeds per note, and each set of reeds is equipped with a stop that can turn the set on or off. The first two sets of reeds are tuned to make the vibrato Cooder speaks of. The third and fourth sets of reeds, however, are tuned one octave higher and one octave lower. While this accordion can produce a rich chord effect, it was considerably more expensive. Not so with the Vienna type, which was made with only two reeds per note, and without stops. Early models of both types of accordions were available with only one or two rows, so it was no accident that, from the earliest days, the Tejano *acordeonistas* chose the less expensive of the two.

Similar situations occurred throughout the world. The effects were startling. Ann Savoy notes in her book *Cajun Music: A Reflection of a People* that the accordion brought a major change in the music itself because of the tuning of the accordion, its musical limitations, and its acoustic power. Referring to how it affected the Cajun fiddle, she notes, "The tunes were full of half tones and complicated note structures that were largely lost after the accordion gained popularity."

More audible in the noise of festive gatherings than the violin, flutes, or a lot of other woodwinds, and certainly more durable than violins, the accordion won what was essentially an economic battle, replacing the melodic strings and woodwinds of many early-twentieth-century music forms.

To the South Texas Chicanos, the changes were stark. The *orquestas típicas* continued playing but became increasingly associated with the wealthier Mexican Americans, which were few in number. Eventually the accordion won out to the point that even some *orquestas* had to include accordions in their makeup. The effect was similar to the one Savoy speaks of. In time, the accordion, which became popular because it could emulate—to a point—the sounds of the horns and strings, turned full circle. The Tejano bands, in many cases, wound up with horn players emulating accordion licks.

Since those days the variety of accordions has increased dramatically. Vienna models with up to three rows and German models with up to two rows are now available. But now accordions are being made which transcend the limitations of diatonic accordions while still remaining diatonic accordions. The "two tone" diatonic accordions have been developed. Essentially two accordions in one, these accordions have both sets of keys that, with a series of switches, give diatonic accordionists the full musical range with only one accordion instead of two.

Yet another interesting development is that of the Rockordeons, or the modified accordions which are being made to certain individuals' specifications, retuning them to their specific needs. Hohner has just introduced a Steve Jordan Tex-Mex Rockordeon. Instead of having a standard and a sharp reed for each note, the Jordan model has both reeds tuned to standard. The bass side of the accordion will be optional, since most people who play conjunto don't use it much. Additionally, the buttons on the Jordan model are flattened to allow for faster finger work and the strap on the left hand is much stronger and adjustable. The strap modification, along with the attaching of the bellows with screws instead of nails, as in standard accordions, is in response to the stress put on the accordion by conjunto players.

These and other modifications have been made through the years by conjunto and other players to give their accordions special sounds, or to adjust notes to their style of playing. Sometimes reeds are changed to make up for the incomplete nature of the diatonics. One of the first of the conjunto players to modify his accordions was Valerio Longoria. Other changes include tuning one reed an octave lower than the standard reed. This gives accordions a deeper voice.

Chromatic accordions are another type of button accordion, with five rows. These are not incomplete instruments, like the diatonic, since they offer a full complement of sharps and flats on the melody side and a wide array of bass accompaniment. Considerably heavier than the smaller diatonics, they are also much more expensive and harder to master.

The piano accordions have also been around for a while. They differ from other types not only in the piano keyboards, but also because they do not work on a push-pull note arrangement. Whether the bellows are opening or closing the notes remain the same. Like the chromatic, these accordions are heavier and more expensive.

The variety of localized or regionally modified accordions is now as diverse as the list of manufacturers. There are Irish types, which feature Irish B-C chromatic tuning, and diatonic accordions with varying amounts of chromatic enhancement, and concertinas, which are the hexagon-shaped little boxes often used in movies to depict Gypsies. Argentines, for example, use the *bandoneón*, a large concertina-like instrument with tuning too complex for this writer to understand.

Accordion makers have been taken by surprise, but they aren't entirely unhappy about it. Top management people for Hohner are delighted with their sales and are finally getting over their Dangerfield complex. For years they have been trying to deal with a product line that was joke fodder by sponsoring and promoting the accordion as a classical instrument. They organized—get this—accordion symphonies to play the classics! The symphony played to critics who were impressed with the acrobatics and to audiences who were polite but generally nonplussed. The president of the U.S.A. division of Hohner said recently that the company is happily accepting that the accordion is more suitably a folk instrument.

Esteban Jordán couldn't agree more, though he did play with a real symphony once. Not surprisingly, they played his music instead of the other way around. He is quick to point out that the accordion's capabilities are in many ways superior to those of the synthesizers: "All this computer stuff is electronic. It's dead, bro, and the accordion is getting hot because people can tell the difference. It gets to people because it's not electric. This thing breathes, it breathes just like we do." Like most conjunto players, Steve is convinced it will never die because accordion sounds are too basic an element of our musical culture. As for Tejano *orquestas,* the accordion is once again returning to many of them, often in tandem with a synthesizer.

As to whether the accordion craze will be a passing fad or a major element in mainstream popular music, it remains to be seen. One interesting development, though, is the recent creation of a diatonic accordion midi. Combining the basic mechanism and chord arrangement of a diatonic accordion, Alex Carozza and other people in Italy have developed a prototype which seems to combine all the elements: the unlimited digital capabilities of computer-generated music voices, the diatonic arrangement of notes, and the life-giving breath that bellows give the instrument.

Only time will tell. In the meantime, you'll pardon me, I think I'm gonna dance.

11

The Accordion

Passion, Emotion, Musicianship

✧

RAMIRO BURR

1990

You heard the high-pitched, reedy sound on Dwight Yoakam's hit last year, "Streets of Bakersfield." Rock artists from the American Midwest like John Cougar Mellencamp and Bruce Hornsby have used it on their albums. Paul Simon fashioned an elegant blend on his *Graceland* album. Other mainstream artists who have incorporated the instrument into their repertoire include the Hooters, Elvis Costello, Ry Cooder, Talking Heads, They Might Be Giants, and Tom Waits.

If you haven't guessed it by now, we're talking about the accordion, a simple bellows-and-reeds instrument with a lot of history and a rich tradition. Considered too square, the boxy instrument was once mostly associated with Lawrence Welk, the top purveyor of unhipness. The accordion was for dinosaurs. Today, however, the accordion is hip again and has been setting trends. *Rolling Stone* magazine called it the hottest instrument in rock music last year.

Other developments have pushed the accordion into the consciousness of mainstream America. Los Lobos, the East L.A.–based Mexican American quintet, received a Grammy for Best Mexican American Performance in 1984 for their single "Anselma." The band, which includes an accordion in their instrumentation, won another Grammy this year for their album *La Pistola y el Corazón*.

Closer to home, veteran conjunto musician and Tex-Mex accordionist Flaco Jiménez won a Grammy in 1986 for Best Mexican American Performance for his *Ay Te Dejo en San Antonio* LP. (Jiménez plays the accordion heard on "Streets of Bakersfield.") Other conjunto artists nominated for Grammys include Narciso Martínez, Santiago Jiménez, Jr., Steve Jordan, and, most recently, Emilio Navaira. And Texas rockers Joe Ely, Ponty Bone, Augie Meyers, Joe "King" Carrasco, and Brave Combo have all used and, in most cases, showcased the accordion in their music.

Still, all this mainstream exposure doesn't explain the instrument's recent ascent in rock music and U.S. pop culture.

Re-emergence

While the Tejano Conjunto Festival en San Antonio has focused attention on the accordion and the genre every year since the first festival in 1982, other musical forms have helped expand awareness of the instrument.

From Southwest Louisiana, in cities like New Orleans, Houma, and Lafayette, the seeds of Cajun and zydeco music evolved from more than two hundred years of blending French, Irish, Spanish, German, Czech, and African American cultures. The late pioneer Clifton Chenier, recognized as the king of zydeco music, did as much to expose the accordion in the past forty years as did conjunto legend Santiago Jiménez, Sr., who died in 1984. In recent years, Cajun artists Beausoleil and new-breed zydeco artists like Buckwheat Dural, Queen Ida, and Rockin' Sidney have further introduced their genre and the instrument into the mainstream.

Another move boosting the growing influence of both the conjunto genre and the accordion was the decision by world-renowned accordion manufacturer Hohner in 1989 to produce a customized model named after speed squeeze-box king Esteban Jordán. Called the Steve Jordan Tex-Mex Rockordeon, the instrument features standard and sharp reeds, flat buttons to allow for speed, adjustable straps, and other modifications.

Also helping fuel the world's pop stew of ethnic squeeze-box flavors is the London-based Globe Style Records label, which is distributing their "Accordions That Shook the World" record series. The series offers music from regions as diverse as Colombia, Lesotho, the Balkans, the Dominican Republic, and Madagascar.

Although these evolvements may help explain the increasing awareness of the instrument, what explains the accordion's comeback?

High-Tech World

The answer, actually, is somewhat simple.

There are two main reasons. First, the accordion is essentially a mechanical instrument producing earthy sounds in an age where electronics and high tech have seemingly come to monopolize the music-industry landscape. In today's rock-and-roll canvas, sophisticated synthesizers, sequencers, midis, and drum machines are the norm.

Secondly, the move toward "real" musical instruments like the accordion goes hand in hand with the larger overall trend by a new wave of bands fascinated by "roots" or regional music and world-beat rhythms. Prime example—the roots-rock band Los Lobos, whose last LP, *La Pistola y el Corazón,* represents a musical salute to their Mexican origins.

The band members reimmersed themselves in the basics of Mexican folk music, playing not only accordions but also other folk instruments like the *vihuela,* violin, *jarana, requinto jarocho, huapanguera, bajo sexto,* and *guitarrón.* In addition to playing two originals, the group recorded various folk songs representative of regional musical forms—like the *jarabe, son jarocho, son huasteco,* and *huapango*—from Veracruz, Guerrero, Michoacán, and other Mexican states.

In an interview during Los Lobos' 1988 *La Pistola* tour, Louie Pérez said learning to play and tune the acoustic instruments was difficult but satisfying work. "We've always recorded a traditional song on all of our albums," he said. "But this album changed the way we work in the studio. Once we got started recording we realized that this was demanding music. It was hard, but we had help from guys like Art Gurst, an instructor at East L.A. College. He's played traditional music for more than thirty years."

Accordionist David Hidalgo told *Frets* magazine in an interview last year that Los Lobos were indebted to veteran musicians like Gurst: "Gurst introduced us to a lot of the instruments and taught us the basic tuning," he said. "Years ago, another guy taught me to play the violin, how to hold it and tune it." The experiences were unforgettable, says Pérez: "It was challenging. But we found out it was a lot more satisfying than spending hours trying to sound like the Doobie Brothers."

Real Music

Top rock stars like Paul Simon and Peter Gabriel are from the school of modern musicians that appreciate the delicacy and originality of ethnic roots music. Gabriel's last album, *Passion,* was an extended work from his soundtrack for *The Last Temptation of Christ,* where he wove third-world melodies and cross rhythms in a Western pop context. That last LP, moreover, was not his first venture into African rhythms. Simon has always had one foot in rock and another in folk music, but his venture into Soweto in South Africa and the resulting album had a large impact in 1987. His *Graceland* LP, which also contained a Louisiana Creole-style zydeco and a homegrown Tex-Mex tune, won a Grammy for best album of the year.

Gabriel and Simon, like the other popsters and rockers on both sides of the Atlantic, are helping create a wider audience for roots music. Like Gabriel's effort, Simon's move sent a message on how far musicians could go to find meaning and authenticity in their craft: there were no limits.

The accordion has also been "discovered" by many contemporary rock, country, pop, jazz, and Tex-Mex artists as a versatile, dynamic instrument that evokes a sense of humanity in a seemingly overprogrammed, computerized world. From the musicians' standpoint, the general consensus seems to be that the accordion is more expressive than even the best touch-sensitive keyboards. In a 1987 *Keyboard* magazine interview, Rob Hyman of the Hooters said he had never played an accordion before recording their *One Way Home* LP: "After playing synths for so long, you get kind of immune to getting dynamics from the feel, even if your synths are touch-sensitive. The accordion, on the other hand, is so expressive because of the bellows and the breathing aspect."

Rediscovering Passion

Other musicians say the accordion is a roots instrument and although the synthesizer can duplicate its sounds, the synthesizer is not a traditional instrument.

"The synthesizers have made things so easy, people have gotten lazy," said Esteban Jordán. "They can't learn, they can't create. The accordion gives you more liberty. It's hot because people can tell the difference. This thing breathes, it breathes just like we do."

Brave Combo's Carl Finch summed it up best: "You can't beat an acoustic accordion," he told *Keyboard* magazine's Bob Doerschuk. "It seems like you can get more passionate on it than on a less physical keyboard and if there's one thing that pop music lacks today, it's passionate conviction. It's like we're more wrapped up in technology and making money than in making music."

12

An Informal History of the Bajo Sexto

⋄

RAMÓN HERNÁNDEZ, JR.
1987

It is difficult to trace the origin of the *bajo sexto* because it is not cited or documented in any musical-instrument dictionaries, encyclopedias, or other reference works. Furthermore, to my knowledge, there is no recognized expert on this subject.

I wrote this article on the *bajo sexto* based on interviews with some of Texas's best-known *bajo sexto* players and manufacturers. I interviewed Alberto Macías, considered San Antonio's foremost *bajo sexto* maker, and his brother Gilberto, who works with him in the shop, primarily making strings for the *bajo*. Both are the sons of Martín Macías, whose skill at making *bajo sextos* is legendary, and from whom his sons learned the trade. Also interviewed were Miguel Orta Acosta, a third-generation *bajo sexto* maker, repairman, and musician, as well as noted *bajo* players Santiago Almeida, Andrés Berlanga, and Toby Torres, and accordionist Valerio Longoria.

According to Alberto and Gilberto Macías, the basic concept of the *bajo sexto* originated in Spain about two hundred years before Christopher Columbus. This places its origin in approximately the year 1200, when it was known as the *bandolón*. Years later, the Spaniards introduced it in Mexico, but it was not until the late nineteenth and early twentieth century that its influence began to be felt in Texas.

The *bajo sexto*, a member of the guitar family, is a twelve-string rhythm-bass instrument. "It is a harmonic guitar," Torres said. "Within the musical high-mid-low range, it covers all the lows and some mids while the guitar covers all the highs and some mids. It's like playing two instruments because you hit the strings in pairs, in a bass-strum combination."

"It's supposed to be played like a bass, not a guitar," insists Almeida, a pioneer in Tejano music. "You have to use the bass strings and it should be played two fingers above and two fingers below."

"You have to know the basics of melody and harmony before anyone makes an attempt to play it," says Acosta. "The harmony is what is most important because people don't dance to the melody. They don't dance to the pretty words a vocalist sings. They dance to the beat; they dance to the harmony."

Physically, the *bajo sexto* looks about the same as a twelve-string guitar. But there are many important differences. For example, the twelve strings of the *bajo sexto,* configured into six pairs, are tuned E, A, D, G, C, and F, low to high, with E, A, and D tuned in octaves and G, C, and F tuned in unison. Furthermore, the *bajo* has a deeper box, a shorter neck, and bigger and thicker strings, and the frets are in different positions. Some *bajo sextos* feature a cutaway, which makes it easier for the player's fingers to reach the lower portion of the neck, extending the player's range. Its bigger box produces a better, more resonant sound, and because it is a bass guitar, it has more boom, more echo, which produces a fuller, richer sound.

The strings are thicker because each one is actually two strings wound together. They can be machine made, but both Acosta and the Macías brothers prefer to continue the traditional method of winding their own strings. The strings are usually bronze wound around another metal, and later magnetized to bring out the sound. Other materials used include brass, steel, and monel.

Before conjuntos originated, two popular musical events of the nineteenth century were weddings and *bailes de regalos* (dances of gifts), according to Valerio Longoria, a conjunto-music pioneer and considered by many to be a genius of the button accordion. Dance music as it was known then was provided by a guitar or *bajo sexto* (already in use in the 1870s) and *tambora de rancho* (tom-tom). The *bailes de regalos* disappeared around 1930.

The 1930s were the formative years of conjunto music. During this time, the two staple instruments used in *bailes de negocio* (business dances) were the accordion and *bajo sexto*. What the *bajo* did for conjuntos was to allow the accordionist free rein in the melody and lead parts by providing dual rhythm and harmony. Since then, it has endured as the standard accompanying instrument to the accordion in the basic conjunto ensemble.

By the late 1940s, the *tololoche* (upright bass) was added. (Later, the *tololoche* would be replaced by the electric bass.) With the addition of drums, the conjunto ensemble by 1950 resembled its present-day counterpart. By the late 1950s another addition to the conjunto, the public-address system, was added.

With the addition of bass and drums, a different type of *bajo sexto* style emerged. No longer did *bajo sexto* players have to carry both the bass and rhythmic loads. Thus, many *bajo* players began to stray away from using the bass strings and started concentrating on the treble, offbeat strums and leads. With this new technique came an evolution of the *bajo sexto* to the *bajo quinto*. The *bajo quinto* is a ten-string instrument with five pairs of strings, tuned in A, D, G, C, and F, low to high. Missing in this newer model are the two E strings of the *bajo sexto*.

The *bajo sexto* (and now the *bajo quinto*) has gained in popularity since Santiago Almeida firmly established it as a principal instrument in the conjunto ensemble in the 1930s. When asked why the instrument had become so popular, Alberto Macías replied, "because of its versatility. It sounds pretty in waltzes, gives good background in polkas, and it can also play melody." Gilberto Macías added that its popularity was due to "its unique style and sound . . . it can also be used in *orquestas*."

13

Macías

The Stradivarius of Bajo Sextos

✧

RON YOUNG

1987

Conjunto music, a spicy, accordion-based style, is a fruit of the marriage between Mexican and European cultures. It is the sound of the Southwest. And just as Nashville is recognized as the country-music capital, San Antonio is known as the Home of Conjunto Music.

A simple but lively dance music, conjunto consists largely of polkas and traditional Mexican song forms such as *rancheras, boleros,* and *huapangos.* It evolved at the turn of the century when Europeans, especially Germans, made contact with Mexican settlers in South Texas, and the accordion became mixed in with traditional Mexican *mariachi* music from northern Mexico. It's a regional music (although it exists wherever there are large populations of Mexican Americans) that is alternately despised as "low class" and treasured as an expression of Chicano art.

In Spanish, the word *conjunto* can have three meanings: the style of music, the musician who plays it, or the group of musicians who play it. The basic conjunto (group) consists of four instruments: the diatonic, three-row button accordion; a modern drum set; bass (usually electric); and the *bajo sexto,* a twelve-string guitar with six pairs of strings. Along with the accordion, the *bajo sexto* is considered to be the coanchor of the modern conjunto.

The history of the *bajo* is not exactly clear, but by some historians' accounts, the instrument was first brought to Mexico by the Spaniards. Others say it evolved from the twelve-string guitar, emerging sometime late in the nineteenth century as native to the Bajío region of Mexico.

In the early development of conjunto music, the *bajo* was used mainly as a bass instrument in conjunction with the bass-chord elements of the accordion. But later, with the addition of bass and drums to the modern conjunto group, the *bajo* players were free to expand its primary use as a rhythm instrument and play it as a solo, melody-line instrument. The first to do so was Santiago Almeida, who played with pioneer accordionist Narciso Martínez in the early 1930s.

The steel-stringed *bajo* is tuned an octave below a standard guitar, and the last two strings are tuned up a half step: E, A, D, G, C, F, low to high, with the first three pairs tuned in octaves and the last three in unison. This gives it a rich tone and a loud, resonant quality.

Don Martín Macías's name is synonymous with the *bajo sexto*. He was a master craftsman who specialized in handmade *bajo sextos* and guitars. While there are many *bajo* makers, a Macías is considered to be the instrument's equivalent to a Stradivarius violin. For more than sixty years Martín Macías dedicated his life to the making of stringed instruments. He died in May 1983, shortly after being inducted into the Conjunto Music Hall of Fame. Today his sons Alberto and Luis carry on the family tradition of *bajo sexto* and guitar making.

Alberto Macías, forty-nine, is not a master guitarist; in fact, he knows only a few chords, just enough to tune his handcrafted instruments. With assistance from his brother Luis, fifty-three, he creates wonderful *bajo sextos* and guitars out of walnut, mahogany, rosewood, and spruce. Both brothers slowly learned the craft of guitar making from their father, and although both worked at full-time jobs not related to their father's craft, in time they joined him in his small shop on San Antonio's South Side. Alberto began working full-time with his father in 1971, and eventually took over the shop when his father passed away.

At the same workbench where his father stood for so many years, Alberto, dressed in a faded blue work shirt, heavy black boots, and work pants, talks about keeping the family tradition alive: "After my father passed away, people got worried about whether the family tradition would keep going. But Luis and I wanted to continue making *bajos* and guitars with the same quality that the Macías name has always implied. We wanted to keep making my daddy proud."

Some people believe in *ánimas*—the spirits of the dead, past mentors who continue to guide from the "other world." Some feel that Martín is guiding the hands of his son Alberto. "Lots of people used to ask me if I was going to make the same instrument as my father made," he says. "I would tell them, 'I'm sorry, but my hands are not the same as my daddy's. But I'm going to do the best I know how.' So far, I've had no complaints. And yes, sometimes I feel that the spirit of my daddy is still in the shop."

Martín was very secretive about his work, and never thought of forcing his craft on his sons, even though he feared the tradition might die with him. But once they began to show an interest, he put them to work doing repairs, something he considered to be the hardest part of the job. "He used to tell me that if I could do all the repairs on a guitar, then it would be easier when I built my first one," says Alberto. "I really was afraid to make a mistake; that's why at first I didn't want to join him. But he would tell me that it's all right to make mistakes, because you'll eventually get it right."

Alberto and Luis spend fourteen-hour days in the shop, mostly working on new orders and repairs. Luis does most of the repairs and finishing, while Alberto builds the guitars and does some repair work. Although they work on all brands of stringed instruments, most of their repairs are for their father's old *bajos*. Alberto beams with pride when he says that so far none of his *bajos* have come in for repair. They get orders for new *bajos* from all over the country and even Monterrey and Michoacán, Mexico, where *bajo* making has its roots.

Alberto has never timed himself on the process of making a *bajo* because so much of his time is taken up by repairs. However, he estimates two to three weeks of solid fourteen-hour days for making just one *bajo*. Only wood parts are used—no nails or screws. Only glue and fine-chiseled wood pieces hold the ornate-looking instrument together. All are fashioned from patterns originally made by Martín. The whole instrument gleams with varnish. "I never use stains on my guitars like they do in the factories," Alberto says. "Why would you want to ruin the real thing?"

Alberto adds that his father didn't want his instruments to look like any others. He tried to break tradition because he wanted to be known "for his unique look." The body is more rounded and the cutaway is tapered down, more to the curve of the guitar's body, giving it a more natural flowing line. The elaborate and delicately curved bridge also follows the body style. Most are embellished with white plastic inlay and detailed line work.

The cost of an average Macías *bajo* is $975, or $800 if there is no cutaway. Most professional players now prefer the cutaway, in order to play more chords and use the *bajo* as a lead instrument. "My daddy was the first *bajo* maker to add the cutaway," boasts Alberto, "but the first person to ask him to do it, my father thought he was crazy. He told him, 'How would you like it if someone cut your arm off of your body?' He thought that it would weaken the instrument, but he found out different, and now most customers prefer the cutaway models."

The Macíases also make an electric *bajo* for $800. While it is more durable and less bulky than the traditional model, it does not have as rich and full-bodied a tone. Also, if a customer prefers elaborate inlay work, the price of the instrument increases approximately $300.

Alberto and Luis make a good living from their trade. Like their father, though, they are averse to publicity. Word of mouth has always sufficed, bringing them more business than they can handle now. Soon they plan to slow down the pace of their seven-day-a-week, fourteen-hour-a-day schedule to that of "normal people." But if his health doesn't fail him, Alberto plans to continue making guitars and *bajos* until he can't anymore—just like his father. And now one of his sons is becoming interested in the business, too, so that perhaps the family tradition won't die with Alberto and Luis.

"My father learned his trade from a master guitar maker from Spain, Don Camerino Villagómez, when he was a young man in Mexico," explains Alberto. "Mr. Villagómez was getting old and wanted to pass his profession on to someone who would be dedicated and who would love guitar making like he did. My father passed the gift on to me, and I'll never forget it. Everything I told you is just what he would have said to you if he had ever given an interview . . . but he never did.

"My father is the main one: he's the originator of the Macías *bajo*," he added proudly. "Like many family trades, when the kids take over there's little they can do to make it better, except maybe making it a little more modern. But there's nothing we can change or want to change on the Macías guitars. They're perfect the way they are."

14

El Saxofón in Tejano and Norteño Music

❖

JOSÉ B. CUÉLLAR
1998

Adolphe Sax died in 1894, over fifty years before his most important invention, *el saxofón,* was introduced into the recordings of the twin Texas-Mexican *frontera* musical traditions called Tex-Mex, or Tejano, and *regional,* or *norteño.*[1] More than a century after Sax's death, the saxophone is now a firmly established element in the extremely popular contemporary sounds of such *norteño* conjuntos as Primavera, Los Tigres del Norte, Los Huracanes del Norte, and Los Rieleros del Norte, and such Tejano music groups as David Lee Garza y los Musicales, Mazz, Roberto Pulido y los Clásicos, Emilio Navaira y Río, and Jay Pérez—to mention just a few. The saxophone has revolutionized and jazzed up most twentieth-century music genres, and U.S.–Mexican borderlands music is no exception.

My project's purpose was to study how the saxophone developed and diffused as part of these twin traditions of *norteño* and Tejano music. My ethnomusicological approach included charting the continuities and changes in the life experiences of the *saxofonistas* and their musical expressions on the sax over time, as well as documenting the distinctions and similarities in Tejano and *norteño* saxophone playing over this past century.

One assumption is that this study can inform us about whether there is one united macro-*cultura* that spans the borderlands from one end to the other, or a number of related micro-*culturas* corresponding to their various urban and rural mini-environments along the border. I am further assuming that by tracing the history of the saxophone's introduction into the Mexican American musical experience this research could concretely help us more clearly understand the concept of transculturation. By transculturation, I mean the complex combination of synchronizing and synthesizing processes that adopt and adapt, meld and blend, combine and fuse diverse cultural elements into somewhat new cultural expressions in innovative and inventive ways. And I also assume that this research's results on the Tejano and *norteño* saxophone will show the extent to which our U.S.–Mexican borderland *cultura,* for all its diversity, is open and receptive to, as opposed to closed and rejective of, outside influences or external elements.

The Findings
EL SAXOFÓN EN LA MÚSICA NORTEÑA

My research found that there were a number of *saxofonistas* throughout northeastern Mexico before the 1940s. But I found little evidence pinpointing exactly when and how the saxophone was brought to the region and by whom.

Some knowledgeable individuals that I interviewed in Monterrey during the summer of 1997 speculated that the saxophone first came to Mexico during the early 1860s with the military bands as part of the would-be-emperor Maximiliano's failed attempt to colonize the country. Some others speculated that *el saxofón* came later, along with the French-influenced *danzones,* to northeastern Mexico from Cuba, through the ports of Matamoros or Tampico. Others suggested that the saxophone first came to Monterrey and the surrounding region from the "over-saxed" and jazz-crazed United States of the 1920s. In sum, it seems the saxophone probably arrived in different ways and at different times to the various *comunidades* of northeastern Mexico. It appears unevenly distributed across communities and years.

Before the 1920s, the saxophone appeared mostly as a military and municipal band instrument in Mexico. By the 1930s, a number of cabaret and municipal *orquestas* throughout the Mexican northeast were playing with one or more saxophones. But only after the late 1940s did the saxophone appear in most northeastern Mexican communities and become really integrated into the new northeastern Mexican music, eventually called *música regional* or *música norteña.*

The sax's actual arrival in northeastern Mexico varied significantly from place to place. For example, historian Gustavo Garza

Guajardo documented a line of saxophonists in Sabinas Hidalgo, Nuevo León, dating back to 1906. There is evidence that Monterrey was exposed during the early 1920s to the jazz-style playing of visiting saxophonists like Tudor Applen with the All American Jazz Orchestra from New Orleans, and locals like Manuel Martha with the El Porvenir Jazz Group. And the noted regional historian and ethnomusicologist Juan Alanís informed me that his documentation shows that the saxophone did not appear in Allende, Nuevo León, until the late 1930s.

That was around the same time that Los Montañeses del Álamo started featuring the saxophone in their music. Yet *norteño* ethnomusicologists agree that it was only after the master *saxofonista* Don Fidencio Almaguer replaced Lencho Gloria, in 1944, that the unique Montañeses style became musically apparent. Fidencio Almaguer's impeccable harmonic sense and semisweet, semibitter sax tone complemented and consolidated the acoustic-oriented violin, flute, bass, and *bajo sexto* with the vocal ensemble sound of Los Montañeses. Their particularly unique blending of sax and flute harmonies and fills behind and between vocals established a tradition still played and appreciated today.

Don Fidencio Almaguer became the much-needed energetic centerpiece of the never-tiring group Los Montañeses, who traveled constantly during the 1940s and 1950s. They played at regional radio presentations and dance halls across the northeastern Mexican states, from Tamaulipas, Coahuila, and Nuevo León to San Luis Potosí, Durango, and Chihuahua. The period between 1945 and 1955 is considered the golden decade of Los Montañeses del Álamo. The group traveled to Mexico City in 1945 and made its first recordings ("De Torreón a Laredo," "Bailando polca," "Del Álamo a San Francisco," and "Sanantoniana") with Don Fidencio on sax.

Fifty years later, everyone agrees that Don Fidencio was one of the best *saxofonistas* in the history of the group and possibly the history of *música regional*. The unique Montañeses style of sax pioneered by Mr. Almaguer can be heard on recorded classics such as "Las golondrinas," "Nochebuena," "Cuando se quiere de veras," and "Sarabia." Other Montañeses recordings feature Don Fidencio in his superb supporting role as the deep but soft second alto voice to the flute, violin, or lead singer.

Otro pioneer saxophonist, Don Santos Ybarra, described Don Fidencio's playing style this way (originally in Spanish, these remarks were translated into English by the author): "Well, one of Almaguer's characteristics is that he didn't stay tied to the melody. He wouldn't tightly follow the way they do today, when the accordion carries the melody and the second plays a third below, very tight. Fidencio wouldn't. He would always play lower. Wow! He gave it that characteristic of the flute playing above, and Fidencio playing more than an octave below. And he would follow precisely—in that very unique style of Don Fidencio's."

Beginning in 1959 Esteban Aguirre Rocha regularly substituted for Don Fidencio on the sax with Los Montañeses. During the 1960s, at least two other saxophonists, Jesús Martínez and Esteban's son, Víctor Aguirre, also regularly played saxophone with Los Montañeses.

The group's 1986 album was publicized as "the new sound of Los Montañeses del Álamo" and was followed by several more. Therefore, despite the passing of both Don Fidencio Almaguer and his long-term substitute, Esteban Aguirre Rocha, another generation of musicians appears committed to maintaining the more-than-fifty-year-old saxophone-based tradition of Los Montañeses del Álamo.

"This maintenance," said Juan Alanís, "is almost by inheritance... The *saxofón* is not learned in school. The melodies, the tunes, are transmitted from generation to generation. Many of them don't know how to read music; that is to say, they memorize and play with mastery as if they were reading the sheet music. But this is from father to son, from musician to musician, how the use of the *saxofón* is transmitted."

Guadalupe Quezada is very proud of the fact that he was the first saxophonist in his hometown of Linares to play *música regional*. According to him,

> Everything changed between 1945 and 1947. A natural disaster, frozen crops that winter, forced many of the *campesinos* to become migrant cotton pickers the following seasons in the United States. They returned with good clothes, leather boots, Tejano hats, plus a desire for fun and lots of money to buy it.
>
> The owners of the three or four nightclub businesses in the so-called tolerance zone of Linares started hiring accordion and *bajo sexto* duos instead of *orquestas* in an effort to attract the returning so-called wetbacks, who showed a definite taste for this *música regional*. The dance promoters and radio stations followed, also hiring conjuntos and pushing the music.

In 1952 Guadalupe Quezada started playing sax with an accordion–*bajo sexto* duo. Their idea was to imitate the extremely popular, first *norteño*-style recordings made four years earlier by alto saxophonist Beto Villa with accordionist Narciso Martínez in South Texas. He said that his goal, as a beginning conjunto saxophonist, was to learn to play Beto Villa's "Monterrey" perfectly. He said, "It was the most difficult piece. I knew that when I could play that tune, I was *un buen saxofonista de música regional!*"

Santos Ybarra, a native of La Paz, San Luis Potosí, and now a longtime resident of Monterrey, for many years has been the only saxophone repairman in all of northeastern Mexico. He has known and repaired the horns of most Mexican saxophonists in and outside of the region for years. Thus, his contribution to the actual maintenance of the *norteño* saxophone tradition is beyond measure.

The son of a musician, Santos Ybarra finally convinced his municipal band director to let him play C-melody sax at age fifteen, after first being forced to study the violin. Almost a decade later, after moving with his wife to work in Donna, Texas, Santos Ybarra performed and recorded with the legendary accordionist Pedro Ayala. He recorded the alto sax part on Pedro Ayala's classic polka "La pecosita" for Discos Falcón in Mission, Texas, in late 1948. Many groups have since performed and recorded distinct versions of it. The legendary Don Manuel Treviño holds the distinction of having recorded a particularly memorable version of "La pecosita" on his *saxofón melódico* with Los Populares de China.

Santos Ybarra remembered Pepe González (also known as El Gorrión) as the first saxophonist to play in what is now considered the characteristic *norteño* or Monterrey style of playing a tight *segunda* harmony, closely following the lead voice a third below. "He had a very unique manner of playing," recalled Don Santos, "because his diaphragm had an impressive air capacity. He could play extremely long phrases without breathing."

Rodolfo (Fito) Hernández from Linares was another great saxophonist, according to Santos Ybarra. Don Fito, who started with Los Regionales de Linares, is best known for his work with three other legendary groups: Los Hermanos Prado, Los Gorriones del Topo Chico, and Los Rancheritos del Topo Chico. "When Rodolfo started playing," Don Santos fondly remembered, "how beautifully he played those tunes. It was very lovely! He had the same melodic tendency as Pepe González, but he also had a very tender and beautiful sound."

Along with that of Rodolfo Hernández, the name of Roosevelt Delgado, the *famoso primer saxofonista* of Los Gorriones del Topo Chico, immediately came to Tacho Carrillo's mind when I asked him to name the best regional saxophonists. Don Tacho is a dedicated organic historian with an encyclopedia's worth of knowledge regarding the region's culture and musicians.

Other saxophonists who helped establish this unique *estilo regiomontano,* or Monterrey style, of sax playing during this foundational period of the 1940s and 1950s include Manuel Treviño, who first played C-melody sax with Los Populares de China; Salomón Quezada (Guadalupe's brother), one of several alto saxophonists who eventually replaced Manuel Treviño with Los Populares de China; Estevan Tirado, the saxophonist with Lalo García y su Conjunto (the backup band for the legendary *norteño* comedian and singer Lalo "El Piporro" González); Julio Prado, who recorded with Los Alegres de Terán but is best known for his sax playing with Los Hermanos Prado; as well as Julio Prado's first cousin Valentín Prado and his son Julio Prado, Jr., both of whom now play sax with Los Nacionales de Linares.

Álvaro Garza of Sabinas Hidalgo, Nuevo León, who played the C-melody sax, cofounded an outstanding group called Los Norteños de Nuevo Laredo with his brother Salomón Garza. Don Álvaro on the alto sax, jelling perfectly with the accordion and supporting the great, out-front, vocal duet harmonization, recorded a number of superb tunes with this classic Monterrey-style *conjunto norteño.* Other less well known *norteño* saxophonists who also made significant contributions as group leaders include Santos Ramírez of Los Canarios and Miguel Arredondo of Los Cardenales.

Santos Ybarra recalled that Fito Olivares once played a "great" melodic sax with the Conjunto Estrella de Miguel Allende. Over the years, Fito Olivares has significantly extended the overlapping musical boundaries of *conjunto norteño* and *conjunto tropical* by writing and recording many now-classic *cumbias* featuring his *sabroso,* tasty, lead saxophone (for example, "La gallina," "La güera Salomé," "Josefina," "Juana la cubana," and "Yo no bailo con Juana").

Recent recordings by Los Norteños de Nuevo Laredo, Los Dinámicos, and Rogelio Gutiérrez contribute significantly to the maintenance of the *norteño* saxophone musical tradition and deserve special note. Los Norteños de Nuevo Laredo and Los Dinámicos recently recorded fresh instrumental takes of such *norteño saxofón* classics as "Los coyotes," "Las tres Conchitas," "La curva," and others.

After first playing the larger, deeper-sounding C-melody sax with Abelardo García Tijerina, the accordionist with García y López, Rogelio Gutiérrez started playing alto sax and assumed leadership of his own group. He became the most productive and influential *norteño* saxophonist-leader to date. He has produced many significant recordings over the years, both as a leader of his own tight Monterrey-style *saxofón y acordeón* conjunto, and as a leader of Lorenzo de Monteclaro's backup conjunto. Four very important recent releases—*Rogelio Gutiérrez: Instrumentales; Norteñas: Polcas Famosas (Dieciocho Éxitos); Polcas y Huapangos;* and *El Rey de las Polcas*—include his classic interpretation of what is arguably the *norteño* sax standard: "El Pávido Návido." Other tunes on these recordings include "Los amores del Flaco," "La tuna," "Los tres negritos," and more. These demonstrate Don Rogelio's ability to either play a tight *segunda,* take the lead, or depart significantly by improvising and harmonizing around the melody in unique and unexpected ways.

Santos Ybarra thinks of Rogelio Gutiérrez as someone whose life story is totally connected to the saxophone—in other words, someone who dedicated his life to the saxophone. "His style was to play some great waltzes," Don Santos remembered. "He always played four or five sets for everyone." If there is one single *saxofonista* who most contributed to both the growth and maintenance of the saxophone in the *norteño* music tradition, and who most deserves the title El Rey del Saxofón Norteño (the King of *Norteño* Sax), it is Rogelio Gutiérrez.

A BRIEF HISTORY OF THE SAXOPHONE
IN TEJANO MUSIC

All the available photographic and other archival evidence dates the saxophone in Texas back to the early 1920s—although the sax may have arrived earlier among other groups, like the Czechs, who started immigrating to South Texas in the 1850s. I found no evidence of the saxophone's presence among Texas Mexicans, or Tejanos, prior to the late 1920s. The only tentative conclusion that we can reach at this time is that the saxophone probably came into Texas-Mexican musical hands from various sources at different times, as also happened in northeastern Mexico.

It appears that one of the most probable sources of the saxophone came into the Texas-Mexican musical experience as a result of the close contact between Czech and Mexican musicians during the late 1920s, when they were both being recorded by the Martin label in San Antonio. As Chris Strachwitz observed, "These two cultures have long lived side by side in Texas, and Mexican-American musicians have adapted many Czech/Bohemian tunes into their repertoire while most Czech bands have learned popular Mexican melodies." Also according to Strachwitz, the sax-flavored "Corrido Rock," recorded by the Joe Patek Orchestra, "is a wonderful example of the cross-fertilization and borrowing of musical ideas which has been an ongoing process over the years." Additionally the evidence shows that accordionist Narciso Martínez often played for Czech as well as for Mexican audiences. This is important because it was Narciso Martínez who first recorded with saxophonist Beto Villa.

Alberto (Beto) Villa, born in Falfurrias, Texas, on October 26, 1915, got his first saxophone from his father, the leader of an *orquesta típica,* who persuaded him to study with a private teacher of Mexican music. As a teenager, when he joined the school band that played only American music, he developed a stronger interest in big jazz bands than in Mexican music. By playing with a number of orchestras all over South Texas, Beto developed into a saxophonist with a clear, fine tone and a well-liked bandleader with a charismatic personality and an excellent sense of his postwar "Mexican American" generation's popular musical taste.

During the four years before World War II, Beto Villa played sax and led his own Mexican American orchestra at a Freer, Texas, dance hall six nights a week. He played in the Navy band during the war. After his discharge from the Navy, Villa gained more popularity and earned more money than ever by playing sax with his own orchestra in his own dance halls.

In November of 1947, Ideal Records producer Armando Marroquín recorded the waltz "Por qué te ríes" and a polka, "Las delicias," with Beto Villa on alto sax and Reymundo Treviño on piano accordion, backed up by drums, trumpet, electric guitar, and contrabass. At Villa's expense, eventually Marroquín reluctantly distributed two hundred records that created such a great demand that

Paco Betancourt, Marroquín's partner, insisted that Beto Villa record some more.

The following February, in 1948, Marroquín recorded four instrumentals, two waltzes and two polkas, with Beto Villa on alto sax but with the popular Narciso Martínez on *acordeón de botón*. Accompanied by a reduced orchestra, Beto and Narciso changed the course and character of Tejano and *norteño* music forever with these recordings. Almost every saxophonist in the region since has imitated Villa's lead interpretations when first learning these songs. Villa's movingly melancholy saxophone made "Rosita" a sixty-thousand-plus single-record seller. It became a big hit and a perennial favorite for him. Nonetheless, it was his smooth version of "Monterrey" that placed the saxophone squarely front and center of the Tejano musical tradition. As noted by Guadalupe Quezada, this piece of musical mastery remains the root paradigm for all the saxophonists in the *tradición norteña*.

Beto and Narciso recorded another set of extremely popular instrumental classics ("Las gaviotas," "La picona," "Tamaulipas," "Rock and Rye Polka") in 1949. Beto Villa also recorded Pedro Ayala's "La pecosita" in November of 1949, exactly twelve months after Santos Ybarra's first recording. Of course, it was Beto Villa's jazzier version featuring two legato saxophones with *bajo sexto* and muted trumpets for backup that remains most popular.

Beto Villa also cut a number of records with other well-known accordionists, like "La chiapaneca" in April 1954, with Tony de la Rosa playing his crisp accented arpeggios, rapid runs, altered scales, and jazzy, syncopated *contrarritmos*. In addition, over the years, Beto Villa recorded sax parts *al estilo Monterrey* with a number of well-known and lesser-known, or unknown, conjuntos.

For the next sixteen years he performed and recorded a truly pioneering, "transcultural" repertoire of saxophone-flavored *música* that appealed greatly to the war veterans and their lovers, *pachucos* and *braceros,* Mexican Americans and *mexicanos* on both sides of the border. He played every style of popular music. This paradigmatic repertoire set the pattern, or model, for dozens of groups that followed.

Beto Villa's transcultural and transnational style of music carried him to the forefront of the heavy, sax-driven movement emerging from the 1940s and 1950s U.S.-rooted Tejano tradition. Other saxophonist and saxophile bandleaders also understood *el gusto del público* for the saxophone's smooth-to-gutsy sound, and they consciously incorporated it into ensemble or solo parts (e.g., Frank Alonzo y sus Rancheros, Balde González, Eugenio Gutiérrez, Pedro Bugarín, Darío Pérez, and Juan Colorado).

Beto Villa quit touring in 1960 because of health problems. During the last four years in which he performed, Beto's son-in-law Wally Armendáriz played saxophone and helped Beto with the band. Beto Villa died in 1986 at age seventy-one, in Corpus Christi. Yet we have his legacy of over one hundred 78s and scores of LPs, and dozens of saxophonists on both sides of the border still reflect his influence.

Exactly three months after Beto Villa recorded "Monterrey," Isidro López turned fifteen years old. Born in Bishop, Texas, on May 17, 1933, he was already playing saxophone in high school. The following brief summary highlights Isidro López's sax contributions to the style of music he loves best.

Isidro studied sax and clarinet in school, and attended college for a year. His first regular playing job was with accordionist Narciso Martínez. He then played second alto with master Tejano saxophonist Eugenio Gutiérrez, and recorded with a number of other conjuntos and bands during the early 1950s.

Isidro López recorded his first lead vocal in 1954 with Juan Colorado's orchestra, when the regular singer did not show up. Before long he was recording on his own, at first with a conjunto featuring Tony de la Rosa on accordion, and later with his own *orquesta* and *mariachi*.

Isidro limited his sax playing after he became a lead singer. But his recorded arrangements always featured his smooth sax along with those of his fellow saxophonists Max Bernal and Chuy Compeán. One excellent example of Isidro's particularly smooth playing style is an instrumental polka called "La callozona."

Isidro continues releasing compilations including both current and earlier recordings. He still performs live occasionally. In 1990 Tejano music's *primer* saxophonist and vocalist was entered into the Texas House of Representatives *Congressional Record,* fifteen days short of his fifty-seventh birthday.

On May 2, 1990, the day Isidro López was entered into the Texas *Congressional Record,* another pioneer Tejano saxophonist, Pancho Villarreal of San Antonio, turned forty-eight. Pancho got his first saxophone when his brother, "Ruco" Villarreal, who already had his own fairly well known conjunto, said to his father, "Buy him a saxophone and I will pay for it."

Like Beto Villa and Isidro López before him, Pancho first started playing saxophone in his school band. At age fourteen, he joined a conjunto called Los Príncipes de Raymundo Valero. He remembers how they wanted to kick him out because, in his words, "no estaba en la onda" (I wasn't in the groove).

Shortly after forming his own group, Panchito Villarreal y su Conjunto, he started appearing regularly on San Antonio's Spanish-language television station KMEX, with "Tío" Laureano: "I spent some time accompanying him, and after that, with Pedro Ybarra, who is now my brother-in-law." Pedro encouraged Pancho to record, resulting in two 45s with the tunes "El herradero," "Dame un besito," and "Con la luz apagada." (Unfortunately, Pancho could not remember the name of the fourth tune.)

Pancho summarized his career as a Tejano saxophonist like this:

> I joined up with my brother "El Ruco" Villarreal *y su conjunto* and that's how my career really got started. I spent about twenty-six years of my life with Ruco. We used to alternate with groups like Isidro López and Agapito Zúñiga, who had two saxes. He was the first group that I saw with two saxes. After that we started using two saxes. After El Ruco stopped playing, around 1965, I went with Flaco Jiménez and Ry Cooder on a tour of California. We went all over the United States and Canada, and played radio and television shows like *Saturday Night Live*.
>
> I should note that after that, my son Panchito and I, together, played *primera y segunda* saxes with Arturo Aldaré y Machismo, and George Rivas. Everywhere we went people would say, "There go *los Panchitos*." We were always very close. He was with me since he was about twelve, and we played almost thirteen years together.
>
> After George Rivas, Panchito went with Emilio Navaira, and I went with Los Tall Boys. They were a bit more my age. I recorded two CDs with them, and then suddenly they separated.
>
> After Los Tall Boys, I went to help my son Javier with his group Sueño. But to tell you the truth, I felt out of it. You know what I mean? I felt out of it because they were young, and in Tejano, it seems that they want younger people. I felt out of place with the kids and so I moved aside.

Describing his personal sax style, Pancho said, "I've never lost that thing of always attacking the notes. That's how I learned. I feel that Tejano has a real strong saxophone, but I've also been told that I play the sax too strong, that I attack the notes too much. I've played with *orquestas* that made me play softer, lighter, and more legato. And I don't particularly like that style." In fact, for Pancho to like a contemporary Tejano group, it has to be one like Rubén Ramos's: "The saxes attack the notes. They sound good, they sound Tejano. For me, that is Tejano!"

The strong, "old school" Tejano sax sound of the Rubén Ramos bands that Pancho Villarreal admires so much has been primarily driven by the saxes of Frank Gómez and Rubén's alto-playing brother, Alfonso Ramos, who has formed and reformed the Texas Revolution with him a number of times over the years. Some recent recorded examples include Rubén Ramos's "El chupachavas" and Alfonso and Rubén's *The Texas Revolution: Together Again.*

Some of the other saxophonists who also contributed to this unique *onda tejana* style of sax playing during its foundational period of the 1960s and 1970s include Louie Bustos and Jimmy Flores with Tortilla Factory; Sal Aguilera, Robert Navarro, Tony Matamoros, and Jimmy Flores with La Familia; Bob López and Manuel Palafox with Ray Camacho; Danny Pérez and Joe Posada with the Royal Jesters and Jimmy Edward; Joey Pérez, Carlos Hernández, and Jimmy Solís with Sunny Ozuna and the Sunliners; and Joseph Rifón and Roy Rositas with Agustín Ramírez.

When asked to speculate on the origin of this most-important sax attack, Pancho is positive that it is a *norteño* influence. Another *norteño* influence that Pancho observed is the wailing or crying style of playing sax. Pancho said the difference is that the Tejano style is calmer and the saxophone plays the *primera* part instead of *la segunda.* "And we don't play quite as rapidly or with as much of the wailing sound."

Pancho also noted the differences in the use of chords between *norteño* and Tejano music:

> *Los conjuntos* play more simple, almost always using the traditional one, five, and four, with the relative minor chord—because they don't go out of the relative key. The Tejano musician started using more ninths, more elevenths, more thirteenths, you know, and combinations with the bass and guitar with the different chords. That's the difference.
>
> On my part, I also used complex chords, you see. But I seem to notice that now I'm going backward, toward the more simple. It seems that's what the people like more. And to tell you the very truth, I think this is correct. It's that there came a period where everyone wanted to make the thing very complex.

Asked generally to name *norteño* influences on his playing, Pancho mentioned Los Gorriones del Topo Chico and Los Rancheritos del Topo Chico, but he was not quite sure of the names of the specific *saxofonistas*. When asked to name the most influential saxophonists in his life, Pancho unequivocally responded, "The one who inspired me was Beto Villa, when he had his *orquesta,* and then Wally Armendáriz, when he started to play solo." When I asked his opinion about the difference between Beto and Wally, Pancho said, "Beto's sax was more wailing and Wally's was more mellow, more separated, and not so weepy."

Assessing the Tejano scene today, Pancho concluded, "Mostly what happened is that they started using the keyboard's synthesized sax sound in place of the sax. That has eliminated much of the work for the Tejano saxophonists. For example, when my son started with Emilio Navaira, I think he was one of the first to double on both keys and sax. *En la onda tejana* the doubling of sax and keys is now used a lot. It gives the conjunto a different flavor. It has the advantage of playing accompaniment with keyboard and the melody with sax."

Of today's Tejano saxophonists, Pancho Villarreal likes "Joe Posada, and a friend, Luis Chávez, who played with Gary Hobbs; Gibby Escobedo, the saxophonist who plays with Jay Pérez; and, of course, my son Panchito Jr."

Frank (Panchito) Villarreal, Jr., is a Tejano saxophone pioneer in his own right, but of a different generation and a different sort. In many respects, he is a prime example of his generation of Tejano saxophonists.

"Music was around us all the time, with my dad playing. Basically we had instruments all over the place, pianos *y guitarras y todo,*" Panchito said.

> Mostly because I heard him playing sax, I wanted to play sax. So he started me at twelve, and I really hit it hard. When I was thirteen I started to play professionally with him. We played professionally together for about thirteen years. We did a lot of duets. He was my mentor and turned me on to different styles of music, like jazz. He had me listen to Charlie Parker, Phil Woods, Chick Corea, and so I started getting into jazz, but I was still more influenced by Tejano.
>
> I first started with a beginner's alto sax, one of those pawnshop horns. Then, through the years, when my dad and I started playing duets, I converted myself from alto to tenor, so that we could do the alto-tenor thing. Now I play mostly the alto.

When Panchito and his dad played in his *tío* Ruco Villarreal's group, "It was more of a brass deal," he said.

> Instead of an accordion, we did the polka with two saxes. People liked to hear it.
>
> Now with my dad, our goal was to sound like one person. My job pretty much was to follow him because he was the lead player. We had to breathe at the same time, tongue together, all that. If we could sound like one, that's what we were looking for.
>
> My dad did a lot more traditional conjunto than I. I've done a lot more of what they are calling now "conjunto progressive." I played with Emilio and Río for four or five years, when he first started. That was my first experience with an accordion player where it was just me and the accordion player, and that was it. That was a totally different experience. That's another way of playing. I had to relearn phrasing because the accordion and sax phrases are totally different than with two saxes together, or playing with brasses, or whatever. It is really up to you, the player, to follow the accordion. I had lots of training with my dad and I am a good follower because for thirteen years I followed his lead. So when it came to the accordion, I said I can do this but it's gonna take more practice, more listening, more hearing.
>
> As far as I'm concerned, there are progressive conjuntos like Emilio and David Lee Garza, and traditional conjuntos like the Tall Boys and Flaco, and *conjuntos norteños* like the Tigres. Everything has some resemblance. The instrumentation is the same. The approach to the music is the same. The only thing is that in Tejano the progressions are different and more challenging, in that they move a lot more.
>
> In traditional and *norteño* conjunto you pretty much stick with a four-five progression. In Tejano, you do the two-five, throw in a six, do a preparation, go to the four, all these minors and stuff comes in. You have all the in-between substitute chords that sound real neat. I find that we overdo it for the people sometimes.
>
> Gosh, it's hard to say who pioneered this progressive style with saxophone. There were lots of groups out there trying to change *la onda*. One of my personal favorites is David Lee Garza. I was listening to him when I was with my dad. In a way I've got to give him credit. But I also got to give credit to Steve Jordan, who was doing this stuff way before anyone else. To me he is the starting point. He was playing all that progressive stuff that's never been done before. Then there were orchestras like Latin Breed and the Royal Jesters also playing totally new stuff with saxophones.

Who were some of the Tejano saxophonists that most influenced me? Well, to be honest, first, I like the way my dad plays best of all. And when we play together we sound the same, and we phrase the same too. And I think Joe Posada is a great player. He is more jazz influenced, and I like that because I like listening to jazz.

Panchito talked about how his personal sax-playing style has changed over the years since he started playing professionally with his dad and uncle. "Back then I had more of a rough sound. I accented a lot back then. Then, as we grew, we started doing more of a jazz kind of feeling, more smooth. And that's pretty much the way I play now. I'm more of a smooth player, I think. Now, if I don't have to accent or tongue it so hard, I won't. I play everything more legato."

Panchito Villarreal played saxophone and keyboards with Emilio Navaira y Río at the first three Tejano Conjunto Festivals of the 1990s. Some of his uncredited sax work can be heard on Emilio Navaira's *Emilio* and *Mis Mejores Canciones: Dieciseite Super Éxitos*, and on La Mafia's *Nuestras Mejores Canciones: Dieciseite Super Éxitos* and *La Mafia: La Historia Musical*.

After he left Emilio, Panchito recorded with a number of other Tejano music groups. An example is the recently recorded Tejano sax duet with Panchito and Gibby Escobedo on Jay Pérez's "Te llevo en mí." He also accepted a recording contract from Capitol.

> They approached me about a record deal to do my own thing. I had been doing the music for Emilio, so they offered me a deal.
>
> I'm also a keyboard player. That's helped me a lot with my arranging and producing. That's what I've been doing with my group Rodeo for the past five years that we've been together, arranging and creating the songs, making them as commercial as possible. That's mainly what our goal is, to sell records in Tejano. We have four compact discs—*Step by Step, Unidos, Nuestro Tiempo,* and *Sobreviviendo*—on Capitol.

Following in the footsteps of David Lee Garza, who won the Most Promising Band Tejano Music Award eleven years before, Panchito Villarreal's Rodeo won the Rising Star Tejano Music Award in 1994. That same year, Emilio Navaira won the Tejano Music Awards for Best Male Vocalist, Male Entertainer, Best Show Band, and Best Conjunto.

In 1994 Joe Posada won the Best Tejano Musician Award for sax. An extremely well respected Tejano saxophonist for years, Joe Posada has an outstanding recording and performance career that goes back to his trailblazing period of Tejano sax work in the early seventies with the Royal Jesters band. Over the decades Posada produced a significant number of his own albums. These discs exhibit his excellent use of jazzy Tejano arrangements as the musical context for his very personal vocal and sax stylings. Although, like Isidro López before him, Joe Posada tends to limit his solo sax work, "Analisa's Smile" on his *Breakaway* album is a welcome exception, and a wonderful example of his rich postmodern Tejano tone and phrasing that continues impressing his contemporaries and admirers like the two Panchitos.

Óscar Montemayor's extraordinary sax playing has obviously contributed significantly to the success of David Lee's Musicales. Together they have won many Tejano Music Awards ever since their first Tejano Music Award for Most Promising Band of the Year on March 6, 1983. When combined with David Lee's accomplished accordion, Óscar Montemayor's unique sax sounds have influenced the articulating and arranging of many other Tejano accordionists and saxophonists, who try to replicate their sound and duplicate their success.

Gibby Escobedo has been influencing the way Tejano-style sax is played for more than twenty-five years, from the early days of Latin Breed to recent recordings and performances with Jay Pérez. Jay Pérez sang with David Lee Garza y los Musicales until he left to form his own group in 1993. Jay's backup conjunto continues in the "progressive" accordion-sax-synthesizer conjunto tradition. As already noted, a number of excellent saxophonists contributed to Jay Pérez's early nominations for Best Tejano/Conjunto Artist of 1994 by Pura Vida Hispanic Music Awards.

In the mid 1990s, two postmodern Tejano saxophonists were integrated into the evolving, progressive accordion-sax-synthesizer conjunto arrangements of both Jay Pérez and Emilio Navaira. Both Marc Martínez and Valentín Maltos have made significant contributions as examples of a new generation of saxophonists who followed Panchito Villarreal's path by doubling on synthesized keys and sax.

Marc Martínez assumed the progressive-style, Tejano alto sax and keyboard playing responsibilities with Emilio Navaira y Río after Panchito Villarreal left to form Rodeo. Marc's sax can be heard on *Emilio: Sound Life,* and *Live: Emilio Navaira y Río.*

Valentín Maltos played saxophone with Jay Pérez at the Fourteenth Annual Tejano Conjunto Festival in 1995. That same year,

Valentín's smoothly polished, postmodern, Tejano-style alto sax was recorded on Jay Pérez's *The Voice*. The next year he recorded *No Limits* with Jay Pérez.

Two of the most popular, award-winning groups in Tejano music, La Mafia and Joe López's Mazz, also used a progressive instrumentation of sax, accordion, and synthesizer on their best-selling recordings. Tommy González played saxophone and congas with Joe López and Grupo Mazz, and Jesse Perales played saxophone with La Mafia.

Three of Tejano music's best-known accordionists—Flaco Jiménez, Valerio Longoria, and Tony de la Rosa—recently released recordings that feature the accordion-saxophone combination. I take this as strong evidence of the continued incorporation of the saxophone in an effort to jazz up the traditional Tejano conjunto mode.

Flaco Jiménez's 1992 Arhoolie album, *Flaco's Amigos,* included two polkas, "Atotonilco" and "La feria," featuring the wonderfully close-harmony *segunda* sax playing of Pancho Villarreal. Flaco's 1992 Reprise album, titled *Partners,* included five tunes featuring the postmodern, Sanborn-like sax of Joe Morales.

Flaco said he planned to record another album with Pancho Villarreal on the sax because Ry Cooder, the producer, loves the sound of the saxophone and accordion together. When asked if he had a personal musical reason for recording with the sax again, he said, "*Porque* it sounds more bluesy, *más* jazzy. When the progressions changed, that's when the saxophone started being used more. My father played with a saxophone once in a while, although he was more traditional. Tony Molina is one of those who first played with *mi papá* in those years."

Valerio Longoria wrote "La Filomena" as an *acordeón-saxofón* duet and recorded a seminal version with Chuy Compeán's lyrical alto in the mid 1950s. During the 1990s, Valerio recorded an album titled *Caballo Viejo,* featuring his son Flavio Longoria on traditional alto sax.

Tony de la Rosa, who recorded with both Beto Villa and Isidro López a decade earlier, recorded "Paloma negra" with his conjunto and two saxes in October 1960 (re-released in 1993). Then in May 1964, he recorded "Una cualquiera" and "Perdí el albur" with the same instrumentation, prefiguring the *acordeón-con-*two-saxes sound that continues gaining popularity into the present. In 1995 Tony released an album of timeless instrumental polkas. Four tracks feature a pair of excellent undocumented saxophonists playing tight *primera* and *segunda* parts in the style of Beto Villa. It also includes a polkacized version of country sax master Boots Randolph's "Yakkety Sax," and a medley of four sax classics: "La cadena" and "Muchachos alegres" blended with Salomé Gutiérrez's "Mi ranchito/ Elodia" medley and "La bomba atómica."

Manuel (Manny) Guerra, drummer and Tejano music producer extraordinaire, and his brother, saxophonist Rudy Guerra, were primarily responsible for producing the Sunglows' classic saxophone polka hit of 1967, "La cacahuata/Peanuts." This song was so successful that it caused an exceptionally popular Corpus Christi group, George Jay and the Rockin' Ravens, to record an instrumental answer called "La pachuca."

Roberto Pulido y los Clásicos provide the Tejano musical link between the postmodern, or "progressive," conjunto sounds of David Lee, Emilio, and Jay; the old-school, power-sax style of Texas Revolution, Latin Breed, and Royal Jesters; and the classic sounds of Beto Villa and Isidro López. For the last twenty years, at the core of the unique Pulido blending of two saxes with accordion is Joel "El Gordo" Pulido on tenor, with Raúl "El Flaco" Pulido or Braulio Jiménez on alto sax. All three have also contributed significantly to the extremely popular live performances and studio recordings produced by Roberto Pulido. While Joel and Raúl are responsible for most of the undocumented Tejano sax playing on Roberto Pulido's early recordings (e.g., Roberto Pulido y los Clásicos' *Greatest Hits!*), in recent years Braulio has ably assumed responsibilities for the alto parts (e.g., Roberto Pulido y los Clásicos' *A través de los Años*). It is important to note that even Roberto Pulido himself has played some *saxofón* on occasion.

The wide appeal of Roberto Pulido's *acordeón con dos saxofones* sound spans geographies and generations, from Seattle to Saltillo, and from seniors to *niños*. It is very important to recognize that the relative influence of Roberto Pulido y los Clásicos is positively heightened by the frequency with which their music is reproduced in compilations of conjunto or borderland music (e.g., *Conjunto: Texas-Mexican Border Music*, Volume 4; *The Best of the Eighth Annual Tejano Conjunto Festival en San Antonio*; and *Borderlands: From Conjunto to Chicken Scratch*).

Finally, there are two more Tejano saxophonists to consider. They are both significant for different reasons. One is the grandson of the legendary alto and baritone saxophonist Ernie Cáceres, David Cáceres, who represents the continuation of the family tradition of playing saxophone with both Tejano and jazz groups (e.g., La Diferenzia and Latin Playerz). The other is Ichiro Nagata, who played tenor saxophone with Los Gatos, a Tejano-style conjunto from Japan, and who is probably the most extraordinary example of the Tejano sax's transcultural transcendence far beyond the U.S.–Mexican *frontera*.

Reflections and Conclusions

My study of the saxophone in Tejano and *norteño* music addressed several sorts of questions. First are those of when, where, by whom, and how the saxophone was first introduced and integrated into this international modern music context. Second are those concerned with the evidence regarding the permanence and salience of the saxophone in Tejano and *norteño* music. These were addressed in the brief narrative tracing the chronology of the saxophone in both the *norteño* and Tejano musical traditions from the 1920s to the present.

The evidence shows that the introduction of the saxophone in Tejano and *norteño* conjunto music during the 1940s and 1950s was not only eminently popular at the time, but an innovation that continues resonating musically among younger and older generations of Mexicans and others throughout the borderland, with two lasting results. First, we have the evolution of some characteristic *norteño* and Tejano styles of playing saxophone that can be distinguished from other saxophone stylings, and from each other. The second is the maintenance and expansion of a well-established repertoire of more than one hundred classic, Tejano and *norteño*, solo and ensemble sax tunes.

My research results support the conclusion that the saxophone's presence has added a new dimension and become an integral part of the sound of the more-popular contemporary *norteño* and Tejano groups, especially during the last two decades. This research also found that the groups found a viable musical model in the early Narciso Martínez–Beto Villa accordion-saxophone combination. Whether you call it "progressive conjunto," as do the Tejano Music Awards and Pura Vida Music Awards, or *conjunto orquestal,* as does Juan Tejeda, the point is that there is abundant evidence of an increase in this type of musical melding, especially since the beginning of the present postmodern music period. Tracing the saxophone's introduction and integration into the Mexican American musical experience also helped us more clearly understand the concept of transculturation. The saxophone's integration into Texas-Mexican music proves an excellent example of instrumental transculturation.

My study's findings are consistent with the notion of a multifaceted *frontera* consisting of mini-environments supporting variants of the larger cultures and societies. It rejects the notion of a single borderland with a common *cultura*. If nothing else, the results show how open and receptive (as opposed to closed and rejective) are the *pueblos* and *culturas* of our U.S.–Mexican *frontera*.

Note

1. Here the author uses the Spanish term *regional* as equivalent to *norteño*. This usage is common in northern Mexico, especially among musicians and others in the music industry. However, as can be seen elsewhere in this book, Tejano musicians may employ the same term to refer to conjunto music. —EDITORS

PART FOUR

Imágenes del Festival

Posters and Photographs

Photographs by Al Rendón

Narciso Martínez, "El Huracán del Valle," considered the father of conjunto music, performs at the Sixth Annual Tejano Conjunto Festival en San Antonio, 1987.

Valerio Longoria, known as the genius of conjunto music for his many innovations, playing at Rosedale Park, 1993. Longoria was the only musician to play at the festival every year since 1982, until his death in 2000.

Rubén Vela y su Conjunto performing in front of the Tejano Conjunto Festival's Quetzalcoatl backdrop. Rosedale Park, 1992.

Fred Zimmerle, on *bajo sexto*, and Narciso Martínez, on accordion, give an impromptu performance, while Daniel Garcés (standing), renowned songwriter and musician, looks on. Rosedale Park, 1991.

Lydia Mendoza accepting the Conjunto Music Hall of Fame award, 1991. A legendary singer of *canciones rancheras* and *corridos*, Mendoza reigned as La Cantante de los Pobres for more than fifty years.

Juan Viesca, "El Rey del Tololoche," ignites his stand-up bass onstage at the Guadalupe Theater, 1988. Viesca, who passed away in 1990, had been "firing up" his *tololoche* since at least 1951.

Flaco Jiménez, the leading ambassador of conjunto music, autographs his photo for an admiring fan. His son David, who plays drums in Flaco's conjunto, stands behind him. Rosedale Park, 1997.

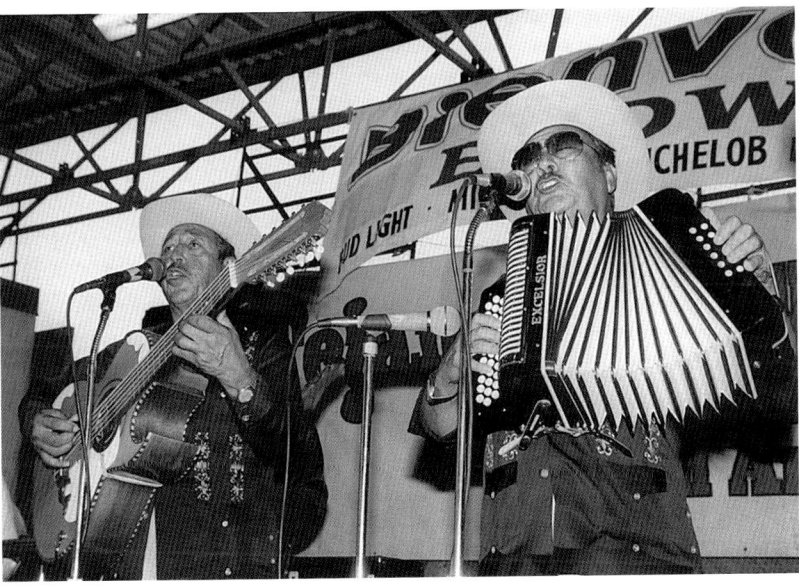

Los Alegres de Terán (Tomás Ortiz, on *bajo sexto*, and Eugenio Ábrego, on accordion) at Rosedale Park, 1985. Los Alegres, pioneers in the *norteño* tradition, were on the same bill with Ramón Ayala y los Bravos del Norte.

Tony de la Rosa, one of the most popular figures in the history of conjunto, concentrates on one of his famous *pasadas*. Rosedale Park, 1989.

FIRST TEJANO CONJUNTO FESTIVAL EN SAN ANTONIO ✧ 1982
Marcelino F. Villanueva, Jr.
Acrylic on canvas

Portrait of Conjunto Falcón, circa 1979

SECOND ANNUAL ✧ 1983
Roberto B. Sosa
Watercolor, airbrush, and rub-off letters on illustration board

THIRD ANNUAL ✧ 1984
James Cobb
Spray paint and stencil on paper

FOURTH ANNUAL ◆ 1985
Roberto B. Sosa
Color pencil on illustration board

Portrait of Don Santiago Jiménez

FIFTH ANNUAL ✧ 1986
Priscilla Reyna-Ovalle
Oil, papier-mâché, wood, and metal on wood

SIXTH ANNUAL ✧ 1987
Thomas Vásquez
Acrylic on illustration board

SEVENTH ANNUAL ✧ 1988
Douglas Jasso
Acrylic on illustration board

EIGHTH ANNUAL ◊ 1989
Thomas Vásquez
Acrylic on illustration board

NINTH ANNUAL ⋄ 1990
Jesse Almazán
Tempera and construction paper on mat board

TENTH ANNUAL ✧ 1991
Roger García
Acrylic on illustration board

ELEVENTH ANNUAL ✧ 1992
Clemente F. Guzmán III
Acrylic on canvas

TWELFTH ANNUAL ✧ 1993
José Esquivel
Acrylic and construction paper on mat board

Portrait of Marcelo Gaona, circa 1985

THIRTEENTH ANNUAL ✧ 1994
Jacinto Guevara
Acrylic on canvas

Portrait of Los Caminantes, circa 1955, with
Flaco Jiménez on accordion, Mike Garza on *tololoche*,
Henry Zimmerle on *bajo sexto*, and Richard Herrera on drums

FOURTEENTH ANNUAL ✧ 1995
Clemente F. Guzmán III
Acrylic on canvas

FIFTEENTH ANNUAL ✦ 1996
Ben Mata
Oil on wood

SIXTEENTH ANNUAL ✧ 1997
Jesús David González
Oil on masonite

SEVENTEENTH ANNUAL ✧ 1998
Rick Hunter
Computer-manipulated photograph

The incomparable Paulino Bernal performing at the Guadalupe Theater on the opening night of the Fifteenth Annual "Quinceañera" Tejano Conjunto Festival, 1996. The opening night was a tribute to the members of the Conjunto Music Hall of Fame.

Esteban Jordán, Doug Sahm, Augie Meyers, the Westside Horns, and Los Lobos jam during the amazing finale of the "New Directions in Conjunto Music" night, 1986.

Accordion wizard Esteban Jordán sitting in with Queen Ida and the Bon Temps Zydeco Band at the close of the "Conjunto Meets Cajun/Zydeco" night, 1989.

Maestro Toby Torres and his *bajo sexto* class, 1987. The Guadalupe Cultural Arts Center has been offering accordion classes since 1981 and various special sessions in the *bajo sexto* since 1983.

Maestro Valerio Longoria and one of his many button-accordion classes, 1984. Longoria taught accordion classes at the Guadalupe for twenty years.

Toby Torres, one of only six *bajistas* inducted into the Conjunto Music Hall of Fame, plays his Martín Macías *bajo sexto*, accompanying Santiago Jiménez, Jr., 1988.

Rubén Vela, "El Chaparrito de Oro," playing his distinctive style of South Texas conjunto. Here he is accompanied by Rubén Garza on *bajo sexto*. Rosedale Park, 1992.

Santiago Jiménez, Jr., stretches his squeeze box to the limit in a special performance at his students' recital at the Guadalupe Theater, 1987. Santiago, Flaco's brother, is a keeper of his father's traditional style.

Dancing is an essential part of conjunto music and, *por supuesto*, of the Tejano Conjunto Festival. Here, the couple in the foreground displays a classic West-Side-of-San-Anto dance style. Rosedale Park, 1986.

Mingo Saldívar, "the Dancing Cowboy," 1985. Saldívar earned this name for his inimitable style of playing the accordion while performing intricate and energetic dance moves.

Master accordionist Eva Ybarra salutes an appreciative audience during her show at the 1992 Tejano Conjunto Festival.

Lupita Rodela, one of the very few women who fronts her own conjunto, sings one of her trademark *piezas* at the Tejano Conjunto Festival, 1985.

Roberto Pulido, a pioneer in the progressive-conjunto sound, performing with his band, Los Clásicos, at the 1990 festival. Combining the accordion with two saxes, Pulido popularized the conjunto-*orquesta* fusion that fueled the Tejano-music explosion of the '80s and '90s.

PART FIVE

Contexto
Cultural and Social Aspects of Conjunto

15

Tejano Music as an Expression of Cultural Nationalism

⟡

JOSÉ R. REYNA
1989

In the historical development of Tejano music from the nineteenth century to the present, there have evolved two principal instrumental types of groups. The older of these forms is the conjunto, which employs the button accordion as the lead instrument and the *bajo sexto,* bass, and drums for rhythm. It reached maturity in the late 1940s and early 1950s.

The *banda* or *orquesta* is a relatively recent form that emerged in the 1930s as a Chicano version of the Anglo swing bands of the big-band era. By the 1950s it had developed its own unique sound, a sound that remained basically intact for several decades.

Thus, even though the repertoires of both conjuntos and bands include Mexican, U.S., and Chicano tunes—from *rancheras,* polkas, and *boleros,* to rock, jazz, *cumbias,* and *salsa*—instrumentally, both types of groups have become distinctively Chicano/Tejano.

In addition to being unique, Tejano music has long been a strong source of cultural identification and pride for the Tejano, and the music has survived, indeed flourished, for this reason. The features that characterize the styles as Tejano, such as instrumentation and orchestration, are significant beyond the more obvious musical and esthetic features and value.

Any examination of the rise of modern nations must take into account the role of formal institutions, political, economic, and educational, and the media—especially electronic media—in promoting national culture and identity, and in nurturing and fomenting regional creative expression.

For many years, Chicanos were denied unrestricted access to many of these institutions by the Anglo, yet artistic expression was left to develop relatively unhampered. Perhaps, as Corky Gonzales said in his epic poem "I Am Joaquín," it was because:

> They frowned upon our way of life
> and took what they could use.
> > Our art,
> > our literature,
> > our music, they ignored—

In Texas, of course, this music was the conjunto and band music that became "the heart and soul of the people of the earth."

For several decades, Texas Chicanos have relied on radio to disseminate, promote, and foment these regional forms. But, for several reasons, Tejano music was not always as ubiquitous as it now is. For many years, Spanish-language radio stations, not only in South Texas but throughout the Southwest, insisted on hiring announcers who were Mexican born and educated. Evidently, station owners considered Mexican Spanish as being more appropriate than the Chicano dialect for broadcasting.

The programming that resulted, obviously, was Mexican oriented. So, in a sense, Spanish-language radio served to promote Mexican culture, broadcasting principally Mexican music such as *mariachi, trío,* and (Mexican) big band. When conjunto music was aired it tended to be *norteño,* from northern Mexico, rather than Tejano. The message was clear: our indigenous conjunto music was as unfit for broadcasting as our dialect.

In spite of these practices, Tejano music continued to flourish in the *plataformas, cantinas,* and *salones de baile* of South Texas. And, although as early as the 1920s some of the better-known groups had recorded with a few national labels such as CBS Records, by the 1940s Chicano entrepreneurs—promoters, businessmen, and aficionados—began building a recording industry which was indigenous, too. By the 1970s, labels such as Ideal, Falcón, Bego, Zarape, Buena Suerte, Freddie, Hacienda, and a host of others were household names among Chicanos.

One effect of the proliferation of Chicano recording labels is the marked increase in Chicano music programming in the last fifteen years or so. Now there are many stations that program Tejano music almost exclusively, and the number is growing. And whether from the general proliferation of Spanish-language radio, or from the demands of more consciously Chicano audiences, most of the stations are employing Chicano announcers and programmers.

In fairness to the broadcasting industry in South Texas, it must be said that there was always some programming which featured Texas conjuntos and bands. But often these programs were short and they were scheduled by different stations throughout the region at different times during the day. It was possible in many places to switch from station to station—from *La Hora de Domingo Peña* to *La Hora de Elpidio Barrera* to *La Hora de Alice*—and listen to Chicano music for most of the day.

Ironically, these programs were initially aired by Anglo stations such as KOPY (Alice) and KINE (Kingsville). A possible explanation for the inclusion of Chicano music in these programs was that the announcers usually bought time blocks from the station and then sold advertising locally and independently of the stations. Getting and keeping audiences was critical, because it meant survival.

It was not until the 1950s and 1960s that Chicano entrepreneurs began building and buying radio stations. Among the earliest was the Dávila family, which established the first Chicano-owned radio station in the country in the mid 1950s, and it carved a niche in the Spanish-language radio market in San Antonio, which already had more than one full-time Spanish-language station. It did this with a predominantly Chicano format. Slowly, the number of Chicano-owned stations grew, and it was these stations that really gave free rein to Chicanos and their music. Other stations, not Chicano-owned, have gradually adapted their formats to include more Chicano music, primarily for economic reasons.

Due mostly to the Chicanos' own efforts, then, Tejano music had come into its own by the 1970s. By then, Texas conjunto and big-band music was being broadcast all along the Texas-Mexico border and had begun to be enjoyed and appreciated by Mexicans in northern Mexico, clearly an instance of Chicano "cultural nationalism." And there is ample evidence that Tejano music has had an impact on the music scene in Mexico.

While there appear to be no studies of Mexican *norteño* conjuntos, they have great similarities with their Texas counterparts. Still, the differences between the typical Mexican conjunto and the typical Texas conjunto are obvious to Tejanos and Mexicans alike. It is equally clear that Mexican conjuntos that succeed in the United States are those that most closely resemble the Texas conjunto.

Therefore, it isn't surprising that some Mexican conjuntos gear their sound specifically to Tejano tastes, and this is simply because it is profitable to do so. Furthermore, success in the United States has catapulted some Mexican conjuntos to even greater success in Mexico, not only in recording but also in movies.

In Mexico, it was not until Tejano musicians, recording companies, and promoters elevated the Texas conjunto to its present status that Mexicans began to use conjunto elements in the *mariachi,* Mexico's most prestigious musical group. Cornelio Reyna would never have had a film career had he not been catapulted to stardom by the prosperous conjunto market in the United States. Until then, conjunto music was viewed by Mexicans as a genre for lower-class people.

In the 1960s, Mexico also imported Texas musicians, albeit on a modest scale. Several Chicano accordionists recorded with Mexican *mariachis* and others toured Mexico, reportedly performing to tremendous receptions. Several individual band leaders—Carlos Guzmán, Freddie Martínez, and Sunny Ozuna—even did cameo appearances in Mexican films. At one time, Freddie Martínez billed himself as "El Embajador Tejano." Admittedly these are isolated instances, but were it not for economic conditions in Mexico and for the fees Tejano groups command, we might have seen a veritable flood of Tejano groups into Mexico.

The Tejano big bands present a peculiar situation with regard to Chicano influence in Mexico. While obvious similarities exist between the *conjunto norteño* and the *conjunto tejano,* there is nothing in Mexican tradition resembling the Tejano band. And, for a number of reasons, it is also highly unlikely that this tradition will be imported by Mexicans in the near future.

First, most Mexican musicians have had neither the type nor quality of training in music that enabled Tejanos to develop a distinctive big-band tradition. For several generations, Chicanos in Texas have thoroughly absorbed the excellent music training provided in public schools in Texas. A review of rosters of all-city, all-district, all-region, and all-state bands in recent decades clearly shows that Chicanos consititute the heart of the music programs of South Texas. Many of these prize band students have gone on to earn music degrees and become school band directors.

More importantly, they have greatly enhanced the Chicano music tradition in Texas. While this training has had a greater impact upon the big-band tradition, which utilizes many of these same band instruments, it has also had a positive effect on conjunto music, and this partially explains the emergence of the more recent conjunto-band hybrids that require more formal training of their players than the strictly traditional conjunto.

The closest thing to a Tejano big band in Mexican tradition would appear to have been those of Luis Arcaraz and Pablo Beltrán Ruiz, which emerged in the 1930s and 1940s in Mexico. But that phenomenon stagnated in the 1950s, and the few that survived now seem to play "society" music. The Tejano big bands, on the other hand, were fomented and nurtured by Chicanos and they have continued to evolve to their present form.

Financial hardship also militated against Mexicans who might have wanted to "borrow" the Tejano band tradition. The capital investment required for equipment used by big bands (amps, speakers, keyboards, sound systems)—not to mention transportation (buses, vans, station wagons, trailers)—is exorbitant in the affluent United States. In Mexico, such capital outlays are unthinkable to all but a handful of performers. In fact, even Chicano bands have nearly priced themselves out of existence.

While promoters and entrepreneurs were advancing the cause of Tejano regional music, musicians were also helping raise the consciousness of Chicanos during the Civil Rights movement of the late 1960s and the 1970s. Around that time the names of groups, especially of the bands, began to reflect the theme of *chicanismo*.

Little Joe and the Latinaires, who had emerged in the 1950s when Chicanos still perceived the "Mexican" label as pejorative, became Little Joe y la Familia in the late 1960s. The new name reflected the respect for that cherished Chicano institution. Another band was called Latin Breed ("breed" is another word for *raza*); yet another group was, simply, La Raza.

Still other groups reflected an awareness of shared cultural values and symbols—La Herencia, the Mexican Revolution, La Patria, La Onda Chicana, Los Chicanos, La Conexión Mexicana, and even Tortilla Factory.

Beyond the use of names, which in any case could be interpreted as either a sign of the times or as opportunism (a *movimiento* bandwagon effect, so to speak), many musicians were genuinely committed to the goals of the movement, and to the spirit of *carnalismo*. At the height of the movement all of the top groups, big bands and conjuntos alike, played at countless Raza Unida Party rallies and at political benefits throughout the region.

As an aside, I should also mention that at an outdoor Chicano music festival near Edinburg I witnessed an extremely heated discussion between several Los Únicos musicians and a gentleman from Mexico, who stubbornly insisted that Chicano music was inferior to Mexican music. Actually, they almost came to blows. This certainly convinced me that the musicians were very much aware of, and proud of, the legitimacy and value of Chicano culture.

Finally, the spirit of *chicanismo* was also seen in a number of lyrical compositions such as "Soy chicano," "Yo soy chicano," "Chicanita," "El corrido del chicano," and at least two parodies I am aware of, "Chicano from Mercedes" ("Okie from Muskogee") and "Chicano Truck Driving Man" ("Truck Drivin' Man"), all of which came out of that period. A cursory view of these songs also shows that they differed markedly from typical *movimiento* songs, which were often songs with Latin American or third-world themes. The songs composed or adapted by Chicanos in Texas dealt with much more familiar experiences, were more appropriate to the regional milieu, and thus reached and affected a broader audience than did songs in the *nueva canción* style.

The 1980s have brought some noteworthy developments in Tejano music. Although much could be said about the continuing evolution of the conjunto and the band from a musicological standpoint, it is more important to note that, in general, the image of Tejano music has improved dramatically. And, again, this has been due to the efforts of Chicano musicians, promoters, and countless devoted fans.

As early as the 1970s, Tejanos began to hold outdoor Tejano concerts and festivals. These events, which often attract thousands, are now commonplace. Although there have been isolated problems, the desired effects have nonetheless been achieved.

Among the oldest and most impressive and prestigious of these events would have to be the annual Tejano Conjunto Festival en San Antonio, sponsored since 1982 by the Guadalupe Cultural Arts Center. This event, which lasts several days and over the years has featured more than a hundred conjuntos, has received official recognition from the state of Texas and the city of San Antonio, and financial support from many businesses and corporations, as well as from the Folk Arts Program of the National Endowment for the Arts.

The Guadalupe Cultural Arts Center has also sponsored two National Heritage Award winners—Valerio Longoria and Pedro Ayala—recognized for their contributions to the conjunto tradition in Texas. The festival regularly features and recognizes many musicians who have made historical contributions to the conjunto tradition in Texas, including Mexicans.

The oldest and, to some, the most prestigious event is the Tejano Music Awards, which annually sponsors a gala awards ceremony and gives recognition to Tejano musicians in a variety of categories. Sponsored by the Texas Talent Musicians Association, the Tejano Music Awards tends to concentrate more on the Tejano bands, or *orquestas*. Like the Tejano Conjunto Festival, the event draws support from an array of corporate sponsors and, unlike the Tejano Conjunto Festival, it has annually produced a TV special which is being aired regionally.

All of these developments have brought national and international recognition to Texas music, musicians, and composers. Several (non-Chicano) record companies which specialize in folk music, notably Arhoolie Records and Rounder Records, have produced impressive collections of Texas conjunto music. Further, in the last five years there has been a renewed interest among the major recording labels—such as CBS and RCA—in recording Chicano music.

The highly acclaimed film *Chulas Fronteras,* produced by Chris Strachwitz, features several Texas musicians. In the last few years, several conjuntos have toured the United States and Europe. Recently, the Hohner accordion company, a regular sponsor of the Tejano Conjunto Festival, announced a new accordion model, the Steve Jordan Tex-Mex Rockordeon, named after Esteban Jordán and made to his specifications.

Tejanos may also take credit for the recent revival of the accordion, principally the button accordion, in U.S. music. It cannot be denied that the use of the accordion by entertainers such as Paul Simon, Talking Heads, Ry Cooder, and Buck Owens, not to mention Los Lobos (a California group once featured at the Tejano Conjunto Festival in their pre–*La Bamba* days), was inspired by Texas conjuntos.

In summary, then, although Tejano music emerged spontaneously and was allowed to evolve more or less freely, recognition and acceptance by mainstream Anglo America has remained elusive and continues to be considerably more difficult to attain. Largely, this has been due to the traditional stigma attached to folk music generally; typically, only "folkloric" forms endorsed by "the state" attain any degree of prestige.

In the absence of a Chicano state that could nurture Tejano regional music, Mexican disc jockeys, perceiving themselves as protectors and promoters of Mexican culture in the United States, for decades engaged in a type of censorship of Tejano music. But this outside interference merely delayed the coming of age of Tejano music.

In the last analysis, Tejanos prevailed—even officially, as city and state proclamations of recent years indicate. Indeed, it is ironic that while Mexicans were busily cultivating other musical genres as preferred national forms, Tejanos beat them to the punch with regard to the conjunto. No one would deny that on an international level "conjunto" is now synonymous with Texas conjunto. The concerted efforts of Texas Chicanos to establish and promote their music is a distinct phenomenon, and reflects nationalistic sentiments not unlike those of full-fledged nations.

The only question that remains is whether the Tejano big band will be promoted in the future as diligently as has been the conjunto. Perhaps because it is more commercial, pop, and "American" than conjunto—and because Mexicans have not laid claim to it—Chicanos have not perceived it as being an endangered species. Yet as a distinctly Tejano phenomenon, this powerful ensemble would certainly merit the same kind of attention that conjunto music has received.

Note

An earlier version of this paper was published in *Revista Chicano-Riqueña* 4, no. 3 (summer 1976): 37–41.

16

The Popular in Conjunto Tejano Music
Changes in Chicano Class and Identity

✧

AVELARDO VALDEZ & JEFFREY A. HALLEY

1991

The increasing popularity of conjunto music is linked to changes in class and identity. This article demonstrates this relationship, examining the growth and influence of conjunto music, particularly over the last decade. This music, through its musicians and audience, plays an important role in shaping the evolving identity of Chicanos.

During the 1980s Chicano music developed from a music that was listened to primarily in the *barrio,* to one which now extends across classes and into the general population. This has come about because of an acceptance of conjunto music, particularly among the rising Mexican American middle class who had previously avoided and ignored this music. These Mexican Americans previously associated conjunto music with the negative image of lower-class and working-class Mexicans (Peña 1985). The acceptance of conjunto music by the general population is illustrated by the crossover of conjunto music with *orquesta tejana,* country and western, rock, *salsa,* blues, and jazz.

Chicano Artists as Intellectuals

Intellectuals are usually thought of as university scholars, writers, and others who are legitimized by societal institutions. These intellectuals often express the interests of those in power. Antonio Gramsci, an Italian philosopher and political leader, developed the notion of the "organic intellectual" to include artists and others who are not necessarily recognized by dominant institutions and who resist the dominant ideology. The "organic intellectuals" for Gramsci are those intellectuals rooted in community, and who represent or express the interests of subordinate groups (Gramsci 1971).

One can expand Gramsci's concept of organic intellectuals to include musicians as they resist the mainstream culture. Chicano musicians, as organic intellectuals, are carriers of a counterideology of and for the Chicano community. In this sense, the activity of organic music intellectuals looks less like traditional intellectual activity because it is connected to the popular, carnivalesque moments of everyday life. In the case of conjunto musicians, they often play in neighborhood icehouses, church festivals, and parks.

If we examine lyrics in much of Chicano music, we find references to particular situations of domination and cultural resistance. Some well-known examples are "El corrido de Gregorio Cortez," the lyrics of Little Joe y la Familia in the 1960s and '70s, the *corrido* describing the shooting of a young Chicano by Castroville police, and, more recently, the musical complaint by Eddie (Lalo) Torres regarding participation in the Gulf War.

In another sense there is an "organicity" between the music and the audience. For these reasons we should not just focus on the musicians as organic leaders. It is the followers, the fans, who are crucial in this process. The fans drive its production, and create forms of life around the music and its cultural meanings.

The crossover of Chicano music into other musical forms is a good example of the process of hybridization. Hybridization refers to a cultural synthesis that takes place without obscuring the culture's originality and origins. The creativity of popular art lies in its openness to a multiplicity of forms, and therefore in its ability to constantly develop into something new, without losing its roots. Chicano music in its many contemporary forms is an example of this process.

This article explores the question of class and musical tastes in conjunto and Tejano music. Manuel Peña maintains that during the 1950s there was a split in the Mexican American community, with the working class listening to conjunto, and the middle class pulled toward *orquesta tejana* (Peña 1985). And he has more recently argued that as Chicano music becomes more commercialized, there is a danger that it will lose its organic connection with the community

(Peña 1989). Rather than assume, as Peña does, that the commercialization of Chicano music will jeopardize Chicano identity and disrupt its connectedness to community, we contend that this hybridization is part of the assertion of Chicano identity.

The Changing Class Structure

The changing social status of the Mexican-origin population is linked to changes in Chicano music. Class differences among this population became more pronounced during the 1980s. During this period we saw a growing middle class and a smaller working class, as well as a growing proportion of this population living in poverty. This class transformation results from the reconstruction of the U.S. economy.

This transformation exacerbated problems of poverty, discrimination, and urban residential segregation among the poor. As a result there was a growing percentage of Chicanos living in poverty, increased numbers of female-headed households, high unemployment rates, and an increased proportion of this group involved in crime and violence.

These changes have also affected the opportunities of the working class. The disappearance of a stable wage-based economy has resulted in downward mobility. Opportunities for working-class Chicanos today are worse now than at any time within the last thirty years.

The middle class, however, has done relatively well during the 1980s. They have experienced increases in family per capita income and years of education, and are less residentially segregated. This segment of the Mexican American community has been able to take advantage of the opportunities created by civil-rights legislation. Also, this group was able to exploit the economic opportunities offered by the new economic order. There are also now more opportunities for assimilation and acculturation for this segment of the community.

The New Assertion of Chicano Culture

Middle-class Chicanos have been identified as part of the "Hispanic Generation" of the 1980s. This generation, as opposed to the "Chicano Generation" of the 1960s and '70s, developed an ideology that emphasizes integration and assimilation. The Hispanic Generation is characterized by the following: a celebration of success, an emphasis on individual achievement, a focus on education (as a means to success), coalition building with other Latino groups, and an acceptance of the corporate world's adoption of Hispanic culture for profit making.

Based on this generation's values and ideology, one would expect a moving away from their ethnic identity, but just the opposite seems to be happening. In fact, many middle-class Mexican Americans have embraced particular aspects of Chicano culture, moving it out of *barrios* into new venues and institutions. This is expressed through an interest in Chicano art, literature, dance, theater, and film by middle-class Mexican Americans and by mainstream cultural institutions.

The Evolution of Chicano Music

Chicano music is defined as music that is played by Mexican American musicians for a Mexican American audience who identify themselves as Mexican American. Although this definition includes a wide variety of musical forms, we focus here on two original types of musical ensembles: conjunto and *orquesta tejana*. Conjunto is music that consists of an ensemble that includes the button accordion, *bajo sexto,* bass, and drums. *Orquesta tejana* music consists of a larger ensemble that includes a horn section (saxophones, trumpets), electric guitar, bass, drums, and an electric piano or synthesizer, and occasionally a button accordion. Songs are predominantly in Spanish in both forms; however, their repertoire includes also English and bilingual lyrics.

Peña describes the historical development of conjunto music from the late 1920s to the mid 1970s, in which there were rapid and stylistic innovations. During this period there was the addition of the *bajo sexto,* electric bass, drums, and vocals to the button accordion. The use of amplification and P.A. systems became standard after the 1950s and distinctive styles developed. The accordion continues to be the basic instrument for the ensemble identified as conjunto. However, since the Conjunto Bernal in the 1970s, there has not been a significant development of the basic musical form. In spite of this lack of change, the popularity of the music has continued to grow.

Conjunto "Scenes" in San Antonio

As a vehicle to discuss contemporary conjunto music and its growing popularity, we will identify venues, or "scenes," audiences, and conjunto groups in San Antonio. The word "scene," as in the expression "making the scene," means more than mere "places" where music is played. They imply a participation that has meaning beyond the particular activity. They are protected spaces. Whether they are at a neighborhood icehouse or at an upscale bar, scenes preserve and create a form of life.

The music, the audience, and the places have different relationships with one another. Some are more community oriented and some are more "upscale." These scenes run on a continuum from modest neighborhood icehouses or dance halls to more affluent, stylish settings.

NEIGHBORHOOD PLACES

What we call "neighborhood places" include venues such as South Side flea markets, local neighborhood *cantinas,* and icehouses. Typical of these scenes is Ramón's, located adjacent to an established East Side Chicano *barrio*. This dance hall and bar caters to local residents, who are primarily poor and working-class Chicanos and Mexican immigrants. In many cases multigenerational audiences attend these neighborhood places. Other locations would be El Venadito, Locomotion, and Treviño's. Typical groups would include the Southside Kid, Joe Allegato, Los Astronautas, Agustín y sus Chicanos, Los Magníficos, and numerous others. Usually these musicians make a living from a straight weekday job and play on the side during evenings and weekends. These groups tend to play primarily at these local venues and are less known outside of San Antonio. Audiences would not necessarily make a special trip outside of their neighborhood to hear this type of group.

NORTEÑO NEIGHBORHOOD PLACES

Norteño neighborhood places constitute a scene similar to neighborhood places, in terms of locality and audience. The difference is that in these places the audience is made up primarily of Mexican immigrants, and border-style *norteño* music is played rather than *conjunto tejano*. The music of Ramón Ayala, for example, is very popular at these places. A typical *norteño* place would be Los Mesquites, by the flea markets at 410, which hires a considerable number of *norteño*-style bands such as Los Diamantes del Norte and Juan Ramos y los Príncipes de Nuevo Laredo. A distinction is made between these scenes and others because the audience is less interchangeable than at other places.

PARKS AND LOCAL FESTIVALS

The park and local-festival scenes attract a cross section of social classes, from lower middle class on down. In fact, they are often family events. Persons of all ages attend: the elderly, middle-aged, young adults, and children with their parents. Typical performers include well-known artists such as Nick Villarreal and Valerio Longoria, and journeyman players such as those mentioned earlier. Venues include Rosedale Park, Mission County Park, Comanche Park, and El Mercado, particularly during Fiesta, Cinco de Mayo, and other special occasions.

CITYWIDE AND REGIONAL CLUBS

Unlike neighborhood places, citywide venues draw hard-core conjunto fans from all over the metropolitan area. Typical clubs are Lerma's, where Henry Zimmerle often plays; King Armadillo, where Eddie (Lalo) Torres plays; Irma's; Eva's Cozy Spot; and several other locations. These are more "respectable" clubs, in that they have a cover charge. Although there are some people in their thirties, most are in their forties and fifties. This clientele is lower middle class, with enough discretionary income to attend such a place.

NATIONAL AND INTERNATIONAL FESTIVALS

One of the major ways in which conjunto music has been legitimized has been through the exhibition of conjunto music at national and international festivals. The major festival, sponsored by the Guadalupe Cultural Arts Center, is the annual Tejano Conjunto Festival en San Antonio. This festival has attracted national and international attention and draws audiences from all around the world. It has also created a Conjunto Music Hall of Fame. Typical performers are Flaco Jiménez, Santiago Jiménez, Jr., Roberto Pulido, Rubén Naranjo y los Gamblers, Rubén Vela, Tony de la Rosa, and Valerio Longoria.

Artists like Flaco Jiménez, Esteban Jordán, and Santiago Jiménez, Jr., have performed in festivals in European countries such as the Netherlands, England, and Germany, and in regional music festivals outside of the Southwest, in states such as Kentucky, Louisiana, and New York, and in Washington, D.C. Festivals include the New Orleans Jazz and Heritage Festival and the American Folklife Festival.

AVANT-GARDE CONJUNTO SCENES

Emerging on the musical scene are a few "avant-garde" places that showcase conjunto artists. Typical of this category is Saluté in San Antonio, and La Zona Rosa in Austin. Saluté is located outside of the Mexican American neighborhoods, on St. Mary's Street, a popular entertainment strip of restaurants and bars catering to San Antonio's young professional middle class.

While Saluté sometimes books middle-rank talent, for the most part the musicians tend to be top conjunto artists like Flaco Jiménez, Esteban Jordán, and Nick Villarreal. These are the most popular groups in the area—that is, in record sales and audience. The music they play is a kind of conjunto, or accordion virtuosic crossover, while remaining within the conjunto style. Nick Villarreal's topical, bilingual lyrics, and his experimentation with blues and country, have made him a favorite of crossover audiences. Esteban Jordán, in his sets in spring 1991, has tended to play fewer polkas and more Afro Cuban, Latin, rock, and jazz, displaying how versatile he can be in all styles. Flaco Jiménez, even when not playing with the Texas Tornados, uses a country-and-western base for many of his songs, singing in Spanish and English. In this sense the music is a dynamic hybrid, with roots in conjunto, but reaching out to other styles.

This is the only club on the strip that is owned by a Mexican American. The audience here is distinctly different from other conjunto venues. Its clientele is middle-class, upscale Mexican American and Anglo. It is a place to go with a date, not with your family. Ages are younger, between twenty-five and forty-five. The typical Chicano participant might be a person who grew up with conjunto music, went to college and drifted away from conjunto, is now about thirty years old, and is again a fan of the music. As a scene for this audience, Saluté relegitimizes the music and makes it accessible. It offers a hip place, not on the West Side, where one can meet other professional types.

A similar place in Austin, on occasion, is La Zona Rosa. Conjunto music is played to an upscale audience, although there is also the University of Texas college crowd who want to get down with the Chicano scene.

Class Scenes and Cultural Generators

What this continuum of scenes shows is the spectrum of conjunto music, beginning with its direct connection with its poor working-class roots, as indicated by neighborhood bars and dance halls. The artists that play here are often from these communities. What is striking, though, is that while the class position of Chicanos has changed and music venues have changed, conjunto music has remained more or less the same.

Along this continuum of clubs and venues, we see that audiences are drawn from different social classes from within the Mexican American community. Clubs such as Lerma's, where the audience tends to be middle-aged, working-class persons, are distinct from those that are neighborhood based. Chicanos drawn to avant-garde venues, on the other hand, tend to be middle class, or artists, students, or semiprofessionals. At this end of the continuum we see more hybridized conjunto music.

The importance of the people in the latter crowd, however, is that as they have moved up the class ladder, they have consciously chosen to listen to conjunto music. These persons are important because they become cultural generators. They now accept the music and become its promoters by their conversion. In this sense, they become reconnected to a fundamental component of Chicano culture.

The Transformation of the Orquesta Tejana

EARLY ORQUESTA TEJANA

Orquesta tejana music began with the big bands of the 1940s and 1950s in South Texas. The Mexican Americans referred to these bands as *orquestas*. Most played standard big-band chart arrangements popular throughout mainstream culture. This music, according to Peña, appealed to middle-class Mexican Americans. These bands, however, were distinct from U.S. big bands in that their repertoire included Latin music such as *mambos, cumbias,* and other *música tejana*. What is particularly distinctive of these *orquestas* is that they also played standard *rancheras* and other conjunto repertoire.

In the early 1950s, such groups as Beto Villa and Isidro López began to develop the sound that would become the modern *orquesta tejana*. This consisted initially of playing fewer U.S. big-band charts, and more *música tropical, rancheras,* and *corridos* with big-band orchestration. This new sound appealed to the Mexican American generation of the late 1950s, who were beginning to forge a Chicano identity distinct from previous generations. This developing identity is manifested through other institutions such as politics, education, and the church.

LA ONDA TEJANA: 1960S AND 1970S

The transition of the *orquesta tejana* sound was completed with a number of bands that emerged in the 1960s in South Texas (Joe Bravo, Sunny Ozuna, Joe Hernández, and others). The most well known of these is Little Joe y la Familia, who developed the prototypic Tejano band. Little Joe's popularity during this period was also based on his association with the emerging identity of the Chicano Generation. Little Joe's musical repertoire included songs with lyrics that often had political themes from the traditional Mexican *corridos* and themes from the 1960s Chicano Movement. Moreover, the pieces were built upon the musical structure of conjunto.

Orquesta tejana music appealed to a broader Mexican American audience than that of *orquesta* during the previous decade. In particular it appealed to the segment of the community that was more upwardly mobile but could not completely identify with either rock and roll or conjunto music. *Orquesta tejana* music offered to its Chicano audience something exciting and innovative without losing its ethnic identity. Tejano bands, however, did incorporate contemporary rock-and-roll sounds. Sunny Ozuna had two all-English hit single records on the national charts during this period. At the same time the Tejano sound of the sixties and early seventies became a vehicle for political and cultural resistance.

THE LULL OF TEJANO MUSIC: THE LATE 1970S

As Tejano music moved toward the end of the 1970s, it began to lose its appeal. There are two main reasons for this transformation. One of the reasons is that the music began to lose its spark and innovation. Economic factors forced many bands to reduce the number of group members. As a result, many Tejano bands began to overuse the synthesizer and other electrical instruments.

Another reason for the loss of its appeal was the changing political climate. The music began to reflect the political conservatism of the late 1970s and 1980s. This period witnessed the decline of the Chicano Movement, with the collapse of many formal barriers that prevented Mexican Americans' equal participation in the society. As a result, Chicano consciousness as a political manifestation was watered down and transformed. Tejano music lost its critical bite and experienced a lull in the late 1970s and early 1980s.

CONTEMPORARY TEJANO MUSIC

Tejano music did not develop its mass appeal until the period 1985–1991. One of the major factors for this increased popularity was corporate America's realization of the market potential of Chicanos. Major record companies like CBS, Capitol EMI, Polygram, and Warner Brothers began to record and promote Tejano bands. The Spanish radio industry capitalized on the market potential of this audience. There has also been a proliferation of radio stations that have primarily conjunto or Tejano formats throughout Texas.

As well, corporations such as Anheuser Busch, GMC Trucks, R.J. Reynolds Tobacco Company, Tony Lama Boots, and others promote and sponsor Tejano bands as a means of marketing their products. The national and international record companies, radio stations, and corporations play important roles in the popularization and commercialization of Chicano music.

Chicanos drawn to contemporary Tejano music are primarily teenagers and young adults. These age groups are the largest segment of the population. These young people are attending Tejano dances and clubs, and going to large concerts. In San Antonio, Tejano music is primarily played at upscale bars such as Desperados and Reflex. This young group is also buying records, tapes, and CDs of popular Tejano groups. A hit Tejano record sells around one hundred thousand units, in comparison with a hit conjunto record, which may only sell twenty-five thousand units.

Today, Tejano's most popular groups—that is, Mazz, Roberto Pulido, Emilio Navaira, and La Mafia—all use the accordion. Why has the accordion been reintroduced into the Tejano ensemble from conjunto music? The increased popularity of the accordion within Tejano music is symptomatic of a reintegration of components of Chicano culture that were previously given less status. Conjunto music continually grounds Chicano music. A parallel might be the continual influence of blues and gospel on jazz and other contemporary musical forms. In this sense, Tejano continually goes back to its roots in conjunto. Tejano music, however, also uses in its repertoire rock, jazz, *salsa,* and *rancheras.* The music is constantly remaking itself by "crossing over" to other forms. In this sense, Tejano music represents an active hybridization.

Conclusion

The popularity of *conjunto tejano* music has different meanings to different segments of the Chicano community. For the middle class it is partly nostalgic, but it is also a political statement in that it reaffirms Chicano identity, independence, and resistance to "Hispanization," as it has always been for the working poor.

Rather than Chicano music representing a process of homogenization (Peña 1986), there has actually occurred a crossover between the conjunto and the *orquesta* tradition, a reconciliation between the roots and the new Chicano music. Today Chicano music can best be described as a postmodern hybridization. This is reflected in different aspects of contemporary Chicano experience, particularly among the young. In Chicano music, it is represented in its drawing from rock, country and western, blues, Latin *salsa,* and jazz without losing its *chicanismo.* This movement points toward an affirmation of ethnic identity rather than a linear assimilation process.

Note

This article was first presented at the conference "Mexican Americans in Texas History," held at the University of Texas Institute of Texan Cultures, San Antonio, May 2–4, 1991.

References

Gramsci, Antonio. 1971. *Selections from the Prison Notebooks.* Edited and translated by Quintin Hoare and Geoffrey Newell Smith. New York: International Publishers.
Peña, Manuel. 1985. *The Texas-Mexican Conjunto: History of a Working-Class Music.* Austin: University of Texas Press.
———. 1986. "Conjunto Music: The First Fifty Years." *Tonantzin* (Guadalupe Cultural Arts Center, San Antonio) 3, no. 3 (May). [Chapter 4 in this volume.]

17

La Voz del Pueblo Tejano
Conjunto Music and the Construction of Tejano Identity in Texas

✧

CATHY RAGLAND

1995

Today is Texas Republic Day. Texas Independence Day más bien dicho, eh. Does that mean we can go back and be a republic, eh? República de los tejanos, ¿verdad? And it's also the start of public school week. Una semana escolar públicamente de Tejas. Todas las mamacitas de los estudiantes pueden venir a la escuela de su hijo y su hija. Right on, right on. Así, pueden conocer a sus maestros, who be teachin' those little midgetitos to stop lookin' at the chiquititititas! Vamos, bien dicho, feliz birthday party. A big happy cumpleaños to—yeah, yeah, party todos, all right—Fred Salazar, hoy su cumpleaños, de parte de su esposa Bertha . . . su guaifa Bertita . . . y sus hijos, sus kiddos, Fred Jr., Roland, Yolanda, and Rick. Let's all go to Kansas City, Kansas City, here we come.
— DJ Rick "Güero Polkas" Dávila (from Dávila's morning radio show on KEDA, March 1992)

For five hours every workday morning San Antonio DJ Rick Dávila, a.k.a. Güero Polkas, entertains listeners with a rapid bilingual rap. It is Spanish radio's version of the "morning zoo" concept heard on most big-city FM rock stations, with some crucial differences: Dávila's Spanglish banter is interspersed with wedding, anniversary, and birthday congratulations, a noontime prayer, and lots of what he calls "accordion abuse." His radio station, KEDA-AM 1540, also known as Radio Jalapeño or La Tejanita (the Little Texan), has promoted conjunto, the accordion-based local music style celebrated as the root of Mexican American music, in San Antonio since 1966. Much of Güero Polkas' rap is focused around empowering *la raza*, the people of Mexican American descent in San Antonio, and reminding them that the roots of Texas-Mexican music lie in the two instruments that make up the core of conjunto music: button accordion and *bajo sexto,* a twelve-string bass-rhythm guitar originally from Mexico.

Güero Polkas (*güero,* meaning a person who is light-skinned, or blond, and "polkas," referring to conjunto's popular dance rhythm) embodies the cultural and musical diversity that has affected the development of the sound as well as asserting its roots on the Texas side of the border. Güero Polkas' charismatic public persona also incorporates Dávila's working-class roots, his formative years assimilating within a dominant Texas-American society, and, finally, his own experience as a Chicano and *tejano* living in San Antonio, Texas. Each day, whether speaking to his audience in Spanish, English, or bilingual, the voice of Güero Polkas is also the voice of Texas Mexicans throughout the state. The station's playlist, which includes rock and roll from the 1950s and 1960s, Texas-style honky-tonk music, Texas-Mexican conjunto music, and contemporary *música tejana,* is also a reflection of the diversity within the local community itself. However, Güero Polkas and other KEDA disc jockeys make a special effort to single conjunto music out as "the music of the people, *la raza*" and "the music of our heritage and our culture."

What Güero Polkas and KEDA seem to suggest is that for many people in the Mexican American communities of South Texas, conjunto music embodies an alternative popular-music history, one which rivals that of U.S. popular-music genres such as rock and roll and country and western. Conjunto pioneers such as Narciso Martínez, Tony de la Rosa, Valerio Longoria, Santiago Jiménez, Sr., and others are often compared locally to U.S. country- and popular-music legends like Elvis Presley, Buddy Holly, Bob Wills, and Hank Williams. Conjunto music, because of its connection to the development of a *tejano* society and its ubiquity at community functions, is valued for its "pioneering" players and its impact on the local society.

As a Mexican American, Güero Polkas emphasizes conjunto's beginnings as rural, working-class music and its continued role in the community. Yet as a disc jockey competing with contemporary rock, country, and *tejano* radio stations in a large U.S. city, he also promotes conjunto as a popular music form unique to Texas.

KEDA was once a Spanish-language station that mixed conjunto with traditional and contemporary Mexican music. However, through the years, KEDA's format has grown to include recordings of U.S. popular music styles such as country, rhythm and blues, and rock along with *música tejana* (a highly produced, mass-marketed style rooted in conjunto, U.S., and Latino pop-music styles and associated with Texas cowboy imagery). It is a musical combination that reflects a strong Texas-Mexican identity and is built on incorporating popular influences rather than assimilating to them. Like conjunto, *música tejana* is sung in Spanish and heard primarily on FM-formatted *tejano* radio stations where, ironically, English is the preferred language of disc jockeys. *Música tejana* is also the music most often recorded by Latin divisions of major record labels with offices now located in San Antonio. On the air, Dávila and other KEDA disc jockeys make distinctions between conjunto and *música tejana*, and they often speak more generally of a *tejano* music which can include both styles. Locally, the terms *tejano* and *música tejana* are more often used interchangeably. Similarly, many Texas Mexicans use *tejano* as a cultural identifier, while others still prefer "Mexican American," "Chicano," or the more universally accepted "Hispanic" identifier.

Beyond the issue of what Texas Mexicans choose to call themselves or their music (which itself is a complex issue that carries with it economic and sociopolitical implications), Rick Dávila's alter ego (Güero Polkas), his powerful image within the local population, and his high regard for conjunto represent, in microcosm, the complexity of Texas-Mexican (or *tejano*) identity in South Texas. He personifies a society that, as folklorist and Texas-Mexican scholar Américo Paredes has argued, created its own history and culture amid the social and political struggle between Mexico, the United States, and Texas. Moreover, he speaks to a people who have a secure sense of self that is built on a shared language, history, and belief system that is at the same time constantly changing and being redefined by the multifaceted world around them.

Manuel Peña's study of conjunto music, *The Texas-Mexican Conjunto: History of a Working-Class Music*, describes the genre's evolution and its connection to social, political, and economic transformations that took place within Texas-Mexican society. Peña says that conjunto music and the two- and three-row button accordions have become powerful symbols of identity among working-class Texas Mexicans. His analysis focuses primarily on commercial conjunto recordings made in the period from 1935 to 1960. Peña asserts that conjunto had, by the end of this period, developed "into a well-defined style that has since remained virtually unchanged" (Peña 1985: 3). While conjunto and the accordion may continue to play an important symbolic role for Texas Mexicans, the conjunto music Peña documented is today also viewed locally as *música folklórica,* a "cultivated" music tradition that has its roots in Texas-Mexican working-class history but is also a cultural operator when constructing a *tejano* identity. With the advent of the Chicano Movement in the late 1960s and into the 1970s, conjunto found itself part of a growing Chicano consciousness, out of which it has played an important role in the rewriting of Chicano/*tejano* history in Texas. In the process it has become one of the most visible and celebrated folk traditions in Texas and the U.S. Southwest. While the music still maintains its working-class, populist audience, it is also celebrated as "traditional" music by middle-class Mexican Americans and is the music most associated with community functions. But as a locally popular music form widely performed and recorded throughout Texas, conjunto also finds itself in a rather ambiguous place, somewhere between the local music industry's definitions of "traditional" and "popular" music.

The constant ebb and flow between American, Mexican, and *tejano* music heard on KEDA at the hands of a fair-skinned, bilingual Texas Mexican is an ideal example of the complexity of relationships between music and social identity. Musical and cultural diversity are at the core of the development of conjunto style and its relationship to *música tejana,* as well as Mexican popular music styles. No simplistic categorization of genres and social strata can provide us with a sufficiently complex understanding of Güero Polkas' sophisticated manipulation of styles. Conjunto music's place is simultaneously entrenched in Texas-Mexican history and community life and in competition with mass-marketed, popular music forms such as *música tejana.* As a result, the music operates as a cultural symbol that is instrumental in the construction of *tejano* identity in Texas, but must also compete in the local music industry as a popular commodity.

Güero Polkas and KEDA play an important role in this ongoing negotiation between multiple sensibilities. As conjunto simultaneously competes with mainstream popular music (this is perhaps more specific to country music given its popularity among Texas Mexicans) and contemporary as well as Mexican popular music styles such as *norteño, banda,* and *tropical,* adjustments are made in performance style, mode of presentation, and production quality. Today, the core of conjunto's instrumentation remains, for the most part, unchanged, as documented by Peña, but it has also been affected by regional distinctions in style (specifically San Antonio, Corpus Christi, and the Rio Grande Valley), an expanded Anglo American and European market, new innovations in recording technology, and musical esthetics that have become associated with the development of conjunto's biggest rival, *música tejana.*

Home Is Where Conjunto Is: Toward a Tejano Construction of a Cultural Universe

In light of these developments, it is time to move beyond Peña's neatly constructed historical schema toward an examination of conjunto music's current position as a symbolic mediator that allows Texas Mexicans to define a geographical home and a cultural universe. As I have already argued, conjunto is currently viewed by middle-class Texas Mexicans and most Anglo Americans as a "folkloric" genre. The accordion and conjunto music are now more solidly ingrained in the definition of *tejano* identity itself and because the music is also a hybrid of German, Mexican, U.S., and Texan musical styles, it is also able to speak to a society that itself is based on a multidimensional view of self. As a result, the music's broader role as a symbol of a Texas-Mexican history and identity brings it into a wider field of interactions and into a complex relationship with Anglo-dominated styles of popular music, as well as with more contemporary Texas-Mexican and Mexican musical genres.

In the work of Américo Paredes on border *corridos* (Texas-Mexican topical and heroic ballads), which documents the history of a people who were misunderstood by both Mexicans and Anglo Texans, these songs revealed a society that set itself apart from both sides of the border. Paredes writes that these songs mirror "the Mexican-American's long struggle to preserve his identity and reaffirm his rights as a human being." In so doing, it has been the Texas Mexican's ability to negotiate a life on the border between two countries with differing attitudes regarding history, culture, language, economics, and politics that has allowed him to construct a society that is both connected to and set apart from a collective Chicano society. It is the work of Américo Paredes, the advent of the Chicano

Movement, and now a growing body of research and writings by other scholars (such as Arnoldo de León, José Limón, David Montejano, and Richard García) that have contributed to the recognition of a Texas-Mexican, or *tejano,* history in Texas.

Much of the research on Texas-Mexican history and identity began in the Rio Grande Valley, an area first settled by American Indians, then by Spaniards in the eighteenth century, and which was once a part of Mexico. This region has always been self-sufficient and self-governing, even after the border lines were drawn at the Rio Grande and the area was taken over by the Texas republic and later by the U.S. government. More recently the work of Arnoldo de León and David Montejano leads us to view the Rio Grande Valley as a sociospatial locus which serves as a unifying base for identity as well as political action in South Texas. Their work has heightened the awareness of a historical "binationality" among Texas Mexicans on the border, which becomes a strong reference point when constructing a distinctive identity away from the border in San Antonio, Los Angeles, Chicago, Detroit, and other urban centers where Texas Mexicans have traveled for work. With conjunto as a vibrant symbolic operator, the Rio Grande Valley (also the documented birthplace of conjunto, as described in Peña's book) becomes a home and point of reference for Texas Mexicans everywhere.

Conjunto evolved initially as an expression of the development of a Texas-Mexican working-class community. As people moved out of the rural Rio Grande Valley and into largely middle-class urban settings, the music was influenced by technology and mainstream popular music. In the Rio Grande Valley and throughout South Texas, conjunto referred to a specific style of music which featured the button accordion and the Mexican *bajo sexto* (a twelve-string bass-rhythm guitar). This instrument, along with the accordion, was popularized on early Texas-Mexican recordings in the Rio Grande Valley by accordionist Narciso Martínez and *bajo* player Santiago Almeida. Today, the modern Texas-Mexican conjunto has expanded to include electric bass and a drum kit as its other core instruments. Traditionally, the music bonded together the Mexican American labor force, like a large chain, linking families and friends from the Rio Grande Valley, to San Antonio, to Corpus Christi, and as far north as Lubbock. Today, it still serves as a bonding force, with the added accoutrements of modern America, that continues to link the lives of Texas Mexicans across the state of Texas and throughout the United States. Through conjunto music, the spirit of the border culture, once disrupted by Anglo encroachment and exploitation, was revived and unified as it had been in the eighteenth century when the Valley was a close-knit, sovereign community.

Crossover Dreams: Flaco Jiménez and the Cross-Pollination of Conjunto

Peña's research indicates that the modern conjunto dance-hall sound, which was solidified by Valley-based accordionist-bandleader Tony de la Rosa with his addition of electric bass and drums in the 1950s, became the model for conjunto groups playing the local circuit as well as those who followed migrant workers across the United States. And while recordings were being made of conjunto music during this period, young Texas Mexicans were beginning to turn to a more contemporary musical style that gave less importance to the accordion and to its working-class roots. This generation, which was growing up in urban centers like San Antonio, was increasingly responding to a sophisticated *orquesta tejana* sound that merged *corridos, canciones,* and conjunto's German-derived polka rhythm with elements of rock, jazz, and rhythm-and-blues styles. Few young people were interested in pursuing the accordion or *bajo sexto* or in continuing the conjunto tradition. By the late 1970s and 1980s, conjunto was not as prominently heard on local Spanish-language radio stations, which were focusing primarily on *orquesta tejana* or contemporary Mexican music styles popular among the next big wave of immigrants into Texas during the 1970s.

In spite of some disinterest among the local community, especially the youth, conjunto emerged among segments of the Anglo American population, who were becoming aware of the growing popularity of San Antonio accordionist Flaco Jiménez outside the state and throughout Europe. In 1976 Jiménez paired up with Anglo American blues-and-folk slide guitarist Ry Cooder to record the classic *Chicken Skin Music* (Reprise 1976). The record was followed by a tour by both musicians and their groups across the United States and in England. A second collaboration, *Showtime,* was recorded the following year (Reprise 1977). By the early 1980s, Jiménez had amassed an enthusiastic following in Europe and was gaining recognition from progressive country and folk-rock enthusiasts.

Jiménez's ability to expand upon the traditional conjunto style, established by Martínez, Longoria, and de la Rosa, endeared him to the college-age, progressive folk and rock audience Cooder had cultivated with his own work as a blues- and country-influenced rock guitarist. Like Cooder, Jiménez was also interested in incorporating elements of rock, rhythm and blues, country, and jazz into his sound. Jiménez's connection to Cooder and his contemporary experimentations endeared him to a contemporary rock audience outside of Texas, as well as in the college student–dominated, "cosmic cowboy" capital of Austin.

By cultivating an Anglo audience and experimenting further with the tradition and the accordion, Jiménez drew mixed emotions within the Texas-Mexican community. Some older musicians felt he had removed himself too far from the tradition while others felt that he had brought a new level of respect and recognition to the music by Anglo American audiences which had been long overdue. Among younger Texas Mexicans, Jiménez's success meant a "return to tradition" but with a firm eye toward change. Many of these young fans had come of age during the Chicano Movement and, at one time or another in their past, had rejected the working-class music of their parents in favor of more popular styles like *orquesta tejana* (a precursor to today's *música tejana*) or U.S. rock. A combination of Jiménez's innovations on the accordion, his association with pop and rock audiences outside of the United States, and his strong devotion (both musically and culturally) to the conjunto tradition instilled a new level of pride among young middle-class Texas Mexicans in Texas. It also helped to heighten awareness among local Anglo Texans to the importance of this tradition in Texas history. However, it must also be noted that Jiménez's passage into the U.S. recording industry has been, and continues to be, closely guarded and tied to the success of mediators like Ry Cooder. Outside of his recordings made on regional and folk labels like Rounder and Arhoolie Records, his previous four-year contract with Warner Brothers stipulated the presence of "known" pop and country artists such as Linda Ronstadt, Dwight Yoakam, Los Lobos, Stephen Stills, and others on his recordings, so the label could be assured of some level of commercial success for these recordings. Though these recordings were not as widely successful as hoped, his subsequent very successful collaboration with the Texas Tornados heightened both his and conjunto's visibility on a national and international level.

In spite of the industry's cautious handling of him, Jiménez's musical crossover success was viewed by Texas Mexicans as a victory over local oppression. After a history of assimilation, the Chicano Movement made it clear that the Mexican American in Texas could never fully assimilate into Anglo American society and should not be forced to. Jiménez's success proved that the Texas-Mexican community had to evolve in order to survive as a coherent entity in Texas and as it did, so it would take in the world around it. The movement also encouraged the Texas-Mexican community to create its own political and economic destiny, a new concept among Texas Mexicans, who had existed under the social, political, and economic control of an Anglo Texan society and culture since the mid nineteenth century. Jiménez's ability to empower himself and his music as an outsider in the Anglo-dominated world of folk and pop music and still remain connected to a past musical history created by Texas Mexicans in Texas was celebrated and embraced within the local community. For Texas Mexicans, he was a symbol of the music's powerful presence in a much larger pluralistic society.

Jiménez's international popularity also brought the accordion back in focus as the important symbol of ethnic identity as described by Peña and other scholars, and renewed interest in conjunto as a form of popular music in Texas. From the Anglo Texan perspective, the Texas Mexican was indistinguishable from the Mexican and historically was held to his second-class citizen status. However, among audiences outside of Texas, conjunto was being described as "pure Texas roots music." Jiménez's high-profile access to the pop-music market gave recognition to the music, both esthetically and culturally, among Texas Mexicans who had once rejected it, among Anglo Texans who disregarded it, and among an international population that was previously unaware of it. This is not to say that the music's cross-cultural popularity represents a diffusing of the local Anglo and Mexican cultural system, but rather that it gave impetus to conjunto's (and the accordion's) re-emergence in popularity among Texas Mexicans and its wider acceptance on the national and international level. It also has exercised some effect on the music's current dual status as "traditional," or "roots" music, and as "popular" music within the local music industry. As a result, the accordion and conjunto's distinguishable polka rhythm (complete with syncopated markers and Texas-style "shuffle rhythm" pace) have re-emerged in the foreground in contemporary *música tejana* styles.

"Tejano and Proud": The Rise of Música Tejana and the Tejano Industry

Peña explains that conjunto's emergence as a symbol of expression among a changing Texas-Mexican society had placed the music, and the accordion, at the core of the construction of a new *tejano* identity in Texas. Conjunto's "pioneers" which he speaks about are accordionists who were born in the Rio Grande Valley border region (with the exception of San Antonio–born Santiago Jiménez, Sr., the father of Flaco and Santiago Jr.) and came from working-class, predominantly migrant backgrounds. Most were born in Texas, or arrived from Mexico at a very young age. In his book, musicians like Bruno Villarreal, Narciso Martínez, Santiago Jiménez, Pedro Ayala, Valerio Longoria, Tony de la Rosa, Rubén Vela, Paulino Bernal, and others are celebrated as cultural heroes representing the voice of the oppressed and the underclass. Today, they are presented at local festivals in San Antonio, such as the Tejano Conjunto Festival, and heard on KEDA radio. Their role now is as cultural monitors, each having contributed to the development of the music, and making it relevant to a changing concept of a Texas-Mexican identity that is fervently celebrated by *música tejana* groups.

Conjunto's ability to spawn a regional music industry in the early 1940s, separate from the Anglo American pop-music industry and remaining completely self-sufficient, has called greater attention to the power and presence of the Texas-Mexican community in Texas for the past fifteen years. Today, its commercial hub is in San Antonio and the "*tejano* music industry" (as it is referred to locally) has developed its own star system, record labels, radio stations, and audiences, though still tied to major label support. The Rio Grande Valley is fervently recognized as the birthplace of conjunto music and likewise *tejano* music in general. San Antonio, once a prominent Spanish settlement, is the hub of a complex *tejano* music industry. San Antonio has been christened by the media and local industry executives as the Tejano Music Capital of the World, and it is predominantly in San Antonio studios that contemporary *música tejana* is produced with the same technology and recording equipment as mainstream U.S. popular music in Los Angeles or New York.

Música tejana (or *tejano* music) is basically Spanish-language popular music which appeals primarily to young middle-class Texas Mexicans. In its present form, it is a strong rival to pan-Latino *cumbia,* New York *salsa,* and Mexican *banda.* Over the last four years, several Spanish-language radio stations in Texas have switched to all-*tejano* music formats. Since 1992, *tejano* radio station KXTN-FM 107 in San Antonio was rated number one overall in the local Arbitron ratings. The station beat out the local country-music station, KCYY-FM, which held the number-one position for several years. In fact, this is the first time in recent history that any Spanish-language station ever ranked number one in the city.

Though *música tejana*'s booming popularity is fairly recent compared to conjunto, it has been evolving on its own since the 1930s. Its musical and historical roots are traced to conjunto music from the Rio Grande Valley and to the sophisticated pan-Latino, big-band sound of *orquesta tejana.* In the 1940s and 1950s, *orquesta tejana* groups filled clubs and concert halls throughout Texas and in communities across the United States where Texas Mexicans migrated. It merged the popular Cuban dance styles like the *bolero* and *danzón* (via Mexico), with Mexican *rancheras* and *canciones románticas,* with U.S. swing and big band. Today, *música tejana* has evolved into a distinctive sound that is rapidly becoming one of the most popular Spanish-language music styles in the United States and Mexico. Though *música tejana* is heard on both AM and FM bands, conjunto music is heard primarily on bilingual and Spanish-speaking AM radio stations like KEDA. The FM *tejano* stations, however, feature English-speaking and some bilingual jockeys who predominantly play *música tejana* and only a select number of conjunto crossover artists. FM radio stations like KXTN and KRIO (formerly a country station) in San Antonio have been instrumental in boosting the popularity of *música tejana,* especially among young people, because it can be heard at a higher fidelity and over a larger distance than the scores of AM stations playing Spanish-language music across the state. For many young Texas Mexicans, *música tejana*'s presence on the FM radio is important because it places the style alongside contemporary rock and country stations and helps validate it in the larger arena of U.S. popular music. Based in large part on the success of KXTN and KRIO, several *tejano* stations have sprung up in urban centers throughout Texas, such as Houston, Dallas, Austin, and Corpus Christi, as well as in other parts of the country.

Música tejana comes in two basic forms: The first is more directly related to the *orquesta tejana* brass-band sound and does not always include the accordion, though its sound is sometimes simulated by keyboards and synthesizers. This style is also more strongly influenced by popular U.S. music such as pop, rock, and jazz, as well as international music imported from Mexico City which features tropical rhythms like *merengue* and *cumbia*. In most contemporary *orquesta tejana* groups the prominent emphasis on the second and fourth beats heard in the polka rhythms of conjuntos remains prominent. Artists who fall in this category include Little Joe, Sunny and the Sunliners, the late Selena, Latin Breed, early Mazz, Liberty Band, and Fandango USA.

The second, and probably more popular, *música tejana* style is often referred to as progressive conjunto. This style includes the accordion, most of the time paired with saxophones or keyboards, and has a loping, polka-inspired two-step dance rhythm at the core of the sound. Other dance styles also played by the progressive conjunto groups include the waltz, *cumbia*, and *huapango*. There is a deliberate country influence, inspired by the modern western-swing sound of George Strait, and it is blended with a "crooner" (a la Tin Pan Alley) singing style. The popularity of this style has been heightened by the revival of the accordion, though the instrument is not as central to the sound as it is in the more traditional conjunto sound. In most cases, the accordionist is not the bandleader, as is usually true with traditional conjuntos. However, many Texas Mexicans will claim that this style represents the "real" country music of Texas. Artists like Roberto Pulido (who pioneered this style), David Lee Garza y los Musicales, Emilio Navaira, La Tropa F (Los Hermanos Farías), and Jay Pérez are also associated with this style.

As a whole, *música tejana* is a tremendous source of pride among Texas Mexicans, after decades of their feeling the pressure to assimilate into Anglo culture. *Música tejana* allows young Texas Mexicans to redefine their identity based on a contemporary, culturally expressive model. The refusal to fully assimilate can be seen in the form of "Tejano and Proud" bumper stickers on the back of Ford Ranger trucks in San Antonio and clubs with names like Tejano Rose, T-Town, and Tejano Rodeo. The reintroduction of the accordion, both as a symbolic identifier and stylistic marker of *música tejana*, can be attributed, in part, to the crossover success of Flaco Jiménez, as well as a new respectability and recognition given to accordion heroes of the past at the Guadalupe Cultural Arts Center's annual Tejano Conjunto Festival. It has also inspired KEDA disc jockey Güero Polkas and his station to call attention to its dedication to conjunto music, the "roots" of *música tejana*. Likewise, the growth of the local *tejano* music industry and its overwhelming popularity in Texas and among settled migrant communities across the United States is part of a renewed construction of *tejano* identity that has been boosted by a strengthening of the community's social, political, and economic presence in the state.

Alongside *música tejana*, conjunto musicians have been put in the position of competing with these well-recorded contemporary groups who also sport accordions somewhere in the mix. *Música tejana* promotes a youthful sensibility and is symbolized by cowboy boots, hats, and big belt buckles, all adopted from a Texan "cowboy" imagery of the past. Since most popular *música tejana* groups are recorded by major labels, they tend to make better-quality recordings and enjoy the promotional backing of multimillion-dollar corporations. As this new style of *tejano* music has consolidated its mass audience, conjunto has been forced to renegotiate its place within the local industry, which doesn't always view it as commercial music or as being within its scope of marketability.

Conjunto: Cultural Mediator or Commercial Commodity?

Since the advent of the *tejano* industry and the commercial domination of *música tejana* in Texas, conjunto has responded by grounding itself more firmly in local community functions and at festivals representing the music and culture of Texas. Its appeal continues to extend well beyond the borders of Texas and the United States, in some cases on the path originally blazed by Flaco Jiménez, but in most cases on the fringes of the local industry. Conjunto music is generally released on cassettes and compact discs by Anglo American folk labels like Rounder Records and Arhoolie (Mingo Saldívar, Santiago Jiménez, Eva Ybarra), or on local Texas-Mexican labels not affiliated with major labels, like Hacienda or Joey (Mingo Saldívar, Nick Villarreal, Ángel Flores). Conjunto (as opposed to *música tejana*) is the style most sought after by Anglo American and European folk- and world-music labels and generally sold to audiophiles. However, these labels have not been able to penetrate the local *tejano*-music distribution network, so they don't compete with local labels, which is why some conjunto artists like Mingo Saldívar record for more than one label. Thus, while the newer genre of *música tejana* controls the regional market and the high end of the local industry, the "middle ground" belongs to conjunto which, in order to survive, has simultaneously reasserted its deep roots in local traditions as music of the people, or "folk" music, and extended its appeal outward into a national and transnational marketplace.

As a historical component of *tejano* music, conjunto has survived and distinguished itself not only through the maintenance of an instrumental core (accordion, *bajo sexto*, bass, and drums), but also by taking in elements of the cultural diversity both locally and transnationally. Today, the instrument of choice among young Texas Mexicans is again the accordion. Through most of the 1970s and 1980s that instrument might have been the electric guitar. These days in both conjunto and *música tejana* there is more experimentation by local players on the accordion such as expanding the melody line, playing more inverted chord progressions, and utilizing electronic effects. Country, jazz, rhythm and blues, rock, and the basic blues scale are not foreign musical elements to the conjunto accordionist, and aspects of these styles are adapted to an expanding conjunto accordion style, especially among the more expressive San Antonio accordionists like Mingo Saldívar, Nick Villarreal, and Eva Ybarra. As far as the songs are concerned, the pressure to compose new "hit" songs is felt by both conjunto and *música tejana* groups. Yet the fact is that conjunto's role is still very much tied to local community functions such as *quinceañeras*, weddings, and family celebrations (though not exclusively), and the conjunto repertoire remains much more devoted to performing and recording traditional songs well known to members of the community.

Conjunto's market is still predominantly confined to middle- and working-class parents of young Texas Mexicans in South Texas. The strong sense of community and family that nurtured early Valley-based conjunto musicians still keeps the tradition alive among all levels of *tejano* society, including a newfound acceptance of conjunto by the youth. The small independent labels must also remain closer to the local community than the major labels, and KEDA radio has devoted much of its airtime to keeping conjunto alive on the AM radio airwaves. In fact, KEDA has taken on the task of keeping listeners aware of the music and its symbolic role within the community by inviting listeners to become members of the "University of Jalapeño," where conjunto is always the subject of the day. The writings of Américo Paredes on border *corridos* and Manuel Peña's study of Texas-Mexican conjunto are filled with references to the role of music in connecting families and friends, first across the border, and then in the agricultural fields of the Rio Grande Valley, as well as in the impoverished West Side of San Antonio. Among Texas Mexicans, wide social networks which include families, extended families, and *compadres* (godfathers, or longtime friends), provide a context for the lives of every individual. Much of the "conflict" Paredes speaks of in his many writings on the subject of conflict and identity on the Texas-Mexican border results from the inability of many Anglo Americans to understand the intricately woven solidarity of family and *compadres* among the Spanish-speaking peoples of Texas.

The diatonic button accordion, the polka rhythms, and the old *corridos* and *canciones* firmly ground conjunto within local values and historical conceptions. Today, both conjunto and *música tejana* groups are closely scrutinized for their interpretations of songs that have long been part of the local repertoire. Traditional conjuntos are expected to develop individualistic renditions of these songs, which is often achieved by developing an identifiable accordion "sound," but the words and melodies for the most part remain intact. Often these songs, which might be recorded by hundreds of local groups, are listed on the local radio hit parade (i.e., KEDA's "Jalapeño Jits") and in many cases multiple versions of the same song, which are recorded by different groups, will compete on the charts simultaneously. This shared repertoire represents a connection to the past while the level of individual interpretation represents a broad spectrum of social interaction and complexity equally important in defining the local society.

The evolution and popularity of conjunto is based on more than class distinctions and struggles over political and economic power. Conjunto and *música tejana*'s current success is also linked to the increasing social and political influence which is currently enjoyed by Texas Mexicans throughout Texas. To understand the relationship between conjunto music and Texas-Mexican society today, one must understand what it is to be bilingual, bicultural, and affected by an array of cultural influences that must be negotiated daily, as Rick Dávila does on the AM radio airwaves in San Antonio.

Manuel Peña writes that the years surrounding World War II marked a shift in rural to urban patterns of residency, a move from agricultural to nonagricultural occupations, and from folk "enclaves" toward a sense of community divided by "class interests." He has further suggested that these processes crucially influenced the development of conjunto. One must also add to these events increased contact with the wider world and the need to symbolically construct a secure place, or point of reference, within the impersonal space of a changing global economy. Today, in spite of major-label promotion of *música tejana,* conjunto musicians continue to play a privileged role in expressing and shaping Texas-Mexican visions of history and place.

Bibliography

Anderson, Benedict. *Imagined Communities.* London: Verso, 1983.
Clifford, James, and George E. Marcus, eds. *Writing Culture: The Poetics and Politics of Ethnography.* Berkeley: University of California Press, 1986.
Council, Kay Francine. "Exploratory Documentation of Texas Norteño-Conjunto Music." Master's thesis, University of Texas at Austin, 1978.
Erlmann, Veit. *African Stars: Studies in Black South African Performance.* Chicago: University of Chicago Press, 1991.
García, Richard A. "Class, Consciousness, and Ideology: The Mexican Community of San Antonio, Texas: 1930–1940." *Aztlán* 9 (1979): 23–65.
Gil, Carlos B. "The Many Faces of the Mexican-American: An Essay concerning Chicano Character." Working paper, Centro de Estudios Chicanos, University of Washington, Seattle, 1982.
León, Arnoldo de. *The Tejano Community, 1836–1900.* Albuquerque: University of New Mexico Press, 1982.
———. *They Called Them Greasers: Anglo Attitudes toward Mexicans in Texas, 1821–1900.* Austin: University of Texas Press, 1983.
Limón, José E. "El Baile: Culture and Contradiction in Mexican American Dancing." *Tonantzin* (Guadalupe Cultural Arts Center, San Antonio) 5, no. 2 (May 1988): 22–25. [Chapter 19 in this volume.]
Manuel, Peter. *Popular Musics of the Non-Western World: An Introductory Survey.* New York: Oxford University Press, 1988.
Marcus, George E., and Michael M. J. Fischer. *Anthropology as Cultural Critique: An Experimental Moment in the Human Sciences.* Chicago: University of Chicago Press, 1986.
Montejano, David. *Anglos and Mexicans in the Making of Texas, 1936–1986.* Austin: University of Texas Press, 1987.
Paredes, Américo. *"With His Pistol in His Hand": A Border Ballad and Its Hero.* Austin: University of Texas Press, 1958.

Peña, Manuel. "Music for a Changing Community: Three Generations of a Chicano Family *Orquesta.*" *Latin American Music Review* 3, no. 2 (1982): 230–245.

———. *The Texas-Mexican Conjunto: History of a Working-Class Music.* Austin: University of Texas Press, 1985.

Roosens, Eugeen E. *Creating Ethnicity: The Process of Ethnogenesis.* Newbury Park, Calif.: Sage Publications, 1989.

Scruggs, Jr., Thomas Mitchell. "Ay, Te Dejo en San Antonio: Conjunto, Anglos, and the Jiménez Family of San Antonio." Master's thesis, University of Texas at Austin, 1985.

Turino, Thomas. *Moving Away from Silence: Music of the Peruvian Altiplano and the Experience of Urban Migration.* Chicago: University of Chicago Press, 1993.

Waterman, Christopher A. *Jùjú: A Social History and Ethnography of an African Popular Music.* Chicago: University of Chicago Press, 1990.

18

Why Are There So Few Women Conjunto Artists?

⋄

AVELARDO VALDEZ & JEFFREY A. HALLEY

1994

Conjunto refers to a music of the Mexican-origin people of the Southwest. The basic conjunto, or performing group, consists of four instruments: a diatonic button accordion, the twelve-string bass-rhythm guitar (*bajo sexto*), the electric bass guitar, and drums. Conjunto music historically derives from a combination of the polka music of early German immigrants and the Mexican *corridos* of the U.S.–Mexican border (Peña 1985, Guerra 1989). From its beginnings in the 1920s and 1930s, conjunto music has survived as a durable and significant cultural expression among working-class and poor Mexican Americans. It has also served as a cultural means for reinforcing sex and gender roles, as other music does in the larger society.

Women in the conjunto-music scene are highly visible as dancers, girlfriends, and wives, but are hardly ever onstage receiving the adoration of fans. When they are performers, they tend to be singers rather than instrumentalists. This situation is also evident in the Tejano-music scene, where virtually all of the women are singers, such as Laura Canales, Selena, Jeanne Le Grand, Shelly Lares, Elsa García, and others. This relative absence of women instrumentalists, particularly accordionists, is a reflection of sex and gender roles in our society.

How can we explain this situation? Is it an extension of Chicano macho culture, in which women occupy a lower status than men—a hypothesis popular among Anglo academics and feminists? Or, is the absence of women in conjunto music a reflection of male-female relations in the larger culture and the musical scene in general?

Our position is that it can be explained by a combination of both these views. Conjunto music does serve as a cultural vehicle for reproducing gender roles in more traditional forms than are typical of the larger society. However, Chicano male-female differences are also products of social and economic issues that restrict the equal participation of Chicanos in society.

GENDER ROLES IN MEXICAN AMERICAN CULTURE

Research has demonstrated that Mexican American culture produces gender roles which are more male dominated than others. This stems from a culture that develops a strong sense of family, which gives overriding importance to the needs of the collective as opposed to individual and personal needs. This value system is given practical significance by traditional gender roles that emphasize husband-father dominance. Does the social world of conjunto music produce similar male-female roles? This is the major question which we examine in this study. We address two aspects of this question: How do individuals acquire the knowledge and skills to become conjunto musicians? Once the skill is acquired, how are they socialized into the profession?

The Acquisition of Knowledge and Skills

The aspiring musician is usually first exposed to conjunto music through family dances celebrating weddings, anniversaries, and birthdays. It is usually also heard on local Spanish-language radio stations. Most regions of the Southwest with large Mexican American populations have radio stations that intermittently have a conjunto format. An individual may have been exposed to the music through records, tapes, and, more recently, compact discs played in the home and car and at social gatherings (Valdez and Halley 1993). One of the consistent aspects of this music is that musicians are predominantly male.

The dominance of men in conjunto music is a reflection of the exclusion of women from musical activity. In discussions with a Chicana who was raised within a family of male musicians, she tells how she was discouraged from even joining the high school band: "I was just beginning junior high and I was interested in joining the junior-high band. My father was somewhat reluctant to allow me to join much of anything. You see, my father is very old-fashioned. My older sister, who is fifteen years older than I, never got to participate in any school functions. Whether it was an athletic sport, or band, my father just did not allow her to do anything. He was and still is very protective of his girls." Typically the segregation of activities by males and females is all-pervasive, and goes beyond musical activities.

This same young woman also explained how she and her sisters were blocked from playing instruments that were considered more "masculine": "Then came the time to choose an instrument; I loved the trumpet and especially the drums. My father told me that that was totally out of the question. He was not going to allow his daughter to play an instrument that should be played by a man. My mother then mentioned the flute or the clarinet, which was the instrument she played when she was in high school."

The accordion in conjunto music is considered an archetypical male instrument within the Mexican American community. This perception of the accordion is a major barrier to young girls learning the instrument. Another barrier that women and girls must overcome is that the accordion is taught informally by other conjunto artists, through a long apprenticeship usually centered around a relative or friend. This mentor-teacher relationship, along with the support from immediate family members and friends, is essential to the learning process.

Therefore, it is important for the child developing the necessary skills to secure this mentor-teacher relationship. The paradox is that, since relationships within Mexican American families have been segregated by sex, this creates a barrier for young girls who desire to learn the accordion, since those who are teachers of the accordion tend to be male. In one family, for instance, the primary mentor-teacher of a young, aspiring male accordionist was a grandfather who, on the other hand, never encouraged his granddaughters to learn the instrument.

Even in those families with long musical traditions, such as the Farías family—whose members constitute La Tropa F, one of the most popular conjuntos in San Antonio—young females are discouraged from learning the accordion and *bajo sexto*. In all, there are ten children in the immediate family, all brothers except for two sisters. All the male children in the family were encouraged to become musicians because, according to one of the sisters, "It was a man thing. None of us were encouraged to play."

Even the few women who finally became successful accordionists had to struggle with their families' initial discouragement and overcome these barriers. In most of the cases, only the persistence of the young girls overcame family obstacles. Like young men, these female musicians were taught to play the accordion by their relatives as early as the age of six. Many of them recount a struggle to overcome the prejudice of the family mentors who objected to their participation. Of course, there are exceptions. For example, one of the major female accordion players, Lupita Rodela, was encouraged to play by her father.

It is often the case that children who study the accordion usually drop it in their teens. The pressure of mainstream music usually draws them away from conjunto music to rock. Many of these do not return to conjunto music until much later. One prominent conjunto artist said, "I used to play accordion as a kid. I stopped playing as a teenager because the others made fun of me." He returned to the instrument in his early twenties and formed his own conjunto.

The problem of maintaining an interest in conjunto music is even more difficult for girls. Since conjunto music is considered a male domain, women who begin to lose interest for the reasons stated above are not encouraged to continue their musical apprenticeship. Aside from these informal mentoring situations, there has recently developed in San Antonio a more formal teaching setting centered at the Guadalupe Cultural Arts Center, sponsor of the annual Tejano Conjunto Festival. Accordion classes are taught by Valerio Longoria, Santiago Jiménez, Jr., and Fred Zimmerle in a classroom setting. The formalization of the instruction has provided a new opportunity for training outside of the old mentoring system. This has the potential to effectively open up the participation of women in the learning process.

Gender Obstacles to Becoming a Conjunto Musician

Acquiring the necessary skills is not the only obstacle faced by women in conjunto music. There are also other obstacles related to the business of becoming a conjunto musician.

CAREER OBSTACLES

Once the instrument is mastered, the musicians who choose to pursue a professional career as conjunto artists will play at clubs, icehouses, dance halls, and other venues such as church festivals. As a conjunto becomes more popular, it may be booked for gigs for the entire weekend, some of these venues in communities throughout South Texas. This creates an organizational structure which restrains women from participation and mobility in these types of situations.

Playing local gigs throughout the week and playing on the road on weekends disrupts family life, particularly for artists who are married (Valdez and Halley 1993). The lifestyle of the musicians demands that they spend long hours away from their family. Playing in a conjunto means that one spends a lot of time in bars and clubs, which presents opportunities for substance abuse, particularly alcohol, but sometimes drugs. This also creates opportunities to meet and socialize with women (and in the case of women, with men). As a result, many of these artists have difficulty leading socially stable lives. The nightlife scene creates the potential to disrupt stable gender relationships.

Many professional male musicians will relate the problems they have with wives, children, and girlfriends, who complain about them being away all the time. Artists who play on a regular basis are often unable to hold a straight job that requires working nine to five, five days a week. Most of these musicians lack formal education that would allow them into more middle-class professions with more flexible work hours. As a result, many of them depend solely on income generated from the conjunto for their livelihood.

The professional lifestyle we have described is essentially a male world and, therefore, not supportive of women's participation. In fact, in the history of conjunto music, and indeed Mexican American music, there have been relatively few women. Those who have participated in conjunto music and other Mexican American genres have been for the most part singers with conjuntos or traditional *tríos*, or soloists who accompany themselves on the guitar. The role of women as singers has been a traditional one in U.S. music. Typically the audience and musicians are comfortable with this role because it fits gender expectations and behavior. A classic example is that of the "torch singer" in jazz and different forms of pop music.

In Mexican American music, a woman who exemplifies this tradition is Lydia Mendoza, a major singer, instrumentalist, and recording artist from South Texas. As indicated in her autobiography (Mendoza 1993), she was one of the first Spanish-language vernacular singers and recording stars of the Southwest. Her career spanned the late 1920s through the 1970s and combined traditional Mexican *corridos* (ballads) with more polished and commercial performances that typify dance-hall, theatrical, and recorded music from the 1930s to the present. This tradition continues in Tejano music, where many popular groups are fronted by attractive and talented women singers, such as Selena.

Although there have been some female lead singers and instrumentalists, conjunto music has remained almost exclusively a male domain. The few women who have succeeded have family and friends who seemed not to accept gender stereotypes regarding the exclusion of women from this music. Women in conjunto music all speak of the encouragement they received from family and key professionals. The few women accordionists we interviewed all came from families of conjunto musicians and were professionally mentored by family members.

Lupita Rodela, a forty-four-year-old blind accordionist from East Texas, leads a conjunto that has been playing for twenty years in small Texas towns such as New Braunfels, Gonzales, Nixon, and Marion. Her group includes her brother, a drummer, and her husband, who manages the conjunto. At a recent performance at a flea market, which we attended, Rodela's husband took song requests from the audience and passed them on to her. During the break Ms. Rodela and her husband sat with an entourage of family members. In fact, during her entire career she has been surrounded and supported by her family, as well as by friends and major conjunto artists such as Flaco Jiménez.

Eva Ybarra is the most active and well-known female accordionist in the conjunto scene today. Eva's conjunto has played throughout the United States and has released a recent Rounder CD, *A Mi San Antonio*. She is also the only woman accordionist featured in this year's (1994) Tejano Conjunto Festival. She was born into a musical family in San Antonio and began to play the accordion at the early age of six. She recently stated, "Many think that I was taught by my brother, but I was actually self-taught, listening to the radio and picking up tunes." Eva was encouraged to play by her dad and brothers, who were musicians. Her mother was a composer and singer, yet discouraged her from playing the accordion. According to Eva, her mother said to her that "women do not have a strong-enough back to play an accordion."

Another well-known female accordionist was Isabel Salaiza, who was based in San José, California. Performing professionally as Chavela, she was called La Dama del Acordeón. Chavela tragically died in an accident in 1992. Like other conjunto artists, she began playing in a family conjunto at nine years of age, with her mother, sister, and grandfather, who played, respectively, *bajo sexto,* drums, and electric bass. She later played with other groups and in 1980 formed her own conjunto, Chavela y su Grupo Express. The experiences of all three of these important women players demonstrate that without strong support from family networks, women cannot break into conjunto music.

PROBLEMS OF LEADERSHIP

Issues of leadership within a conjunto concern day-to-day factors such as booking gigs, negotiating payments, selecting repertoire, determining lengths of sets and breaks, setting practice sessions, and engaging in numerous other organizational and business tasks, not to mention defining general codes of behavior and dealing with individual egos and personal crises of band members. These are difficult-enough tasks for established musical groups to accomplish.

Conjunto groups have the characteristics of informal rather than formal organizations. Because of the informal structure and hierarchy of these groups, interpersonal relationships are key to the continuity of the conjunto. A major conjunto promoter, when asked what it takes to keep a group together, stated: "It's a struggle and work. So that you need to be tight because the pay is not good. You cannot survive on it so you usually have to have another job. You really have to love it, to put up with all the bullshit that goes on night after night. You don't get home till three or four in the morning, going out of town, doing rehearsals, and all the interpersonal conflicts that exist within the group. You gotta get it together."

Gender-role conflicts complicate this kind of organization. In particular, when we find women who lead conjuntos, we find that these women frequently have difficulty carrying out leadership functions. When asked about a prominent female accordionist's relationship with her musicians, a male conjunto promoter said, "I don't think she's been able to keep musicians, or keep a steady group, and I hate to say it, because she's so good, but I think the fact that she is a woman had a lot to do with it, because of the attitudes of a lot of conjunto musicians in a mainly male conjunto-music world." He goes on to specify that she's having trouble keeping musicians because the men in her group don't want to take orders from her.

The more-successful female conjunto artists who lead their own conjuntos are seen by the men as aggressive and assertive, qualities more frequently associated with maleness. One of the most widely respected female accordionists, who has fronted her own group for the last three years, was described in this way. An agent who booked her for a major concert relates his experience: "I talked to her one time when I booked her for a dance. I felt like I was talking to a guy. I remember her saying to me, '*Hey*, me tienes que pagar. Estos chavos creen que estoy jambando la feria.' Like she was saying, quit screwing around. I need this money, the guys might think that I am stealing it." Acting in ways associated with men is no doubt one strategy women use to overcome gender domination. The price paid by women artists for leading conjuntos is often the inability to retain male musicians, as well as finding themselves with reputations for being too male and insufficiently female.

Where we have found more stability is where women are linked with men, usually family members. These men often function as managers and act as buffers to the larger world. This allows for the women to retain their traditional female roles within this male domain. For example, one famous singing conjunto duo is a husband-wife team that has been playing together for twenty years. The interview we conducted with this couple at an established club was clearly controlled by the husband, who, in doing almost all the talking, effectively did not allow her to express her thoughts and opinions.

Another prominent woman accordionist's situation is similar in that she has maintained a stable conjunto whose core is composed of herself and her brother. As well, her husband manages the group even though he is not a musician. Even within this network of family, however, this woman has experienced conflict with male musicians who would not accept her leadership because of her gender. She stated, "It's not easy for men to accept a woman giving orders. This is why I think that many women become singers; they don't want to play the accordion, which means they have to give orders." She goes on to explain how she has had to fire musicians because they didn't like the idea of her displaying her versatility: "This one *bajo sexto* player didn't like my style, but, my style is crossing frontiers and I am not going to change because of what he thinks." In our discussion with her, she constantly referred to the difficulties she had with male members of her conjunto.

PROBLEMS OF SEXUAL TENSION

Another hindrance in the professional socialization of female conjunto players is male performers' perception of sexual tension caused by their presence on the scene. A prominent conjunto artist discussed one aspect of this issue: "Once I had a girl that I wanted to bring into the band as a singer. I thought it would be a very good idea and she sang good, but as soon as I asked the band members, they said, 'Well, if you're gonna do that, that's fine.' But then I asked 'Why?' and they said, 'Well, you know, my old lady.' I said, 'Yeah, but this is business.' They said, 'Yeah, but she doesn't understand that.' They think that because they're out there with a woman . . . there's going to be hanky-panky." Based on the reaction of his band members, he reluctantly decided not to hire the singer.

Another informant speaks about the potential sexual tensions that may arise when a woman joins a band:

> A good-looking woman creates a situation with her band members where they may try to get into her pants. Unfortunately, this might start to create problems. It creates a whole different set of interpersonal circumstances as opposed to if it was all men in the group.
>
> Now if she's going with one band member, she now has to deal also on different levels with all the other band members. If she's not just going out with one band member, then she's available maybe for all of them to try to hit up on her. So a woman in a band creates a social situation that could easily lead to problems.

This description indicates some of the barriers that women and men need to overcome for there to be gender equality in conjunto.

The experience of one female recording artist exemplifies the social and professional costs to women who cross gender roles. She has suffered a reputation as "pretty wild," and has been said to have had various relationships with her band members, including "partying, alcohol, and drugs." She has experienced major setbacks in her career and has had difficulties in keeping her group together and in retaining record contracts. Many observers of the scene point to her unstable lifestyle as a cause of the trouble.

This strategy of being assertive and aggressive, described earlier, is now played out in the sexual realm. In fact, she is thought to epitomize the permissive lifestyle which attracts men to the conjunto scene. In this case, however, because a woman is seen to embody these characteristics, she is devalued.

The perceived possibility, or actuality, of sexual tension creates another obstacle in the professionalization of women in conjunto music. This, along with issues of leadership and gender-based career obstacles, helps explain the scarcity of women in conjunto music.

Conclusion

This article has examined the role of gender in conjunto music. Restrictions on women in this Mexican American musical genre are pervasive, and stem from factors of both race and class. In the course of the acquisition of knowledge and skills, women are consistently excluded from a mentoring relationship.

Once in the profession, there are profound gender-based career obstacles. The professional lifestyle is essentially a male world. There are very few women in conjunto music. Those that have succeeded have been helped by networks of family and key professionals. Yet the informal nature of the musical organization makes it more difficult for women to carry out leadership functions. The more-successful female players tend to take on the assertive gender roles more commonly associated with men. A major obstacle to women is the perceived sexual tension that a woman's presence might create.

This research has shown the pervasiveness of dominant gender roles within the everyday life of conjunto music. However, like other arenas of struggle, the terrain is contested. We have indicated that some women are successful in resisting and surmounting the traditional gender roles, and are creative in constructing new roles. We have found that when the study of conjunto music is formalized in institutions, women's participation significantly increases. Formalization of participation, therefore, reduces the socially constructed barriers that have historically restricted women's opportunities.

Although the music has been discussed in positive terms as an expression of Mexican American resistance and affirmation of ethnicity (Valdez and Halley 1991), it also is an arena in which conventional gender roles and gender inequality are reproduced and reinforced.

References

Guerra, Carlos. 1989. "The Unofficial Conjunto Primer for the Uninitiated Music Lover, Revised." *Tonantzin* (Guadalupe Cultural Arts Center, San Antonio) 6, no. 2 (May). [Chapter 1 in this volume.]

Mendoza, Lydia. 1993. *Lydia Mendoza: A Family Autobiography*. Compiled by Chris Strachwitz and James Nicolopulos. Houston: Arte Público Press.

Peña, Manuel. 1985. *The Texas-Mexican Conjunto: History of a Working-Class Music*. Austin: University of Texas Press.

Valdez, Avelardo, and Jeffrey A. Halley. 1991. "The Popular in *Conjunto Tejano* Music: Changes in Chicano Class and Identity." *Tonantzin* (Guadalupe Cultural Arts Center, San Antonio) 9, no. 1 (May). [Chapter 16 in this volume.]

———. 1993. "Career and Identity in Mexican American Conjunto Musicians." In *Current Research on Occupations and Professions: Creators of Culture*. Vol. 8, edited by Muriel Cantor. Greenwich, Conn.: JAI Press.

19

El Baile
Culture and Contradiction in Mexican American Dancing

✧

JOSÉ E. LIMÓN
1988

To speak of a contemporary dance in the Mexican American community is to speak centrally of a regional variant of the European polka as the major form, of the public commercial dance hall as its primary performance context, and of a dualistic ensemble as its chief musical source.

On any weekend night and often midweek or on Sunday afternoon, largely working-class Mexican Americans in the Southwest, Midwest, and Northwest will pay admission to enter commercial, usually Mexican American–owned public halls to dance. In between dances they may momentarily sit in kinship or friendship groups at tables surrounding a large dance floor, talking and drinking beer purchased from concessions in the hall or from liquor bottles brought into the dance. However, during the three-to-four-hour dance, most of their time will be spent dancing.

They will dance in male-female couples primarily to a Mexicanized polka which, according to Américo Paredes, the best scholar on Mexican American culture, has become something very close to a native folk form in the twentieth century. While other dance forms may be performed—for example, slow-rhythm Mexican *boleros*, waltzes, Latin American *cumbias*, country and western, and rock and roll—the polka predominates. The latter is danced with the male leading his partner with a gliding step (the feet rarely leave the floor) in a counterclockwise direction around the dance floor. This gliding forward motion is punctuated and elaborated with body dips and swinging turns, the latter possibly borrowed from 1940s-style

American swing dance. Particularly skillful execution of all of these moves may occasion conversation and calls of approval (*gritos*) from other dancers and from those sitting at their tables as the dancers glide by.

People dance to the music provided by two different kinds of ensembles: the conjunto, composed of lead accordion, guitars, and rhythm, and the orchestra, with varying combinations of brass, reeds, guitars, electric keyboard, and rhythm. Since the 1920s the conjunto has been traditionally associated with the working classes, the orchestra with more middle-class audiences. Recently a clear convergence is taking place between the two ensembles, while the audience and dancers tend to be increasingly working class. The middle and upper classes seem more inclined to take up Anglo American social dancing performances and contexts, for example, discos, strictly country and western, et cetera. It would appear that dancing and its associated music and social context has been increasing since the turn of the century.

We describe Mexican American dancing culture in the way I have done, but it is just that, a description which is useful for cultural "outsiders" and obvious to "insiders." Lately, however, as a cultural anthropologist I have become interested in understanding more deeply how this community feels and thinks about its dancing. What values do they attach to it? At one level, the answer is obvious. They *enjoy* it, or at least it would seem so, otherwise, one could reasonably ask, why do they participate in it so intensively? And, normally, that might have ended the matter, except that something not quite normal (please note I did not say "abnormal") began to occur in intimate connection with dancing that, as an anthropologist, made me rethink this question and to go beyond the seeming fact that people enjoy dancing, as true as that may be. What follows is my account from my field notes as I tried to probe deeper into this unnormal occurrence.[1]

"¡Es puro pedo de viejas!" (It's all women's crap!) Mendieta told me as we sat at the bar in the mostly empty dance hall on a Monday morning in the summer of 1979. We were effectively alone as we each sipped a late-morning beer, save for an elderly janitor cleaning up after the Sunday *tardeada* (afternoon dance). Mendieta, part-owner of this slightly decrepit dance hall, continued to talk: "Mira,

Limón, el pedo pasó allá" (Look Limón, the shit happened over there), motioning toward the far corner of the dance floor; "pero, pa' mí . . . que un vato le metió mano a la ruca" (but, if you ask me, some dude grabbed the broad's ass), telling me with a yellowed toothy grin while grabbing a hammy handful of air. He paused and leaned toward me, "Pero eso que dicen del diablo . . . ¡es puro pedo! ¡Pedo de viejas!" (But all the stuff they're saying about the devil is just a lot of crap! Women's crap!). "Y si quieres saber la verdad, anda ver a la ruca; se llama Sulema y es mesera en el restaurante San Miguel" (And if you want to know the truth, go see the broad; her name is Sulema and she's a waitress at San Miguel's restaurant). "¿Quieres otra vironga, carnal?" (Would you like another beer, bro?) he asked and without waiting for my answer, he half waddled to the other side of the bar and pulled another two out of the ice, dismissing my effort to pay with a wave and a flash of a ring-laden hand. However, he was only part-owner of El Cielito Lindo (the Beautiful Little Heaven) dance hall, so, from a well-loaded money clip extracted with some difficulty from a deep pocket of his yellow matching leisure-suit pants, he peeled off a couple of dollars and put them in the cash register, taking his change as well. One beer and a few pleasantries later, I was off to San Miguel's restaurant in search of Sulema and the devil, but not without Mendieta's parting shot, "No se te olvide, Limón, es puro pedo" (And don't forget, Limón, it's just a lot of crap).

In the early summer of 1979, I had returned to do fieldwork in my native, hot, poverty-stricken South Texas from cool, distant, hip Westwood, California, where I had been spending a postdoctoral year at UCLA. I had gone to UCLA as a cultural anthropologist interested in folklore, particularly Mexican American folklore, but I had spent the year fighting traffic and doing a lot of reading and thinking about the Mexican American dancing culture that I had grown up in as a teenager in Corpus Christi and also as a student at the University of Texas at Austin. As a student of Mexican American culture, the deep and intense attachment of the community to its dancing had both involved me personally and intrigued me anthropologically, but now I began to sense a problem, namely, that the dancing was not always a scene of total enjoyment but contained some possible cultural contradictions, some conflicting values.

Shortly before leaving Texas, I had begun to gather data on a devil figure that had recurrently appeared among Mexican Americans in

South Texas since the mid seventies, and, I soon discovered, had not disappeared during my absence. A relative had told me about one of many reported recent appearances, this one at El Cielito Lindo dance hall in a medium-sized town (population 90,000) in deep South Texas that I shall fictitiously call Limonada since so many of my relatives live there.

Now as I finished a delicious *fritada* (goat-blood pudding) at San Miguel's restaurant, Sulema, to whom I had briefly introduced myself already, was done with the lunch rush hour and she had a little time to come over and talk to me during her own thirty-minute lunch break. While Señor San Miguel checked his Rolex and eyed us both suspiciously, she munched her tacos, sipped her *tamarindo* water, and began to tell me about the devil.

As it turned out, according to her, Mendieta was mistaken. Nothing, she said, had actually happened to *her*. It was some other *muchacha* (some other girl), though she knew her. "Nos salimos de *high school* al mismo tiempo, hace seis años" (We dropped out of high school about the same time, six years ago), she added with only the slightest trace of embarrassment crossing her face, which looked older than the twenty-four to twenty-seven years of age I now calculated her to be. But how did she know about the incident? Well, while she wasn't involved in it, she had been at the dance at El Cielito Lindo the night it happened. "Tocaron Shorty y los Corvettes y andaba con mis amigas" (Shorty and the Corvettes played that night and I was with my girlfriends). But did she actually see the devil? I asked, in a silly, too-hurried anthropologically adolescent fashion. "Pos, no, pero una de mis amigas lo vio" (Well, no, but one of my girlfriends saw him), "yo nomás sé lo que dice la gente" (I only know what people say).

I was about to ask her just what it was that people say, but our lunchtime had run out and Señor San Miguel and dirty dishes waited. Could I see her again and, perhaps, her girlfriends? I inquired. Long pause . . . and I knew. I had made another mistake. She didn't have to say it; her long hesitation said it all: ¿Familia? (Family?) ¿Quién eres tú, y qué quieres de de veras? (Who are you and what do you really want?) and, the ultimate deep normative structure of greater Mexico, ¿Qué va a decir la gente? (What will people say?) I pulled back slightly in silence as we stood at the restaurant door. Perhaps sensing my discomfort, she quickly and expertly negotiated this tricky cultural terrain for both of us. Well, she said, she lived with her parents since she was single, so she wasn't so sure about my coming to their house, since they didn't *know* me, nor, we had established earlier, did they know my relatives well, although one of her brothers had known my cousin Tony in high school before he was killed in Vietnam. There was the restaurant as a place to meet like today but there were only the lunch periods like today . . . and then there was Señor San Miguel. As for some other places . . . after hours . . . well, *¿qué va a decir la gente?* She didn't have to say it.

Then she had a bright thought. Could we meet Wednesday night at the Denny's restaurant on the highway? She and her friends went there almost every Wednesday night for lemon meringue pie and coffee. Good pie, she assured me. I couldn't, at least not this Wednesday. I was on a preliminary field scouting trip, making initial contacts such as these and establishing a place to live for the summer. And, I had to return to Austin for the rest of the week but I would be back Friday, I explained to Sulema, and I would see her at the Denny's the following Wednesday. She had another bright thought. There was a dance at El Cielito Lindo this Friday night, and, if I liked dances, maybe I could come and maybe she and her friends would be there and maybe we could talk. "A lo mejor. ¿Quién sabe?" (Maybe. Who knows?) San Miguel glared and waited impatiently. His $2.50 an hour was being used up with no labor in return. Later, I would discover that he, in his married state, periodically tried to get Sulema to go to bed with him. "See you there," I said. As we parted she told me with a smile, "¡Y no se preocupe del diablo, nomás se le aparece a las mujeres!" (And don't worry about the devil, he only appears to women!)

That Friday night, after paying my $10 admission, being frisked for concealed weapons, and making my way past a huge bouncer who wholly engulfed the stool he was sitting on, I met Sulema and her friends Ester, Blanca, and Dolores, or Lola. I politely asked if I could join them and there were introductions all around, with Sulema prefacing the whole thing with a "This is the professor I told you about, *es* anthropologist *y quiere saber del diablo*" (He's an anthropologist and he wants to know about the devil). Ester, a hairdresser, wanted to know what that had to do with digging up old bones, since the local newspaper had run a story about a team of anthropologists who had a dig going near the town. (Damn those archeologists, I thought to myself, they always get the headlines!) On the other, subdisciplinary hand, Lola, a salesperson at Woolworth's, wanted to know was it really true that anthropologists could teach monkeys to speak English like she had read in the *Time* magazine in the beauty shop. Blanca, who worked at the ticket window of the local theater, made a joke that such anthropologists should come to South Texas if they really wanted a challenge. Everyone laughed. I mumbled something about the different kinds of anthropologists and somehow explained my interest by saying in not-too-convincing fashion that cultural anthropology is something like history.

Throughout the evening we talked when Los Cadetes de Linares (the Cadets from Linares) weren't playing a particularly loud polka, or between their sets. We only drank a little. Me, to keep a clear head; they, perhaps as well and as a matter of social discretion. One would inevitably run into cousins. I had beer while they shared one purse-sized pint bottle of Bacardi rum (bought for them by Blanca's older brother, just recently released from prison). They passed the bottle around either under or flat across the table and carefully poured tiny amounts into mostly Coca-Cola and ice–filled cups. With a small pen knife, Ester cut up slices of Mexican lemons since the establishment did not provide any with their setups. (This also led to the usual conventional personal joke about not cutting up Limón.)

We danced. By dancing with each of them and moving myself around the table each time we returned from the floor, I tried to solve a probably cultural problem. I wanted other men to feel quite free to come up to ask any of them to dance, the ostensible reason everyone was here. However, I suspect I produced another possible cultural problem for myself. After all, I was just one guy dancing with four women. I could just hear the men, particularly the large group of unaccompanied men gathering around the bar, saying "O es muy chingón, o es joto" (either he's a big fucker or he's a fag), that dark fate that haunts so many men at the edge of their masculine consciousness. In terms of the local principles of homosexuality, I'm sure my slight build, buttoned-down shirt, and glasses didn't help. (I was reminded of the times when I visited my parents and went out to drink and shoot pool with my two-hundred-pound working-class brother. "Damn it," he says after drinking a few beers, "why don't you get some fucking contact lenses?") At any rate, I negotiated myself past this possible dark fate throughout the night with only occasional slightly amused glances and, perhaps paradoxically, with Mendieta's unsolicited help. He was serving behind the crowded bar resplendent in another, this time light blue, leisure suit. As I came to get another beer and a second setup for the women, he gestured "hello" with outstretched hands, rolled his eyes and head toward the women, and, in front of all the men, made an obscene gesture with his hand suggesting sexual intercourse.

But amidst drink, dance, and talk, I was after the devil and he indeed appeared, not in any visible dramatic form, but as the principal figure in a collective narrative produced by the women that night and reproduced in varying versions throughout my summer. Amidst moments of intense concentration, nervous laughter, and occasional glances toward the dance floor, this is how I came to know the devil. I offer it as a general dialogue of voices, including my own.

Dice la gente (the people say) that sometimes at night when a Mexican American dance is in full swing in southern Texas as so many are, especially on weekend nights; as couples glide in almost choreographed fashion counterclockwise around the floor to the insistent, infectious rhythm of conjunto polka music; as men, women, music, and not small amounts of liquor all blend in heightened erotic consciousness, it is then that the devil may appear.

He comes in the form of a well-dressed, quite handsome man. "Estaba bien *cute*" (He was real cute), says Blanca, but hastens to add that she didn't really see him, this is what she was told by a female cousin. The devil is tall and strong in appearance. "Con *shoulders* así" (with shoulders like this), demonstrates Ester with outstretched fingers. Sulema cannot resist. "¿Estás segura que nomás los *shoulders?*" (Are you sure you're only talking about the shoulders?) Laughter. Embarrassed looks and glances. It's a few moments before we can continue and they can look at me again without laughing. What does he look like? How is he dressed? I ask. "¡Muy elegante con *suit* y todo!" (Very elegant with a suit and everything!) "Es güero así como Robert Redford" (He's blond like Robert Redford). I think of Robert Redford, as I take note of the young Mexican American men around me, at best one or two in inexpensive suits, most with thick dark hair and shirts open to mid chest or lower revealing, on some, the Virgin of Guadalupe resting on Indian bare, brown skin.

The narrative stops, perhaps because I have been looking away. So what else happens? I finally ask. Is that it? A handsome guy appears? Oh no, then comes the good part, Ester continues. They say that after he comes in right over there (motioning to the entrance to El Cielito), a girl sitting with her friends spots him and she really wants to dance with him. Blanca interrupts. "Well, everyone does!" "I know," Ester replies, "*pero ésta le hace ojos*" (but this one makes eyes at him). I ask them to slow down as I try to jot down at least the main points of the story and their reactions. "So," Ester continues, "she makes eyes at him and he comes over to ask her to dance." In parody and with a laugh, Lola flicks her own heavily made-up eyelids quickly up and down. "So he asks her, *y salen a bailar*" (and they go out to dance). At this point Sulema covers her eyes. Blanca whispers, "This is the good part, this is the good part" and gets a "Shh!" from Lola.

Up on the bandstand, Los Cadetes de Linares are coming back from their break and around us, men (and very occasionally a woman) walk by carrying beers and setups to their tables. The few all-female groups like the one I am with will try to get a male friend or relative to bring them beer and setups to avoid going to the male-crowded bar. "And so," Ester continues, "as they're dancing, *la* girl *le mira los* feet" (the girl looks down at his feet) "*y tiene* feet *de* chicken!" (and he has the feet of a chicken!) "Goat!" Sulema says loudly, trying to correct her. Clearly exasperated, Ester sharply replies, "¡Chingado, lo que sea!" (Goddamn it, whatever!) and apologizes for using a bad word. On my small pad I scribble as fast as I can, missing a lot but concentrating on the narrators. Ester continues: "Y cuando le vio los *feet,* la *girl* gritó" (And when she saw his feet, the girl screamed). "And then she faints right there on the floor," Sulema quickly adds and gets a dirty look from Ester for her unsolicited contribution. "And then she fainted, Mr. Limón," Ester continues (who can't seem to call me José), "and he ran to that corner over there and disappeared in a puff of smoke!" Lola adds a denouement. "My brother says that he was in that corner that night but he only heard the scream, he didn't see smoke or nothing. *¿Quién sabe?*" A puzzle remains. I say to them: Sulema told me that one of you did see the devil. Which one was it? "¡Qué *liar,* Sulema!" Blanca exclaims. "You told us you saw him when you were going to the ladies' room." Sulema looks embarrassed. In the final analysis, however, the issue is not really that important, and I decide to leave it alone, as well as the true identity of the woman who encountered the devil on the dance floor.

The Devil, the Dance, and the Contradictions of Culture

What is important is that a recurrent belief exists in the form of an emergent collective narrative—that it exists for these women and, to judge from other less-systematic data, for women like these throughout South Texas, including San Antonio and the extensions of Texas everywhere, for the devil has also been reported in the agricultural labor camps of California and Wisconsin. In another fashion it exists for men as well, as I will show in a moment, but first let me say a bit more about these women and their interpretive perceptions of the devil as I continued to engage them in later conversations, principally over too many lemon meringue pies at Denny's. What is the devil all about? What does it mean, if anything, for you? Why do you think such an unusual thing happened? Why does the devil appear to women like yourselves at dances? Before answering me directly, they first summarize what *la gente dice* (people say), which really turns out to be synonymous with what the elders say, as I will show in a moment. However, in more extended conversation, it turns out that Sulema, Ester, Blanca, and Lola have their own distinctive consensus perception of this figure and its relation to their lives. Ester: "I don't know . . . I kinda like him!" Why? (I feign surprise.) He's a devil, isn't he? "Sí, pero, *he's so different!*" (Different from what? I think to myself. Do I need to really ask, or having met Mendieta is the answer evidently clear?) "Está bien chulo" (He's so cute, attractive), Ester continues. Lola adds, "Once I met a guy like that in Houston." "What do you think he would be like? I mean, as a person?" I ask. "Te apuesto que es bien suave" (I bet he's real kind, soft, sweet, suave). "But he's a devil!" I insist, in mock argument. "What about the goat's feet?" "Ay, *who cares?*" says Sulema. And Blanca adds, with a nice laugh, "¡Nomás le pones zapatitos!" (You just need to put little shoes on him!)

But, as I say, there are other perceptions of the devil in this community. Let me briefly summarize three others. For example, there are the elderly, both male and female. Here, I talked to eight people. The devil, they say, comes today because things are out of hand. Girls go to dances by themselves. *En nuestro tiempo, no se veía eso* (In our time, you didn't see that). There is too much drinking. Outside the dances and even inside, you see *mariguanos* (marijuana smokers). A seventy-four-year-old man tells me: "La última vez que fui, tuve que ir al excusado, y allí estaban los cabrones fumando mugrero" (The last time I went to a dance, I went to the restroom and there were the bastards smoking trash). "And the music is so loud," says another, "*con todos esos aparatos*" (with all those electronic things). "And, for all this, they charge so much!" "Se imagina usted, señor Limón, ¡diez dólares! ¡Ni que fuéramos ricos!" (Can you imagine, Mr. Limón, ten dollars! As if we were rich!) "Ya no son como los bailes de antes" (They are not like dances used to be [in our time]). "Por eso viene el diablo" (That's why the devil comes). "Se acabaron los bailes de regalo" (The "gift dances" are no more).

I carried my same questions to another social scene: the daily afternoon, all-male, quiet, slow-drinking scene at the bar at Mendieta's place. Here is another view, more or less shared by the married and the single men who drink there. Like Mendieta, they think of the story as women's noise, chatter, crap, and, they claim, they do not go around telling the story, although they've heard it from women. Nonetheless, what do they think the devil is all about?

They seem to see it as women imagining what they think the women would like to have but can't or shouldn't have. To some extent, the single men see the issue in more sexual terms but with an element of race. "Las viejas quieren vatos así, tú sabes, vatos gabachos" (Broads want guys like that, you know, like Anglos). It is the married guys at the bar who offer a more extended analysis. "Women, you know, always want more of everything. They're never satisfied." "It's like my wife," one tells me, "*cómprame esto, cómprame el otro*" (buy me this, buy me that). "Se vuelven locas con las *credit cards*. Chingue, chingue, con que vamos al *mall*, vamos al *mall*" (They go crazy with the credit cards. Nag, nag, let's go to the mall, let's go to the mall), says another.

I don't quite see the connection. What does that have to do with the devil? "It's like the church says, like Eve," tells another one. "*¡Quería la pinche manzana!*" (She wanted the damn apple!) "So this rich white guy, real high society, appears and he tempts them but he disappears *pa' que aprendan que no pueden tener todo*. But they think they can, or they want to. *Por eso se imaginan todo este pedo*" (So that is why they imagine all that shit).

Finally, and frankly, here my data is weakest for it comes from a few married women and ample access to them required delicate negotiations, so that I really wound up talking to very few wives of relatives and close friends. What do they think? The devil is moral retribution, they tell me. God's way of punishing all those loose women who try to entice men. "You see how she made eyes at him in the story, right, José?" a married cousin asks me. "They shouldn't be at the dances out like that. The girls who go to the nightclub at the Holiday Inn are even worse. They're just out to get men." (The Holiday Inn nightclub is where my cousin's husband does his drinking, by the way.) "They should stay at home. If the devil appears, *¿quién les manda que anden allí?*" (who forced them to be there?) "*¡Viejas feas!*" (Dirty broads!)

We can perhaps begin to appreciate how the dance is a scene that can elicit contradictory values and understandings; that the dance, while on the surface a scene of enjoyment and fun, can also conceal other perspectives. These perspectives can only be revealed by the projection of a devil figure that historically in religious culture has always stood for the negative. Thus, while they attend and like the dances, the working-class men I interviewed also see them as zones of cultural resistance into which the devil, understood as an "Anglo," intrudes. Yet at the same time, it is an area in which they, exemplified by Mendieta, feel in control of women. The women, on the other hand, or at least the single ones, see the dance and the devil as a potential zone of liberation from this male sexual domination. I'm not convinced that they actually want an "Anglo"; what they seem to want is kind men who will treat them fairly. The married women, however, see dances as places that threaten their married stability.

Finally, however, it is the elders that I found the most interesting. They are the most critical of the dances, and they take the appearance of the devil as a sign that Mexican American culture has changed for the worse. To make their point clear, however, they contrast the contemporary dance to an older form of dance they used to know. These were *los bailes de regalo* (the gift dances), which differed from contemporary dances in several ways. *Bailes de regalo* were organized by families, not by promoters; there was no admission, although they were open to people beyond the extended family; drinking was very minimal and highly regulated (men could leave the dance and go have a drink outside and at some distance from the dance); sexual conduct was also highly regulated through the presence of chaperones; and, finally, symbolically, a woman was honored for agreeing to dance with a particular man. After he returned her to her seat, he was obligated to present her with a small gift, usually a piece of candy. I asked the old people if the devil ever appeared at these dances, and, as one told me, "Nunca, el diablo nunca entra en lugares de respeto y amistad" (Never, the devil never enters places of respect and friendship).

In my remarks, I have tried not only to describe Mexican American dances but also to say something about the way these dances can also contain and reveal different value perspectives articulated through the appearance of a devil figure. The very projected appearance of the devil suggests that while these are scenes of intense culture expression and enjoyment, they also disclose something of the cultural contradictions Mexican Americans feel about living in an Anglo, class-dominated society.

Note

1. All personal names and place references in this article are fictitious.

PART SIX

Platicando con los Grandes

Interviews with Conjunto Legends

The following interviews were originally published in Spanish, the language in which they were conducted. We are including here the original Spanish-language interviews as well as English translations, by Max Martínez with Víctor Guerra and Martha Vogel.

20

Santiago Jiménez, Sr.

✧

JUAN TEJEDA
1982

(English translation: page 267)

Lo siguiente es una entrevista con Don Santiago Jiménez, Sr., el famoso acordeonista de San Antonio. Se llevó a cabo el 26 de febrero en la casa del señor Jiménez.

Santiago: Soy Santiago Jiménez, uno de los primeros acordeonistas que empezó la música norteña aquí en San Antonio. Yo nací en 1913, y ahorita tengo setenta y . . . perdón, tengo sesenta y siete años.
Juan: ¿En qué fecha de 1913?
Santiago: El veinticinco de abril de 1913.
Juan: ¿Aquí en San Antonio?
Santiago: Aquí en San Antonio, sí.
Juan: ¿Cuándo aprendió a tocar el acordeón usted?
Santiago: Bueno, aprendí el acordeón cuando tenía la edad de doce años. Y en esos tiempos mi padre era el que tocaba en los bailes, y yo mirándolo a él, empecé a aprender así polcas, redovas y chotís. Y luego, ya después, este, como a los veinte años, empecé a grabar los primeros discos aquí en San Antonio.
Juan: Su papá, entonces, ¿tocaba el acordeón?
Santiago: Sí, mi papá tocaba el acordeón.
Juan: ¿Él aprendió de quién?
Santiago: Bueno, él aprendió, tal vez, mirando a otros tocar el acordeón, porque él siempre iba a los bailes alemanes donde se tocaban las polcas. Y de allí para acá, él empezó a aprender, y empezó a tocar en los bailes.

Juan: ¿Y las polcas, entonces, de los mexicanos acá son diferente que las del alemán?

Santiago: Bueno, sí es un poco diferente, pero, como le he dicho yo, siempre viene esa música de Alemania, porque, este, mi papá la aprendió de los alemanes, y luego otros acordeonistas, oyendo a mi padre tocar, empezaron a tocar las mismas, el mismo ritmo, ¿verdad?, pero creo yo que vino esa música de Alemania.

Juan: ¿Su papá, se llamaba qué?

Santiago: Patricio Jiménez.

Juan: Y antes de él, ¿sabía usted de alguien, un mexicano, que tocaba acordeón también?

Santiago: No. Allí en el barrio donde yo nací, él era el único acordeonista que había.

Juan: ¿Aquí en San Antonio?

Santiago: Aquí en San Antonio, sí. Le nombraban el barrio de la Piedrera. Precisamente por eso es que hice yo la polca esa "La Piedrera". Y en ese tiempo se hacían los bailes nada más en las casas. No había micrófonos, no había *amplifiers,* nada de eso. Nomás el acordeón y la guitarra. De la manera que se hacían esos bailes, en aquel tiempo, sería como el 1920, o '25, cuando yo tenía apenas como unos diez años . . . mi papá tocaba en el barrio de la Piedrera cada ocho días, cada sábado. Los muchachos de allí del mismo barrio se juntaban todos, y los bailes como los hacían era de mover el *furniture,* o ya sea los muebles, a otro cuarto, y dejar un cuarto libre para bailar. Y así duraban los bailes, muchas veces, desde las ocho de la noche, hasta las siete de la mañana.

Juan: ¿Su papá era de San Antonio, también?

Santiago: Sí, él nació en Eagle Pass, luego se vino para acá pa' San Antonio.

Juan: ¿Usted fue a la escuela aquí en San Antonio?

Santiago: Sí, fui a la escuela. La escuela donde fui yo estaba por la calle Magnolia, para acá pa' rumbo de Brackenridge Park. Se llamaba la escuela González. Todavía existe, pero, no sé si todavía dan escuela allí, pero está el *building* todavía allí.

Juan: ¿Y a qué edad empezó allí?

Santiago: Tenía yo como siete años cuando empecé ir a la escuela.

Juan: ¿Y fue hasta qué?

Santiago: Pues, nada más llegué hasta el número seis.

Juan: ¿Y es toda la educación formal que tiene, vamos a decir?

Santiago: Exactamente, sí. Porque en ese tiempo mi padre empezó a estar enfermo. Nosotros empezamos a crecer un poco y tuvimos que sostener la casa, yo y un hermano mío. Por eso no tuve mucha escuela.

Juan: ¿Y empezó, entonces, a tocar cuando tenía como diez años?

Santiago: Sí, como unos diez o doce años. Pero no era conocido todavía, nomás allí en la casa tocaba. Como allá, a la edad de veinte años, como dije ahorita, empecé a hacerme conocido porque el señor Dávila, de la estación KEDA, él fue el que me llevó la primerita vez a los micrófonos que me oyeran por la radio. Y allí fue donde me empecé a hacer conocido yo. Y le agradezco mucho a ellos porque ellos fueron los que de veras me abrieron el camino para llegar donde llegué yo, de grabar discos. Cuando se enteraron de escuchar mis piezas y todo por radio, muchas compañías de discos luego luego se informaron dónde vivía yo y todo para grabar discos.

Juan: ¿Entonces, antes que había grabado, empezó a tocar en la radio, aquí en radio KEDA?

Santiago: Exactamente. En ese tiempo no se llamaba KEDA, le nombraban *La Hora Anáhuac* . . .

Juan: Ah, sí.

Santiago: . . . que ahora comenzó otra vez en la estación.

Juan: Sí, claro. Y entonces era como 1933, ¿no?, cuando empezó a tocar por radio.

Santiago: Exactamente, sí, como en '36. No, como en '33, como en '33, porque ya pa' el '36 fue cuando lancé el primer disco al mercado.

Juan: ¿Cuál fue el primer disco?

Santiago: Pues no tengo la seguridad, no estoy muy seguro, pero, parece que fue una polca que le nombrábamos "El aguacero polca". [*Después se acordó que era la polca "Dices pescao".*]

Juan: ¿Era composición de usted?

Santiago: No, era una pieza que mi papá tocaba. Yo no sé quién será el compositor de esa pieza, pero mi papá tocaba esa pieza y a mí me gustó para grabarla. Y grabé varias que mi papá tocaba también, como el vals "La tuna", y así.

Juan: ¿Y de dónde salieron esas canciones?

Santiago: Pues, esas canciones no sé de dónde mi padre las aprendió. Yo se las aprendí a él, y como él nunca grabó discos, este, a mí me gustaron esas piezas para grabarlas, y fue un éxito. Bueno, también, se vendió bastante. Todavía hasta la fecha las han grabado otros artistas y todavía se venden esas piezas.

Juan: ¿Y con qué grabó? Los instrumentos: acordeón, y ¿qué más?

Santiago: Acordeón, bajo sexto y el contrabajo, que le dicen el tololoche.

Juan: A mí me decían que antes se usaba nomás el acordeón, el bajo o guitarra y un tambor, también. Que en diferentes lugares usaban un tambor de cuero. ¿Sabe usted de eso?

Santiago: Bueno, sí. Algunos usaban tambor, también. Pero yo nada más usé bajo sexto, y hasta la fecha todavía lo uso cuando grabo, y el contrabajo, y el acordeón.

Juan: ¿Con quién grabó esos primeros discos?

Santiago: Los primeros discos que grabé yo fue en la compañía Decca.

Juan: ¿De aquí en San Antonio?

Santiago: No, eran, yo creo, de California ellos. Ellos me vinieron a grabar aquí en San Antonio.

Juan: ¿Todavía tiene discos viejos usted?

Santiago: Pues, sí . . . fíjese que no . . . este, sí tendré, tendré alguno que tengo, por allí que anda, de los primeros que grabé yo. Algunos los emprestaba y ya no volvían, y así.

Juan: ¿Quién tiene esos discos? ¿No sabe de alguien?

Santiago: Pues, sí tengo un primo hermano mío que los cuida como cuidar su casa. Tiene como unos cinco o seis discos de los primeros que grabé yo.

Juan: Entonces se levantó mucho usted en esos tiempos, ¿no?

Santiago: Sí, bueno, los primeros discos, como . . . pues, fue una admiración, porque en aquellos tiempos no habían muchos que tocaban ni hacían grabaciones. Los primeros discos que grabé yo fue un éxito grande luego luego. Y como fui muy conocido aquí en San Antonio, pues . . . la gente siempre me apoyó mucho y empezaron a comprar discos. Y hasta la fecha todavía el último álbum que grabamos yo y Flaco Jiménez se ha vendido bastante.

Juan: Durante esos tiempos, temprano, cuando salió de la escuela, ¿empezó a trabajar? ¿Qué estaba haciendo?

Santiago: Bueno, trabajé mucho, pues, así nomás en trabajitos que yo desempeñaba, como el primer trabajo que hice yo, ya después, fue de waxear pisos y lijar pisos. Eso me gustaba hacer yo, lijar los pisos y ponerlos nuevos otra vez y todo eso. Y trabajé como cinco años durante la guerra en Fort Sam Houston. Eso fue después.

Juan: Y cuando empezó a tocar, ¿estaba trabajando?

Santiago: Tocaba y trabajaba. Había un *nightclub* aquí en la calle de, me parece, Laredo, cerca de la calle Camarón, por allí, se llamaba Perales Nite Club. Allí toqué un año. Tocaba allí y trabajaba, también. En la noche tocaba, y en el día trabajaba. Hasta que una vez me decidí más a tocar, y hice mi vida tocando por como . . . yo creo unos doce o trece años. Hice mi vida tocando, nada más.

Juan: ¿Eso viene siendo como de qué año?

Santiago: Bueno, fue como el 1940, hasta como el 1952, algo así.

Juan: ¿Tocaba todo alrededor del estado, pa' fuera?

Santiago: Bueno, en ese tiempo no salía muy lejos yo, nada más alrededor de aquí: Seguín, San Marcos, Cotulla, Dilley, Devine, Carlota [Charlotte], todos esos pueblitos cercanos de aquí, y en San Antonio, era donde tocaba yo. Donde toqué muchos años de regla fue en El Gaucho. Le nombraban El Gaucho, en la calle de Navidad y El Paso.

Juan: A ver, ¿puede nombrar unas de las primeras polquitas que grabó, así en una lista, nomás los nombres?

Santiago: Bueno, sí, como le dije anteriormente: "El aguacero", "El Cotulla", "La Piedrera", "Una mañana de abril", "Margarita", y por ahí va. No me acuerdo de las demás, pero, por ahí va.

Juan: Sí, y esas son unas grabaciones, o composiciones, de usted, ¿verdad?

Santiago: Algunas, sí.

Juan: ¿Acuáles?

Santiago: Bueno, la que hice muy popular y que todavía se escucha mucho es "Viva Seguín", "La Piedrera" y "El aguacero", que grabé la primer vez. Ésa nunca ha muerto tampoco, siempre se escucha mucho aquí. Pero, una de las más famosas que todavía se oye por dondequiera, y la han grabado muchos artistas, orquestas también, es "Viva Seguín".

Juan: "Viva Seguín", yo la toco también. Pues, yo vengo de la tradición de usted, también. Su hijo me enseñó, Santiago Jiménez, Jr.

Santiago: ¿De veras?

Juan: Cuando yo tenía diez años de edad. Y toqué con él, también.

Santiago: Fíjese, ¡qué bueno!

Juan: ¿Cuándo se casó usted?

Santiago: Yo me casé en el '36.

Juan: ¿Aquí en San Antonio?

Santiago: Aquí en San Antonio, sí.

Juan: ¿Y cuántos hijos tuvieron?

Santiago: Bueno, teníamos ocho. Ocho hijos, sí. Nomás dos mujeres. La mayor se llama Antonia, y luego el Flaco Jiménez, luego Luis, y luego Rubén, Roberto, Adriana. Bueno, pues, todos crecieron, gracias a Dios, y algunos se casaron, y están viviendo con sus familias.

Juan: Y de ellos, ¿qué tantos se hicieron músicos?

Santiago: Pues, de los más famosos . . . casi todos mis hijos tocan un poco —el que no toca guitarra, toca acordeón. Pero los más conocidos fue el Flaco Jiménez y Santiago Jr.

Juan: ¿Ahora el Santiago Jr. está rifando, no?

Santiago: También está rifando muy bien. Y ojalá que Dios lo ayude y se vaya pa' arriba.

Juan: Bueno, después de 1952, ¿qué pasó? ¿Comenzó a trabajar otra vez? ¿Siguió tocando?

Santiago: Bueno, sí, paré de tocar por un tiempo y me fui pa'l pueblito este de Dallas. Allá estuve once años trabajando en un seminario, mayordomo de un seminario. Allí casi no se halla trabajo, pero, como conocía el trabajo, como le expliqué, de lijar pisos y todo, es lo que hacían allí, y yo les decía cómo lo hicieran. Y tuve once años allí.

Juan: ¿Hasta cuándo?

Santiago: Tuve hasta el '79. Y luego me vine pa' acá pa' San Antonio otra vez, y ya tengo aquí como tres años que me vine de allá.

Juan: ¿Y paró de tocar todo ese tiempo?

Santiago: Todo ese tiempo paré de tocar. Nada más tocaba así cuando había alguna boda, un *party,* pero, de regla no tocaba yo ya, nomás trabajaba. Y de allí me retiré ya. Cumplí la edad de sesenta y cinco años allí, y luego me retiré de trabajar. Y nomás vine a San Antonio, y pues mucha gente que me conoce aquí . . . me contrató Jimmy's Restaurant que está por la calle Rittiman Road. Quería que le tocara allí yo, y parece que no, pero fíjese, ya tengo tres años de estar con Jimmy, tocando desde que vine de allá de Dallas. Empecé otra vez con la música. Y ahora toco allí cada en cuando. No quiero agarrar muchas tocaditas porque yo ya me canso un poco.

Juan: ¿Qué tantos *albums* grabó?

Santiago: Álbums grabé muy pocos. Ahorita tengo como unos tres nomás. Casi eran puros *forty-fives* en esos tiempos pa' acá.

Juan: ¿Grabó más *forty-fives*, no?
Santiago: Sí, muchos.
Juan: ¿Qué tantos, aproximadamente?
Santiago: Bueno, de grabaciones de discos, poco más o menos tengo arriba de cien discos grabados.
Juan: ¿Con acuáles compañías grabó?
Santiago: Grabé con varias compañías. Grabé con Decca, grabé con Mercury, grabé con Corona, con RCA Victor, también con Columbia.
Juan: Columbia es compañía grande, ¿verdad?
Santiago: Sí, la RCA Victor también. Bueno, yo tengo más de doce discos grabados con RCA Victor.
Juan: Muchas composiciones . . .
Santiago: Composiciones mías y algunas de algunos otros compositores también. Pero, casi lo que he grabado yo son puras composiciones mías.
Juan: ¿Cuándo iniciaron al tamborero ustedes?
Santiago: Bueno, el tamborero ya vino despues de los treinta, yo creo. Así todo el tiempo se usaba nomás el acordeón y la guitarra, y el bajo. Yo nunca he grabado con tamboras. No, nomás con tololoche, bajo sexto y acordeón, hasta la fecha, porque me gusta que se oye así lo que yo toco. No, porque la tambora también se oye mucho muy bonito, pero yo me impuse a oírme así, y me gusta. Y todo el tiempo que voy a grabar, me dicen que si quiero poner tambora, o algo, y les digo, pues, prefería mejor el tololoche y el bajo sexto, pero, si es necesario, pues, ponemos tamboras también. Pero casi todo el tiempo grababa nomás bajo sexto, contrabajo y acordeón.
Juan: ¿Y cantando también?
Santiago: También canto. Tengo nomás unas grabaciones cantadas también, que han salido así, regulares. Regulares digo porque en los *royalties* que me pagan, se venden bien. Se han vendido muy bien.
Juan: ¿Sí? ¡Qué bueno! Y antes se tocaba nomás sentado, ¿verdad?
Santiago: En ese tiempo, cuando yo comencé, se tocaba sentado. No se paraban para tocar. Nomás el tololoche, nomás parado, pero cuando se acababa así la pieza, o algo, pues se sentaban un rato a descanzar. Y era más fácil así que ahora, porque ahora tienen que estar parados. Digamos, yo para la edad que tengo, ya no puedo aguantar mucho.

Juan: ¿Quién cree usted que fue el primer acordeonista que empezó a tocar parado, así? ¿Sabe?

Santiago: ¿Lo cree? que no tengo ninguna idea quién fue el que empezó así.

Juan: Me dicen que antes también no cantaban mucho, que era puro instrumental.

Santiago: Instrumental, exactamente, así era. No había mucha canción en ese tiempo.

Juan: Cuando vino pa' atrás aquí a San Antonio, después de estar allá en Dallas, ¿comenzó a tocar otra vez?

Santiago: Sí, así es. No duré ni dos meses sin que luego luego me hablaron para tocar. Y me han hablado en varias partes, pero, es como le digo, ya no aguanto yo mucho. Con una tocada que hago cada semana es suficiente para mí. Lo hago para que no se me olvide.

Juan: Empezó a grabar también, ¿no? ¿Grabó unos *albums*?

Santiago: Sí, pues, el último álbum que grabamos en la . . . esta, ¿cómo se llama ese disco?, se me olvida a mí el nombre . . .

Juan: ¿Arhoolie Records?

Santiago: Sí, ése fue el último que grabé, yo y Flaco Jiménez [*Don Santiago Jiménez, with Flaco and Juan Viesca*].

Juan: ¿Tiene planes de grabar otras cosas?

Santiago: Pues, el señor ese mismo quería grabarme otra vez, pero, no sé cuándo vendrá otra vez, porque es compañía de California.

Juan: Entonces, aquí el chicano ha agarrado la música de los alemanes y ha hecho algo distinto con él, ¿no?

Santiago: Sí, algo diferente, pero siempre de allí viene esa música. Yo siempre lo he dicho, no sé si estaré bién, o estaré mal, pero, esa música viene de Alemania. Nomás que aquí la hemos nosotros arreglado de otra manera, ¿verdad? Pero, así viene de por allá.

Juan: ¿No ha escrito canciones nuevas ahora pronto?

Santiago: Sí, escribí algunas que van a venir en un álbum. Se las di yo a Flaco Jiménez pa' que las grabara él, y muy pronto las van a oír ustedes. Son como unas cuatro o cinco canciones mías que van a salir en disco. Joey se las grabó. Joey López se las grabó a Flaco, y creo que en este mes quizás salga ese álbum nuevo por Flaco Jiménez. Allí incluye canciones mías que yo compuse.

Juan: ¿Y cómo mira la música ahorita?

Santiago: La música de acordeón, a como está ahorita, es para mí . . . esa música ya no va a morir más. Se va a quedar para siempre, porque el acordeón ahorita está muy fuerte por todo el mundo. Ya si no hay un ritmo de acordeón, ya la música ya no sirve. Según entiendo yo, el acordeón entra en cualquier orquesta, mariachis . . . y siempre ha tenido el acordeón un ritmo muy alegre, que es lo que le gusta a la gente, la alegría de la música esa. Y yo, cuando comencé a tocar el acordeón, yo nunca creía que iba a llegar el acordeón . . . a hacerse tan famosa esa música como está ahorita.

Juan: ¿Yo leí en un estudio tocante la música de acordeón, que antes la música de acordeón era como para los rascuachis, o era para la gente de abajo, opuesto a la música de orquesta. ¿Qué piensa usted, había ese sentimiento, algo asina?

Santiago: Bueno, yo nunca lo pensé así, pero, mucha gente, digamos que escribía mucha música, como hay todavía ahorita, ellos decían que la música de acordeón, no . . . para ellos, pues, no era nada, era nomás un son cualquiera. Pero yo nunca lo pensé así, porque yo desde un principio pensé que a mí me gustaba toda clase de música. Pero, el alegría del acordeón era más, era más todo el tiempo, arriba de cualquier otra música que estaban tocando, como el rock and roll, en aquellos tiempos, ¿cómo decir? . . . el charlestón. Pero mucho pitío para acá y pitío para allá, y para mí era nomás, también como decían ellos, que era un sonsonete.

Pero, siempre el acordeón, pensaba yo —no porque yo la tocaba y mi papá también— pero, yo pensaba que la música de acordeón traiba un ritmo muy alegre aunque fuera muy sencillo, pero muy alegre, que es lo que alegra en la música: la alegría. Porque de qué sirve que sepa uno tocar mucho muy bien y no tiene que . . . no le sale a uno de aquí, ¿verdad?, del pecho, ¿verdad?, o sea el cantante, o sea el que está tocando. Y sí es cierto así lo que dice usted. Yo oí decir muchas cosas así. Pero, para mí, yo nunca pensé que iba a ser así. Y ahora, pues, lo están viendo toda la gente, y lo están oyendo, escuchando día con día, que la música de acordeón es una música muy alegre, y nadie puede decir que no.

Juan: Bailable, también.

Santiago: Muy bailable, sí. Allí se podía acompañar todo, también. Ahora más por los acordeonistas destacados que han salido ahora, como Ramón Ayala, y todos esos muchachos. Tocan mucho muy bonito.

Juan: ¿Qué piensa de Esteban Jordán?

Santiago: También es un acordeonista pero ¡qué bárbaro!, de los mejores también. Para mí, me gusta mucho como toca él.

Juan: Le ha metido muchas cosas al acordeón, ¿no?

Santiago: Mucho, mucho. Cosas que yo nunca podía creer que iba a salir en un cajoncito tan chiquito, como es el acordeón.

Juan: El chotís, ¿de dónde viene ese tipo de música?

Santiago: Precisamente, el chotís viene de Alemania. Sí, señor. El chotís, las polcas, las redovas, vienen también, los valses.

Juan: No hay, entonces, una música que viene más de aquí y no de Alemania, con el acordeón, ¿verdad? ¿El huapango?

Santiago: Bueno, el huapango, yo creo, viene de México, con los mariachis. Los corridos también vienen de por allá. Pero, lo que es música muy antigua viene, que yo sé bien, que viene por allá de Alemania.

Juan: Yo pensaba que el chotís tenía otra cosa, porque lo bailan muy indio, muy indito.

Santiago: Bueno, ahora sí hay diferentes modos de bailar el chotís, pero, cuando yo miraba mi papá que tocaba los chotís, y la gente lo bailaban mucho muy diferente a como los bailan ahora. Ahora los bailan sueltos de a tiro, y en aquel tiempo, no. Se agarraban la bailadora y el bailador, y daban dos, tres pasos pa' adelante, y dos, tres pasos para atrás, y luego las vueltas en puntas, en las puntas de los pieses. Los valses también en las puntas de los pies los bailaban. No ponían el tacón abajo ni en el piso, nunca. El vals...

Juan: Ha de haber sido muy duro, ¿no?

Santiago: Muy bonito que lo hacían. Y ahora, pues, se baila de todas maneras. Y ya, bueno, yo digo por mi parte, muchas cumbias que salieron ahora —que yo nunca en mi vida había sabido ni lo que era una cumbia, ni nada, en aquellos tiempos no se oía nada de eso— pues, ahora me fijo yo que el mismo ritmo... hay unas, algunas cumbias que son muy aprisa, y hay unas cumbias que son más despacio, y se puede mirar casi como una polca. La cumbia, también, se puede bailar igual, nomás que tienen otros nombres que le han sacado allí. Pero, lo que yo sé de la música vieja, yo nomás sé como chotises, valses, redovas y polcas. Y los huapangos, bueno, los huapangos ya vienen de por México, de por allá. Esos son los bailes de más antes.

Juan: Siempre he visto a la raza aquí bailar asina: en un círculo, alrededor. ¿Siempre se ha hecho eso? ¿O empezó a un cierto tiempo que la raza empezó a bailar alrededor, asina?

Santiago: Bueno, eso es lo que le dicen el Paul Jones, yo creo, ¿verdad? Eso sí es precisamente como le digo yo, eso también lo he visto yo. Lo vide muchos años pa' atrás. También los alemanes trai-ban eso. Eso lo sacarían después ellos aquí, pero, ellos le nombraban el Paul Jones, que todavía le nombran, yo creo, así. Pero ya muy poca gente he visto yo que lo baila. En aquellos tiempos, cuando yo tenía allá como los treinta y cinco años, por allí, todavía bailaban el Paul Jones.

Juan: Yo me acuerdo que tocábamos el Paul Jones con Jimmy [Santiago Jr.] en los bailes, pero era cuando se metían las mujeres adentro y los hombres afuera, y daban vuelta. Luego pitaban un pito y bailaban con quien estaba en frente. Ése es el Paul Jones que me acuerdo yo.

Santiago: Exactamente, sí, así es.

Juan: Pues, tal vez de ahí por ahí este estilo de que cuando bailamos, bailamos *counterclockwise,* alrededor pa' la izquierda, y todavía . . . y estaba pensando que tal vez salió del Paul Jones.

Santiago: Sí, del Paul Jones viene eso.

Juan: ¿Y el Paul Jones vino del alemán?

Santiago: Sí, vino del alemán, porque yo me acuerdo que yo miraba allí en el Brackenridge Park, allí se hacían los bailes en veces, y allí venían muchos alemanes de aquí de New Braunfels. Todos esos venían aquí a Brackenridge Park a los bailes, y así lo bailaban.

Juan: ¿Y por qué le decían el Paul Jones?

Santiago: No tengo ni idea dónde salió eso, Paul Jones.

Juan: ¡Quién sabe quién era Paul Jones! Y decían que el alemán no quería mucho al mexicano.

Santiago: No, en ese tiempo, no. Mi papá tuvo, yo creo, muchos amigos alemanes aquí en New Braunfels, todo eso. Precisamente allí fue donde él aprendió a tocar el acordeón. Él tenía muchos amigos alemanes, de manera que algunos no los querían, y algunos sí. Pero, sí es cierto que el alemán no quería muy bien a los mexicanos.

Juan: ¿Qué piensa usted hacer en el futuro, ahora?

Santiago: Pues, esperando nomás la buena suerte, porque ya uno, ya cuando entra a una edad así como la que tengo yo, pues, no puede uno trabajar, nomás de hacer cualquier cosa alrededor de la casa. Porque yo ahorita como estoy operado, también, no puedo trabajar, y además de eso, que ya, pues, yo ya trabajé bastante. Y treinta y cinco, cuarenta años de trabajo en mi vida, y creo que es bastante. Así es que la pasamos yo y mi señora, Virginia, nada más paseándonos cada en cuando.

Juan: Y con su música, ¿qué son los planes?

Santiago: Pues, seguir así para distraerme nada más. Pero es como le digo, no tocar mucho, porque ya muchas desveladas, ya no las puedo aguantar como las aguantaba más antes. Así es que, muchas veces con un sábado que toque, es bastante para practicar y no olvidarme de a tiro. Y cuando hay unas grabaciones de disco, pues, también. A ver si ahi algún día de estos hacemos otro álbum para dejarles recuerdos.

Juan: Ándale, ¡eso es lo bonito! Pues, me da mucho gusto haber tenido la oportunidad de estar aquí, hablando con usted, ya que usted es uno de los meros grandes en la música de conjunto aquí en Tejas, y pues, por todos los Estados Unidos. Y creo que van a haber muchas cosas bonitas todavía que va a dejarnos a nosotros que estamos siguiendo esta tradición de la música de conjunto. Le deseo suerte.

Santiago: Muchas gracias. Así que sea.

Santiago Jiménez, Sr.

⬧

JUAN TEJEDA
1982

(Entrevista original: página 255)

The following is an interview with Don Santiago Jiménez, Sr., the famous accordionist from San Antonio. The interview was conducted on February 26 at the home of Don Santiago.

Santiago: I am Santiago Jiménez, one of the first accordionists to play *norteño* music here in San Antonio. I was born in 1913 and I am now seventy . . . no, excuse me, I am now sixty-seven years old.
Juan: What date in 1913?
Santiago: April 25, 1913.
Juan: Here in San Antonio?
Santiago: Yes, here in San Antonio.
Juan: When did you learn to play the accordion?
Santiago: Well, I learned to play the accordion at the age of twelve. Back then, my father played at dances and I, watching him, started to learn the polkas, redowas, and schottisches. And then, some time later, well, maybe at the age of twenty, I began to make the first recordings here in San Antonio.
Juan: Your father, then, played the accordion?
Santiago: Yes, my father played the accordion.
Juan: From whom did he learn?
Santiago: Well, he learned, perhaps, by watching others play the accordion, because he always went to the German dances where they played polkas. And from then on, he started to learn, and he started to play at dances.

Juan: And the polkas, then, of *mexicanos* here are different from German polkas?

Santiago: Well, they are a little different, but as I've told you, that music always came from Germany. Because, well, my father learned it from the Germans, and then other accordionists, hearing my father play, started to play the same ones, with the same rhythm, right? But I think the music came from Germany.

Juan: Your father, what was his name?

Santiago: Patricio Jiménez.

Juan: And before him, did you know of anyone, a *mexicano,* who also played the accordion?

Santiago: No. There in the *barrio* where I was born, he was the only accordionist there was.

Juan: Here in San Antonio?

Santiago: Yes, here in San Antonio. They called it the *barrio* of La Piedrera [the Quarry]. That is precisely why I composed that polka "La Piedrera." And in those days dances were just held in people's homes. There weren't any microphones, there weren't any amplifiers, nothing like that. Just the accordion and guitar. In the way they held those dances, back in those days, it would've been about 1920 or 1925, when I was barely ten years old . . . My father played in the *barrio* of La Piedrera every eight days, every Saturday. The young people from there in the same *barrio* would all get together, and the way they did the dances, they would move the furniture into another room and they'd leave one room clear for dancing. And then the dances would last, oftentimes, from eight at night until seven in the morning.

Juan: Was your father also from San Antonio?

Santiago: Yes, he was born in Eagle Pass, then he came here to San Antonio.

Juan: Did you go to school here in San Antonio?

Santiago: Yes, I went to school. The school I went to was on Magnolia Street, over here by Brackenridge Park. The school was called González. It's still there, but I don't know if they still hold classes there, but the building is still there.

Juan: And at what age did you start there?

Santiago: I was about seven years old when I began to go to school.

Juan: And you went until when?

Santiago: Well, I only got to number six.

Juan: And, let's say, that's all the formal education you have?

Santiago: Exactly, yes. Because at that time my father started to be ill. We started to grow up a little and we had to maintain the house, me and one of my brothers. That's why I didn't have much schooling.

Juan: So then you started to play when you were about ten years old?

Santiago: Yes, about ten or twelve years old. But I wasn't known yet, I only played at home. Somewhere around the age of twenty, as I just said, I began to become known, because Mr. Dávila, of the radio station KEDA, he was the one who took me for the very first time to the microphones, so that people could hear me on the radio. And that's where I started to become known. And I am very grateful to them because they were the ones who really opened the door for me, to get to where I got, making records. When they found out about listening to my songs and all on the radio, right away many record companies inquired about where I lived and all to make records.

Juan: So before you had recorded, you started to play on the radio, here at Radio KEDA?

Santiago: Exactly. In those days, it wasn't called KEDA, they called it *La Hora Anáhuac* . . .

Juan: Ah, yes.

Santiago: . . . which they've started up again at the station.

Juan: Yes, of course. So then it was about 1933, right, when you began to play on the radio?

Santiago: Yes, exactly, about '36. No, about '33, about '33, because it was about '36 when I launched my first record out on the market.

Juan: What was the first record?

Santiago: Well, I'm not certain, I'm not too sure, but it seems that it was a polka that we called "El aguacero polca." [*He later remembered that it was the polka "Dices pescao."*]

Juan: Was it your own composition?

Santiago: No, it was a tune that my father played. I don't know who the composer of that tune would be, but my father played that tune and I liked it enough to record it. And I recorded several others that my father played, like the waltz "La tuna," and so on.

Juan: And where did those songs come from?

Santiago: Well, I don't really know where my father learned those songs. I learned them from him, and since he never recorded, well, I liked them and made records out of them, and it was a success.

Well, they also sold pretty well. Even to this day other artists have recorded them, and those tunes still sell.

Juan: And what did you record with? The instruments: accordion, and what else?

Santiago: Accordion, *bajo sexto,* and the contrabass, which they call the *tololoche.*

Juan: They used to tell me that early on they used only the accordion, *bajo* or guitar, and also a drum. That in different places they used a drum made out of hide. Do you know anything about that?

Santiago: Well, yes. Some of them used a drum too. But I only used the *bajo sexto,* and even to this day I use it when I record, and the contrabass, and the accordion.

Juan: With whom did you make those first records?

Santiago: The first recordings I made were with the Decca company.

Juan: From here, in San Antonio?

Santiago: No, they were, I believe, from California. They came here to San Antonio to record me.

Juan: Do you still have any old records?

Santiago: Well, yes . . . actually no . . . well, I might have, I might have one somewhere from those first records I made. Some I would loan out and they wouldn't come back, and like that.

Juan: Who has those records? Do you know of anyone?

Santiago: Well, I do have a first cousin who takes care of them as you would your home. He's got about five or six of the first recordings I made.

Juan: Then you hit it pretty big in those days, right?

Santiago: Yes, well, those first records were . . . well, it was really something because in those times, there weren't many who played or made records. The first records that I made became hits right away. And since I was very well known here in San Antonio, well . . . people always gave me a lot of support, and they started to buy records. And even to this day, the last album that Flaco Jiménez and I recorded has sold very well.

Juan: In those days, early on, when you left school, did you start to work? What were you doing?

Santiago: Well, I worked a lot, just in little jobs that I would carry out, like the first job that I had, later on, was waxing floors and sanding floors. I liked doing that, sanding floors and making them new again and all that. And I worked about five years during the war at Fort Sam Houston. That was later.

Juan: And when you started to play, were you working?

Santiago: I would play and I would work. There was a nightclub over here on, I believe it was, Laredo Street, close to Camaron Street, thereabouts, it was called the Perales Nite Club. There I played for a year. I would play there and I would also work. At night I'd play, and during the day I'd work. Until one day I decided to concentrate on playing, and I made my living playing for something like . . . I think some twelve or thirteen years. I made my living playing, and that's all.

Juan: That would be in what year?

Santiago: Well, it was about 1940, until about 1952, something like that.

Juan: Would you play all over the state, out of town?

Santiago: Well, in those days I didn't go too far, just around here: Seguin, San Marcos, Cotulla, Dilley, Devine, Carlota [Charlotte], all those little towns close by, and in San Antonio, that's where I would play. Where I played regularly for many years was at El Gaucho. They called it El Gaucho, at Navidad Street and El Paso.

Juan: Let's see, can you name some of the polkas you recorded, just in a list, the names only?

Santiago: Well, yes, as I told you earlier: "El aguacero," "El Cotulla," "La Piedrera," "Una mañana de abril," "Margarita," and so on. I don't remember the others, but, it's along those lines.

Juan: Yes, and those are your own recordings, or compositions, right?

Santiago: Some of them, yes.

Juan: Which ones?

Santiago: Well, the one that I made very popular and which is still heard a lot is "Viva Seguín," "La Piedrera," and "El aguacero," which I recorded first. That one has never died either, it's still heard a lot around here. But, one of the most famous that is still heard everywhere, and which has been recorded by many artists, *orquestas* too, is "Viva Seguín."

Juan: "Viva Seguín," I play that one myself. You see, I'm also following in your tradition. Your son taught me, Santiago Jiménez, Jr.

Santiago: Is that so?

Juan: When I was ten years old. And I played with him, too.

Santiago: Imagine that. How nice!

Juan: When did you get married?

Santiago: I was married in '36.

Juan: Here, in San Antonio?

Santiago: Yes, here in San Antonio.

Juan: And how many children did you have?

Santiago: Well, we had eight. Eight children, yes. Only two girls. The eldest is named Antonia, and then Flaco Jiménez, and then Luis, and then Rubén, Roberto, Adriana. Well then, all of them are grown, thank God, and some got married, and they're living with their families.

Juan: And of them how many became musicians?

Santiago: Well, of the most famous . . . almost all my children play a little—those that don't play guitar, play the accordion. But the best known was Flaco Jiménez, and Santiago Jr.

Juan: Now Santiago Jr. is making it big, right?

Santiago: He's also making it pretty big. And hopefully God will help him and he'll do even better.

Juan: Well, after 1952, what happened? Did you start back to work again? Did you keep playing?

Santiago: Well, yes, I stopped playing for a time and I left for this little town of Dallas. I was there for eleven years working in a seminary, head of the janitorial staff. There's hardly any work there, but since I knew the work, as I explained to you, of sanding floors and everything, it's what they did there, and I would tell them how to do it. And I was there for eleven years.

Juan: Until when?

Santiago: I was there until '79. And then I came back here to San Antonio again, and I've been here for about three years now, since I left there.

Juan: And did you stop playing for all that time?

Santiago: All that time, I stopped playing. I would only play when there was a wedding, a party, but I wasn't playing regularly, I was just working. And I already retired from there. I turned sixty-five there, and then I retired from working. And I just came to San Antonio and, well, a lot of people know me here . . . Jimmy's Restaurant, which is on Rittiman Road, hired me. He wanted me to play for him, and it doesn't seem like it, but look here, I've been with Jimmy for three years now, playing ever since I came back from over there, from Dallas. I started with the music once again. And now I play there every once in a while. I don't want to take on too many gigs because I get a little tired now.

Juan: How many albums did you record?

Santiago: I recorded very few albums. Right now I only have about three of them. They were mostly just 45s in those days.

Juan: You recorded more 45s, right?

Santiago: Yes, a lot of them.

Juan: How many, approximately?

Santiago: Well, of recordings, I've made more or less over a hundred records.

Juan: For which companies did you record?

Santiago: I recorded with several companies. I recorded with Decca, I recorded with Mercury, I recorded with Corona, with RCA Victor, also with Columbia.

Juan: Columbia is a big company, isn't it?

Santiago: Yes, RCA Victor, too. Well, I've made more than twelve records for RCA Victor.

Juan: Many compositions . . .

Santiago: My own compositions and some by some other composers, too. But, almost everything I've recorded are only my own compositions.

Juan: When did you begin using a drummer?

Santiago: Well, the drummer came in after the thirties, I believe. So before that, it was always just the accordion and the guitar, and the *bajo*. I've never recorded with drums. No, just with the stand-up bass, *bajo sexto*, and accordion, to this day, because I like it that what I play sounds like that. No, because the drums also sound very very nice, but I got used to hearing myself that way, and I like it. And every time I go in to record, they ask me if I want to put in drums, or something, and I tell them, well, I would prefer the stand-up bass and the *bajo sexto*, but if it's necessary, well, we'll put in the drums too. But for the most part, I would just record with the *bajo sexto*, contrabass, and accordion.

Juan: And singing, too?

Santiago: I sing, too. I only have a few recordings where I also sing, which have come out, you know, okay. I say okay because from the royalties I get paid, they sell well. They have sold very well.

Juan: Really? That's good! And early on, everyone played sitting down, right?

Santiago: At that time, when I began, you played sitting down. You wouldn't stand up to play. Only the stand-up bass, only on your feet, but when the song was over, or something, well, then you would sit down to rest a while. And it was easier that way than it is now, because now you have to be on your feet. That is, at my age, I can't take much anymore.

Juan: Who do you think was the first accordionist to play standing up like that? Do you know?

Santiago: Would you believe, I don't have any idea who it was that started like that.

Juan: They tell me that early on there wasn't much singing either, that it was just instrumental.

Santiago: Instrumental, exactly, that's the way it was. There wasn't too much singing in those days.

Juan: When you came back here to San Antonio after being over there in Dallas, did you start to play again?

Santiago: Yes, that's right. I wasn't even here two months when right away they called me to come play. And they've called me from various places, but, as I told you, I don't have the stamina anymore. One gig a week is enough for me. I do it so that I won't forget it.

Juan: You also started to record, right? Did you record some albums?

Santiago: Yes, well, the last album that we recorded on the . . . let's see, what is the record called? I forget the name . . .

Juan: Arhoolie Records?

Santiago: Yes, that was the last one I recorded, me and Flaco Jiménez [*Don Santiago Jiménez, with Flaco and Juan Viesca*].

Juan: Do you have plans to record other things?

Santiago: Well, that same man wanted to record me again, but I don't know when he'll come back again, because it's a California company.

Juan: So, here the Chicano has taken the Germans' music and made something different out of it, right?

Santiago: Yes, something different, but that music has always come from there. I've always said it, I don't know if I'm right or if I'm wrong, but that music comes from Germany. It's just that here we've arranged it in another way, right? But it still comes from over there.

Juan: Have you written any new songs lately?

Santiago: Yes, I wrote a few that will be coming out in an album. I gave them to Flaco Jiménez so that he could record them, and you'll be hearing them very soon. They're four or five songs of mine that are going to come out on a record. Joey recorded them. Joey López recorded them for Flaco, and I think that perhaps this month, that new album by Flaco Jiménez will be out. It will include my songs, which I wrote.

Juan: And what do you think of music today?

Santiago: Accordion music, as it is today, for me . . . that music will never die. It will last forever, because the accordion right now is very strong throughout the world. If there's no accordion rhythm, the music just isn't any good. As I understand it, the accordion can fit into any *orquesta, mariachi* . . . and the accordion has always had a very joyful rhythm, which is what the people like, the joy of that music. Now me, when I began to play the accordion, I never thought that the accordion would become . . . that the music would become as famous as it is now.

Juan: I read in a study about accordion music that early on accordion music was kind of for common people, or it was for low-class people, as opposed to *orquesta* music. What do you think? Was that attitude there, something like that?

Santiago: Well, I never thought about it that way, but a lot of people, let's say, who wrote a lot of music, as there still are today, they would say that accordion music, no . . . to them, well, it was nothing, it was just a very ordinary sound. But I never thought of it that way, because from the very beginning I thought that I liked all kinds of music. But the joy of the accordion was greater, it was greater all the time, more than any other music that was being played, like rock and roll, in those days, for instance . . . the Charleston. But a lot of horn blowing over here and horn blowing over there and, to me, it was just like they used to say, that it was monotonous.

Now, the accordion, I always thought, not just because I played it and my father did too, but I thought that accordion music had a very happy rhythm, simple though it might have been, but very happy—which is the thing in music that makes people happy: happiness. Because what good is it to be able to play really, really well and not . . . if it doesn't come from here, right, from the heart, right, whether it's the singer or whether the one who's playing. And what you say is indeed true. I heard many things like that said. But for me, I never thought it would be that way. And now today, all the people are seeing it, and they're hearing it, listening to it day after day, that accordion music is very happy music, and no one can say that it isn't.

Juan: Danceable, too.

Santiago: Yes, very danceable. You could accompany everything too. Today even more because of the accomplished accordionists who are out there, like Ramón Ayala, and all those young people. They play so very well.

Juan: What do you think of Esteban Jordán?

Santiago: He's also one of the best accordionists, he's just tremendous! As far as I'm concerned, I really like how he plays.

Juan: He's done a lot of things on the accordion, right?

Santiago: A lot, a lot. Things that I could never believe would come out of such a little box, like the accordion is.

Juan: The schottische, where does that kind of music come from?

Santiago: The schottische, to be exact, comes from Germany. Yes, sir. The schottische, polkas, redowas, also come [from there], waltzes.

Juan: So then, isn't there any music that comes more from here and not from Germany, with the accordion, right? The *huapango?*

Santiago: Well, the *huapango,* I believe, comes from Mexico, with the *mariachis. Corridos* also come from over there. But as to very old music, it comes, as far as I know, it comes from over there from Germany.

Juan: I thought that the schottische had something else, because the way it's danced is Indian, very Indian.

Santiago: Well, now there are different ways to dance the schottische, but when I saw my father playing the schottische, and the people danced it very different from how they dance them today. Today they dance them real loosely, but not back then. The woman and the man would hold each other, and take two, three steps forward, and two, three steps back, and then the turns on tiptoe, on the tips of their feet. Waltzes, too, they danced on tiptoe. They didn't put their heels down or on the floor, never. The waltz . . .

Juan: It must have been very hard, right?

Santiago: It was beautiful, the way they did it. And now, well, it is danced in all kinds of ways. And now to me, well, many *cumbias* out there today—I never in my life even knew what a *cumbia* was or anything, in those days you didn't hear any of that—well, now I see that the same rhythm . . . there are some, some *cumbias* that are very fast, and there are some *cumbias* that are slower, and you can see it as a polka. The *cumbia,* too, can be danced the same way, it's just that they have other names that they've come out with there. But as far as I know about old music, I only know like the schottisches, waltzes, redowas, and polkas. And the *huapan-*

gos, well, the *huapangos* come from around Mexico, from over there. Those are the dances from long ago.

Juan: I've always seen people dance like this: in a circle, going around. Has that always been done? Or did it begin at a certain time that people began to dance in a circle like that?

Santiago: Well, that's what they call the Paul Jones, I think, right? That is exactly how I would say it, I've seen that, too. I saw it many years back. The Germans also had that. They might have started it later over here, but they called it the Paul Jones, which it's still called, I believe. But now I see very few people dancing it. Back in those days, when I was about thirty-five, around there, they still danced the Paul Jones.

Juan: I remember that we'd play the Paul Jones with Jimmy [Santiago Jr.] at the dances, but it was when the women got inside and the men outside, and they would go in a circle. Then they would sound a horn and they would dance with whoever was in front. That is the Paul Jones I remember.

Santiago: Yes, exactly. That's it.

Juan: Well, maybe, from thereabouts, this style that when we dance, we dance counterclockwise, around and to the left, and still . . . I was thinking that maybe it came from the Paul Jones.

Santiago: Yes, that comes from the Paul Jones.

Juan: And the Paul Jones came from the Germans?

Santiago: Yes, it came from the Germans, because I remember that I would see there in Brackenridge Park, they had dances there sometimes, and many Germans from here in New Braunfels would come there. All of them would come here to Brackenridge Park to the dances, and that's the way they danced it.

Juan: And why did they call it the Paul Jones?

Santiago: I have no idea where that came from, Paul Jones.

Juan: Who knows who Paul Jones was! And they'd say that the German didn't care much for the *mexicano*.

Santiago: No, not at that time. My father had, I believe, many German friends here in New Braunfels, and all that. That is precisely where he learned to play the accordion. He had many German friends, so that some didn't like them, and others did. But yes it's true that the Germans didn't like Mexicans very much.

Juan: Now what do you plan to do in the future?

Santiago: Well, I'm just waiting for good luck, because when you, when you reach an age like mine, well, you can't work, just do odd jobs around the house. Because right now, since I've also been operated on, I can't work, and on top of that, well, I already worked a lot. And thirty-five, forty years of work in my life, and I think that's enough. So me and my wife, Virginia, spend our time just going out once in a while.

Juan: And with your music, what are your plans?

Santiago: Well, to kind of keep on, just to amuse myself. But it's like I'm saying, to not play very much, because too many late nights, I can't handle them like I used to handle them before. So that oftentimes, with just playing one Saturday, that's enough to practice and not forget completely. And when there are some recordings, well, also. Maybe one of these days we'll make another album to leave the people some memories.

Juan: There you go, that's the beauty of it! Well, I am very pleased to have had the opportunity to be here, talking with you, since you are one of the greats in conjunto music here in Texas and, well, all of the United States. And I believe that there'll still be many fine things that you will leave to those of us who are following this tradition of conjunto music. I wish you luck.

Santiago: Thank you very much. Let it be so.

21

Valerio Longoria

✧

MAX MARTÍNEZ
1983

(English translation: page 287)

En la última década se ha visto mucho interés en la música chicana, particularmente la música llamada "música de conjunto". Por primera vez en la historia chicana, hemos visto esta música —que originó en el norte de México y el sur de Tejas— intelectualizada a través de estudios académicos, lecturas, artículos, discursos y demás. En este discurso formal sobre la música de conjunto surgen varios individuos quienes han contribuido al desarrollo y el avance de esta música.

Uno de los primeros músicos, realmente acordeonista, es Valerio Longoria. Justamente es apodado como el "genio" del acordeón. Si Narciso Martínez llevó al conjunto desde los ranchos, los salones y los barrios a los estudios de grabación, Valerio Longoria llevó la música de conjunto a otro nivel, tan complejo como progresivo.

Platicando con Valerio Longoria, luego luego da la impresión de que es, aunque con sesenta años encima, un hombre inquieto, lleno de energía, un hombre amante de la vida, siempre buscando las novedades del mundo. Será esa actitud, quizás desarrollada desde muy joven, que le sirvió como impulso para llevar la música de conjunto a una complejidad inesperada, tomando en cuenta las limitaciones del instrumento principal, el acordeón.

Valerio Longoria es responsable por las siguientes innovaciones en la música de conjunto: fue el primero, y aún es uno de los pocos, en cantar y tocar el acordeón al mismo tiempo; fue el primero que grabó con batería; fue el primero que experimentó con el tono del acordeón, afinándolo en nuevos tonos; fue el que introdujo al bolero en la música de conjunto.

Valerio Longoria tiene casi cincuenta años de estar tocando el acordeón, y casi cuarenta años de estar grabando, principalmente sus propias composiciones. Hace dos años regresó a su estado natal, Tejas, para empezar de nuevo aquí su carrera como recording artist. *Le sigue con el entusiasmo de uno mucho más joven. Durante su ausencia de Tejas, su música siguió viva, la siguieron tocando otros conjuntos.*

El año pasado, Valerio Longoria fue homenajeado al ser admitido al Conjunto Music Hall of Fame.

La siguiente entrevista se llevó a cabo el 11 de abril.

Max: ¿Cuándo comenzó a tocar el acordeón?

Valerio: Tenía como algunos siete, ocho años cuando me compró una acordeón mi padre. Era una acordeoncita que compró en unos diez dólares, de dos teclados. Y, con esa acordeoncita me fui enseñando poco a poco.

Max: ¿Solo? O hubo alguien quien . . .

Valerio: No, nadie me dio clases de acordeón. Yo solo aprendí, mirando otros músicos como Narciso Martínez. Yo pienso que Narciso Martínez es el primer *recording artist* en el estado de Tejas, ¿verdad?, porque grabó muchísimos discos.

Max: ¿Cuándo tocó en público por primera vez?

Valerio: Pos, desde muy chico. Desde que aprendí el acordeón. En otras palabras, cuando estaba chamaco ya me ocupaban para tocar en porecitos así que hacían allí en el pueblo. Me enseñé allí en Harlingen, en el Valle de Tejas, y de muy chico comencé a tocar en bailecitos, así, bodas, bautizos y qué sé yo . . . fiestecitas que hacían, cumpleaños que hacía la gente.

Max: ¿Solo, o acompañado?

Valerio: Acompañado con guitarra, y bajo sexto a veces. Entonces no usábamos tambora. Usábamos un *bass*. Entonces, *bass*, guitarra, bajo sexto y acordeón.

En aquel tiempo, me acuerdo que comenzábamos nosotros a tocar en las plataformas que había en los ranchos. Empezábamos a las siete, las ocho, y tocábamos hasta las siete, las ocho del otro día. Tocábamos toda la noche y me acuerdo que nos pagaban cuatro dólares. A mí, sólo del acordeón, me pagaban cuatro dólares, y al de la guitarra le pagaban cuatro dólares también, y a los demás.

Pos, no me acuerdo cuánto cobraban por el baile. Cuando andaban bailando, allí les cobraban cada pieza. Eso sería a daime cada pieza, y las muchachas que bailaban también acostumbraban ganar un nicle, ¿verdad?, del bailador. La casa les pagaba a las muchachas, la casa le cobraba al bailador. Solo que se rayaban.

¡Imagínate, nomás, tantas horas que había y las piezas que hacíamos! Las empresas nos decían que hiciéramos las piezas cortitas, solo que unas dos vueltas y ¡*boom!*, se acaba la pieza y a cobrar. Y nomás se acababa de cobrar, y allí había un pito que nos pitaba, y ya sabíamos que cuando pitaba el pito nos arrancábamos tocando otra vez de vuelta. Pitaba el pito y nos parábamos. A veces la hacía cortita y ahí está el pito de vuelta, nos paramos, y asina.

Max: ¿Qué composiciones tocaban? ¿De ustedes, o de moda, o qué?
Valerio: Las polcas, pos, de las que aprendíamos, ¿verdad? Unas de Narciso y otras de otros músicos que aprendíamos, y le revolvíamos del pico al mozo con "El clavelito" y todas esas piezas. Y así fuimos trabajando, diremos, hasta ahorita. Comenzamos en Harlingen. Yo vivía en Harlingen y salíamos a tocar en Raymondville, a un lugar que se llamaba Los Coyotes. Allí en un ladito había una plataforma que le decían La Princesita y otra plataforma que le decían Los Jacalitos. Tú sabes, este, en Raymondville era pura plataforma. Pos, nosotros mexicanos, antes, en esos años, qué íbamos a ocupar un salón, ¿no? A veces era piso de tierra.

Entonces, debajo de un árbol, colgaban las lámparas, de esas de gasolina. Cada rato andaban echándole aire a las lámparas para que dieran luz. Colgaban tres, cuatro lámparas en un cordón de alambre, de un árbol a otro. Y pos daba mucha luz.

Pero, el piso era de tierra. Antes de llegar a los bailes se miraba el polvadero. Allá nomás mirábamos el polvadero y sabíamos que era el baile. Porque cuando andaban bailando todos, levantaban el polvo. Las muchachas salían con medias. No necesitaban medias entonces, porque salían con medias de tierra.

Pos, la gente nomás se rodeaba y se paraba. No había asientos para sentarse. Nomás ponían banquillas alrededor del patio. Allí se sentaban las mujeres nomás. Los hombres siempre andaban parados al aire libre, era todo al aire libre. Los hombres andaban ahí, con la botella en la mano, bailando. Nomás bailaban y se salían, bailaban y se paraban.

Entonces, nosotros nos juntábamos en un lado o debajo de un arbolito, y con unas sillas o algo que nos ponían, y allí comenzábamos a tocar.

Max: Bueno, después de ese comienzo, ¿cuándo llegaron a tocar en un salón?

Valerio: Pos, de salones hasta muy después, diremos. Sí, más o menos, ya cuando comenzamos a grabar aquí en San Antonio. El caso es que llegué aquí en San Antonio a fines del '45. Llegué del *army*, ¿verdad? Fue cuando me llamó el ejército aquí. Como me vine a registrar el '42 aquí en San Antonio, de ahí a fines de '45 me llamaron ya para entrar. Pero, yo estuve corto tiempo en el *army*. Fui a Alemania. Cuando fui para allá, este, no llevaba acordeón. Allá conseguí una y también toqué en lugares alemanes, en *nightclubs*, ¿verdad? Pos, me recibieron muy bien, porque la gente de allá aprecia mucho a la acordeón. Pos de allí viene el acordeón. Me miraban tocar a mí, y yo moreno y ellos güeros, ¿me entiendes cómo te digo?, les caía grato a aquéllos que yo tocara la acordeón, ¿verdad?

Tocaba las polcas que aprendí aquí. Simplemente, pos "El barrilito" lo aprendí aquí, pero "El barrilito" es alemán. Ellos lo hicieron allá, es netamente alemán. Les tocaba "El barrilito" y n'hombre, ¡les gustaba mucho!

Entonces, después de Alemania me vine para acá el '46 y fue cuando comencé a hacer por grabar aquí. Vestido de soldado, toqué en un lugar que le decían La Estrellita. Yo creo que sería uno de los primeros lugares de San Antonio donde tocaban la acordeón o, diremos, polcas. Estaba por aquí por la Castroville, para allá, pa' afuera. Y allí tocaban Los Hermanos Villarreal, quienes fueron los primeros que conocí aquí tocando en San Antonio, en bailes.

Naturalmente que también existía "El Gallito", Jesús Casiano, uno de los más viejos acordeonistas de aquí de San Antonio. Entonces vivía él, pero no tocaba mucho, no sé por qué. En otras palabras, tocaba de cada en cuando el señor, pos ya era señor grande cuando yo era joven, ¿verdad? Yo lo alcancé a ver tocando, en ocasiones, en bailecitos asina de aquí.

Como te digo, comencé tocando en La Estrellita, y de ahí hicieron un lugar más pa'l centro, por la Castroville, que le pusieron El Cielito Lindo. Entonces, yo hice una polca que se llamaba "Cielito polca", para el lugar ese. Era un lugar grandísimo y se llenaba de mucha gente. Pos, era el único lugar grande que había entonces de polca en San Antonio.

Max: ¿Cómo se hizo el contacto para grabar?

Valerio: Pos, el señor me oyó una vez que iba pasando por ahí, cuando estaba tocando en una cantina por la calle Santa Rosa. La cantina se llamaba El Topo Chico, el dueño era el señor Víctor Olivares. Tal vez, este señor Rangel iba pasando por ahí y me vio tocar. Él fue el que me habló que si quería grabar. Le dije que ¡sí, cómo no! Entonces fue cuando fuimos y grabamos la primer grabación.

Max: ¿Cómo se llama la grabación?

Valerio: La primer grabación con el señor Rangel fue una polca mía que se llamaba "El polquerito". Por el otro lado, canté una canción que se llamaba "Jesús Cadena", que aquí le decían "La güera Chavela", ¿verdad?, pero que es "Jesús Cadena". Ése fue el primer disco. Con ésa pegué bastante, y después pegué con "Chiquitita", una canción de Manuel Apodaca de Nueva York. Y después seguimos grabando así, ¿verdad?, varias canciones. No me acuerdo de todos los nombres, para qué echarle más que la verdad. Tantos años, ¿verdad?

Max: ¿Cómo pagaban los discos que grababan?

Valerio: Quince dólares por los dos lados. Le grababa el disco por los dos lados, me daba quince dólares. Mucho tiempo estuve grabando por quince dólares el disco, aquí en San Antonio, con el señor Rangel. De ahí, me pasé al Ideal. Los cuantos años que pasé con la compañía Ideal, me pagaban veinticinco el disco. La compañía que me pagó más fue la Falcón. La Falcón me pagaba a mí . . . me parece que nos daba setenta y cinco dólares a cada uno, a mí y al guitarrero.

Cuando grabamos el primer disco por quince dólares, asegún entiendo, en quince días, o dos semanas, vendió el señor dos mil copias. Sería como a sesenta y nueve centavos el disco. Ya estaba carito el disco porque era grande. Me figuro que eran . . . que valían cerca del dólar los discos de setenta y ocho revoluciones. No había *cassettes,* ni *eight-tracks,* ni nada en esos años.

Había LPs, pero las compañías mexicanas, diremos de aquí de este lado, de los Estados Unidos, no los hacían. Apenas estaban comenzando las compañías y lo que rifaba era el disco grande para las pianolas.

El primer LP lo grabé con Falcón. Fueron los primeros que me sacaron LP. Ya cuando iba sacando el LP Falcón, el Ideal sacó uno con los discos que ya tenía grabado con ellos. Sacó uno la compañía Ideal y la compañía Falcón sacó otro, y así me fui.

Pos, en el Valle fui muy conocido porque de ahí era la compañía Ideal. Solo que salía disco de la Ideal y luego luego se desparramaba por todo el Valle de Tejas. Ya había grabado con el señor Rangel aquí, pero yo hice la primer grabación de la compañía Corona aquí en San Antonio. Ya estaba fuerte en fama cuando comencé con la Ideal.

Max: ¿Ve alguna diferencia en esos días y hoy?

Valerio: Bueno, la diferencia, pos casi ni tiene diferencia. Nomás es que el equipo se amejoró, ¿verdad? En otras palabras, los micrófonos que usábamos simplemente para grabar, pos, para todo el conjunto usábamos uno o dos micrófonos. Nos rodeaban a todos al micrófono para grabar, imagínate. No había máquinas grandes para grabar en los Estados Unidos. Tal vez nomás en las compañías grandes, como la Columbia, la Victor, tenían todo. Las compañías tenían estudios muy grandes, pero las compañías que comenzaban aquí en Tejas, pos, diremos, comenzaban a grabarte, pero en máquinas chicas, no en máquinas grandes como ora. Grabábamos en uno o dos canales. Ahora hay hasta treinta canales para grabar.

En esas ocasiones, si hacías un equívoco, muchas veces así lo dejaban en el disco. Un equívoco poquito. Porque era mucho trabajo arrendarte y comenzar todos otra vez de nuevo. Ahora, no. Ahora si haces un equívoco o algo cuando estás grabando, le sigues grabando hasta que acabes el disco. Después arriendan el *tape* y allí se compone el equívoco por el que lo hizo. Con bastantes canales, si se equivocó uno de los compañeros, no necesita uno pararse hasta que termine la pieza, y después se arrienda el *tape* en el canal donde se equivocó el otro, y nomás le parcha. Es como parchar el tubo de una llanta.

Max: ¿Qué ocasionó su ausencia del estado de Tejas?

Valerio: El '59 me fui para Chicago. Iba contratado nomás por tres meses. Pensaba ir y venir, pero me gustó mucho Chicago y me quedé siete años allí en Chicago.

Estuve tocando y grabando. Grabé un LP con una compañía que se llama Firma. Salí en una gira para Florida y en Miami me quedé tres años, y grabé otro LP y muchos discos chicos.

Después de tres años me fui a Chicago de vuelta, y de ahí me salí en otra gira para rumbo a Colorado, Arizona, hasta Los Ángeles. Allí me quedé siete años más, en Los Ángeles. También tengo discos grabados en California, tengo LPs grabados con una compañía que se llama Volcán.

Nomás que mis discos no llegaban a Tejas, solo que en Tejas se fue acabando la música mía. Entonces, este, muchos dijieron que ya me había matado allá en donde estaba, que en Chicago me habían matado. Entonces, Tony de la Rosa grabó como unas cuatro piezas en un disco que se llama *Polcas Inolvidables*. Ese disco que grabó Tony de la Rosa fue porque creían en verdad que me habían matado. Luego que me les voy apareciendo en Tejas de vuelta. Ya se dieron cuenta que no era cierto que me habían matado. Pero ya estaba viviendo allá, en Chicago, solo que me fui pa' atrás.

Entonces, tengo un amigo aquí que me manda a decir, cuando estaba en Los Ángeles últimamente, que Los Dos Gilbertos andaban grabando todas las piezas mías. El señor Albino Arredondo, de aquí en San Antonio, me trajo de California de vuelta, hace dos años. Pos tenía más de veinte años de no estar en Tejas de pie, diremos, viviendo. Solo que me vine de un jalón a Tejas, a quedarme, y comencé a grabar con Discos Joey. Ahorita ya tengo dos LPs con Joey. Mis últimas grabaciones han tenido mucho resultado. Pero Los Dos Gilbertos grabaron toda mi música. La quisieron grabar igual, porque se copiaron de grabaciones mías, ¿verdad? Un compadre de Gilberto le pasó los discos. De allí los sacó Gilberto, y los sacó con las mismas pasadas mías. Ahí nomás le revuelve otra cosita.

Ya estoy aquí de vuelta. Se está dando cuenta que estoy aquí de vuelta y muchos van a ver si es el mismo, porque comencé a muy temprana edad a grabar. Dicen, "Ese hombre no puede ser Valerio Longoria", y van y se desengañan, y dicen, "Pos sí, es cierto, es Valerio Longoria todavía".

Max: ¿Cuáles de los conjuntos actuales te gustan más?
Valerio: Jordán. Esteban Jordán. No ha habido otro acordeonista en los Estados Unidos. Yo no creo que haiga habido otro acordeonista, ni en México, que toque como toca Esteban Jordán. Está muy liviano para tocar, y toca muchas clases de música, comenzando con *soul* y todo eso. Fue el primero que sacó a pesa de lo electrónico, comenzó a meterle electrónica al acordeón. En otras palabras, trae muchos instrumentos electrónicos que hacen el acordeón que haga diferentes sonidos. Como, trae eco, trae *phaser*, trae todo eso.

Max: ¿Qué opina de los conjuntos de México?

Valerio: Bueno, pos, yo he visto conjuntos de México que están tremendísimos, muy fuertes, como Ramón Ayala. Toca mucho muy bien Ramón.

Max: ¿Adónde va el conjunto?

Valerio: A todo el mundo. Tengo un aparato que agarra a Colombia, agarra a London, agarra a Brasil, agarra a todo el mundo, y oigo acordeón. La acordeón, 'ondequiera se oye. ¿Adónde va? A todo el mundo.

Valerio Longoria

MAX MARTÍNEZ
1983

(Entrevista original: página 279)

In the last decade, there has been a lot of interest in Chicano music, particularly what is called "conjunto music." For the first time in Chicano history, we have seen this music, which originated in the north of Mexico and in South Texas, intellectualized in academic studies, lectures, articles, discourses, and more. In these formal discussions of conjunto music, several individuals emerge who have contributed to the development and advance of this music.

One of the first musicians, in truth an accordionist, is Valerio Longoria. He is justly known as the "genius" of the accordion. If Narciso Martínez took the conjunto from the farms, the dance halls, and the barrios to the recording studios, Valerio Longoria took conjunto music to another level, as complex as it was progressive.

Speaking with Valerio Longoria, one quickly gets the impression that, although over sixty years old, he is a restless man, a bundle of energy, a man who loves life, always looking for new things the world might offer. It could be this attitude, perhaps acquired at a very young age, that helped him to take conjunto music to an unexpected complexity, considering the limitations of its principal instrument, the accordion.

Valerio Longoria is responsible for the following innovations in conjunto music: He was the first, and still is one of the few, who sing and play the accordion at the same time; he was the first to record with drums; he was the first to experiment with the tone of the accordion, tuning it in different keys; he was the one who introduced the bolero *to conjunto music.*

Valerio Longoria has been playing the accordion for nearly fifty years, and he has been recording for almost forty years, mainly his own compositions. Two years ago, he returned to his native Texas to begin anew his career as a recording artist. He pursues it with the enthusiasm of a much younger man. During his absence from Texas, his music stayed alive, maintained in the repertoire of other conjuntos.

Last year, Valerio Longoria was honored by being inducted into the Conjunto Music Hall of Fame.

The following interview was conducted on April 11.

Max: When did you start to play the accordion?
Valerio: I was about seven, eight years old when my father bought me an accordion. It was a little accordion that he bought for some ten dollars, with two rows of buttons. And, with that little accordion, I began to teach myself, little by little.
Max: By yourself? Or was there someone who . . .
Valerio: No, no one gave me lessons on the accordion. I learned on my own, watching other musicians, like Narciso Martínez. I think that Narciso Martínez was the first recording artist in the state of Texas, right, because he made so many records.
Max: When did you play in public for the first time?
Valerio: Well, since I was very young. Ever since I learned to play the accordion. In other words, when I was a young boy they were already hiring me to play for little parties that they would have there in town. I taught myself there in Harlingen, in the Valley, and as a very young boy I started to play for little dances, like that, weddings, baptisms, and who knows what . . . small *fiestas* that they had, birthday parties that people gave.
Max: Solo, or accompanied?
Valerio: Accompanied by guitar, and sometimes *bajo sexto*. We didn't use a drum back then. We used a bass. Back then, bass, guitar, *bajo sexto,* and accordion.

In those days, I remember that we started playing on the [dance] platforms that they had on the ranches. We would start at seven, eight, and we'd play until seven, eight the next day. We'd play all night, and I recall that they'd pay us four dollars. Me alone on the accordion, they'd pay me four dollars, and the one on guitar, they'd pay him four dollars too, and to the others.

Well, I don't remember what they charged for the dance. When people were dancing, there they'd charge them for each dance. That would've been a dime per tune, and the girls who would dance were accustomed to getting a nickel, right, from the partner. The house would pay the girls, the house would collect from the [male] dancer. So they made out real well.

Just imagine how many hours it was, and the tunes we played. The management would tell us to make the tunes short, so one or two turns and boom, the tune is over and off to collect. And as soon as the collecting was done, and there would be a horn that would blow for us, and we already knew that when the horn blew we'd start playing once more again. The horn would blow and we would stop. Sometimes, they'd make it short and there's the horn again, we stop, and like that.

Max: What compositions did you play? Yours, or popular ones, or what?

Valerio: The polkas, well, the ones that we learned, right? Some by Narciso and others by other musicians that we learned, and we'd mix it up across the board, with "El clavelito" and all those tunes. And that's the way we worked, let's say, until today. We started in Harlingen. I lived in Harlingen, and we would go to play in Raymondville, to a place called Los Coyotes. There, to one side, was a [dance] platform which they called La Princesita, and another platform that they called Los Jacalitos. You know, in Raymondville it was just platforms. Because back then, how were we *mexicanos* ever going to get into a dance hall, right? Sometimes it was a dirt floor.

So then, under a tree, they'd hang lanterns, those gasoline ones. Every now and then they would pump air into the lanterns, so they'd stay lit. They'd hang three, four lanterns on a wire cord, from one tree to another. And so it gave a lot of light.

But it was a dirt floor. Before getting to the dances, you'd see the clouds of dust. As soon as we saw the clouds of dust we'd know that it was the dance. Because when they all got to dancing, they'd whip up the dust. The girls would leave with stockings. They didn't need stockings back then, because they'd leave the dance with dirt stockings.

Well, the people would just mill around and stand around. There were no seats to sit on. They'd just put old benches around the patio. Only the women would sit there. The men were always standing outdoors, everything was outdoors. The men would be there, bottle in hand, dancing. They would just dance and leave, dance and stand around.

So we would gather to one side or under a little tree, and with some chairs or something that they'd put out for us, and there we'd start to play.

Max: Well, after that beginning, when did you first get to play in a dance hall?

Valerio: Now, dance halls, not until long afterward, let's say. Yes, more or less, not till we began to record here in San Antonio. The thing is, I got here to San Antonio toward the end of '45. I came out of the army, you know. That was when the army drafted me here. Since I came here to San Antonio to register in '42, from there until the end of '45 they finally called me in. But I was only in the army for a short time. I went to Germany. When I went over there, I didn't take an accordion. I got one there, and I also played in German places, in nightclubs, you see. Well, they received me very well, because the people over there really appreciate the accordion. Of course, the accordion comes from there. They would see me play, and me brown skinned and them light skinned, if you know what I'm saying, it was pleasing to them that I played the accordion, really.

I would play the polkas that I learned here. Frankly, well, I learned "El barrilito" here, but "El barrilito" ["Beer Barrel Polka"] is German. They composed it over there, it is purely German. I'd play "El barrilito," and man, they loved it!

Then after Germany, I came here in '46 and that's when I started trying to record here. Dressed as a soldier, I played in a place called La Estrellita. I think it was one of the first places in San Antonio where they played the accordion, or, let's say, polkas. It was over here on Castroville, on the way out of town. And Los Hermanos Villarreal played there. They were the first ones I met playing here in San Antonio, at the dances.

Of course, there was also "El Gallito," Jesús Casiano, one of the oldest accordionists from here in San Antonio. He was still living then, but he didn't play much, I don't know why. In other words, the gentleman played from time to time, as he was already an older man when I was a young man, you see. I managed to see him playing here, on occasion, at little dances and the like.

As I told you, I began playing at La Estrellita, and after that they built a place closer in to downtown, on Castroville, which they named El Cielito Lindo. Then I composed a polka which was called "Cielito Polka," after that place there. It was a huge place and it would fill up with a lot of people. Well, it was the only large polka place there was in San Antonio back then.

Max: How did you make the contact to record?

Valerio: Well, the man heard me once when he was passing by, as I was playing in a saloon on Santa Rosa Street. The saloon was called El Topo Chico, the owner was Mr. Víctor Olivares. Maybe this Mr. Rangel was passing by there and he saw me play. He was the one who called me, about whether I wanted to record. I told him, yes, of course! It was then that we went and made the first recording.

Max: What's the recording called?

Valerio: The first recording with Mr. Rangel was a polka of mine which was called "El polquerito." On the flip side, I sang a song called "Jesús Cadena," which here they called "La güera Chavela," right, but which is really "Jesús Cadena." That was the first record. It was a big hit, and then we had a hit with "Chiquitita," a song by Manuel Apodaca of New York. And after that we kept recording, you know, different songs. I don't remember all the titles, no point in saying any more than the truth. So many years, right?

Max: How were you paid for the records you made?

Valerio: Fifteen dollars for both sides. I'd make both sides of the record, he'd give me fifteen dollars. For a long time, I recorded for fifteen dollars a record, here in San Antonio, with Mr. Rangel. From there, I went on to Ideal [Records]. The few years I spent with the Ideal company, they paid me twenty-five per record. The company that paid me the most was Falcón. Falcón would pay me . . . I think they'd give us seventy-five each, me and the guitarist.

When we made the first record for fifteen dollars, as I understand it, in fifteen days, or two weeks, the man sold two thousand copies. That would be at sixty-nine cents a record. Records were getting expensive because they were large. I figure that they were . . . that the 78-rpm records cost close to a dollar. There weren't any cassettes, or eight-tracks, or any of that in those years.

There were LPs, but the Mexican companies, let's say from here on this side, in the United States, they didn't make them. The companies were just starting out, and what was going over were the big records [78s] for the jukeboxes.

I recorded my first LP with Falcón. They were the first to come out with an LP of mine. Just as the Falcón LP was coming out, Ideal came out with one from the records I had already made with them. The Ideal company came out with one and the Falcón company came out with another, and it went on like that.

So, I became very well known in the Valley because the Ideal company was from there. So when a record came out on Ideal, right away it was distributed throughout the entire Valley. I had already recorded with Mr. Rangel here, but I made the Corona company's first recording, here in San Antonio. I was already pretty famous when I started with Ideal.

Max: Do you see any difference between those days and now?

Valerio: Well, the difference, there is hardly any difference. It's just that the equipment has gotten better, you see. In other words, the microphones that we used simply for recording, why, we only used one or two microphones for the entire conjunto. They'd group us all together around the microphone to record, if you can imagine that. There weren't any large machines to record with in the United States. Maybe just at the big companies, like Columbia, Victor, they had everything. Those companies had very large studios, but the companies that were starting here in Texas, well, let's say, they would record you, but on small machines, not on the large machines like today. We would record on one or two tracks. Today they have as many as thirty tracks to record on.

In those sessions, if you made a mistake, they'd often leave it that way on the record. A little mistake. Because it was a lot of trouble to go back, and have everybody start all over again. Not today. Now if you make a mistake or something while you're recording, you keep recording until you finish the record. Then they rewind the tape and right there the mistake is fixed by the one who made it. With lots of tracks, if one of the guys makes a mistake, it isn't necessary to stop until the tune is over, and then they rewind the tape on the track where the mistake was made, and they just patch it. It's like patching the inner tube of a tire.

Max: What led to your absence from Texas?

Valerio: In '59 I went to Chicago. I only had a contract for three months. I thought I'd go and come back, but I liked Chicago a lot, and I stayed there in Chicago for seven years.

I played and I recorded. I recorded an LP with a company called

Firma. I went on a tour in Florida, and I stayed for three years in Miami, and I recorded another LP and lots of singles.

After three years, I went back to Chicago again, and from there I went on another tour, bound for Colorado, Arizona, all the way to Los Angeles. I stayed there seven more years, in Los Angeles. I also made records in California, I recorded LPs with a company named Volcán.

Except that my records didn't make it to Texas, so that in Texas my music began to disappear. Then, many began to say that I had gotten killed out where I was, that I'd been killed in Chicago. Then Tony de la Rosa recorded some four tunes in a record called *Polcas Inolvidables*. That record that Tony de la Rosa made was because they really believed that I had been killed. Then all of a sudden I show up in Texas again. Then they realized that it was not true that I had been killed. But I was already living over there, in Chicago, so I went back.

Then, I have a friend here who sent word to me, when I was in Los Angeles the last time, that Los Dos Gilbertos were recording all my tunes. Mr. Alvino Arredondo, from here in San Antonio, brought me from California again, two years ago. Well, it had been more than twenty years since I'd last stood in Texas, let's say, living here. So I came in a straight shot back to Texas, to stay, and I began to record with Joey Records. Right now, I've already got two LPs with Joey. My last recordings have had great results. But Los Dos Gilbertos recorded all of my music. They tried to make it the same, because they copied my recordings, you see. A buddy of Gilberto's gave him the records. Gilberto got them [the tunes] from there, and he recorded them with my own riffs. He just mixes in a little something else there.

Now I'm back again. It's getting around that I'm back again, and many people come to see if it's the same one, because I started to record at a very early age. They say, "That man can't be Valerio Longoria," and they come and they see for themselves and they say, "Well, yes, it's true, it's still Valerio Longoria."

Max: Which of the current conjuntos do you like the best?

Valerio: Jordán. Esteban Jordán. There's not been another accordionist in the United States. I don't believe that there has been another accordionist, not even in Mexico, who can play like Esteban Jordán plays. He's very nimble in his playing, and he plays many kinds of music, starting with soul and all that. He was the first to weigh in with electronics, he began to add electronics to the accordion. In other words, he's got a lot of electronic equipment that allows the accordion to make different sounds. Like, he's got an echo, he's got a phaser, he's got all of that.

Max: What do you think of the Mexican conjuntos?

Valerio: Well, I've seen Mexican conjuntos that are just terrific, really dynamic, like Ramón Ayala. Ramón plays really, really well.

Max: Where is conjunto going?

Valerio: All over the world. I have a set [shortwave radio] that picks up Colombia, it picks up London, it picks up Brazil, it picks up the whole world, and I hear the accordion. You can hear the accordion anywhere. Where is it going? All over the world.

22
Eva Ybarra

✦

JUAN TEJEDA
1986

(English translation: page 298)

Esta corta entrevista con Eva Ybarra, "La Reina del Acordeón", se llevó a cabo en abril de este año.

Juan: Eva, ¿dónde y cuándo naciste?
Eva: Mira, Juan, yo nací aquí en San Antonio el día dos de marzo de 1945. Así es que soy orgullosa de ser sanantoniana cien por ciento.
Juan: 'Ta bueno. ¿Qué son tus primeras memorias dentro de la música, cuando estabas chiquita?
Eva: Bueno, yo empecé a la edad de cinco años. Es que a mí me gustaba mucho el ambiente de la música. Mis hermanos, mi papá, mi mamá —todos eran músicos. Así es que yo les seguí los pasos a ellos.
Juan: ¿Acuál instrumento empezaste a tocar?
Eva: A la edad de seis años empecé a tocar el acordeón, porque mi hermano Pedro tocaba el acordeón y me gustaba mucho. Siempre estaba atrás de ellos y me corrían, en veces, porque había muchos hombres y no había mujeres. Pero yo estaba por el ambiente del acordeón. Por eso lo seguía, y me sentía triste porque me corrían y yo quería estar viendo, escuchando la música.
Juan: ¿Qué fue lo que te atrayó al acordeón?
Eva: No sé exactamente, pero siempre me ha gustado el acordeón, el sonido. Creo que como me gustaba el piano, y no había piano, entonces elegí al acordeón, que es una adaptación del piano. Si hubiera habido un piano, tal vez hubiera elegido al piano.
Juan: ¿Cómo aprendiste a tocar el acordeón?

Eva: Bueno, pa' empezar, nomás viendo, escuchando, tocando. Aprendí yo sola, y después, si yo quería que mi hermano Pedro me ayudara, él me ayudaba. Me daba pisaditas o diferentes polcas.

Juan: ¿Cuándo empezaste a tocar profesionalmente?

Eva: Pues a la edad de seis años, mi papá ya me traía por dondequiera. Después, formamos un grupo, yo y mis hermanos Pedro y David. Todos estábamos jóvenes. No me acuerdo muy bien, pero creo que tenía algunos quince o dieciséis.

Juan: ¿Y después?

Eva: Después, nos separamos yo y mis hermanos, y le seguí de cantante y canté con mariachi, y también toqué acordeón con mariachi. Fui a México y Puerto Rico como solista, y después regresé y toqué con otro grupos, como Rangel and Company y otros. Y ahorita estoy tocando con La Familia Fama, y preparando mi propio conjunto.

Juan: ¿Acuáles acordeonistas han sido tus mayores influencias, vamos a decir, como acordeonista?

Eva: Pues, Óscar Hernández, Paulino Bernal y mi hermano Pedro Ybarra. No es porque sea mi hermano, pero porque es un gran acordeonista también. Y hay muchos acordeonistas buenísimos que me gustan también.

Juan: ¿Y cómo clasificas el acordeón que tocas tú?

Eva: Bueno, no es que yo diga, pero mucha gente me dice que acaricio el acordeón, y otros han dicho que la hago llorar, y así me siento, como me dicen ellos.

Juan: ¿Por qué crees que no hay muchas mujeres acordeonistas?

Eva: Quizás sí haya, nomás que no se han dado a conocer. Pero como dicen todos, hay pocas. Son pocas las que son.

Juan: ¿Por qué crees que existe así?

Eva: No sé cómo decirte. Sé que a mí sí me gustó el acordeón, siendo mujer.

Juan: ¿Y has sabido tú de otras mujeres acordeonistas?

Eva: ¡Sí, cómo no! De California, Chavela, muy buena también. Lupita Rodela, de aquí de San Antonio. Y hay otras, como te dije, pero no se han dado a conocer. En el futuro, va a haber. No van a haber nomás una, o dos, o tres, sino que asina como hay hombres, van a haber muchas mujeres. Es mi opinión. Así lo veo.

Juan: ¿Qué piensas de la música de acordeón, de conjunto? Hay unos que dicen que la música de conjunto y acordeón se está muriendo porque a los jóvenes no les gusta escuchar esta música hoy en día. ¿Qué piensas de eso?

Eva: Pienso que depende en el gusto de cada quien. Para mí, la música de acordeón nunca va a morir. Siempre va a seguir adelante. Es más, yo pienso hacer un día un grupo de muchos acordeones, como una orquesta de acordeones. Para mí, la música de acordeón nunca va a morir, porque es una música muy bonita.

Juan: ¿Qué piensas hacer en el futuro con tu vida musical, tu carrera artística?

Eva: Pues, pienso seguir adelante, seguir estudiando. Nunca se acaba de aprender, como dicen, hasta que los dedos estén parejitos, es cuando se acaba de aprender. Así es que pienso seguir estudiando, seguir adelante.

Juan: Bueno, ¿no hay alguna otra cosa que le gustaría decir?

Eva: Nomás que yo sé que tú me diste la oportunidad de trabajar contigo, dando clases de acordeón. Y así es que me siento muy orgullosa de trabajar contigo, enseñando clases de acordeón. Y ojalá que en el futuro haiga más acordeonistas. No importa que sean hombres o mujeres, pero que no se acabe el acordeón. Para mí, nunca va a morir. Siempre va a seguir adelante.

Eva Ybarra

JUAN TEJEDA
1986

(Entrevista original: página 295)

This short interview with Eva Ybarra, "the Queen of the Accordion," was conducted in April of this year.

Juan: Eva, where and when were you born?
Eva: Look, Juan, I was born here in San Antonio on March 2, 1945. So I am proud to be 100 percent San Antonian.
Juan: That's good. What are your first memories within music, when you were little?
Eva: Well, I started at the age of five. You see, I really liked the musical environment. My brothers, my father, my mother—they were all musicians. So I followed in their footsteps.
Juan: What instrument did you first play?
Eva: At the age of six I started to play the accordion, because my brother Pedro played the accordion and I liked it very much. I was always tagging along after them, and sometimes they'd run me off, because there were a lot of men and there weren't any women. But I was there for the accordion atmosphere. That's why I followed them, and I'd feel sad because they'd run me off, and I wanted to be watching, listening to the music.
Juan: What was it that attracted you to the accordion?
Eva: I don't know exactly, but I have always liked the accordion, the sound of it. I think that since I liked the piano, and there wasn't a piano, I then chose the accordion, which is an adaptation of the piano. If there had been a piano, maybe I would have chosen the piano.

Juan: How did you learn to play the accordion?

Eva: Well, to start with, just by watching, listening, playing. I learned by myself, and later, if I wanted my brother Pedro to help me, he would help me. He'd teach me little runs or different polkas.

Juan: When did you start to play professionally?

Eva: Well, at the age of six my father was already taking me all over the place. Later, we formed a group, me and my brothers Pedro and David. We were all young. I don't remember exactly, but I think I was maybe fifteen or sixteen.

Juan: And afterward?

Eva: Afterward, my brothers and I split up, and I continued as a singer and I sang with a *mariachi,* and I also played the accordion with the *mariachi.* I traveled to Mexico and Puerto Rico as a soloist, and then I returned and played with other groups, like Rangel and Company and others. And right now I'm playing with La Familia Fama, and preparing to start my own conjunto.

Juan: What accordionists have been your major influences, let's say, as an accordionist?

Eva: Well, Óscar Hernández, Paulino Bernal, and my brother Pedro Ybarra. It's not because he's my brother, but because he's also a great accordionist. And there are many excellent accordionists that I like too.

Juan: How would you classify the accordion you play?

Eva: Well, it's not that I'm saying it, but a lot of people tell me that I caress the accordion, and others have said that I make it weep, and that's the way I feel, like they've said.

Juan: Why do you think there aren't many women accordionists?

Eva: Perhaps there are, except that we just don't know about them. But as everyone says, there are just a few. There are only a few of them.

Juan: Why do you think that is?

Eva: I don't know how to tell you. I do know that I liked the accordion, being a woman.

Juan: And have you heard of other women accordionists?

Eva: Yes, of course! From California, Chavela, also really good. Lupita Rodela, from here in San Antonio. And there are others, like I said, but they haven't become known. In the future, there will be. There won't be only one, or two, or three, but just as there are men, there will be many women. That's my opinion. That's how I see it.

Juan: What do you think of accordion music, of conjunto music? There are some who say that conjunto and accordion music is dying out because these days young people don't like to listen to it. What do you think about that?

Eva: I think it depends on individual tastes. As far as I'm concerned, accordion music will never die. It will always keep going. What's more, some day I plan to form a group of many accordions, like an accordion orchestra. As far as I'm concerned, accordion music will never die, because it's a beautiful music.

Juan: What do you plan on doing in the future with your music, with your artistic career?

Eva: Well, I plan to keep going, keep on studying. You never finish learning, as they say, until your fingers are all the same length, that's when you're done learning. So I plan to keep on studying, keep going.

Juan: Well, is there anything else that you would like to say?

Eva: Only that I know you gave me the opportunity to work with you, teaching accordion classes. And so I feel very proud to work with you, teaching accordion classes. And I hope there will be more accordionists in the future. It doesn't matter whether they're men or women, as long as the accordion doesn't disappear. As far as I'm concerned, it will never die. It will always keep going.

23

Bruno Villarreal

❖

CLAYTON T. SHORKEY
1987

(English translation: page 308)

Bruno Villarreal, conocido como El Azote del Valle, nació el 21 de mayo de 1912, en La Grulla, un pueblito en el sur de Tejas, cerca de la frontera mexicana. Casi completamente ciego toda su vida, tenía un talento para la música y empezó a tocar el acordeón de dos líneas de botones desde muy joven. En algún momento de su carrera, cambió al acordeón de piano. De acuerdo con Manuel Peña, autor de The Texas-Mexican Conjunto, *"entre los acordeonistas, el honor de la primera grabación —al menos con las grandes compañías norteamericanas— le pertenece [a Villarreal]. Eso fue en 1928". Para 1935, él ya había hecho alrededor de cincuenta grabaciones, la mayoría de ellas instrumentales, incluyendo "La bella Italia" (polca), "La varsoviana" (mazurca), "La coyota" (vals bajito) y "Los siete pasos" (chotís).*

 La vida era difícil para Bruno Villarreal en esos días. Peña escribe que su padre "lo recuerda, en los 1930, viviendo en un ranchito a tres millas de Santa Rosa, en la punta norte del Valle del Río Grande, y caminando diariamente al pueblo —medio ciego como estaba— a tocar su acordeón por cualquier cantidad de dinero que le ofrecieran. A veces lo ocupaban para tocar en los bailes de negocio u otros tipos de celebraciones". Chris Strachwitz escribió en 1975 que "Bruno Villarreal . . . es recordado hoy por gente tan al norte como Amarillo, Tejas, tocando con una taza de lata atada a su acordeón de piano".

 Clayton T. Shorkey es profesor de trabajo social en la Universidad de Tejas en Austin y presidente del Texas Music Museum.

Acompañado por Rudy Martínez, miembro de la mesa directiva del Texas Music Museum, estaba haciendo una investigación sobre la música de conjunto cuando encontró a Bruno (que ahora carece del uso de las piernas) viviendo en el albergue Retama Manor Nursing Home en Robstown, Tejas. Llevó a cabo esta entrevista el 30 de agosto de 1986, con la ayuda de la sobrina de Bruno, Tomasa (Tammy) Gutiérrez. También estaba presente Bárbara Rodríguez, hermana de Bruno.

Bruno Villarreal será admitido al Conjunto Music Hall of Fame en el Sixth Annual Tejano Conjunto Festival en San Antonio, 1987, por ser el verdadero "padre" de la música de conjunto con acordeón grabada. —J.T.

Tomasa: Vinieron unos señores a buscarte, unos señores que quieren saber de tus discos.
Bruno: ¿De acuáles discos?
Tomasa: Pues los que hiciste con el acordeón.
Bruno: ¿Y cómo no vinieron aquí?
Tomasa: Aquí están.
Bruno: ¿On'tán?
Tomasa: Vinieron a hablar contigo.
Bruno: ¿Cuándo?
Tomasa: Orita.
Bruno: ¿Cuándo?
Tomasa: ¡Aquí están!
Bruno: ¿Dónde?
Tomasa: ¡Aquí!
Bruno: ¿Quién?
Tomasa: ¡Los señores estos!
Bruno: Pues quién sabe qué señores serán. Hay muchos señores.
Tomasa: Pues aquí están parados. Quieren hablar contigo.
Bruno: ¿Sí?
Tomasa: Sí.
Bruno: ¿Son de estatuas, o qué?
Rudy: He's a professor from the University of Texas.
Tomasa: Es un profesor.
Bruno: ¿Profesor?
Tomasa: Sí.
Bruno: De mañas, ¿cómo fue? [*se ríe*]

Bárbara: Los señores estos quieren hablar contigo, Bruno, tocante de su vida.
Tomasa: Te van a hacer famoso. Te van a poner en un libro.
Bruno: ¡Ah, qué hijos de . . . !
Tomasa: Sí, aquí están. Quieren hablar contigo, de veras.
Bruno: Pues, que le pregunten a Tomás Acuña.
Tomasa: ¿Dónde grabaste el primer disco, Bruno? ¿Te acuerdas?
Bruno: Ay . . . pues en San Antonio, hombre. Bueno, y los señores estos no hablan, ¿o qué?
Tomasa: Sí, pero son bolillos.
Bruno: ¿Y qué tiene que sean bolillos? ¡A poco dices que no saben hablar en bolillo!
Clay: Let's see . . . my name . . . mi nombre es Clay Shorkey y soy profesor en *the University of Texas in Austin and we have a project . . .*
Bruno: Dile que de qué se trata, nomás, más o menos.
Tomasa: Pues, de eso. Quieren saber de tu vida, que ¿por qué te hiciste famoso y dónde hiciste tus discos?
Bruno: Ah, pues dile que . . . lo famoso . . . que me hice famoso nomás pa'l trago, por la buena dirección que me dio mi padre. Nunca me mandaron a ninguna escuela ni a ninguna parte.
Tomasa: Sí, pero dice que tú eres el número uno con el acordeón. Él ha oído. Por eso viene a hablar contigo.
Bruno: ¿Sí? Ah . . .
Clay: We're going to have an exhibit for the Texas Museum de música, y tú es muy famoso en, *for the* música *of accordion . . .*
Bruno: Pues, ora no tengo acordeón, ni tengo nada.
Tomasa: Sí, pero nomás quieren saber. Quieren aprender de tu vida, porque ellos oyeron que tú eras el número uno con el acordeón.
Bruno: Ajá. Pues, sí lo era, pues soy todavía, nomás que no tengo acordeón.
Clay: Ask him when he first got an accordion, when he first played the accordion.
Tomasa: ¿Cuándo comprates tu primer acordeón?
Bruno: Ay . . . el primero que compré, yo creo que fue como en '28, yo creo '29, algo así.
Clay: Ask him if he remembers where he bought it.
Tomasa: ¿No te acuerdas dónde la comprates, o te la dieron, o qué?
Bruno: Que me dieron, nada. A mí nunca me dieron nadie nada.

Tomasa: Bueno, ¿dónde la comprates?

Bruno: ¿La primera? La compré en Montgomery Ward.

Clay: Ask him if he took lessons, or if somebody taught him.

Tomasa: ¿Te enseñaron cómo tocar, o tú solo?

Bruno: Yo solo.

Clay: Ask him when he first played for people in groups, like parties, or something like that.

Tomasa: ¿Y no te acuerdas qué tantos años tenías cuando primero empezaste a tocarle a la gente?

Bruno: Pues, ¿sabe qué?, la mera verdad de las cosas, las acordeones chiquitas las toqué como unos ocho años, de esas chiquitas. Y luego, de esas de piano, las toqué hasta como el año antepasado, el año pasado.

Clay: Was it a one-row accordion, or a two-row?

Tomasa: Bueno, la primerita que tocaste, la chiquita que tenías, ¿era de un zurco o de dos?

Bruno: [*se ríe*] Era de dos, hombre, y luego comencé a comprar de tres, y así. Yo compré muchos acordeoncillos pa' enseñarme a tocarlas. Compré varias acordeones.

Clay: Did he learn by listening to the music of other people?

Tomasa: ¿Cómo aprendiste? ¿Con el radio, oyendo a alguien más o . . . oyendo a quién?

Bruno: Pues, oía y compraba discos también, que tenían música de acordeón. Diles que yo aprendí solo.

Tomasa: Te acuerdas cuando comprabas discos para aprender, ¿no te acuerdas de quiénes eran?

Bruno: No, las compraba en las casas ahí de discos.

Tomasa: Sí, pero ¿quién las tocaba? ¿No sabías quién?

Bruno: ¡Pos, las vecinas, hombre!

Tomasa: Sí, pero ¿quién tocaba en los discos? ¿De quién era la música?

Bruno: Había música de varios acordeonistas, ¿ves? Acordeonistas italianos y de cuanto había. Dile que yo me enseñé a tocar solo, que yo no . . .

Clay: When did he make his first record?

Tomasa: ¿No te acuerdas cuándo hiciste tu primer disco?

Bruno: ¿Cuándo hice el primer disco? No . . . yo creo que fue como en el '29 o el '30, algo así.

Clay: What song?

Tomasa: ¿Cómo se llamaba la canción que tocaste?

Bruno: Ay, Dios . . .
Tomasa: ¿No te acuerdas?
Bruno: Yo hice varios discos, ahí.
Tomasa: ¿Cómo se llamaban?
Bruno: Pues, es mucho eso, oiga. Este, a don Tomás Acuña, es a quien le grababa yo, de ahí de San Antonio, la casa de música mexicana que había ahí. Era muy buen hombre conmigo.
Clay: Ask him if he made a lot of money putting out records.
Tomasa: ¿Hiciste dinero, Bruno, haciendo discos?
Bruno: Sí, pero yo ayudé mucho a mi gente. Yo nunca pude juntar dinero.
Clay: What were some of the best things that he remembers when he was having a lot of success?
Tomasa: ¿Qué es lo más que te acuerdas cuando tú estabas haciendo discos? ¿Qué es lo más que te gustaba?
Bruno: Pues yo grabé varias piezas, como por ejemplo le grabé "La cucaracha", "La Adelita", "La rielera", y grabé varias piezas, "La chivatore" y muchas piezas. Grabé como en cuatro compañías de discos. Mira que don Tomás Acuña lo ponía en la compañía que le daba la gana, ¿ves? Era muy buen hombre conmigo, él.
Clay: What is his favorite type of music?
Tomasa: ¿Qué clase de música te gustaba más?
Bruno: Bueno, la música clásica nunca la practiqué, ¿ves? Tocaba asina que otra, como valses altos y cosas básicas, como . . .
Tomasa: ¿Pero qué es lo que más te gustaba tocar?
Bruno: No, pos la música popular.
Clay: What advice would he give young musicians starting out today?
Tomasa: ¿Qué dices de la música de los jóvenes hoy? ¿Qué les dijeras?
Bruno: Orita, la juventud toca ahi lo que le da la gana. A cualquier cosa la hacen cumbia. Si van a cantar una alabanza, la hacen cumbia ahi también, ¿ves? Van a cantar un canto de Dios, y la hacen cumbia. Cuando yo tocaba, en los tiempos en que yo tocaba, por eso a mucha gente le gustaba como tocaba yo, porque yo tocaba al estilo antiguo todo el tiempo.
Clay: Ask him if he knows Esteban Jordán.
Tomasa: ¿Te acuerdas de Esteban Jordán?
Bruno: Lo he oído mentar nomás. De lo que sí puedo darle cuenta es una botella de trago. Nomás probándola un tantito . . . yo le

digo . . . no, este, ya no puedo hacer nada ya de cuestión de andar en la tomada, ni nada, porque no puedo.

Tomasa: ¿Pero tocar sí?

Bruno: Tocar, sí puedo tocar. Tocar sí puedo, porque es como una estufa, ¿ves?, mientras la mecha esté buena, tiene que prender.

Clay: Did he write his own songs?

Bruno: Diles que casi todo el tiempo anduve tocando yo solo nomás.

Tomasa: Las canciones que tú hacías, Bruno, ¿eran tuyas o de alguien más?

Bruno: Pues, hubo varios músicos que anduvieron conmigo, pero ahi nomás en ratitos, nomás. Casi lo más del tiempo, yo toqué solo.

Tomasa: Pero lo que quieren saber es que si ¿tocabas canciones tuyas o de otras personas también?

Bruno: Pues cantaba de todo. Yo era como las pianolas de esa niclea, ¿ves?, tocaba de todo. Conmigo no hay que . . . yo y mis acordeones no se nos dificultaba nada.

Clay: What is his favorite type of music?

Tomasa: ¿Qué es lo que te gusta tocar más? ¿Polcas, cumbias o qué?

Bruno: Pues, me gusta tocar todo. Lo que yo toco, lo toco porque me gusta, ¿ves?

Tomasa: Bruno, ¿todo el tiempo vas a ser músico? ¿Todo el tiempo has sido músico?

Bruno: Todo el tiempo he sido músico.

Tomasa: ¿Todo el tiempo vas a ser, hasta que te mueras?

Bruno: ¡Hasta que me muera! Habiendo qué tocar. Pues si no hay qué tocar, pues así me la paso molineando. No crean, no ha sido tan bonita nuestra vida. Ha sido más bien una vida de sufrimiento, pero, pos bueno, nunca vi otro oficio nomás que el de la música. Pues, yo no pude trabajar, ¿ves?, por la falta de la vista, ¿ves?

Tomasa: ¿Y le gusta que le vengan a preguntar de tu vida?

Bruno: ¿Que si me gusta?

Tomasa: Ajá, ¿a platicar de toda la música que has tocado y todo?

Bruno: Bueno, pos, no ofenden. No le hacen ofensas a uno, ni nada. No, si malos que vinieran aquí y lo agarraban a garrotazos, como un señor que me dijo que si yo le hacía quién sabe qué al hermano, que venía y me mataba. Pues, 'ta bueno. Dichoso el que pueda matar a uno como un piojo. [*se ríe*]

Clay: Where did he play? At parties, outside people's houses?

Tomasa: Bruno, el señor quiere saber dónde tocabas el acordeón, ¿en pores, en bailes o . . . ?

Bruno: En todas partes.

Tomasa: Pero ¿dónde tocabas más? ¿Dónde le gustaba la gente que tocabas más?

Bruno: Pues en la calle. En las banquetas . . . y en los pores y todo. En bodas, en bailes y cuanto.

Clay: Tell him that it's an honor to be able to come here and talk to him, because many people that know about his music and such . . . that he has made a very important contribution.

Tomasa: Dicen estos señores que ellos están gustosos de estar hablando contigo, porque mucha gente te conocen y hablan de ti, que eres número uno y que ellos están gustosos de haberte hallado, porque te andaban buscando.

Bruno: Oyes, pues ¡fíjate! No me lo dicen. Bruno, número uno, ¿ves? [*se ríe*]

Tomasa: Dicen que ellos están bien gustosos de haberte hallado. Creían que no te iban a hallar.

Bruno: Ah . . . ¿no sabes tú que cosa mala nunca muere?

Tomasa: Bruno, ¿te pueden retratar?

Bruno: ¿Eh?

Tomasa: ¿Te pueden retratar?

Bruno: ¿Cómo, aquí, así on'toy?

Tomasa: Sí, nomás un retratito, es todo, pa' que salgas en el papel.

Bruno: ¿En calconzillos, o cómo? [*se ríe*]

Tomasa: ¿Te pueden retratar?

Bruno: Pues, ¿por qué no? Ya te lo haiga si se quiebra la cámara. [*se ríe*]

Tomasa: Nomás vinieron a hablar contigo, de tu música y cómo te fue en tu vida.

Bruno: Mi vida todo el tiempo fue una de sufrimiento, nomás que como dice la gente, que sólo el que trae el morral, sabe lo que trae adentro, ¿ves?

Bruno Villarreal

✧

CLAYTON T. SHORKEY
1987

(Entrevista original: página 301)

Bruno Villarreal, known as El Azote del Valle (the Scourge of the Valley), was born on May 21, 1912, in La Grulla, a village in South Texas near the Mexican border. Almost completely blind all of his life, he had a talent for music and began playing a two-row button accordion early in his youth. At some point in his career he switched over to the piano accordion. According to Mañuel Peña, author of The Texas-Mexican Conjunto, *"among accordionists, the first recording honor—at least with the large American companies—belongs to [Villarreal]. That was in 1928." By 1935 he had already made about fifty recordings, primarily instrumentals, including "La bella Italia" (polka), "La varsoviana" (mazurka), "La coyota" (waltz), and "Los siete pasos" (schottische).*

Life was hard for Bruno Villarreal in those years. Peña writes that his father "remembers him in the 1930s, living on a ranchito *three miles from Santa Rosa, at the north end of the Rio Grande Valley, and walking every day into town—half-blind as he was—to play his accordion for whatever money was offered. At times he was also hired out to play at* bailes de negocio *or other kinds of celebrations." Chris Strachwitz wrote in 1975, "Bruno Villarreal . . . is today remembered by people as far north as Amarillo, Texas, playing with a tin cup attached to his piano accordion."*

Clayton T. Shorkey is a professor of social work at the University of Texas at Austin and president of the Texas Music Museum. Accompanied by Rudy Martínez, a board member of the TMM, he was doing research for an exhibit on conjunto music when he found Bruno (now without the use of his legs) living in the Retama Manor Nursing Home in Robstown, Texas. He conducted this interview on August 30, 1986, with the assistance of Bruno's niece Tomasa (Tammy) Gutiérrez. Also present was Bruno's sister Bárbara Rodríguez.

Bruno Villarreal will be inducted into the Conjunto Music Hall of Fame at the Sixth Annual Tejano Conjunto Festival en San Antonio, 1987, for being the true "father" of recorded accordion conjunto music. —J.T.

Tomasa: Some men came to see you, some men who want to know about your records.
Bruno: About which records?
Tomasa: Well, the ones with you on the accordion.
Bruno: And why didn't they come here?
Tomasa: They are here.
Bruno: Where are they?
Tomasa: They came to speak with you.
Bruno: When?
Tomasa: Right now.
Bruno: When?
Tomasa: They're here!
Bruno: Where?
Tomasa: Here!
Bruno: Who?
Tomasa: These men here!
Bruno: Well, who knows who these men are. There are lots of men.
Tomasa: Well, they're standing right here. They want to talk to you.
Bruno: Is that right?
Tomasa: Yes.
Bruno: Are they statues, or what?
Rudy: [*in English*] He's a professor from the University of Texas.
Tomasa: He's a professor.
Bruno: A professor?
Tomasa: Yes.
Bruno: Of vices, is that it? [*laughs*]
Bárbara: These men here want to speak with you, Bruno, about your life.
Tomasa: They're going to make you famous. They're going to put you in a book.
Bruno: Oh, what sons of . . . !

Tomasa: Yes, here they are. They want to speak with you, really.
Bruno: Well, they should ask Tomás Acuña.
Tomasa: Where did you make your first record, Bruno? Do you remember?
Bruno: Oh . . . well, in San Antonio, man. So, these men here can't talk, or what?
Tomasa: Yes, but they're gringos.
Bruno: And what of it if they're gringos? Are you saying they can't speak gringo?
Clay: [*mixing English and Spanish*] Let's see . . . my name . . . *mi nombre es* Clay Shorkey and I am a professor at the University of Texas in Austin and we have a project . . .
Bruno: Ask him what it's all about, more or less.
Tomasa: Well, it's about that. They want to know about your life, about why you became famous and where you made your records.
Bruno: Well, tell him that . . . about being famous . . . that I became famous only for my drinking, because of the fine guidance my father gave me. They never sent me to school or anywhere.
Tomasa: Yes, but he says that you're number one on the accordion. He's heard. That's why he's come to speak with you.
Bruno: Really? Uh . . .
Clay: [*mixing English and Spanish*] We're going to have an exhibit for the Texas Museum of Music and you are very famous on, for accordion music . . .
Bruno: Well, I don't have an accordion now, or anything else.
Tomasa: Yes, but they just want to know. They want to learn about your life, because they heard that you were number one on the accordion.
Bruno: Uh huh. Well, yes, I was, and I still am, except that I don't have an accordion.
Clay: [*in English*] Ask him when he first got an accordion, when he first played the accordion.
Tomasa: When did you buy your first accordion?
Bruno: Oh . . . the first one I bought, I believe it was about '28, I believe '29, something like that.
Clay: [*in English*] Ask him if he remembers where he bought it.
Tomasa: Don't you remember where you bought it, or did someone give it to you, or what?
Bruno: Nothing was given to me. No one ever gave me anything.
Tomasa: Okay, where did you buy it?

Bruno: The first one? I bought it at Montgomery Ward.
Clay: [*in English*] Ask him if he took lessons, or if somebody taught him.
Tomasa: Did someone teach you how to play, or you by yourself?
Bruno: Me, by myself.
Clay: [*in English*] Ask him when he first played for people in groups, like parties, or something like that.
Tomasa: And can you remember how old you were when you first started to play for people?
Bruno: Well, you know what? The real truth is, I played the little accordions for about eight years, those little ones. And after that, those piano ones, I played them until about the year before last, or last year.
Clay: [*in English*] Was it a one-row accordion, or a two-row?
Tomasa: Well, the very first one you played, the little one you had, was it a one-row or a two-row?
Bruno: [*laughs*] It was a two-row, man, and then I started to buy the three-row, and so on. I bought a bunch of accordions to teach myself how to play them. I bought several accordions.
Clay: [*in English*] Did he learn by listening to the music of other people?
Tomasa: How did you learn? From the radio, listening to someone else, or . . . listening to who?
Bruno: Well, I listened to records and also bought them, the ones with accordion music. Tell them that I learned by myself.
Tomasa: Do you remember when you bought records to learn from, can you remember whose they were?
Bruno: No, I bought them at those record stores.
Tomasa: Yes, but who played them? Didn't you know who?
Bruno: Well, the ladies in the neighborhood, man!
Tomasa: I know, but who played on the records? Who was the music by?
Bruno: There was music by different accordionists, you see. Italian accordionists and whatnot. Tell him I learned to play by myself, that I didn't . . .
Clay: [*in English*] When did he make his first record?
Tomasa: Do you remember when you made your first record?
Bruno: When I made my first record? No . . . I think it was about '29 or '30, something like that.
Clay: [*in English*] What song?

Tomasa: What was the name of the song you played?
Bruno: Oh dear! . . .
Tomasa: Don't you remember?
Bruno: I made a lot of records there.
Tomasa: What were they called?
Bruno: Well, that's too much, you know. Uh, Don Tomás Acuña, that was who I recorded for, from there in San Antonio, the Mexican-music company that was there. He was very good to me.
Clay: [*in English*] Ask him if he made a lot of money putting out records.
Tomasa: Did you make money, Bruno, making records?
Bruno: Yes, but I helped my family a lot. I was never able to keep any money.
Clay: [*in English*] What were some of the best things that he remembers when he was having a lot of success?
Tomasa: What do you remember most when you were making records? What did you like the best?
Bruno: Well, I recorded various tunes, like, for example, I recorded "La cucaracha," "La Adelita," "La rielera," and I recorded various tunes, "La chivatore," and many tunes. I recorded with about four record companies. Look, Don Tomás Acuña would put them out with whatever company he felt like, you see? He was a very good man to me, he was.
Clay: [*in English*] What is his favorite type of music?
Tomasa: What kind of music did you like best?
Bruno: Well, I never performed classical music, you see. I would play, you know, one or another, like fine waltzes and basic things, like . . .
Tomasa: But what did you like to play the best?
Bruno: No, well, popular music.
Clay: [*in English*] What advice would he give young musicians starting out today?
Tomasa: What do you think of the music of young people today? What would you say to them?
Bruno: Today, young people just play whatever they feel like. They make a *cumbia* out of anything. If they're going to sing a hymn, they also go and make it into a *cumbia*, you see. They're going to sing a song about God, and they make it into a *cumbia*. When I played, back in the days when I played, that's why many people liked the way I played, because I played in the old style all the time.

Clay: [*in English*] Ask him if he knows Esteban Jordán.

Tomasa: Do you remember Esteban Jordán?

Bruno: I've just heard him mentioned. What I can really tell him about is a bottle of liquor. Just tasting it a little bit . . . I can tell him . . . no, well, I can't do anything anymore that has to do with drinking or anything, because I can't.

Tomasa: But you can play?

Bruno: Play, I can still play. I can still play, because it's like a stove, you see, as long as the wick is good, it's got to fire up.

Clay: [*in English*] Did he write his own songs?

Bruno: Tell them that most of the time I just went around playing alone.

Tomasa: The songs that you used to do, Bruno, were they your own or someone else's?

Bruno: Well, there were several musicians who went around with me, but just for short spells, that's all. Just about all the time I played alone.

Tomasa: But what they want to know is if you played your own songs or some by other people, too?

Bruno: Well, I sang a little of everything. I was like those nickelodeons, you see, I played everything. With me, there's no need to . . . me and my accordions, there was nothing too difficult for us.

Clay: [*in English*] What is his favorite type of music?

Tomasa: What do you like to play most? Polkas, *cumbias,* or what?

Bruno: Well, I like to play everything. What I play, I play it because I like it, you see?

Tomasa: Bruno, will you always be a musician? Have you always been a musician?

Bruno: I have always been a musician.

Tomasa: Will you always be one, until you die?

Bruno: Until I die! As long as there's something to play. 'Cause if there isn't anything to play, well, I pass the time fidgeting. But really, our life hasn't been so very nice. It's been a life of suffering, rather, but then, well, I never thought of any other occupation except that of music. 'Cause I couldn't ever work, you see, because of my poor eyesight, you see.

Tomasa: And do you like people to come and ask you about your life?

Bruno: Whether I like it?

Tomasa: Uh huh, to talk about all the music you've played and everything?

Bruno: Well, it's not offensive. They don't offend me, or anything. No, bad guys would come in here and take a club to you, like the guy who told me that if I did who knows what to his brother, that he'd come and kill me. Well, okay. Lucky is he who can kill you like a bug. [*he laughs*]

Clay: [*in English*] Where did he play? At parties, outside people's houses?

Tomasa: Bruno, the man wants to know where you played the accordion, at parties, at dances, or . . . ?

Bruno: Everywhere.

Tomasa: But where did you play most often? Where did people like you to play most often?

Bruno: Well, in the streets. On the sidewalks . . . and at parties, and everything. At weddings, at dances, and whatnot.

Clay: [*in English*] Tell him that it's an honor to be able to come here and talk to him, because many people that know about his music and such . . . that he has made a very important contribution.

Tomasa: These men say that they are happy to be speaking with you, because many people know about you and talk about you, that you are number one, and that they are glad to have found you, because they have been looking for you.

Bruno: Well, imagine that! You don't say. Bruno, number one, see? [*he laughs*]

Tomasa: They say they are very glad to have found you. They thought they wouldn't find you.

Bruno: Oh . . . don't you know that you can't kill a bad weed?

Tomasa: Bruno, can they take your picture?

Bruno: Huh?

Tomasa: Can they take your picture?

Bruno: What? Here, just like this?

Tomasa: Yes, just a little picture, that's all, so you can be in the paper.

Bruno: In my undershorts, or what? [*he laughs*]

Tomasa: Can they take your picture?

Bruno: Well, why not? It's your problem if the camera breaks. [*he laughs*]

Tomasa: They just came to talk to you, about your music and how your life was.

Bruno: My life was always one of suffering, except that, as people say, only the one who carries the sack knows what's inside, right?

24

¡Conjunto! Estilo y Clase
Narciso Martínez, Valerio Longoria, Tony de la Rosa, Paulino Bernal, Flaco Jiménez y Esteban Jordán

✧

JUAN TEJEDA
1988

(English translation: page 333)

*E**stilo. Algunos lo tienen, otros no.*
Cuando uno habla de la música de conjunto, esa música chicana distintiva que usa el acordeón de botones como su instrumento principal, que se desarrolló en el área fronteriza de Tejas y México a comienzos del siglo, es claro que hay ciertos individuos que han desempeñado un papel importante en la creación de estilos únicos dentro de este género.

Por ejemplo, si te gusta la música de conjunto y la escuchas, sabes que Flaco Jiménez (ganador del premio Grammy en 1987) toca ese viejo acordeón de manera diferente que, digamos, Esteban Jordán. O que Valerio Longoria no toca esa cajita como Nick Villarreal. Son diferentes. Han desarrollado sus propios estilos. Hay los que prefieren el estilo de Rubén Vela y los que aman la música de Los Alegres de Terán. Que haya estilos distintivos entre la música de conjunto es algo que los amantes de la música de conjunto dan por hecho, pero poco se ha escrito sobre ello.

El profesor Manuel Peña, autor de un estudio notable sobre la música de conjunto, The Texas-Mexican Conjunto: History of a Working-Class Music, *dice que la historia del conjunto se puede dividir en tres distintas fases. La primera, hasta 1935, se puede llamar la formativa, cuando el acordeón se tocaba solo o se combinaba con diversos instrumentos de una manera ad hoc. La segunda fase empezó en 1935, con la aparición de las primeras grabaciones de Narciso Martínez. Conocido entre la generación más joven como "el primero", Martínez fue primordialmente el responsable por llevar al emergente conjunto más allá de su estilo germánico anterior. La fase final de la música de conjunto empezó a tomar forma durante la década posterior a la guerra, cuando el ensamble moderno se cristalizó en una unidad coherente. Para mediados de los cincuenta ya había adquirido una forma y un estilo que han permanecido virtualmente iguales hasta hoy en día.*

Además de destacar a Narciso Martínez, que es llamado el "padre" de la música de conjunto, Peña se enfoca en varios otros músicos que, según él, jugaron papeles importantes en el desarrollo estilístico de la música de conjunto. Entre ellos están Valerio Longoria, el "genio" de la música de conjunto, recordado por sus innovaciones; Tony de la Rosa, "cuyas polcas se convirtieron en el ideal contra el cual otros se medían", y uno de los acordeonistas más populares en la historia de la música de conjunto; y Paulino Bernal, quien, con el Conjunto Bernal, "creó un sonido sumamente popular basado en una mezcla única de lo tradicional y lo innovador. El resultado fue un grupo que es reconocido hasta la fecha como 'el único de su tipo'".

Cuando estábamos pensando en un artículo para incluir en el programa del Tejano Conjunto Festival de este año, decidimos que sería interesante enfocarnos en los estilos distintivos que se han desarrollado en la música de conjunto. Pero ¿de qué manera lo haríamos? Sentimos que ya que éramos lo suficientemente afortunados de tener todavía vivos a la mayoría de los pioneros estilísticos de conjunto, quién sería mejor para hablar sobre el tema que los estilistas mismos. Se decidió que entrevistaríamos a seis de los estilistas del conjunto: Narciso Martínez, Valerio Longoria, Tony de la Rosa, Paulino Bernal, Esteban Jordán y Flaco Jiménez. Y que les hiciéramos a cada uno las mismas preguntas.

Supusimos que sus respuestas individuales a las mismas preguntas nos brindarían una buena base de comparación. Las cinco preguntas iniciales fueron:

1. ¿Se han desarrollado estilos distintivos en la música de conjunto?
2. ¿Cuáles estilos se han desarrollado y quién los creó?
3. ¿Y el estilo suyo? ¿Usted cree que desarrolló un estilo distintivo?
4. ¿Eran populares estos pioneros estilísticos, y era usted popular?
5. ¿Cuáles estilos existen hoy, y qué nos espera en el futuro de la música de conjunto? ¿Cambiarán los estilos o permanecerán iguales?

Decidí hacer las entrevistas yo mismo, en parte porque no había nadie más disponible en el tiempo necesario y en parte porque, en el fondo, creo que yo simplemente quería hacerlas. Para mí fue un gran privilegio y un honor el poder sentarme personalmente con estos grandes del conjunto para hablar de estilo. Hablamos de varias cosas, muchas de las cuales fueron más allá del límite de las preguntas iniciales. Se hicieron algunos comentarios muy básicos e importantes.

Las entrevistas se llevaron a cabo en febrero y marzo de este año. Los siguientes "monólogos" fueron editados de las entrevistas, muchas de las cuales resultaron bastante largas. Nos hubiera gustado incluir más de lo que dijo cada uno, pero el espacio y el tiempo no lo permitieron. De todos modos, estamos seguros que ustedes disfrutarán y serán ilustrados por los comentarios sobre estilo de seis gigantes del conjunto que definitivamente lo tienen.

Y ahora, en sus palabras . . .

Narciso Martínez

Sí, ¡cómo no! Para mi opinión, sí. Ahora hay muchos grupos de acordeón que tocan puro regional, puro estilo . . . hay varios grupos que nomás tocan puro cumbia, *you know?* . . .

Santiago Jiménez fue el único, el primero que oí de todos. Santiago Jiménez viejo. Santiago Jiménez y sus Valedores. Pero Santiago Jiménez . . . lo que lo hizo fuerte a él fue "La Piedrera", "Rumbo a Roma", "Viva Seguín". Tenía un gran estilo. Sus muchachos son buenos muchachos. Me trató muy bien cuando 'tuvimos allí. El tacuachito vino naciendo en San Antonio. Era pura polca en aquellos años . . . cuando comenzó en San Antonio. Y Santiago Jiménez, pos era su comida de él.

Yo vine a oír música, músicos, ya como el 1948, '49. Yo todavía iba a tocar. Y oía a los Donneños, a Mario, Ramiro, Pedro Ayala, Los Alegres de Terán —fueron los primeros que comencé a oír, ya después que había pegado yo. . . .

Bueno . . . como Pedro Ayala, Valerio Longoria, más o menos van con el mismo . . . más o menos . . . van con el mismo estilo. Hay otros que han metido . . . otros grupos como Óscar Hernández, Esteban Jordán, varios otros, orita están poniendo mucho estilo de negro . . . en los arreglos. Bueno, como Esteban, no es que tenga tanto de estilo, es que toca muchas piezas nuevas que hay ahora . . . lo que ha grabado son muchas piezas viejas . . . piezas como "El zopilote mojado", ¿ves?, y 'ta bien, tiene su estilo. Pero en esas piezas, es más estilo viejo.

Ya, estilo nuevo es, como dije orita, Óscar Hernández, y hay otros que con el mismo estilo ese que tocan . . . y muy distinta a la mía, creo yo que es muy distinta a la mía. Paulino Bernal, Óscar es el que lo conoce. . . .

Un buen músico . . . Tony de la Rosa comenzó, era muy amigo mío, tiene su estilito, también. . . .

No podía oír a nadie en discos. No había nadie. Yo grabé en el 1935 para el Bluebird y no había de nadie nada, nada. No había ni radio en ese tiempo. Sí había discos, pero muy poco de . . . era como de tríos . . . Pues allá en San Antonio, que es un pueblo muy extenso, fue donde grabé la primera vez yo . . . Como cinco o seis veces grabé en San Antonio . . . Mis primer grabaciones, fueron un montón de todo . . . Y allí se desarrolló mucho, mucho en San Antonio . . . muchísimo, mucho talento.

Pues la acordeón, yo puedo decir que fui el primero que empecé a figurarlo en grupo. Pero como le dije orita, yo toqué por años con la pura acordeón solo, de sol a sol. Allá por el mil novecientos cuarenta y . . . ocho, cuarenta y nueve, fue cuando comenzaron a hacer grupos, conjuntos. Puedo decir que fui uno de los primeros.

Mi hermano tocaba. Él tenía una acordeoncita muy . . . No sabía, pero como quiera, yo le hacía y le hacía y hasta que comencé a tocar y ya pa'l mil novecientos . . . veintiséis, veintisiete, ya la dejó él, y seguí yo . . . Es que me gustaba la música. Cantaba . . . canté en un disco . . . Yo todavía no puedo ni hablar, pero, pues yo canté en varios discos . . . Pero yo sé que fui el primero que introducí la acordeón en discos grabados . . . acompañado con acordeón . . . porque más antes sí había como orquestas o grupos de violines y todas esas cosas, mariachis . . . pero no . . . acordeón mezclada con canciones en disco yo no vi, nunca.

En 1935, me preguntaron: "¿Cómo te dicen?" "Pues me llamo Narciso Martínez." "Bueno, pero usted es ¿qué?" Jue el '35, como en septiembre, y en ese tiempo vivía muy fregadito, fregadito . . . todavía. Peor, porque ahora por la edad. Bueno, el que me grabó fue Enrique, de aquí de Brownsville. Fue el que me puso el apodo ese, El Huracán del Valle. Fue el '35. El '34 había pasado un chubasco por aquí, y por eso pasó. . . .

Ahorita aquí . . . están muy entusiasmados con la cumbia. Hay casi sesenta, de setenta por ciento más pa'l lado de la cumbia que pa'l lado de la polca. . . .

Actualmente, puede ser el mismo estilo, pero no es el mismo músico. Un músico toca de una manera y otro toca de otra. Puedo tocar yo y puede tocar él con la misma . . . pero cada quien tiene su estilo.

Como por ejemplo . . . el vals. El vals fue muy popular, pero ya ahorita no lo aprecia la gente. La gente baila y no lo aprecia. El vals es bueno como para una boda, una quinceañera, y una o dos, nomás. Sí, son muy bonitos, pero la gente quiere que corra la sangre recio.

Digo yo, no voy a hablar de mí mismo, porque yo ya acabé, yo ya estoy pa' irme. Pero no nomás por eso. Yo lo que creo que el acordeón ya no va, se me hace a mí. Ojalá y sigan jalando igual, pero ya hay menos gente de acordeón que de orquesta.

Más antes la gente era de puro orquesta típica, pero cuando entró el acordeón fuerte, allá por el '38, el '39, '40 y '44, y todos esos, las orquestas se cayeron de a tiro. Pero luego entró Beto Villa, Balde González, con orquestas de aquí. Luis Arcaraz de México venía aquí. Yo toqué muchas veces con ellos.

En mi concepto mío, ahorita lo que está tan . . . ahorita es Roberto Pulido, y todos esos. Pienso que la orquesta le está quitando bastante al grupo, al conjunto.

Yo miro muy poco pa'l acordeón en lo de adelante. No se morirá de a tiro, pero a como estaba diciendo antes, se oía muy poco el acordeón, nomás en ranchos. Allá en el rancho se oía el acordeón nomás, un violín y un acordeón sólo.

Es lo que tocaban. No había grupos en aquellos años. Y el acordeón posiblemente, eso es lo que pienso yo, pero quién sabe más adelante cómo vaya a estar. Yo los he oído en radio, en televisión, que nunca va a morir. Pues, ojalá nunca muera, pues, eso fue mi comida por muchos años. Ya ahora, pues ya ahora no, pero por muchos años yo viví de ello.

Quería nomás decirles mucha suerte a los que tocan . . . y a los que no tocan también, naturalmente. Sí, que Dios los bendiga y que, pues . . . porque yo ya puedo decir ¡qué va!, ya voy a alzar la carabina [*y se ríe*]. Ya hace mucho casi ni toco. Sí toco, pero muy poco . . . ya muy poco . . . como en baile de promoción, no toco ni quiero tocar. Hay veces que voy con Gilberto Pérez a tocar, porque me vienen a llevar y me pagan por un rato. Sí les ayudo.

Valerio Longoria

Sí, nosotros agarramos [el acordeón] en Estados Unidos porque —no sé por qué—, pero la culpa la tienen los alemanes por haber mandado esas acordeones para acá. . . .

Se han desarrollado varios estilos, y muchos todavía existen, pero aún, sin embargo, la misma música, la primera, todavía existe. Es la misma.

El estilo de antes era apresurada la música, porque simplemente se bailaba taconeado. Ahora bailan de otro modo, no se baila taconeado. Ahora se baila más corridito, entonces la música es más despacio.

Cada músico tiene su estilo. Es duro para pronunciar todos estos estilos que salen, porque hay muchisísimos músicos que quieren tocar como el otro, como toca el otro . . . entonces ya no es estilo de ellos, ya es estilo del otro.

Claro que se han estado cambiando estilos . . . antes tocábamos muy apresurado. Las polcas eran muy apresuradas y se bailaban diferente. Después Tony de la Rosa grabó más despacio, otro estilo más despacio, y lo aceptó la gente.

El tiempo de Tony de la Rosa, Rubén Vela también lo agarró . . . pero ahora después, Rubén tiene su estilito, pero ahora parece que agarró de tocar un poquito más alegre, más de prisa que como tocaba antes.

El estilo de Esteban es distinto. Muchos no entienden la clase de música . . . Está avanzado en la música americana . . . eso es la cosa, y Esteban se crió al lado de los americanos. Él vivió mucho tiempo en West Texas, en Big Spring, Texas, y allí puro inglés, puro rock and roll y gente de color. Y ahi fue donde Esteban agarró la onda de tocar algo así como toca.

Paulino Bernal, ni se diga, es un gran músico . . . otro estilo diferente, avanzadisísimo, avanzado, muy inteligente para la acordeón. Paulino desarrolló otras cosas a través del trío. Casi nunca cantaba en su conjunto. Metía cantantes. Había un muchacho que le decían La Pulga, de Kingsville. "Mi único camino", La Pulga estaba en primer voz y el hermano de Paulino estaba en segunda, y . . . realmente no sé quien fue él, pero [se hizo] un trillito, y ya era otro estilo.

Hay dos estilos muy diferentes, el de Paulino y el de Esteban. Como Óscar Hernández . . . otro estilo bueno, aunque eso era ya acordeón cromática, pero es otro estilo también bien pesadísimo, pero es de un acordeón completa. Un acordeón cromática es completa.

También ahi tienen a Los Cachorros, ¿verdad? Ellos tienen su propio estilito muy sabroso. Diferentes moviditas, diferentes pasadas, diferentes a las otras pasadas que damos nosotros. Muy diferentes, muy alegres, muy bien y sin embargo . . . bueno, otro estilo como el de Ramón Ayala.

Flaco Jiménez es otro estilito. El también toca apresuradito . . . como se tocaba un poquito antes, pero un poco más despacio.

El estilo de Los Lobos es otro estilo ya mucho más apresurado. Quizás más aprisa que antes, pero sin embargo son otro estilo. Cada quien tiene su estilito. Como Los Pavos Reales tiene su propio estilo. Como Lalo, él tiene estilo muy propio. Salvador García tiene estilo muy propio. . . .

Narciso fue uno de ellos [músicos que influyeron a Longoria] y algunos otros acordeonistas que oía por la radio. Se oía acordeonistas que no los alcancé a conocer. Iba a un lugar, habían pianolas, oía una pieza tocar, y se me pegaba. Y fue como comencé yo en la música.

Yo me sentía que quería cantar y tocar a la vez, meter solfeo y estar cantando a la misma vez, dar la pasada cuando estoy cantando. A muchos se les dificulta, créemelo . . . eso de cantar y tocar a la misma vez, darle solfeo y . . . ir cantando, o luego ir dándole pasaditas al mismo tiempo sin destonarse, sin salirse del riel.

De esa manera aprendí. Esa manera comencé yo, tratando de hacer eso . . . de no pararme cuando estaba cantando, de seguir tocando. Por eso me preguntan, "Valerio, ¿cómo le haces para estar cantando y estar dándole pasadas a la misma vez?" Es tan fácil para mí, es facilísimo de a tiro, porque yo así aprendí. Así me gustaba. . . .

Hay, de estilo en México, muchisísimos. La mayoría de los conjuntos de México tocan diferente a los de Tejas. Lo tejano es diferente el estilo aunque, por ejemplo, hay muchos aquí en Estados Unidos que copean a Ramón Ayala, que es otro estilo propio de Ramón, el estilo de Los Cachorros . . . después de Los Cachorros . . . Los Alegres de Terán, ya ése es otro estilo, porque son corridos . . . pero pura música mexicana con puros pistoleros y qué sé yo.

Cada quien agarra su estilito, pero la música es casi la misma. Sí, pero no sé como aclarar eso de los estilos muy bien, porque está en el que tiene más talento, el que puede desarrollar más música. Ahí es donde cambia el estilito. El sonido nunca cambia porque es el mismo, aquel sonido sabroso del acordeón. Pero otras pasaditas, diferentes pasaditas, ya es otro estilo.

Y a eso le nombro estilo. Que sacaron estilos porque sacaron diferentes pasadas que no están iguales a como las de Narciso, iguales como a las de Tony o iguales como las de Esteban. Porque ellos ya nos dejaron este estilo. Por eso digo, no hay muchos que cambien a lo de ellos, que saquen su propio estilo, sus propias pasadas, sus propias movidas.

He visto a Carlos y José venir pa' acá de México y tocan sencillo. Y cuando tocan, pues la gente se levanta y comienza grite y grite, y todo eso.

Como Rubén Naranjo, es fácil el estilo de él, es fácil. Son sus propias pasaditas, pero es facilito. Dos pasaditas, una pasadita y ahi para cantar. Canta y de ahí vuelve a tocar otra vez sus dos pasaditas iguales. . . .

Todo tiene que ir cambiando, todo va cambiando. Antes no se tocaba lo que ahora se toca. No había cumbias. No hace mucho tiempo que nació la cumbia. Bueno, en Colombia tal vez había. Pero aquí en los Estados Unidos, no había cumbias. Había polcas, chachachás, porros, antes.

Quisiera que nunca, esto del acordeón, que nunca se acabe, y que hubiera más progreso en eso, que salieran más músicos buenos como los que tiene que salir. Ese es mi sueño, que nunca se acabe la música de acordeón y que siga adelante.

Tony de la Rosa

Bueno, para los que yo me recuerdo, ¿verdad?, el primer acordeonista que yo escuché fue Narciso Martínez. El señor Narciso Martínez, para mí, es el señor del acordeón. En seguida me tocó la oportunidad de oír a don Santiago Jiménez, ¿verdad?, Benito Espinoza, El Gallito.

Comenzamos a oír conjuntos de San Antonio ya después, Valerio Longoria. Puros estilos propios, únicos. En fin, está don Pedro Ayala. Crió su propio estilo. Tanto de compás de la música regional, como el compás que tenía don Narciso Martínez, que todos pasamos por ese compás de música . . . todas estas personas, que yo sepa, ellos fueron creadores de su propio estilo.

De los estilos sale un estilo original, como el de don Narciso Martínez, ¿verdad? Entonces ése lo reconoces dondequiera que tú escuchas una de las selecciones de él. . . .

'Tamos hablando de mucho tiempo pasado. Valses, polcas, chotís, redovas, danzas, ochos, escuadrillas, bailes de escoba, lo que usted quiera. Antes, era un bajo sexto, una guitarra y el acordeón, nomás . . . que era todo y era pulmón.

Me preguntaste cuál es la diferencia de Narciso . . . cuando la época del señor Longoria, un gran amigo mío, compañero de trabajo. Él es el único que yo escuché que estaba cantando y tocando su acordeón al mismo tiempo. Esa onda a mí me llamó mucho la atención.

Don Esteban [Jordán] es la crema del acordeón en la forma esta . . . él, desde *blues, jazz, country* . . . él te va a tocar lo que tú pidas. Si están de acuerdo los muchachos, ¡Échale! Como estábamos hablando antes, de que Valerio Longoria tocaba algo difícil, algunas cosas difícil, allí está este muchacho. Para mí, él y Óscar Hernández, ¿verdad?, y Paulino Bernal . . . nos creamos de esos estilos.

Ahora, Jordán, todavía hasta la fecha, no hay quien lo siga. Él está muy avanzado en su mente, con su música, y nosotros estamos detrás de él. Pero a nosotros no nos conviene seguirlo, por la simple razón de que la mantequilla de nuestro pan es otra.

Bernal introdució —ya había otros, pero no eran reconocidos— las tres voces. Y un estilo muy único de ellos, en acordeón, en voces, en los arreglos, señor. El compás de mi compadre Paulino Bernal, yo bailaba muy a gusto con él.

Hablando de cremas y acordeones, tienes que hablar de Esteban Jordán, tienes que hablar de Óscar Hernández. Otro muchacho que se desarrolló tremendísimamente en progresar es Bobby Naranjo, otra generación. Las tres son diferentes generaciones.

Hay otro muchacho, que no está por aquí, pero también tienes que darle su respeto, es Beto Salinas, que anduvo por un tiempo allí trabajando. En Laredo, el que trabaja orita muy allegado a lo de nosotros es Bernardo Martínez [y sus Compadres].

Desde Narciso Martínez hasta Jiménez, Valerio, Cuco Borjas, Gil Borjas . . . una persona que yo estimo y aprecio es don Manuel Guerrero. Hay otros, Flaco Jiménez, no se diga. . . .

El estilo mío, yo más o menos lo saqué de los acordeonistas. Sí, no lo niego. Pero pa' distinguirle también tenía diferente compás a los demás conjuntos. Fue más lo que me hizo ser diferente a los demás, porque tocaba lo mismo que tocaban los demás, pero mi onda era otra, otro compasito, otra cosa. Aparte del acordeón, mi mayor influencia del estilo, fue el *country, country music.*

Por eso me quedo yo en la misma parte de donde siempre estoy. Por eso me reconocen. Porque saben, al escuchar, que es Tony de la Rosa que está tocando. . . .

Ahorita, como yo la miro, es que sale un grupo y está pegando, y se forman como cinco o seis grupos que lo van a arremedar. Van a tocar, no igualito que aquél, pero cerquita. Yo digo que el conjunto tiene su tiempo, la orquesta tiene su tiempo, esos grupos nuevos tienen su tiempo. Y todos son compañeros, pero todos tienen su tiempo. Y unos la hicimos y unos no la hicimos, pero todos anduvimos allí. Todos anduvimos allí, ¿me entiendes? Ahora si me preguntas orita que quién miro yo que esté fuerte, no miro nada mientras que los demás sigan haciendo lo que los demás están haciendo. Tienen que ser diferentes.

Esteban sí es popular, dentro de la generación que escucha lo que él está desarrollando por parte de la música americana. Hay el cambio ese en la onda, que chicana, y la música que se está revolviendo, hasta la música de los de color, *rock,* tú nómbralo. Ya hay grupos chicanos, mexicanos también, que te tocan toda esa clase de música. Te la tocan. . . .

Sí, señor, así como cambió de la época de don Narciso, el señor Jiménez, a la época a donde estamos orita, así va a ser para adelante también. Pero cada santo tiempo se va a repetir, también. Se queda el acordeón allí atrás y al rato viene, y se queda un rato [*se ríe*], luego viene otra cosa. Es como decir cuando estaba el chachachá, el mambo, ¿verdad?, tropical, mariachi —que siempre ha estado allí—, las sonoras, tú nómbralo.

El repertorio va a cambiar, de la forma de que mientras que haiga acordeonistas, y haiga músicos, ¿verdad? —sea de bajistas, sea acordeón de piano, de pito, de aire, lo que quieras—, se van a dar a conocer y es donde va a cambiar, porque esa persona es la guía. Y me preguntas que si va a cambiar, en la forma de compases, de esto y el otro. Repertorio no es nomás decir tengo mucho repertorio, sino todo el tiempo tienes que estar agregando y [es] la cosa más simple que hay y la más dura.

No miro yo que va a haber muchos que van a crear su estilo, que van a ser pioneros también más delante. Si son diferentes, van a ser pioneros. Si no hay diferencias, no van a ser pioneros.

Lo único es que hoy en día yo miro una cosa muy mal entre los compañeros de música. Ya los compañeros de música que teníamos antes no son iguales como estábamos impuestos nosotros, por la simple razón de que ahora no están tocando para gustar y que les guste tocar. Por más que te guste, por más que te guste tocar y ser músico, lo miro muy mal yo que lo hacen únicamente para enseñarle al otro músico que toca más que el otro.

No piensan así, esos muchachos, que piensan del público. Porque en mi carrera, los he visto que vienen y los he visto que van. Y yo también vine y yo también me voy.

Muchas gracias.

Paulino Bernal

Han habido personas que se han destacado por su estilo, como Narciso Martínez, Tony de la Rosa, Valerio Longoria, Esteban Jordán, Pedro Ayala, personas que han sabido saber distinguirse, de una manera o otra, y eso les ha causado éxito.

El estilo de Narciso Martínez, de la música de los bailes allá en los patios de los ranchos, era bien alegre, proyectando alegría, la familia, la comunidad. Veo gente en el patio bailando la redova, los chotís. En el tiempo de Narciso, nomás él estaba tocando. Pedro Ayala empezó a grabar cosas que también grababa Narciso, nomás que como había tanto campo, porque eran pocos los acordeonistas.

Valerio Longoria es muy agradable, porque, para mí, era la música al tiempo del novio, la novia. Y Valerio sacaba la canción o el bolero que más te caía. Para mí fue muy clásico lo del bolero moderno y el estar cantando y tocando al mismo tiempo. Eso lo distinguió bastante.

Tony de la Rosa *slowed it down a little bit*. Más despacio que Valerio o Narciso, muy alegre, con una música bien marcadita en tiempo. Es un estilo ni mexicano —mexicano de México— pero tampoco americanado.

Eugenio [Ábrego, de Los Alegres de Terán] es un buen acordeonista, pero su estilo es más campesino, más tradicional, mexicano.

Esteban Jordán combinó todo, y podía tocarlo todo. Empezó a sacar notas que no las estaban usando. Allí estaban, pero no las estaban usando. Fue el primero que hizo combinación de todo, metió tropical, *jazz*, mariachi, con el acordeón. Hizo tantas combinaciones, rock and roll con el acordeón. Agarró de aquí, de allá, de todas partes, y lo metió al acordeón y lo metió bien hecho, y se puede mantener con sus canciones rancheras también, y irse de un extremo al otro.

No conocí mucho la música de don Santiago Jiménez. He conocido mucho más de su hijo, Flaco, un músico típico de San Antonio, pero está sintiendo lo que está tocando y proyectando a la gente con sus movimientos y su cuerpo. Hace que la gente se meta. No es complicado. Es bien sencillo lo que toca él, y ha logrado distinguirse. . . .

Cuando empecé, tenía a Narciso Martínez, a Tony de la Rosa y a Valerio Longoria tocando. Yo dije, "Yo no puedo tocar lo que ellos tocan porque nunca los voy a superar en lo que ellos están tocando. Tengo que sacar algo mío".

Empecé a sacar polcas mías, empecé a escuchar, me empecé a juntar con otros músicos, empecé a viajar con una orquesta muy famosa por todo Estados Unidos, y me pegaba a los acordeonistas, a los trompetistas. Un trompetista muy amigo mío, Louie Gasca, me enseñó mucho.

Entonces dije, "Voy a tener que distinguirme de otra manera, voy a sacar música que no se está tocando", *chords* que no tocaban los demás acordeonistas. Empecé a sacar otra música y me gustó la música de Los Panchos, Los Tres Reyes, todos esos tríos buenos. Comenzamos a distinguirnos en las voces también, del dueto que siempre cantábamos, a un trío moderno y con *chords* en el acordeón, y polcas más complicadas que lo que estaban sacando los demás.

Me ayudó salirle al acordeón de tres líneas. Todos siguieron con la de dos líneas. Me fui rápidamente a la de tres líneas, pero no me quedé allí. Cuando salió el acordeón italiana llamada Rino, fui el primero que tuve esa acordeón y eso me dio un sonido moderno, más clásico. Tenía los cambios para que sonara más *mellow*, más dulce. Eso fue una de las cosas, el acordeón cromática, y otra fue las polcas complicadas que empecé a grabar. . . .

Tiene que ver mucho la cultura de la gente. Yo creo que tiene que ver mucho el área donde viva una persona. Nosotros del Valle tenemos influencia de México y la influencia de los Estados Unidos. Aquí sale otro sabor, otro estilo del acordeón al de San Antonio. Simplemente, el bajista . . . tocar el bajo sexto en San Antonio es muy diferente que tocarlo acá.

[El conjunto tejano] es una música completamente distinta [al mexicano], en el ritmo, y en la música. Se distinguen los tejanos en que es un poco más avanzado como tocan el acordeón.

El conjunto es una combinación de toda la música, ¿pa' qué más que la verdad? No hay nada nuevo bajo del cielo, no nos podemos tapar —todo está descubierto, ¿no? Cada quien agarra de aquí, de allá, ¿verdad?, y hace una creación que brota de él. Pero todo viene de aquí, de allá, de todas partes.

Cada vez que hacíamos cambios radicales y drásticos, siempre teníamos gente que decía, "No, ya no me gusta porque ya cambió". Pero *that's the only way* para progresar, *you have to take chances. You know you're going to lose a few,* pero a la vez, te vas a abrir un campo más amplio y te vas a distinguir. . . .

No he oído que alguien más se haya destacado. Quizás hayan algunos, pero yo no sé. Quizás ha sido porque ahora aquí en Estados Unidos se ha modernizado mucho la música. Se han ido por el lado del *rock* y se han ido por un lado más chicano. Si acaso hay jóvenes que se interesen en el acordeón, que saquen cosas nuevas. Yo estoy viendo que no hay mucho futuro, porque alguien va a tener que sacar algo pronto para seguir. Si no, van a seguir allí siempre con la misma música, las mismas pasadas, las mismas canciones. Son las mismas cosas básicamente.

Conjunto music will always be there but I'm just hoping que alguien saque algo moderno. ¿Por qué no un joven combina toda esa música de *rock* y todo eso que anda orita con el acordeón? *Why not?* Ahorita ya hay una cosa más avanzada todavía que lo que está sacando Esteban. *Esteban had the right ideas.* Pero ahorita hay música de juventud que podía andar un acordeonista allí en mero medio y dándoles, dándoles lo que quieren, pero con el acordeón.

Sobre todo, quisiera animar a todos los acordeonistas y todos los músicos que usaran su talento para proyectar la música en cualquier estilo —no importa en qué música, cabe una acordeón— pero que lo usaran con un propósito positivo a la gente.

Flaco Jiménez

Los estilos —comenzando del estilo legítimo de mi papá, don Santiago Jiménez, que fue el pionero de la música del sonsonete, del acordeón, tejana— sí se han desarrollado bastantes estilos.

A mi parecer, y entre los años que yo he vivido entre la música de acordeón, creo que Narciso Martínez fue un estilista primero, y luego participó Ramón Ayala en la época nueva. Pero en la época vieja, que fue Pedrito Ayala, Bruno Villarreal, Valerio Longoria, y para nombrar tantos estilos, está difícil, porque en este ramo de la música de acordeón sanantoniana o tejana hay muchos estilos que han desarrollado.

Está difícil, diremos, para *pinpoint* cada estilo. Pero [hay] Esteban Jordán, que está en lo progresivo de esta clase de música. Y hay muchos estilistas ahorita que a través de escuchar varios acordeonistas en ocasión de que yo escuché cuando estaba yo joven. Escuché a Manuel Guerrero en el acordeón, que me inspiró. Escuché a Eugenio Ábrego, que me inspiró también.

Tony de la Rosa es un estilista bien original y, este, Tony hizo su época, y la sigue haciendo todavía. Y hay muchos que lo imitan o hay muchos que quieren no nomás imitar, pero querer seguir el sentido de aquel acordeonista que es Tony. Lo admiro yo, siendo diferente estilista, pero como quiera, en diferentes acordeonistas ellos también echan un poquito de Tony de la Rosa, porque está muy agradable.

Paulino Bernal en ese tiempo, cuando ya dejó de tocar el tipo de Armando Armendáriz, lo puchó más en sabiduría de música, en hacerlo más profesional, más progresivo. Así que creo que Paulino Bernal fue uno de los pioneros pa'l *progressive*.

Esteban sí es popular y lo respeto por su sabiduría en su acordeón. Y ha puesto más que un granito de arena para exponer la música *jazzy* y algo avanzado en el detalle. . . .

Mi estilo vino en escuchar a varios estilos. Yo cuando comencé, tenía para empezar el estilo de mi papá, don Santiago Jiménez, al tipo . . . no digo [de] antaño, pero cuando comenzó el detalle de la música del sonsonete del acordeón. Y luego comencé a escuchar [otros] acordeonistas. Después de mi papá fue Salvador García Torres, "El Pavo" de Los Pavos Reales. Escuché mucho a Narciso, escuché mucho a Paulino, a Valerio. Escuché muchos. Manuel Guerrero, de Los Tres Reyes de Daniel Garcés. Así que todo eso lo combiné y quizás de aquí, de allá, de todos esos amigos de música de acordeón . . . de repente salió el estilo mío. . . .

Realmente, sí hay diferencia [entre lo norteño y lo tejano]. Porque, no ofendiendo a nadie, diciendo la verdad, lo original se exploró, y la cuna de ese acordeón que vino de por allá de europa, el *pioneer* fue mi papá, don Santiago Jiménez. De allí pa' allá se desarrollaron diferentes estilos. Pero sí hay diferencia en cierto sentir, pero en sabiduría de acordeón, tanto hay buenos aquí como hay en México. Pero a mi parecer, es Tejas en que originó el estilo diferente, todo lo que es estilos en general.

[Mexicanos y tejanos] tenemos el mismo sentir, el mismo sentir, sea tejano o mexicano. Naturalmente que sí hay poquito de diferencia por el detalle que el mexicano incluyó —sea el tipo norteño y todo eso— incluyó el saxofón combinado con acordeón, que fue lo que siguió al original de aquí de Tejas.

Yo creo que es la hermandad, las combinaciones dentro acordeonistas, que nos ponemos de acuerdo y estamos en armonía, de platicarnos y decir y sentir lo que siente uno en el Valle, en México, aquí en Estados Unidos, Tejas, dondequiera. Todo se hace una flor acordeonísima bien bonita que florece, y cada quien tiene su estilo. Pero luego, cierra en que todos estamos unidos en ese detalle.

En cada región es la misma cosa. Si acaso habla uno en un tal acento, y vas a otra parte y se oye diferente el lenguaje, sea el sonsonete de como estamos hablando, es la misma cosa del acordeón. Tenemos nuestro diferente acento para introducir ese mensaje musical. . . .

La afinación no tiene que ver mucho en el arte que . . . el *individual* toque. Sí es, si acaso en un acordeón afinada diferente, es idea de tomar diferente sonido en el acordeón. Pero lo que sabe uno es lo que toca en acordeón. Si acaso se oye diferente es porque está afinada diferente. O a la mejor le enfadó a uno nomás el oído y dice, "Chihuahua, quisiera tener otro sonido, nomás para cambiarle un poquito, aunque sea mis tocados la misma cosa". Pero el sentimiento está todavía igual. Está como Gilberto García, el de Los Dos Gilbertos. Él tiene su onda de afinar su instrumento que está muy bien afinado. Toca igual a nosotros, ¿verdad?, al tipo polcazo, al tipo redova, canción ranchera, bolero, pero cada quien tiene sus ideas para mejorar su sonido.

Los Chamacos son unos de ellos, ellos combinan en detalle. Lo bonito es que cada cabeza es un mundo y, musicalmente, cada quien tiene su acordeonista favorito. . . .

As far as the acordeón, no creo yo que la gente vaya a cambiar de opinión . . . con el sonido del acordeón.

El estilo —desde don Santiago Jiménez, que fue lo más simple pero bonito, hasta mero arriba, como a Esteban Jordán y Valerio

Longoria— no creo que va a cambiar. Todo se va a quedar encerrado en un cierto *atmosphere*.

Va a haber algo nuevo en *exposure*. Va a haber *exposure* en no nomás penetrarnos aquí, trabajando nomás así como hemos trabajado durante los años. No, el detalle del acordeón, acordeonistas chamacos, acordeonistas jóvenes que ahorita están para hacer su debut . . . los vamos a ver en lo internacional. No va a ser nomás aquí local.

El sentimiento, todo el tiempo, debe de estar allí. Está como el detalle del sentimiento de *country-western* cuando entra el detalle de Hank Williams. El *country-western* y eso, nunca se ha ido, y nunca se va a ir. Conjunto *is here to stay! Of course,* ¡con acordeón!

Esteban Jordán

En cada región, el tiempo de los músicos es muy importante . . . como si vas a Corpos, broda, allí la misma polca que yo te toco en Houston, la toco diferente en Corpus . . . no diferente, sino el compás nada más, el tiempo va abajo. Yo sé dónde y dónde no. En el Valle lo subo un poquito más. Yo te conozco de bailes. En Houston es tacuachito, en San Antonio es el serruchito, en West Tejas es el tieso [*se ríe*], ¡el tieso, loco! Yo me las sé todas, vato.

La música, bro, 'ta muy curiosa, *because there's only twelve notes to it. It's what you do with those twelve notes.* Pero las doce notas son pa' todos —es pa' ti, es pa' mí, pa' Óscar [Hernández, quien estaba presente durante la entrevista] . . . y el que la barajea— y de allí, de esas notas, bro, salen dialectos.

Ahora hay muchos que oyen un pedacito de éste, un pedacito del otro y el otro, y hacen un estilo. Pero esos son oportunistas, esos ya no son estilistas . . . Orita hay estilistas falsos . . . Lo mío, muy pocos lo pueden copiar, por eso no lo han copiado. . . .

Bueno, mira, en Tejas nació, vamos a decir, nació el estilo, el estilo de conjunto, porque lo trajo el alemán para acá, tú sabes, cuando los concentraron aquí.

El estilo que sacó . . . Ramón Ayala viene de Los Alegres de Terán. Fíjate, ¡ése es el original! Ramón Ayala y Cornelio Reyna, Los Alegres, La Rubia y la Morena, toda esa bo', ellos son los meros machín.

Y acá, pa' acá pa'l la'o de Corpos fue Tony de la Rosa, El Alacrán, ¿cómo se llama?, Ángel Flores. Ora el chavo acá de Laredo se oye igual a Tony de la Rosa —Bernardo. Ora, te vas pa' San Antonio, oyes las pasadas del viejón, Santiago. Ahora aquel chavo quiere arremedar un poco de lo mío, vamos diciendo, Nick Villarreal. Pero siempre se oyen las pasadas del viejón. Se le abre la onda y de repente se le apaga el foco, y cuando se le apaga al vato, se va con Santiago y usa las pasadas de él, ¿ves?, porque *that's basic, because it goes back to his basics.* . . .

Me gusta tocar de todo, *that's what I like to do,* pero, *sometimes,* le revuelves mucho. Si estás en el Valle, no puedes 'tar tocando *jazz, rock* y luego voltearte y tocarles una salsita bien sabrosa y luego un buen bolerazo, como un danzón, y luego una polca *because they'll kill you! There's no such thing as that.* Pero en California, sí. Ahora en Califas, una polca o dos por noche y ¡ya! . . .

Un estilista pesa'o, que sobresalió, es Valerio Longoria, porque fue el que modernizó. Antes de eso, Narciso Martínez trajo polcas . . . un estilo que sacó él. Y de allí comenzó, vamos diciendo, don Pedro Ayala. Estilista él, pero pa' los valses, redovas, broda, para esas ondas. ¡Jijo!, ¡qué bonito! Pero no lo podías sacar de allí, y ¿para qué lo quieres sacar de allí?

Santiago Jiménez, Sr., sacó ese estilo . . . sanantoniano, loco, broda . . . muy loco ese estilo, muy corridón, muy sabrosón . . . parecía norteño, pero no es, ¿me entiendes cómo te quiero decir? *Similar* al norteño pero no es norteño. Es sanantoniano.

Valerio aprendió, se avanzó. ¿De dónde? De él, quizás, no sé. Todos tenemos que oír y escuchar algo para poder reaccionar. El hombre se quebró la cabeza pa' sacar estilos, él mismo, en ese tiempo y en esa época. . . .

Entonces yo oía, yo oía todos los estilos, porque yo ya tocaba guitarra. Cuando comencé a agarrar la acordeón, yo oí la de Valerio y de allí aprendí yo. El único que *I was influenced by was him.* . . .

Después de Valerio, despuesito de Valerio, Tone [de la Rosa] fue el que siguió la tradición, la combinación de la onda. Porque ése es un estilo, es un estilo de la Kineña, estilo Kineño, tacatacataca, piquetia'o —y se conoce. Y de allí salió Rubén Vela. De allí salió Gilberto Pérez. De allí salió Rubén Naranjo. De allí salió Chano Cadena.

Paulino is good, man! Paulino is a very good man. He brought a style. From all the styles, he picked something of his own . . . había un estilo de sangre. *That made it all together.*

Yo oí a Paulino tocar, en unas grabaciones que yo nunca había oído. Igualito a Valerio Longoria, *man! Wow! I couldn't believe it! And that's beautiful.* El vato podía tocar toda la onda. *And then he grabbed* el tiempo que había en los tríos . . . y se hizo. *In other words,* hizo un conjunto, estableció la onda del trío dentro del conjunto. Porque traiba muy buenos elementos [músicos] también —eso le ayudó mucho. Estilistas como cantantes, hacían un estilo, *overall* —Juan Sifuentes, El Macho, La Pulga. . . .

Tito Puente, Machito, Tito Rodríguez, Count Basie, en *big bands, you know,* arreglos, como te digo, Buddy Rich, vato. ¡Jijo de su, 'taba cabrón! Como es tamborero, jijo, pitaban los pitos, hacía lo mismo a las tamboras que los pitos. *That influenced me, bro.*

Lo meto en polca, lo meto en redova, onde me dé mi chingada gana. Yo hago lo que yo quiera. *Okay, for soul, Ray Charles. For drummer, Buddy Rich. For wild, Jimmy Smith.* Agarra la onda. Henry Mancini, yo aprendo de allí, yo aprendo de *anywhere, Dixieland.*

Bro, I'm a universal stylist. Yo orita, pa' onde yo me quiera ir, me voy, broda. Yo tengo una *freedom* muy loca . . . *It's so hard for me to* seguir un estilo. Soy muy estilista de todo. Y nunca paro de aprender.

The only new style you're gonna see is me. I'm comin' out with a new style, for me—not for the musicians, only for me. See, I'm bringing out the style that I did in the fifties, sixties, okay?

El conjunto va a seguir, bro. Las polcas y toda la onda va a seguir. *All they're gonna do is recycle mainly what they did.* No se va a acabar. *It's not going to stop.* Orita 'tan metiendo *combination,* los violines y todo ese jale, con la acordeón. *It's cool. They're using little pieces of it.*

It's our time to move it! To learn from ourselves. Find out what you got. Find out about your own self. ¿Qué tanto traes en la chaveta? *You think just because you got a pocketful of money, you think you're it. And it's not where it's at, at all. If you're going to create, it doesn't take money to create. Just go out and grab a book,* o vete pa' las montañas, vato. *Do something, go break your head, you'll find it. Look for it, you'll find it.*

Conjunto! Style and Class
Narciso Martínez, Valerio Longoria, Tony de la Rosa, Paulino Bernal, Flaco Jiménez, and Esteban Jordán

✦

JUAN TEJEDA
1988

(Entrevistas originales: página 315)

*S*tyle. Some have it, some don't.
When you talk about conjunto music, that distinctive Chicano music that uses the button accordion as its principal instrument, which developed around the Texas-Mexican border during the turn of the century, it is clear that there are certain individuals who have played a significant role in creating the unique styles within the genre.

For example, if you like conjunto music and listen to it, you know that Flaco Jiménez (1987 Grammy Award winner) plays that ol' accordion different than, let's say, Esteban Jordán. Or that Valerio Longoria doesn't play that squeeze box like Nick Villarreal. They're different. They've developed their own style. There are those that prefer the style of Rubén Vela and those that love the music of Los Alegres de Terán. That distinctive styles exist within conjunto music is taken for granted among conjunto music lovers, but little is written about it.

Dr. Manuel Peña, author of a landmark study on conjunto music, The Texas-Mexican Conjunto: History of a Working-Class Music, states that the history of the conjunto may be divided into three distinct phases. The first, to 1935, may be called the formative, when the accordion was either played solo, or combined with sundry other instruments in an ad hoc fashion. The second phase began in 1935, with the appearance of Narciso Martínez's first recordings. Known among the younger generation as El Primero, Martínez was chiefly responsible for moving the emergent conjunto beyond its earlier Germanic style. The final phase of conjunto music began to take shape during the decade after the war, when the modern ensemble crystallized into a cohesive unit. By the mid fifties it had acquired a shape and a style that has remained virtually unchanged to this day.

Besides highlighting Narciso Martínez, who is called the "father" of conjunto music, Peña focuses on various other musicians who he says played important roles in the stylistic development of conjunto music. They include Valerio Longoria, the "genius" of conjunto music, remembered for his innovations; Tony de la Rosa, "whose polkas became the ideal by which others were measured," and one of the most popular accordionists in the history of conjunto music; and Paulino Bernal, who with the Conjunto Bernal "created a highly popular sound based on a unique blend of the traditional and the innovative. The result was a group that is recognized to this day as 'the only one of its kind.'"

In thinking of an article to include in this year's Tejano Conjunto Festival program, we decided that it would be interesting to focus on the distinctive styles that have developed in conjunto music. How would we approach it, though? We felt that since we are fortunate enough to still have most of conjunto's stylistic pioneers living, who would be better to speak on the subject than the stylists themselves? It was decided that we would interview six of conjunto's stylists—Narciso Martínez, Valerio Longoria, Tony de la Rosa, Paulino Bernal, Esteban Jordán, and Flaco Jiménez—and ask each the same questions.

We assumed their individual responses to the same questions would provide a basis for comparison. There were five initial questions:

1. *Have distinctive styles developed within conjunto music?*
2. *What styles have developed and who were they created by?*
3. *How about your own style? Do you think you developed a distinctive style?*
4. *Were these stylistic pioneers popular and were you popular?*
5. *What styles exist today and what does the future hold for conjunto music? Will the styles change or remain the same?*

I decided to do the interviews myself partly because no one else was available within the necessary time, and partly because deep down inside I guess I wanted to do them. I consider it a great privi-

lege and honor to have been able to sit down personally with these conjunto greats to discuss style. We talked about a number of things, many of which went beyond the limits of the initial questions. Some very basic and important comments were made.

The interviews were conducted in February and March of this year. The following "monologues" were edited from the interviews, many of which turned out to be quite lengthy. We would have liked to include more of what each said, but space and time did not permit. Nonetheless, we feel certain that you will enjoy and be enlightened by these comments on style from six conjunto giants who definitely have it.

And now, in their own words . . .

Narciso Martínez

Yes, of course. In my opinion, yes. Today there are many accordion groups that play only *regional,* sheer style . . . there are several groups that just play only *cumbias,* you know? . . .

Santiago Jiménez was the only one, the first of all of them that I heard. Santiago Jiménez, Sr. Santiago Jiménez y sus Valedores. But, Santiago Jiménez . . . what made him famous was "La Piedrera," "Rumbo a Roma," "Viva Seguín." He had a great style. His boys are good boys. He treated me very well when we were there. As it turns out, the *tacuachito* was born in San Antonio. It was all polka in those years . . . when it started in San Antonio. And Santiago Jiménez, well, it was his meat and potatoes.

I came to hear music, musicians, by about 1948, 1949. I still went out to play. And I'd listen to Los Donneños, Mario, Ramiro, Pedro Ayala, Los Alegres de Terán—they were the first ones I began to hear, after I had already made it big. . . .

Well . . . like Pedro Ayala, Valerio Longoria, they more or less play. . . more or less . . . play the same style. There's others who have used . . . other groups like Óscar Hernández, Esteban Jordán, several others, they're using a lot of Black style right now . . . in their arrangements. Well, like Esteban, it's not that he has so much style, it's that he plays many of the new tunes that are around today . . . what he's recorded are a lot of old tunes . . . tunes like "El zopilote mojado," you see, and that's good, he has his style. But in those tunes, it's more old style.

Now, a new style, as I said just now, is Óscar Hernández, and there are others who with that same style that they play . . . and very different from mine, I think it's very different from mine. Paulino Bernal, Óscar is the one who knows him. . . .

A good musician . . . Tony de la Rosa began, he was a very good friend of mine, he has his style, too. . . .

I couldn't listen to anyone on records. There was no one. I recorded in 1935 for Bluebird, and there was nothing of anyone, nothing. There wasn't even radio at that time. There were records, but very little of . . . it was like *tríos* . . . Well, over there in San Antonio, which is a very large city, is where I recorded for the first time . . . I recorded in San Antonio about five or six times . . . My first recordings, they had a bunch of everything . . . And it grew a lot there, a lot in San Antonio . . . A whole lot, a lot of talent.

Well, the accordion, I can say that I was the first to begin to include it in a group. But, as I just said, I played for years alone with just the accordion, from dusk to dawn. Then around nineteen forty . . . eight, forty-nine, was when they started to form groups, bands. I can say that I was one of the first.

My brother played. He had a little accordion, very . . . I didn't know, but anyway, I tried and I tried until I began to play, and so by nineteen . . . twenty-six, twenty-seven, he dropped it, and I continued . . . It's that I liked music. I would sing . . . I sang on a record . . . I still can't even talk, but well, I sang on several records . . . But I know I'm the first to introduce the accordion on recordings . . . accompanied by an accordion . . . because before that there were like orchestras or violin groups and all those things, *mariachis* . . . but not . . . I never saw the accordion combined with songs on a record, never.

In 1935, they asked me, "What do they call you?" "Well, my name is Narciso Martínez." "Okay, but you are what?" That was 1935, in about September, and at that time I was pretty hard up, hard up . . . still. Worse now, because of my age. Well, the one who recorded me was Enrique, from here in Brownsville. He's the one who gave me that nickname, El Huracán del Valle. It was in '35. In '34, a big rainstorm had passed through here, and that's why it happened. . . .

Today here . . . they are very enthusiastic about the *cumbia*. There's almost 60, 70 percent more on the side of the *cumbia* than on the side of the polka. . . .

In truth, it can be the same style, but it's not the same musician. One musician plays in one way and another plays in another way. I can play and he can play with the same . . . but each one has his style.

For example . . . take the waltz. The waltz was very popular, but today people don't appreciate it anymore. People dance and they don't appreciate it. The waltz is good for a wedding, a *quinceañera,* and just one or two. Yes, they're very beautiful, but people want to get worked up.

I want to say, I'm not going to talk about myself, because I'm already done, I'm about ready to go. But not just because of that. What I believe is that the accordion isn't in anymore, it seems to me. I hope they keep on working like before, but already there are fewer people into the accordion than into *orquesta.*

Before, people only went for the *orquesta típica,* but when the accordion started getting popular, around '38, '39, '40, and '44, and all those [years], the *orquesta* plumb went out of favor. But then came Beto Villa, Balde González, with their *orquestas* here. Luis Arcaraz, from Mexico, would come here. I played with them many times.

The way I see it myself, right now what is so . . . right now it's Roberto Pulido, and all those guys. I think the *orquesta* is taking a lot from the group, from the conjunto.

I see very little for the accordion from here on. It won't die altogether, but as I was saying earlier, you heard the accordion very little, except on the ranches. There on the ranch, you'd only hear the accordion, just a violin and an accordion.

That's what they played. There weren't any groups in those years. And possibly the accordion, that's what I think, but who knows how it will be down the road. I've heard them on the radio, on television, that it will never die. Well, I hope it never dies, because that was my meal ticket for many years. Now today, well not anymore, but for a lot of years I lived off of it.

I'd just like to say good luck to those who play . . . and to those who don't play, too, of course. Yes, may God bless them and, well . . . because I can now say, just imagine, I'm going to put away my rifle soon [*and he laughs*]. For a long time now I've hardly played. I do still play, but very little . . . very little now . . . like at a commercial dance, I don't play nor do I want to play. There's times when I go out to play with Gilberto Pérez, because they come to get me and they pay me for a little while. I'll help them out.

Valerio Longoria

Yeah, we took up [the accordion] in the United States because—I don't know why—but the Germans are to blame for sending those accordions over here. . . .

Several styles have been developed, and a lot of them are still around, but yet, however, the same music, the original music still exists. It's the same.

The old style, the music was hurried, simply because it was a heel-tapping style of dancing. Today they dance another way, they don't do the heel tapping. Today they dance more fluidly, so the music is slower.

Every musician has his own style. It's hard to articulate all these styles that crop up, because there are so many musicians who want to play like the other guy, like the other guy plays . . . then it's not their style, it's now the other guy's style.

Clearly the styles have been changing . . . before, we played very fast. The polkas were very hurried and they were danced differently. Later, Tony de la Rosa recorded slower, another, slower style, and the people accepted it.

Tony de la Rosa's tempo, Rubén Vela also took it up . . . but now, later, Rubén has his own style, but now it seems that he's taken to playing a little happier, faster than how he played before.

Esteban's style is different. Many people don't understand the kind of music . . . He's very knowledgeable about American music . . . that's the thing, and Esteban grew up around Americans. He lived for a long time in West Texas, in Big Spring, Texas, and there it was only English, only rock and roll and Black people. And that's where Esteban got into the groove of playing sort of like he does.

Paulino Bernal, it goes without saying, is a great musician . . . another, different style, extremely advanced, advanced, very gifted on the accordion. Paulino developed other things by means of the *trío*. He almost never sang with his conjunto. He'd bring in vocalists. There was a young man called "La Pulga" [the Flea], from Kingsville. "Mi único camino," La Pulga was the lead voice and Paulino's brother was the second, and . . . actually I don't know who it was, but [they formed] a little *trío*, and that was already another style.

There are two very different styles, Paulino's and Esteban's. Like Óscar Hernández . . . another good style, although that was now a chromatic accordion, but it's another very heavy style, but it's with a complete accordion. A chromatic accordion is complete.

You also have Los Cachorros, right? They have their own very delightful style. Different little moves, different riffs, different from the other riffs that we have. Very different, very joyful, very good, and, however . . . well, another style like Ramón Ayala's.

Flaco Jiménez is another style. He also plays a little fast . . . like they used to play not too long ago, but a little slower.

The style of Los Lobos is another style that's much faster. Perhaps faster than the old days, but nevertheless they're another style. Everyone has his own style. Like Los Pavos Reales have their own style. Like Lalo, he has a style very much his own. Salvador García has a style very much his own. . . .

Narciso was one of them [Longoria's influences], and some other accordionists that I would hear on the radio. You'd hear accordionists who I never got to know. I'd go into a place, there would be jukeboxes, I'd hear a tune playing, and it would stick. And that's how I got my start in music.

I felt that I wanted to sing and play at the same time, play solfeggio and be singing at the same time, play the riff while I'm singing. Many find it difficult, believe me . . . that thing of playing and singing at the same time, playing solfeggio and . . . singing, or then doing riffs at the same time without losing the pitch, without going off the track.

That's the way I learned. That's how I began, trying to do that . . . not to stop when I was singing, to keep playing. That's why they ask me, "Valerio, how do you manage to be singing and playing riffs at the same time?" It's so easy for me, plumb easy, because that's how I learned. I liked it that way. . . .

Styles . . . there are so many of them in Mexico. The majority of conjuntos from Mexico play different from those in Texas. *Tejano* is a different style, although, for example, there are many here in the United States who copy Ramón Ayala, which is Ramón's own style, the style of Los Cachorros . . . after Los Cachorros . . . Los Alegres de Terán, that's yet another style, because they're *corridos* . . . but pure Mexican music, full of gunfighters and whatnot.

Everyone acquires his own style, but the music is almost the same. Yes, but I don't know how to clear up the matter of styles very well, because it comes down to who has the most talent, the one who can create more music. That's where the style changes. The sound never changes because it's the same, that sweet sound of the accordion. But other riffs, different riffs, then it's another style.

And that's what I call style. They created styles because they came up with different riffs that aren't the same as Narciso's, or the same as Tony's, or the same as Esteban's. Because they already left us this style. That's why I say, there aren't many who change what they did, who develop their own style, their own riffs, their own moves.

I've seen Carlos y José come here from Mexico and they play simple. And when they play, well, the people get up and they start screaming and shouting, and all that.

Like Rubén Naranjo, his style is simple, it's simple. They are his own riffs, but it's very simple. Two riffs, one riff, and then he sings. He sings, and then he goes back to playing his same two riffs again. . . .

Everything has to keep changing, everything is always changing. Before, no one played what's played now. There weren't any *cumbias*. It wasn't so long ago that the *cumbia* was born. Well, maybe in Colombia they had them, but here in the United States there weren't any *cumbias*. There were polkas, cha-cha-chas, *porros*, back then.

I would like for this accordion thing, for it to never end, and that there would be more progress with it, that more good musicians would come along like the ones who have to come along. That's my dream, that accordion music will never end and that it will continue going forward.

Tony de la Rosa

Well, of the ones I remember, right, the first accordionist I heard was Narciso Martínez. Mr. Narciso Martínez, to me, is the master of the accordion. Shortly after, I had the opportunity to hear Don Santiago Jiménez, you know, Benito Espinoza, El Gallito.

We started hearing conjuntos from San Antonio later, Valerio Longoria. Nothing but individual, unique styles. Finally, there's Don Pedro Ayala. He created his own style. The tempo of *regional* music as well as the tempo that Don Narciso Martínez had, we all experienced that musical tempo . . . all these people, as far as I know, they were creators of their own style.

From the styles comes an original style, like that of Narciso Martínez, you know? So then you recognize it wherever you hear one of his selections. . . .

We're talking about a long time ago. Waltzes, polkas, schottisches, redowas, *danzas, ochos,* quadrilles, broom dances, whatever you want. Back then, it was just a *bajo sexto,* a guitar, and the accordion . . . that was all, and it was hard work.

You asked me what is the difference with Narciso . . . during the time of Mr. Longoria, a great friend of mine, a fellow worker. He's the only one that I heard who was singing and playing his accordion at the same time. That's something that really caught my attention.

Don Esteban [Jordán] is the cream of the crop on the accordion in this form here . . . from blues, jazz, country, he . . . he'll play you whatever you ask. If the guys go along with him, "Go for it!" Like we were talking earlier about how Valerio Longoria played somewhat complicated, some difficult things, this young man is right there. To me, he and Óscar Hernández, right, and Paulino Bernal . . . we're formed by those styles.

Now Jordán, no one comes near him, even to this day. He's very advanced mentally with his music, and we're in back of him. But it's not to our advantage to follow him, for the simple reason that that's not where our bread is buttered.

Bernal introduced—there were already others, but they weren't known—the three voices. And a very unique style of theirs, on the accordion, in the voices, in the arrangements, sir. The tempo of my *compadre* Paulino Bernal, I danced very comfortably to it.

Speaking of the cream of the crop and accordions, you have to talk about Esteban Jordán, you have to talk about Óscar Hernández. Another young man who has made phenomenal progress in his development is Bobby Naranjo, another generation. All three are different generations.

There's another young man, who's not around here, but you have to respect him, that's Beto Salinas, who was around there playing for a while. In Laredo right now, the one whose work is closely related to my style is Bernardo Martínez [y sus Compadres].

From Narciso Martínez to Jiménez, Valerio, Cuco Borjas, Gil Borjas . . . a person I esteem and appreciate is Don Manuel Guerrero. There are others, Flaco Jiménez, of course. . . .

My own style, I more or less took it from the accordionists. No, I can't deny it. But to distinguish it, I also had a different tempo from that of the other conjuntos. That's what most made me different from the others, because I played the same things they played, but my style was another, another tempo, another thing. Apart from the accordion, my major influence in style was country, country music.

That's why I stay in the same place where I always am. That's why they know me. Because they know, when they hear it, that it's Tony de la Rosa who's playing. . . .

Right now, the way I see it is that a group shows up and starts getting popular, and about five or six groups will form that are going to copy it. They'll play not exactly the same as that one, but close. I'd say that conjunto has its time, *orquesta* has its time, those new groups have their time. And they're all buddies, but they all have their time. And some of us made it and some of us didn't make it, but we were all there. We were all there, you understand. Now if you ask me right now who I see that's strong, I don't see anything as long as the rest are doing what the rest are doing. They've got to be different.

Esteban is really popular, with the generation that listens to what he's developing in the direction of American music. There's that change in the trend, call it Chicano, and the music is becoming mixed, even Black people's music, rock, you name it. There are already Chicano groups, Mexican too, who'll play you all that kind of music. They'll play it for you. . . .

Yes, sir, just as it changed from the time of Don Narciso, Mr. Jiménez, to the time we're in right now, that's the way it'll be from here on also. But every blessed time will be repeated, too. The accordion falls behind and a moment later it comes back, and it stays behind for a while [*he laughs*], and then something else comes along. It's like saying that when there was the cha-cha-cha, the mambo, right, *tropical, mariachi,* that it's always been there—the *sonoras,* you name it.

The repertoire is going to change in such a way that while there are accordionists, and while there are musicians, right—whether it's *bajo* players, whether it's piano accordion, horns, winds, what have you—they're going to become known and that's where the change will come, because that person is the guide. And you ask me if it's going to change, in the area of tempos, in this, that, and the other. Repertoire is not just saying, "I've got a big repertoire," but you have to be adding all the time, and it's the simplest thing there is and the hardest.

I don't see that there'll be many more who will create their own style, who will also be pioneers further on. If they're different, they'll be pioneers. If there aren't any differences, they're not going to be pioneers.

The only thing is that nowadays I see something very bad among my fellow musicians. The fellow musicians we had back then aren't the same as we were used to, for the simple reason that today they're not playing to please or because they like to play. No matter how much you may enjoy it, no matter how much you may enjoy playing and being a musician, I think it's very bad if you do it just to show another musician that you can play better than him.

They don't think that way, those young people who think of the public. Because in my career, I've seen them come, and I've seen them go. And I also came, and I'm also gonna go.

Thanks very much.

Paulino Bernal

There have been people who have stood out for their style, like Narciso Martínez, Tony de la Rosa, Valerio Longoria, Esteban Jordán, Pedro Ayala, people who have figured out how to distinguish themselves, one way or another, and that has brought them success.

Narciso Martínez's style of music, from the dances on the ranch patios over there, was very joyful, projecting joy, family, community. I see people on the patio dancing the redowa, the schottische. During Narciso's time, he was the only one playing. Pedro Ayala began to record things that Narciso also recorded, it's just that there was plenty of room, because there were few accordionists.

Valerio Longoria is very pleasant because, to me, it was music in the bridegroom's, or the bride's, tempo. And Valerio would play the song or *bolero* that you liked the best. In my opinion, the matter of the modern *bolero* was very classical, and singing and playing at the same time. That really made him stand out.

Tony de la Rosa slowed it down a little bit. Slower than Valerio or Narciso, very joyful, with music that had a nice strong beat. It's a style that's neither Mexican—Mexican from Mexico—but nor is it Americanized.

Eugenio [Ábrego, of Los Alegres de Terán] is a good accordionist, but his style is more rural, more traditional, Mexican.

Esteban Jordán combined everything, and he could play everything. He began to use notes that weren't being used. They were there, but they weren't being used. He was the first to do a combination of everything, he mixed in *tropical,* jazz, *mariachi,* with the accordion. He put together so many combinations, rock and roll on the accordion. He took from here, from there, from everywhere, and he did it on the accordion and he did it really well, and he can keep up with his *ranchera* songs, too, and go from one extreme to the other.

I didn't get to know the music of Don Santiago Jiménez very well. I've gotten to know a lot more about his son, Flaco, a typical San Antonio musician, but he's feeling what he's playing, and he's communicating with his movements and his body. He makes the people get into it. He's not complicated. What he plays is very simple, and he's managed to distinguish himself. . . .

When I started, I had Narciso Martínez, Tony de la Rosa, and Valerio Longoria playing. I said, "I can't play what they play because I can't ever outdo them in what they're playing. I have to come up with something of my own."

I started to come up with my own polkas, I started to listen, I started to get together with other musicians, I started to travel with a very famous *orquesta* all over the United States, and I'd stick with the accordionists, with the trumpet players. A trumpet player who's a good friend of mine, Louie Gasca, taught me a lot.

Then I said, "I'm going to have to distinguish myself in some other way, I have to come up with music that's not being played," chords that other accordionists weren't playing. I started to come up with another kind of music, and I liked the music of Los Panchos, Los Tres Reyes, all those good *tríos.* We began to distinguish ourselves with the vocals, too, from the duets that we always sang to a modern trio, and with chords on the accordion and polkas more complicated than what others were coming out with.

It helped me to move on to the three-row accordion. Everybody continued with the two-row. I quickly moved to the three-row, but I didn't stay there. When the Italian accordion called Rino came out, I was the first to have that accordion and that gave me a modern sound, more classical. It had the changes to make it sound more mellow, more sweet. That was one of the things, the chromatic accordion, and another was the complicated polkas I began to record. . . .

The culture of the people has a lot to do with it. I think that the area where a person lives has a lot to do with it. Those of us from the Valley have influences from Mexico and influences from the

United States. Another flavor emerges here, another accordion style different from San Antonio's. Simply, the *bajista* . . . to play the *bajo sexto* in San Antonio is very different from playing it here.

[*Tejano* conjunto] is completely different [from Mexican conjunto], in its rhythm, and in the music. *Tejanos* distinguish themselves in that the way they play the accordion is a little more advanced.

Let's be honest, conjunto is a combination of all kinds of music. There's nothing new under the sun. We can't escape it—it's all been discovered, right? Everyone takes from here, from there, right, and makes a creation that springs from within. But it all comes from here, from there, from everywhere.

Every time we made radical and drastic changes, there were always people who'd say, "No, I don't like it anymore, because it's changed now." But that's the only way to progress, you have to take chances. You know you're going to lose a few, but at the same time, you're going to open up a wider space for yourself, and you're going to distinguish yourself. . . .

I haven't heard of anyone else who has really stood out. Perhaps there are some, but I don't know. Perhaps it's because here in the United States music has become greatly modernized. They've gone over to the side of rock and they've gone over to a more Chicano side. If there are young people who are interested in the accordion, let them come up with new things. I'm seeing that there isn't much of a future, because someone has to come up with something soon to keep on. If not, they're just going to go on forever with the same music, the same riffs, the same songs. They're basically the same things.

Conjunto music will always be there, but I'm just hoping that someone will come up with something modern. Why doesn't a young person combine all that rock music and all that stuff going on right now with the accordion? Why not? Right now there's already something even more advanced than what Esteban is playing. Esteban had the right ideas. But today there's young people's music that an accordionist could be right in the middle of, and giving, giving them what they want, but on the accordion.

Above all, I would like to encourage all the accordionists and all the musicians to use their talent to convey the music in whatever style—no matter what kind of music, there's room for an accordion—but that they use it for people in a positive way.

Flaco Jiménez

Styles—starting with the legitimate style of my father, Don Santiago Jiménez, who was the pioneer of accordion-sound, *tejano* music—a lot of styles really have been developed.

The way I see it, and in the years that I've lived in the midst of accordion music, I think that Narciso Martínez was among the first stylists, and then came Ramón Ayala in recent times. But in the old period, there was Pedro Ayala, Bruno Villarreal, Valerio Longoria, and to name so many styles is difficult, because in this branch of San Antonio or *tejano* accordion music there are many styles that have been developed.

It's difficult, I'd say, to pinpoint each style. But [there is] Esteban Jordán, who is in the progressive camp of this type of music. And there are many stylists right now, various accordionists who I had occasion to listen to when I was young. I listened to Manuel Guerrero on the accordion, who inspired me. I listened to Eugenio Ábrego, who inspired me, too.

Tony de la Rosa is a very original stylist and, well, Tony made a place for himself, and he continues doing it. And there are many who imitate him, or there are many who want not just to imitate but to follow the feeling of that accordionist who's Tony. I admire him, being a different stylist, but anyhow, among different accordionists they too throw in a little of Tony de la Rosa, because it's so pleasing.

Paulino Bernal during that time, when he'd stopped playing Armando Armendáriz's style, he pushed it further in musical knowledge, making it more professional, more progressive. So I believe that Paulino Bernal was one of the pioneers of progressive conjunto.

Esteban really is popular and I respect him for his knowledge of the accordion. And he's put in more than a little grain of sand toward presenting music that is jazzy and kind of advanced in the details. . . .

My style came from listening to various styles. When I began, I had, to start with, the style of my father, Don Santiago Jiménez, a style . . . I won't say [of] long ago, but when that particular accordion-sound music began. Then I started to listen to [other] accordionists. After my father it was Salvador García Torres, "El Pavo" of Los Pavos Reales. I listened a lot to Narciso, I listened a lot to Paulino, to Valerio. I listened to a lot of them. Manuel Guerrero, with Daniel Garcés's Los Tres Reyes. So I combined all of that and perhaps from here, from there, from all those friends in accordion music . . . suddenly my style emerged. . . .

Actually, there is a difference [between *norteño* and *tejano*]. Because, without wishing to offend anyone, the truth is, the original music was explored, and the cradle of that accordion that came from over there from Europe, the pioneer was my father, Don Santiago Jiménez. From then on, different styles were developed. But there is a difference in a certain sense, but in knowledge of the accordion, there are as many good ones here as there are in Mexico. But in my view, it's in Texas where a different style originated, everything that's style in general.

We [Mexicans and *tejanos*] have the same feeling, the same feeling, be it *tejano* or *mexicano*. Naturally, there is a little bit of difference in the fact that the Mexican included—that is, the *norteño* type and all that—the Mexican included the saxophone combined with the accordion, which is what followed the original from here in Texas.

I believe it is the brotherhood, the relationships among accordionists, that we're in agreement and we're in harmony, to talk with each other, and to say and to feel what one feels in the Valley, in Mexico, here in the United States, Texas, wherever. It all becomes a beautiful, very accordionate flower that blooms, and each one has his style. But then, it closes up with all of us united on that point.

In each region it's the same thing. If you happen to speak with a certain accent, and you go somewhere else and the language sounds different, be it the rhythm of how we talk, it's the same thing as with the accordion. We have our different accents to convey that musical message. . . .

Tuning doesn't have much to do with the art that . . . the individual might play. It is, if it happens to be an accordion that is tuned different, it's the idea of getting a different sound on the accordion. But what one knows is what one plays on the accordion. If it happens to sound different it's because it is tuned differently. Or maybe he just got annoyed with the sound, and says, "Doggonit, I'd like to have another sound, just to change things a little, even though my playing might be the same." But the feeling is still the same. It's like Gilberto García, of Los Dos Gilbertos. He has his thing of tuning his instrument so that it is really well tuned. He plays the same as we do, right, the heavy polka style, redowa style, *canción ranchera, bolero,* but each one has his own ideas for improving his sound.

Los Chamacos are one of those, they blend the details. The beautiful thing is that each mind is a universe and, musically, each one has his favorite accordionist. . . .

As far as the accordion, I don't think that people will change their mind . . . about the sound of the accordion.

Style—from Don Santiago Jiménez, which was really simple but beautiful, up to the very top, like Esteban Jordán and Valerio Longoria—I don't think it's going to change. Everything will remain enclosed in a certain atmosphere.

There is going to be something new in the exposure. There's going to be exposure in not just a local breakthrough, working just like we've worked over the years. No, the matter of the accordion, accordionists, youngsters, young accordionists who are about to make their debut . . . we're going to see them on the international scene. It's not going to be just here, local.

The feeling should always be there. It's like the particular feeling in country-western when the Hank Williams sound comes along. Country-western and all that has never disappeared, and it will never disappear. Conjunto is here to stay! Of course, with the accordion!

Esteban Jordán

In each region, the musician's tempo is very important . . . like if you go to Corpus, brother, there the same polka that I play in Houston, I play it different in Corpus . . . not different, except just the tempo, the tempo slows down. I know where, and where not to. In the Valley, I pick it up a little more. I do know about the dances. In Houston, it's the *tacuachito*, in San Antonio it's the *serruchito*, in West Texas it's the *tiezo* [*he laughs*], the *tiezo*, dude! I know all of them, man.

Music, bro, is very weird, because there's only twelve notes to it. It's what you do with those twelve notes. But those twelve notes are for everyone—it's for you, it's for me, for Óscar [Hernández, who was sitting in on the interview] . . . and the one who can mix it up—and from there, from those notes, bro, dialects emerge.

Today there are many people who hear a bit of this, a bit of that and the other, and they create a style. But those people are opportunists, those people aren't stylists anymore . . . Right now, there are false stylists . . . My thing, very few can copy it, that's why they haven't copied it. . . .

Well, look, it was born, I'd say, in Texas, the style was born, the conjunto style, because the Germans brought it over here, you know, when they got settled here.

The style that was created by . . . Ramón Ayala comes from Los Alegres de Terán. Look, that's the original one! Ramón Ayala and Cornelio Reyna, Los Alegres, La Rubia y la Morena, all that bunch, they're the real deal!

And over here, over here by Corpus, it was Tony de la Rosa, El Alacrán, what's his name? Ángel Flores. Now the guy over here from Laredo sounds the same as Tony de la Rosa—Bernardo. Now you go to San Antonio, you hear the riffs of the old man, Santiago. Now that guy wants to imitate a little of what I do, we're talking Nick Villarreal. But you always hear the old man's riffs. He finds a groove, and all of a sudden he goes blank, and when the guy goes blank, he goes back to Santiago and uses his riffs, you see, because that's basic, because it goes back to his basics. . . .

I like to play everything, that's what I like to do, but, sometimes, you mix it up too much. If you're in the Valley, you can't be playing jazz, rock, and then turn around and play them some real tasty *salsa,* and then a good, solid *bolero,* like a *danzón,* and then a polka, because they'll kill you! There's no such thing as that. But in California, yes. Now in Califas, one or two polkas a night and that's it! . . .

A heavy stylist, who really stood out, is Valerio Longoria, because he was the one who modernized. Before that, Narciso Martínez brought polkas . . . a style that he created. And from there, I would say, Don Pedro Ayala began. A stylist, he is, but on waltzes, redowas, brother, for those kinds of things. Wow! How beautiful! But you couldn't get him out of there, and why would you want to get him out of there?

Santiago Jiménez, Sr., came out with that . . . San Antonio style, far-out, brother . . . that style was very far-out, very fast-paced, really sweet . . . it was like *norteño* but it isn't, you understand what I'm trying to say? Similar to *norteño* but it's not *norteño.* It's San Antonio.

Valerio learned, he progressed. From where? From himself, perhaps, I don't know. We all have to listen and to hear something to be able to react. The man knocked himself out to create styles, he himself, at that time and in that era. . . .

So I would hear, I would hear all the styles, because I already played the guitar. When I began to take up the accordion, I heard

Valerio's accordion, and that's where I learned. The only one I was influenced by was him. . . .

After Valerio, a little after Valerio, Tony [de la Rosa] was the one who continued the tradition, the combination of the whole thing. Because that's a style, it's a style from La Kineña [the King Ranch], Kineño style, *tacatacataca,* choppy-like, and you recognize it. And from there came Rubén Vela. From there came Gilberto Pérez. From there came Rubén Naranjo. From there came Chano Cadena.

Paulino is good, man! Paulino is a very good man. He brought a style. From all the styles, he picked something of his own . . . the style was in his blood. That made it all together.

I heard Paulino play, on some records that I'd never heard before. Exactly like Valerio Longoria, man! Wow! I couldn't believe it! And that's beautiful. The guy could play it all. And then he grabbed the *trío* tempo . . . and it came together. In other words, he formed a conjunto, established the *trío* sound within the conjunto. Because he had very good elements [musicians], too—that helped him a lot. Singers who were stylists, they created a style, overall—Juan Sifuentes, El Macho, La Pulga. . . .

Tito Puente, Machito, Tito Rodríguez, Count Basie, in the big bands, you know, arrangements, like I'm saying, Buddy Rich, man. Son of a, he was bad! Since he's a drummer, man, the horns would sound, and he'd do the same on the drums as the horns. That influenced me, bro.

I mix it into the polka, I mix it into the redowa, wherever I fucking feel like it. I do whatever I want. Okay, for soul, Ray Charles. For drummer, Buddy Rich. For wild, Jimmy Smith. Get with it. Henry Mancini, I learn from there, I learn from anywhere, Dixieland.

Bro, I'm a universal stylist. Me, right now, wherever I want to go, I go, brother. I have a very crazy freedom . . . It's so hard for me to follow one style. I'm very much a stylist of everything. And I never stop learning.

The only new style you're gonna see is me. I'm coming out with a new style, for me—not for the musicians, only for me. See, I'm bringing out the style that I did in the fifties, sixties, okay?

Conjunto is going to continue, bro. Polkas and the whole thing will go on. All they're gonna do is recycle mainly what they did. It's not going to end. It's not going to stop. Right now they're using combination, violins and all that stuff, with the accordion. It's cool. They're using little pieces of it.

It's our time to move it! To learn from ourselves. Find out what you got. Find out about your own self. How much have you got inside your head? You think just because you got a pocketful of money, you think you're it. And it's not where it's at, at all. If you're going to create, it doesn't take money to create. Just go out and grab a hook, or go to the mountains, man. Do something, go break your head, you'll find it. Look for it, you'll find it.

PART SEVEN

Visiones de Conjunto

Personal Histories, Poems, and Short Stories

25

Confessions of an Accordion Abuser

✧

ISMAEL DOVALINA

1992

I suppose I can trace my affinity for accordion music back to my father, who grew up in Laredo, Texas. He worked half his life at Kelly Air Force Base. One of his favorite albums was a collection of Polish polkas, which included "El barrilito," or, "Beer-Barrel Polka."

My tastes, on the other hand, for the last two decades, have tended more toward rock and roll. During high school, I bought a Hohner Echo Harp harmonica and learned to play hits like "Oh! Susanna" and "Like a Rolling Stone." This experience with the harmonica would come in handy later because an accordion is similar to a harmonica. Both are reed instruments with similar scales; various tones are produced when the lungs or the hand-operated bellows push air past the reeds. The accordion is the more versatile instrument.

My appreciation for Mexican music became aroused during a higher-education sojourn in the northeastern United States. It was during that period that I learned how *mariachi* standards, such as "Guadalajara," could bring a lump to my throat and make my eyes water. My leftist Chicano *camaradas* and I would listen to songs of the Mexican Revolution: "La Adelita," "Carabina 30-30," "El corrido de Felipe Ángeles." Those great old songs made us feel revolutionary. Even more importantly, this music evoked a homesickness and a nostalgia for South Texas, which is a truly unique region that some people must leave in order to truly appreciate. During this period, I also learned that there were *colonias* of *mexicanos* in Michigan, Chicago, Ohio, and even in New York City.

In 1979, my lovely wife and I moved to El Valle de Tejas, the Rio Grande Valley. I remember seeing La Mafia, Mazz, and other Tejano groups play at the Weslaco High School stadium. I started watching Johnny Canales, the Ed Sullivan of Tejano music.

On a trip to New York, I saw an old Hohner accordion in a pawn-shop window on Broadway. It was selling for less than one hundred dollars. I bought it and immediately discovered that it was not as easy to play as I had anticipated.

We moved back to San Cuilmas in 1985. I took the family to several free events, Cinco de Mayo and the Accordion Abuse Fest, at the historic downtown Market Square. It dawned on me that conjunto music is the "soul music" of South Texas.

About two years ago, I bought the *Gato Negro* compact disc by Santiago Jiménez, Jr. It made a positive impression on me. Santiago is pictured on the cover, smiling, holding a black accordion in what is obviously a West Side hubcap shop.

Summer, 1991. The sun is going down after another hot day. I've just finished mowing my mom's lawn, sweeping the clippings, when barely audible strains of conjunto music waft through the air. It must be coming from a church festival at Saint John's, several blocks away. I pause to listen more closely. The songs I can barely make out are from the *Gato Negro* CD. It is almost like a sign from God saying, "Study the accordion."

Not long before, I had learned that the Guadalupe Cultural Arts Center offered beginning accordion lessons taught by Santiago Jiménez, Jr. The Guadalupe is without doubt one of the leading institutions promoting Chicano, Mexican, and Latino culture in the country, and probably the world. I usually don't make New Year's resolutions, but my 1992 resolution was to study the accordion.

I took my wife and two young sons to the Guadalupe on a gray January Saturday to register for the classes. Registration was easy. However, as the first class approached, I began to get anxious. I knew nothing about the accordion. I'd probably be the weakest player in the class. I was determined to go. As Edward James Olmos says in *Stand and Deliver,* "Tienes que tener ganas," or, "You must have the will."

Santiago's accordion class met at his Chief Recording Studios on South Presa Street, just south of downtown. Santiago has been playing professionally for over thirty years. He has over a hundred 45s and thirty-something albums and cassettes to his credit. He has twice been nominated for Grammys. He is part of a great music family.

His grandfather was a noted accordionist and his father, Santiago Jiménez, was a conjunto-music giant, recording songs in the 1930s that are still popular to this day.

On that first night, Santiago played several songs for us. He told us that he plays *al estilo tradicional,* or, "in the traditional style." When he played, I heard strains of classical music. I visualized finely dressed nineteenth-century couples dancing to a waltz, as well as border-town *bailes de patio,* held in someone's backyard with the hosts periodically splashing water on the hard earth in order to keep the dancing couples from raising too much *polvo.* Through his music, Santiago reminded me that the accordion is essentially a European instrument. His polkas would not sound out of place in a German *biergarten* or echoing across Alpine vales.

All of the students were honored to have an accordion legend, a true virtuoso, as our instructor. Santiago is a friendly and unassuming individual. He is a star who does not act like a star. Throughout the class, he circulates around the room, trying to spend some time with each student. He takes a humanistic approach to education. He recognizes that the students are at different levels and are progressing at separate paces. There are no tests, there are no grades. Santiago always has a smile and a kind word.

The students are an interesting group. At first, we were somewhat formal and serious with each other. It is mostly men, several women, and a young man of eleven years. Carlos is a very good player. He has been playing since his high-school days in Dilley. Abel works at Kelly, Santos works in a hospital, Robert works for City Public Service, Raúl is an assistant principal in a high school, Joe works for Ma Bell, Debra is a pharmaceutical tech, and Imelda is a secretary. Nick goes to middle school. One evening, Gabriel presents Santiago with a brightly colored painting depicting a conjunto group surrounded by vignettes of working people.

All of us have one thing in common: we love the music. We look forward to the classes; the accordion is becoming a part of our lives. We don't discuss politics or religion, or gossip much. However, we freely share melodies and playing tips with each other. Together, we are creating an accordion subculture.

After studying the accordion for just a few months, I realize that music is very multicultural. Music is a global crossroads where cultures meet, intertwine, clash, and yes, sometimes even blend. The accordion is a very international instrument.

On March 7, many of the students participated in an accordion contest held at the Dacbert Music Company on Nogalitos Street. We played on a stage with amplification and colored lights, in front of a crowd of about one hundred friendly people. Students from our class took first and third place. Afterward, Santiago and his conjunto played. It was great to hear him play accompanied by a full complement of conjunto all-stars, Cookie Martínez on the drums, Mark Rubin on the *tololoche* (upright bass), and Toby Torres on the *bajo sexto*.

I currently have a repertoire of approximately five songs. The first song I learned is a polka named "Recuerdos de mis tiempos." Next, I learned "Daddy's Polka" and "Quiero dinero." I've learned most of the "Salvador Waltz." It is a slow but difficult piece which has taken me about a month to learn. It goes well at weddings. I'm currently trying to learn the "Cotulla Polka."

My friends have constantly encouraged me. David Catacalos, an accomplished jazz bassist and part-time Jungian analyst, accompanied me late one night over a few beers. Miguel Nacel, a well-known keyboardist and composer (and my *cuñado*) accompanied me on a guitar today and told me only two things are required of an aspiring musician: heart and a good ear.

I have come to realize that San Antonio is to conjunto music what Nashville is to country music. We have Hispanic art, Spanish newspapers, and a thriving broadcast industry. I find myself listening to radio stations such as KCOR; La Fiera, KVAR; and Radio Jalapeño, KEDA. San Antonio is also home to other great accordionists, such as Esteban Jordán and Valerio Longoria.

As I write this, I'm listening to the Texas Tornados on a CD. Like most other things in life, the accordion is difficult and challenging. I suppose I'll have to study it for some years before becoming an even mediocre player. That does not concern or deter me. I am objective enough to know that I am not a good accordionist (yet), but I am nevertheless a happy accordionist.

I am in search of an answer to a timeless question: Why do Mexicans love accordion music so much? I began this search as an attempt to recover my Mexican roots. I agree with the feminist poet Adrienne Rich, who wrote: "The real art or literature of any group comes into being when the members of that group cease feeling the need to explain and justify themselves to a dominant culture and begin to reclaim their own culture, for themselves."

26

An Odyssey through the Magical Land of Conjunto, El Movimiento Xicano, and the Tejano Conjunto Festival

✧

JUAN TEJEDA

1996

Ometeotl. Con el permiso de Dios, primeramente.

Ika tlen niyazki
Amitla ni ten yotiliu tlakuitlapan tlalipan
Kenin ki chua no yolotzin
Azeh motopalli tiualah nemiliz
In kueponiz tlalipan
Ti nezkayotitiuh xohimeh
Ti nezkayotitiuh kuikameh

¿Con qué he de irme?
¿Nada dejaré en pos de mí sobre la tierra?
¿Cómo ha de actuar mi corazón?
¿Acaso en vano venimos a vivir?
¿A brotar aquí en la tierra?
¡Dejemos al menos flores!
¡Dejemos al menos cantos!

With what should I go?
Will I leave nothing after me on the earth?
How should my heart act?
Did we come to live in vain, perhaps?
To sprout here on the earth?
We should at least leave flowers!
We should at least leave songs!

   —poema de Nezahualcoyotl
     "Coyote Hungry for Justice"
      Poet-King of the Texcocos

A mí me nombraron por la Virgen de San Juan. Me pusieron John.

I was born in 1953 on the South Side of San Anto to poor, proud, humble, and hardworking *mexicano* parents. My father, Francisco Mariano Tejeda, *que en paz descanse,* once began an oral history I was doing on him for the University of Texas at Austin by saying, "Fui sembrador y cazador" (I was a planter and a hunter). He was much more than this, of course, but this was important to him and so began our conversation on that day a long time ago. *Mi mamá,* Lillie Cisneros Tejeda, used to clean rich people's houses on the North Side and later became a beautician and businesswoman.

They loved music and dancing. Especially *música de conjunto. Música de acordeón.* I can still recall my parents taking us to the *bailes* at Torres Place, a *salón* in the deep South Side of San Antonio, and dancing to the music of Los Gallardos, or some other conjunto that was playing there on any particular weekend. My father could dance. *Polcas, valses, redovas,* and this in spite of the fact that he was almost completely paralyzed in his left leg and wore a brace from the knee down, a constant and painful reminder of his army days in World War II. When he danced with my mother it was as if they were gliding on the clouds. There weren't too many couples that could dance a *chotís como mis padres. ¡Así como se debe bailar un chotís!*

It is no wonder that *el jefe* loved music so much. His father, *mi abuelo,* José Antonio Tejeda, whom I never met because he died when my father was about nine years old, was a musician and played the violin and guitar and sang. *Mi abuela,* Santa Martínez Tejeda, also played the *acordeón.* Her brothers were all musicians and they tell me that she used to get up and play at some of the *bailes* so that her brother could take a break and go out to dance. My father's brother, Tío Rogelio, was the main musician of the family. He played the guitar, *bajo sexto,* and bass. Family gatherings inevitably ended with my *tío* Rogelio breaking out the guitar or *bajo sexto* and singing with my father and other members of the family. "El ausente" and "Soldado razo" were a couple of their favorite songs. My mother would even join my father and sing "La barca de oro." Those were magical times of *música, comida, cerveza, canciones y familia.*

The Early School Years: El Acordeón, Cultural Genocide, and Rock and Roll

My parents were poor, but they worked hard and sacrificed to send all five of their children to Catholic school. My oldest brother, Frank; Mary Alice; myself (I am the middle child); and my two younger brothers, Ernesto and Richard, all went to the South Side *barrio* Catholic school of Saint Leo's. It was a typical Catholic *barrio* school with grades from first through eighth. While the great majority of students were *chicanitos,* a noticeable number of *gabachitos* went to school there. African Americans were rare, if any. The school was run by White nuns in black habits. Of the few lay teachers that taught there, I recall only one African American among them. No Chicanas. Actually, I think there was one Chicana, or Latina, nun. I don't know where she was from but she was tough. Slender, strict, classy for a nun, and she played the piano. She was the music teacher. I wish I could remember her name. Sister Estelle, I think.

When I was nine years old, my father wanted me to learn how to play the button accordion. Not only did he want me to learn how to play, but he wanted me to learn from Don Santiago Jiménez, Sr., *el mero mero pionero de San Cuilmas* (San Antonio) and father to Flaco and Santiago Jr. My parents searched for Don Santiago but he was nowhere to be found. They did, however, locate Santiago Jiménez, Jr., who informed us that his father was living and working in Dallas. We were in luck, though. If I really wanted to learn, Santiago Jr. himself would teach me. He was a young, seventeen-year-old accordionist at the time and hadn't even begun his professional career.

Santiago Jiménez, Jr., had recently gotten married and was living in a tiny home on Rivas Street on the West Side of San Anto. My father drove me there for my first lesson. I didn't even have an accordion then. Santiago Jr. explained to my father that I could use his accordion during the lessons and that he was going to charge us three dollars for each new tune that I learned. My first lesson began with a *polquita:* "La Piedrera," the now famous and classic *polquita* that Don Santiago wrote during the late thirties for the *barrio* where he lived, La Piedrera, near Brackenridge Park. I learned it in two sittings, then moved on to "Viva Seguín," "Montelongo vals," and so many other instrumentals that now I can't even remember their names.

It seemed that I had an aptitude for music and the accordion, and it got to the point where I could pick up a tune in one lesson. It was around this time that my parents bought me my first button accordion: a two-row, black Hohner that they bought for forty dollars at a pawn shop. One day my father took me to my regularly scheduled lesson and, while Santiago Jr. was getting ready, I began playing the *bolero* "Days of Wine and Roses." Santiago came over to me and asked me who had taught me that *bolero* and I told him that I had learned it myself, from memory. He was surprised and pleased. I was proud.

Over the next three years, Santiago Jiménez, Jr., and my family developed a very special relationship. Santiago Jr. was forming his first conjunto and needed musicians. When he found out that my cousin Bobby played the guitar and *bajo sexto,* he enlisted him in the band. Bobby, who is now a county commissioner here in Bexar County, was fifteen years old at the time. Later, when Santiago's drummer dropped out, my cousin Tony, Bobby's brother, began playing drums in the conjunto. Fred was on bass. Santiago Jiménez Jr. y su Conjunto began playing at parties, weddings, and small clubs in and around San Antonio. Our family would go to the dances and inevitably I would be called to the stage to perform a couple of *polquitas,* a *chotís,* or a *vals.* I was about eleven years old and the audience loved it. They would give me money and hugs and pinch my cheeks, something that I didn't particularly like because I was already *chato* enough as it was and I felt that they were going to make me even more *chato.* My *tío* Rogelio, Bobby and Tony's father, would sometimes play bass or drums, and my father would also get up on stage and sing "Los laureles" or "Dos palomas al volar" with Chago (Santiago Jr.).

When my cousin Tony had to drop out of the conjunto, I took over playing drums. Over the next two years I played drums with Santiago Jiménez Jr. y su Conjunto. I still played the accordion occasionally when we would switch over on instruments, but my main job was on drums. I was twelve, thirteen years old and playing in these sometimes seedy nightclubs until two in the morning. El Venadito was a favorite and then there was El Capri Nite Club, Medrano's, and others. It was fun most of the time and the money was good for a *chavalón.* Sometimes I would make fifty to sixty dollars on a weekend. I was able to help out my parents and still have spending money for the movies, clothes, and other things that I needed.

⋄◆⋄

I don't know exactly when, why, or how it happened, but it did. This constant feeling in my young mind that something was not right. That we were not right. That my family, my parents were not right.

Why? Why was speaking Spanish in school wrong? Why were we punished for speaking our first language? Why was I ashamed of my father because he spoke primarily *mexicano* (as he called it) and I didn't want him going to the PTA meetings? Why was I ashamed of taking *tacos de frijol* and *chorizo con huevo* to school for lunch, so much so that I had to hide underneath the stairwell and eat them? I loved *tacos de papas con huevo con tortillas de harina*. Why then did I ask my mother to give me baloney-and-white-bread sandwiches for lunch so that I could eat in the cafeteria with the other kids? Why was I ashamed of playing the accordion and playing in a conjunto band? Where was this coming from? Why did some of the children, much of the time *chicanitos* themselves, ridicule me for playing the accordion? Why was conjunto music inferior to rock and roll? Why were *tacos* inferior to sandwiches? Why was English better than Spanish? Why was white skin better than brown? Why did I feel this way? Where was it coming from? Why did I feel ashamed of my parents, my music, myself?

I never played the accordion at any of the school talent shows, nor at any of the school functions. I never told too many of my peers after this that I played the accordion and that I played drums with Santiago Jiménez Jr. y su Conjunto. I quit the conjunto shortly thereafter. When I told my parents that I had to get out of the band, they wanted to know why but I really couldn't explain it to them. What was I going to tell them, that I was ashamed of the music they loved so much? That I was ashamed of playing the accordion, of playing with Santiago Jiménez, Jr.? Why? They tried to get me to reconsider but I knew that it was over. I was thirteen years old and I cried, right there, in front of my parents. It would be a long time before I understood and was able to play the accordion again.

I went to Central Catholic High School, supposedly one of the best college-preparatory high schools in the city. Played football my freshman year, then joined the Lloyd Rifles, the freshman drill team. At Central it was mandatory to be in ROTC for two years. I liked it in the drill team because most of the members were Chicanos. There was a connection, camaraderie. *Camaradas*. During the late sixties everyone had long hair and there we were with shaved heads. It was tough. Those were my rock-and-roll days: Jimi Hendrix, Led Zeppelin, Grand Funk Railroad, Jethro Tull, Chicago, and Carlos Santana. We may have been gung ho, Central Chicano, shaved-head drill team members, but we were *locos* and we were rockers. I even had a relatively short, unmemorable stint as a singer with two rock bands: Stoned Creek and Free Enterprise. Yeah, that's right, Free Enterprise. Being in a band was a cool way to meet chicks.

My senior year they made me EX-O (Executive Officer) of the Chaminade Guard. After one of our competitions at Loyola University in New Orleans, the colonel there at the university offered me and the commander a full four-year military scholarship to go to Loyola when we graduated, but by that time I had had enough of the "military." The war, or should I say the conflict, in Vietnam was still going on, I had just missed being drafted in the last official mandatory military draft that the United States ever had, and they had just accepted me at the University of Texas in Austin.

The University Years: El Movimiento Xicano, Conjunto Aztlan, and Xinachtli

Moving to Austin right out of high school was an awakening, a rebirth. It was the first time I had really been away from San Antonio and *mi familia*. The university was big, a student body of about forty-five thousand students at that time, and Chicanos were less than 1 percent of that. Though I was rooming with a *camarada* from San Anto in a small efficiency apartment, the overwhelming feeling that first year was one of isolation. In San Antonio, Chicanos were the majority. At the University of Texas in Austin, we were almost nowhere to be seen. Needless to say, the few Chicanos who were there gravitated toward each other.

My first encounter with the Chicano Movement was when I went and heard this Brown Beret from California speak at one of the off-campus buildings. He spoke of the Chicano nation, Aztlan, and that Chicanos had to defend ourselves against the racist attacks and take back the land that rightfully belonged to us. He spoke of defending ourselves against police brutality and that we had to take up weapons to protect our people, as was our right. He spoke of an armed revolution. While I wasn't quite ready to take up arms at that time, I was ready to take every Chicano-studies course that the university was offering: Chicano history, government, literature, folklore, and more. I was ready to learn and get involved. I became a freshman representative in student government. I got involved with MAYO, the Mexican American Youth Organization. I was on the first Mexican American Cultural Committee at UT, and I campaigned extensively for Ramsey Muñiz in 1972 when he ran for governor of the state of Texas for the Raza Unida Party.

The turning point for me, though, was when I enrolled in a creative writing course that was being taught by the already famous Xicano poet Alurista. ¡Órale! It was like coming home! Here were a group of Chicanos and Chicanas *locas, poetas, escritores, pintores, músicos y más* all getting together to think, discuss, create, write poems, *¡tirar onda y hacer movimiento!* This was the Movimiento Chicano! I was a Chicano. For the first time in my life I began to understand *el por qué*. Why was I here? *¿De dónde vine? ¿Quiénes éramos como un pueblo? ¿Cuál era nuestra historia?* The answers were harsh! Racism, sexism, genocide *y la pobreza entre la gente*. Why were over 50 percent of *chicanitos* dropping out before they graduated from high school? Why did a policeman kill twelve-year-old Santos Rodríguez in Dallas? We began to write and get organized *entre los estudiantes, los artistas, con la comunidad chicana*. The answer was in *la lucha. La lucha por la justicia. La lucha por nuestra tierra. La lucha por nuestra libertad. Y la lucha estaba en el Movimiento Chicano. ¡Que viva Aztlan libre! ¡Que viva nuestra raza!* Never again would we be led to believe that our arts and our culture are inferior! Never again would we be ashamed of playing the *acordeón*. We had to make sure that our children understood that we come from a proud race of American Indians *y españoles*. Of warriors and poet-kings. Of pyramid builders and astronomers. Of mathematicians, artists, revolutionaries, and dancers that have God in their hearts and search for truth, dignity, love, and peace in these times of war.

We studied and learned and we got organized. First at the university with CASA (Chicano Art Students Association, a name that we later changed to Chicanos Artistas Sirviendo a Aztlan). Later, within the Chicano community in East Austin: LUChA (League of United Chicano Artists) and the Brown Berets. We did a lot of work. Organized benefits, art exhibits, and poetry readings. We were in *marchas* against police brutality, *marchas* against the boat races in East Austin, *la marcha de los campesinos*. We organized the Festival

Estudiantil Chicano de Arte y Literatura and Floricantos, and published books: *Trece Aliens, 'Ta cincho,* and *Tejidos* (a journal). We painted murals and played music. This was the Chicano Renaissance. We believed we could do anything and everything, and many times we did. We were artists, activists, organizers, and cultural warriors. It was in this spirit that I began playing music again.

A bunch of us Trece Aliens musicians formed a band we called In Lak' Ech (a Mayan term meaning *tú eres mi otro yo*). I began by playing congas and percussion. We all wrote poems and were experimenting with writing songs. Devon Peña on guitar, Alfredo Cruz on flute. Later Bobby Ramírez joined us on bass and his brother Kiko on guitar. We played here and there, and later changed our name to Reforma o . . . Revolución. At some point I remembered that I could play the accordion and on one of my visits to my *jefes* in San Anto I took that little, two-row, black button Hohner accordion out of the closet and brought it back up to Austin. It was like riding a bicycle. Once you learn how to play it, you never really forget, but I had lost a lot of time. I was twenty-two years old, a beginning accordionist again, and we were about to form the Conjunto Aztlan.

We were a *conjunto de Movimiento Xicano*. Alurista, *tlamantinime* (Aztec wise man) that he is, taught us well to search for our roots, our traditions. We played everything from *cantos indígenas* with *tambores* and *flautas,* to traditional conjunto accordion music, to folk, blues, jazz, and beyond. Hey, we were Chicanos, after all. Danny Mendoza was doing the drums and when José Flores Peregrino, a *poeta*, songwriter, guitarist, and *bajo sexto* player from Laredo, joined the Conjunto Aztlan, we were jamming. We played the university and local club scene in Austin: Raul's, the Royal Coach. Fiestas del Barrio. Fundraisers for *carnales:* the Brown Berets, Quintanilla House. We played at NACS (National Association for Chicano Studies) conferences and we were the first conjunto to play at Harvard. The Chicano law-student association flew us up there. It was a period of intense activity and creativity. We were all writing songs, going to school, working in the *barrio,* organizing classes and projects, and playing music at night. We worked hard and we partied even harder. This was my training ground: the university, Austin, El Movimiento Chicano, *poetas*, cultural arts organizations, *y el* Conjunto Aztlan. I had found my roots. I learned about life and love. *Amor, dolor y el trabajo que teníamos que hacer.*

It was during this time that I became a *danzante conchero,* a traditional, ceremonial Aztec dancer, *y me encontré con Dios otra vez.* It was inevitable. All life leads back to the origin, the beginning, *las raíces, lo todo.* I became a part of Xinachtli (*semilla que germina* in Aztec Nahuatl), and over the next eight years we became apprentices in *la tradición.* Andrés Segura, now a *capitán general de la danza,* became our spiritual teacher and guide. We participated in all of the ceremonies in Mexico and did a lot of work and ceremonies in Austin and San Antonio, and in many other parts of the United States. Without a doubt, this was one of the most significant times in my life. Through *la danza,* we not only found our native culture, language, and traditions, but more importantly we found our spiritual connection. This completed the cycle for me. It all came together. *¡Él es Dios!* We believed. In ourselves, *en el movimiento,* in our people, in our culture and traditions. We believed in dignity and respect for all people and all living things. We believed in *nuestra tierra, justicia y libertad para todos!* It was through *la danza, la música, la poesía, nuestras artes* that we found our spirituality, our creative connection, the Creator. It was through *las artes* that we preserved and passed on our proud culture, history, language, and traditions to all of our children and their children's children for generations to come.

Times were a'changing, *como dice la canción.* We worked with the Conjunto Aztlan and Xinachtli through the early to mid eighties. But this was 1979. I had already received my B.A. in Chicano studies and English, I had just broken up with the last of my Austin loves, there were hassles on the horizon, and I was ready to come back home. San Antonio, San Cuilmas, Yanaguana.

El Guadalupe Cultural Arts Center y Casi Quince Años del Tejano Conjunto Festival

San Antonio is the Chicano cultural capital of the world. It is the capital of Aztlan. It is the conjunto-music capital of the world. It is all of this and much more. *¡Aquí la raza rifa!* We are the majority, not a minority. I was home. *La tierra de mi nacimiento. Mi familia.* I rented a little house on the deep South Side of San Anto *cerquita de la Misión Espada,* right next to the aqueduct that the *indios* built for the Spanish missionaries back in the 1700s. I was still playing *acordeón* with the Conjunto Aztlan and doing *danza,* and getting settled in. Nineteen eighty was a good time to be in San Antonio in spite of the fact that the Reagan era was just beginning. It was supposed to be the Decade of the Hispanic and I guess it was, *porque ¡qué chinga nos dieron!* More importantly for me, though, it was the decade of the Guadalupe Cultural Arts Center.

A group of Chicano artists and organizations were getting together to form a coalition and ask for funds from the City of San Antonio. The city had rarely given any money to the Chicano arts, but they sure as hell had been funding the symphony, the ballet, and the museums to the tune of millions of dollars for many, many years. Remember that Chicanos constitute more than 50 percent of the city population. We pay taxes too! Why weren't the Chicano arts being funded? The time was ripe, however, because around 1978 San Antonio had gone from an at-large election system for city council, in which there was only one token Chicano representative, to a single-member-district representation (ten single districts and one mayor) plan in which that very first election year saw about four Chicanos elected to city council, plus one Black representative. All they needed was one vote and they could pass anything they wanted. The politics were ready, the backing was there, and the initial grant proposals were written.

Thirteen Chicano-arts organizations were funded that first year in 1980–81. Amongst those thirteen organizations were the consortium of groups that would later become the Guadalupe Cultural Arts Center: Performance Artists Nucleus, Inc., Centro Cultural del Pueblo, San Antonio Consortium for the Hispanic Arts, Latin American Theatrical Association, and the Mariachi Project. I knew many of the artists that were involved in this initial organizing and proposal-writing phase, and when they got funded a Chicana poet friend of mine called me and told me to apply for the music position. It turned out to be a Mariachi Project director's position and, though I was more of a conjunto artist, I was hired in August of 1980. Anyway, the job required an arts administrator more than a *mariachi*, and I had gained that experience in Austin. I implemented a *mariachi* project in the community whereby we offered classes, organized presentations, and worked with developing young *mariachi* groups in the city.

About midway through my first year at the center I got a call from Ben King, who was a music writer for the *San Antonio Express-News*. He was taking accordion classes from Santiago Jiménez, Sr., around this time and he asked me if I would be interested in working with him in organizing a conjunto festival. Hey, this was my *mera neta,* remember? I agreed, on the condition that I would hire the bands, since I knew many of them personally; and that the Performance Artists Nucleus, Inc., the organization I worked for (prior to changing its name to the Guadalupe Cultural Arts Center), would be a cosponsor along with the *Express-News;* and that the Conjunto Aztlan could play. The first conjunto festival was in 1981, though it wasn't that much of a festival, more of a concert. Valerio Longoria y su Conjunto played on a weekend night at the Sunken Gardens in Brackenridge Park and Santiago Jiménez Jr. y su Conjunto, Conjunto Aztlan, and Los Paisanos de Chalito Johnson played the following night at the Arneson River Theater. It was a success, though I had other ideas about what a conjunto festival should be.

Toward the end of 1981 we moved into the Guadalupe Theater, the Performance Artists Nucleus became the Guadalupe Cultural Arts Center, and the Mariachi Project became the Xicano Music Program. The organization was going through some growing pains, the arts wars began in earnest, and plans were laid to produce the first Tejano Conjunto Festival en San Antonio.

From the beginning, plans for the Tejano Conjunto Festival were methodical. The Guadalupe would take over the festival, and the *San Antonio Express-News* and KEDA Radio would cosponsor the event and provide the publicity and promotional support. The center was on a mission. The Tejano Conjunto Festival had to do more than just present conjuntos; we were going to educate the public and our own children about the beauty of our culture and our music. The schools weren't doing it. It was up to us to give our children a positive understanding of who they were, who we are. This was a psychological war as much as it was a political, economic, social, cultural, and artistic war.

You have to understand that conjunto music was much maligned up to this point. It was *cantina* music. It was *música del rancho, de la gente pobre.* It was lower-class music. It was inferior to other forms of music, or so they told us, and that's why I had felt ashamed of playing the accordion. The festival had to counteract these racist notions and bring rightful respect to this unique form of music. The respect that conjunto music deserved. Conjunto music is the original Chicano music. It is a unique form of American music that we Chicanos created and gave as a gift to the world. We borrowed the button accordion from the European settlers, combined it with a *bajo sexto* guitar that the Spanish introduced us to, and began singing *corridos,* playing Mexican and indigenous rhythms, and creating something new, exciting. It deserved respect.

Toward this end, the Tejano Conjunto Festival's goals that we implemented that first year, and which still stand, were to preserve and promote that unique form of traditional Chicano music known as conjunto; to give proper recognition and respect to those artists who pioneered this musical genre; to showcase the best in conjunto music; and to foster a better appreciation and understanding of Chicano music and culture. From the very beginning we set out to accomplish these goals by developing and initiating some important mechanisms as part of the festival: the Conjunto Music Hall of Fame to recognize and pay tribute to those artists who pioneered and contributed profoundly to the creation and development of conjunto music; and a poster contest for junior-high, high-school, college, and open-level participants by which we would select the official poster for the festival each year. The poster contest worked on many levels: educational, cultural, and artistic, to begin with. We also began a program-magazine publication for the festival that included scholarly articles, interviews, and, later, biographies of the performers. We also made it a point to document the festival in audio, video, and photography for historical documentation and, possibly, commercial purposes. That first year we also began the community classes in button accordion and we hired Valerio Longoria as the master accordion instructor.

The first Tejano Conjunto Festival en San Antonio was held May 22–24, 1982: three days at El Mercado, Mission County Park, and Rosedale Park. We presented seventeen different conjuntos, among them Flaco Jiménez, Manuel Guerrero, Los Paisanos, Conjunto Aztlan, and a very young conjunto known as Los Hermanos Farías, later to be known as La Tropa F. We inducted Narciso Martínez, "El Huracán del Valle"; Santiago Jiménez, Sr.; Valerio Longoria; Pedro Ayala, "El Monarca del Acordeón"; Tony de la Rosa; and Esteban Jordán into the Conjunto Music Hall of Fame. We gave them each a brand-new accordion and a framed copy of the festival poster with a plaque on it. Of course, all of these masters of the accordion performed at the festival. It was an unqualified success. Thousands of people came out to the festival. Never before had there been a festival of this type and of this magnitude in the history of conjunto music. One of the highlights of the festival was when the three Jiménezes—Santiago Sr. (accordion), Flaco (*bajo sexto*), and Santiago Jr. (bass)—performed together in a grand finale jam. It was history. It was magical. *¡Andaba en las nubes!* I had met my heroes, the accordion greats, and worked with them for the first time in my life. It would be the first of many more to come.

To cover the almost fifteen years of the Tejano Conjunto Festival, *y uno de pilón,* would be an impossibility, especially in these pages. *Pero, si me lo permiten,* I would like to take you all through a few of the photographs in my mind. Some of the highlights and lowlights of the festival from a cultural worker's, arts administrator's, festival organizer's perspective. There have been many magical memories such as the one I mentioned above at the first TCF. The second year, for instance, we went from a three-day festival to five days. We held our first symposium on conjunto music at the Centro de Artes at which we gave away five hundred free dinners, plus drinks! Bar drinks, too, baby! *¿Teníamos feria, o qué?* We also had the only religious service that has ever been a part of the TCF, when Paulino Bernal and El Conjunto Bernal held their "Música, Cantos y Testimonios de su Nueva Vida en Jesucristo" at the Sunken Gardens Amphitheatre. Sadly, however, Martín Macías, the legendary *bajo sexto* maker, whom we inducted into the Conjunto Music Hall of Fame that year, did not make it to the induction ceremonies. He was in the hospital at the time. His daughter accepted the award on his behalf and took it to him in the hospital. He got to see the award before he died. His daughter later told me that when he saw the award, he smiled. He was eighty-seven years old. I used to visit him at his home and shop on the South Side of San Antonio. He made my twelve-string guitar for me.

The year 1986 was memorable because we held our first "New Directions in Conjunto Music" night at the festival, which featured Doug Sahm, Augie Meyers, and the Westside Horns (Rocky Morales, Louis Bustos, and Al Gómez), along with Esteban Jordán y su Río Jordán and Los Lobos. What a night! The monster jam at the end had everybody up there onstage, all three bands, jamming, taking turns, taking leads! It was a mystical, almost out of body experience for me and I think everybody else that was there that night. West Side sound meets West Coast Chicano rock a la conjunto Jordán. *¡Jíjole!*

It was in 1987 that we first started including short biographies of each of the bands that performed at the festival in our program-magazine. We had switched to a tabloid-size magazine format in 1985, and the TCF issue became one of four *Tonantzin* magazines we produced per year back then. The *Tonantzin* program-magazine for the festival has always been a very important part of the TCF. It is an educational and historical tool. We have published some of the most noted Chicano scholars, such as Manuel Peña, José Limón, and José Reyna. We've included interviews with Santiago Jiménez, Sr., Valerio Longoria, Eva Ybarra, Esteban Jordán, and more. Short stories, poems, and articles on conjunto music have also been included. While it is an important aspect of the festival, it is also one of the most demanding and labor intensive. Many a night we've spent burning the midnight oil trying to make publication deadline. There were some years that the graphics department (David, *el* Diamond), myself, and others worked around the clock, all night long, and turned in the completed manuscript to the printer at 9:00 a.m. one year and at 12:00 noon another year. We put it out, though. I think there has only been one year that we didn't have the publication by opening day. As I write, we are four days away from the opening night of La Quinceañera at the theater. Burn, baby, burn!

Quickly, some more highlights. In 1988, we finally got the official Conjunto Music Hall of Fame award. Cecilia Rangel, an Austin-based artist, designed a sculpture, cast in bronze, depicting the button accordion and *bajo sexto* mounted on a mahogany base with an engraved plaque. In 1989, we held the first "Conjunto Meets Cajun/Zydeco" night at the TCF. Dubbed "Where the *Barrio* Meets the Bayou," this evening put together four conjunto bands (Test Tube Babes, Nick Villarreal, Mingo Saldívar, and Esteban Jordán) with three Cajun/Zydeco bands (Savoy-Doucet Cajun Band, Michael Doucet and Beausoleil, and Queen Ida). Esteban jamming with Queen Ida and her band at the very end was another memorable moment. The first and only "Conjunto in Film and Video" night was held in 1990. This same year we also produced the first and only live cassette recording: *The Best of the Eighth Annual Tejano Conjunto Festival en San Antonio, 1989*. In 1991, we expanded to a seven-day festival, Monday through Sunday, and we presented forty-three bands! Not to be outdone, in 1992 we presented forty-five bands in seven days! This is the record. We went back down to five days in 1995 and the first and only festival video was produced this same year: *The Best of the Eleventh Annual Tejano Conjunto Festival en San Antonio, 1992*.

Over the years we have witnessed the passing of some of the all-time greats in conjunto and Tejano music. Among the Conjunto Music Hall of Fame members that we have lost, Martín Macías was the first in 1983, then Santiago Jiménez, Sr., in 1984. Ismael Gonzales was posthumously inducted in 1985. Eugenio Ábrego, accordionist from Los Alegres de Terán, died in 1988. The year 1990 dealt a severe blow to conjunto music when we lost five pioneers: Bruno Villarreal, "El Azote del Valle"; Pedro Ayala, "El Monarca del Acordeón"; Armando Marroquín from Ideal Records; Manuel Guerrero, "El Sargento Que Canta"; and Juan Viesca, "El Rey del Tololoche." In 1992, *perdimos nuestro papá,* the Father of Conjunto Music, Narciso Martínez, "El Huracán del Valle." He was getting ready to perform at the Tejano Conjunto Festival (for the eighth time) when he took ill. He died on June 5, 1992. He was going to be eighty-two years old. In 1993, in his honor, we renamed the Conjunto Music Hall of Fame Award the Narciso Martínez Award. Other important figures who are now in conjunto heaven are Chavela, one of the few female accordionists who fronted their own conjuntos, and Raúl Johnson, bass player and vocalist for Los Paisanos, among many others.

The Creator has blessed me in many ways and for this I give him thanks constantly. It has been my great honor and privilege to have known, on a personal basis, and worked with, all of these amazing musicians. I remember sitting in Narciso Martínez's home in La Paloma, a tiny South Texas town, with Óscar Hernández, who had taken me there so that I could do an interview with Narciso. It turned into an almost surreal scene at one point when we were laughing about something Narciso said, and I thought to myself: Here I am with two of the greatest accordionists in the history of conjunto, in Narciso's home, and we are all laughing. Narciso's wife walked by at that time and acknowledged Narciso's laughter and sarcasm with a quick smile, half-smirk, in his direction. I remember sitting in Valerio Longoria's home on the South Side of San Antonio. Pieces of accordions, reeds, tools, and cigarette butts were scattered all over the kitchen table and we were sitting side by side. He was teaching me "Cielito Polka," his original *polquita,* which was the first tune he ever recorded, in 1947. I remember when they stole Toby Torres's *bajo sexto* from the festival, the only time something like this has ever happened. I remember taking Tony de la Rosa to the hospital in my van after he had a heart attack onstage at last year's festival. When the EMS came, he refused to go with them. He had a second heart attack while in the hospital, at 2:00 a.m.

There have been many memories, both personal and professional. They weren't always good, as you can imagine. There have been funding woes and technical nightmares. Disappointments, disillusions, and *desmadres*. I prefer, however, to look on the bright side. My children, Zitlalli Aztlan Libre and Juan Francisco Tonatiuh—two of the greatest creations I've ever played a part in—were born right after the first two TCFs. When they were very young, I would sit with them in our living room and play the accordion. I taught both of them how to play the polka "La barranca."

Para Cerrar

Looking back, I think that the Tejano Conjunto Festival has fulfilled its goals, if not completely, at least in good measure. We are preserving conjunto music, not only through the festival, but also through the accordion and *bajo sexto* classes we offer the community at the Guadalupe Cultural Arts Center. We've inducted thirty-one of the conjunto greats into the Conjunto Music Hall of Fame. We've presented over 140 of the very best conjuntos from both the United States and Mexico, even Japan! Through the center, the poster contest, the classes, the hall of fame, our audio-video productions, the media, and our publications, we've educated everyone, including ourselves, about *nuestra cultura, nuestra música*. In fact, we're in the process of publishing an anthology of the collected writings of the Tejano Conjunto Festival's *Tonantzin*s over the last fifteen years. I believe that we have the best published material in the world on conjunto music.

A few final words about identity and labels, about conjunto, *orquesta tejana,* and Tejano music.

Chicanos have created two unique, original, American musical ensembles: the conjunto and the *orquesta tejana*. The conjunto, which developed around the turn of the century and into the twenties and thirties, utilizes the button accordion (most of the time) as its principal instrument, along with the *bajo sexto,* sometimes guitar, as its companion instrument. Bass and drums round out the basic conjunto ensemble. The *orquesta tejana* developed during the thirties and forties and was initially modeled after the U.S. big bands of this period. Horns (saxophones, trumpets, trombones), sometimes piano, and guitar were the lead instruments. As the *orquestas* evolved into the fifties, the large horn sections were scaled down, and they played a varied repertoire of U.S. jazz, pop, and rock music, along with *polcas, boleros, cumbias,* and the like. Beto Villa began it all, then Isidro "El Indio" López and Little Joe. In the sixties and seventies, which were the heyday of the *orquesta tejana,* bands such as Sunny and the Sunliners, Latin Breed, Tortilla Factory, and others took *orquesta* music to new heights. Conjunto and *orquesta tejana* music had a parallel development after the forties up until the mid seventies. While there was some experimentation with using the accordion combined with the saxophone and integrating the accordion into the *orquesta,* they pretty much remained separate musical ensembles, each with their own hard-core audiences.

In the seventies, when the synthesizer groups came into prominence, many people thought that the synthesizer was going to replace the accordion and the horns. That, of course, didn't happen. What did happen was an interesting phenomenon. During the late seventies and into the eighties the conjunto and the *orquesta tejana* merged into a distinctive ensemble. I call it a *conjunto orquestal,* and people like Roberto Pulido y los Clásicos pioneered this sound, combining the accordion with two saxophones. It was something new. This is the third phase in the development of Chicano music and it is the one we are still into in 1996. It's called Tejano music and the popular groups are Emilio Navaira, David Lee Garza y los Musicales, La Diferenzia, Elsa García, Mazz, and others. In some fashion, these bands all combine horns and the synthesizer with the accordion. Everyone thought that the accordion was going to fall by the wayside. Instead, it came back stronger than ever. Revenge of the Squeeze Box, Part One. It had to be. Everything returns to its roots, its origins, in one way or another. Tejano music is on the rise, *carnales,* and rightfully so. It is unique, original, innovative, bilingual, experimental, crossing over, and traditional all at the same time. It's our turn!

For those people who keep asking me if this music, or this band, is conjunto or Tejano? Let me just say this: Conjunto music is Tejano music. It is the original Tejano music. *Las raíces.*

You've heard me throughout this article refer to myself as a Chicano and also use the word "Xicano." They're one and the same, only different spellings. "Xicano" comes from the Mexica Indians, who were the Aztecs. In Azteca Nahuatl (the language of the Aztecs) the *x* is pronounced with a "ch," or sometimes "sh," sound. Thus, you have *mechica, mechicano,* "Chicano." *Mexica, mexicano,* "Xicano." *Yo soy xicano por nuestras raíces indígenas.* No *soy* Hispanic, though I have Hispanic blood in me. *Soy xicano: mexicano en los Estados Unidos, no mexicano en México. Es diferente, aunque tenemos las mismas raíces.*

The legacy that the Guadalupe Cultural Arts Center and the Tejano Conjunto Festival en San Antonio leave will ultimately be measured in our children and our children's children for generations to come. The fact that hundreds of young *xicanitos* and *xicanitas* are now playing the *acordeón* as a result of our classes and are proud of it is enough for me, though I know we have a long way to go and a lot more work to do. The war is not over yet, by a long shot.

If I had to pick my favorite aspect of the Tejano Conjunto Festival, it would have to be the accordion students' recital. An image stands out in my mind of a nine-year-old *xicanito* accordionist performing in public for the first time at the Teatro Guadalupe at one of our student recitals. The young accordionist's father brought his own father, the accordionist's grandfather, to hear him play. When this *xicanito* started playing the *vals* "Honor y gloria," the grandfather started to audibly cry. I cried too, silently. This then nine-year-old *xicanito* is Xavier Trejo. He started playing the accordion through the lessons we offer at the Guadalupe. Fred Zimmerle was his first instructor. He's now about sixteen years old and one of the hottest young accordionists in the Tejano-music scene. He was playing with Óscar G. y Grupo Sol and recently started his own band, X-Men y Presente Band.

La tradición de la danza azteca taught me that there have been four suns that existed before this sun, the one we currently live in. We are in the fifth sun: *nahuiollin* (four movement), the sun of conscience, the sun of war, that is governed by the god of war, Huitzilopochtli. All of these previous suns have been destroyed by some cataclysmic event. All of humanity was destroyed also, except for a chosen people who were destined to lead humanity into the new sun. This sun, the fifth sun, will also be destroyed by "terremotos, y la gente va a padecer hambres." The hope for our future and for our children is that there will be a new sun, the sixth sun, *nahuicoatl* (four serpent), and it will be the sun of justice.

I never thought I'd be working here at the center for this long, *¡casi dieciséis años!* Me and my *primo* Armando are doing a gig tonight. We play traditional conjunto music *con acordeón y bajo sexto*. It looks like the Conjunto Aztlan might be reuniting to record our long-overdue Movimiento Xicano CD this summer. I'm ready to retire and write some poetry, some songs.

Gracias, Señor. ¡Él es Dios!
Ometeotl.

27
Un Recuerdo a Valerio

✧

LONNIE GUERRERO
1985

Oyes, Valerio, aquí te mando un telegrama
Desde hace tiempo que yo quiero hablar contigo
Porque yo debo soportar mi tía Juana
Te pido chamba porque sé que eres mi amigo

Yo toco el bajo, la guitarra y las maracas
De vez en cuando el acordeón y la tambora
Yo soy neutral entre las gordas y las flacas
Por ser casado y serle fiel a mi señora

Como yo soy admirador de tu conjunto
Y de tus discos que han tenido tanta fama
Hoy me he animado a escribirte de este asunto
Y por lo pronto te mando este telegrama

Este corrido no lleva ningún misterio
No hay intención para ofender con estos versos
Son nada más unos recuerdos a Valerio
Se los dedica este señor de pocos pesos

Y cuando vengas a pasearte aquí a mi pueblo
Al disponer tienes tu casa, por supuesto
Nomás preguntas dónde vive ese Guerrero
Que escribe versos y rasguña el bajo sexto

Sinceramente,
Lonnie Guerrero
Austin, Texas

28

Esteban

❖

EDÉN TORRES

1986

There's this cat, see
brown-amazing man
got words pouring out
make you laugh
make you like his smile
make you know
he's heavy Chicano
brings that squeeze box
and your body
got to move
"You dig, man?"
he is bad
been playing so long
always coming back
coming home
to Texas
like an old tomcat, see
got scars and jazz
lickin' and clickin'
those rings
against those buttons
always coming back
conjunto, man
exploding that rich
Chicano color

all over
music
squeeze-box king coming
and coming
gonna hit you, *mano*
and the pattern
echoes lightning
98-pound man
o' sugar
playin' sweet
fine music
young girls
feel the energy
like wild Spanish ponies
running free across Texas
and they wait
hoping in the alley
behind the *cantina*
whispering and singing
"El Parche"
wanting him to play
their bodies
the way he
fingers that accordion
they got no way
of knowing
he can't love them
like he loves
that music
he might try
but that *norteño* sound
is the magic
in his bones, man
and he's
always coming back
coming home
conjunto, man
exploding that rich
Chicano color
all over

29

Steve Jordan

✧

JERRY TUMLINSON

1992

Midnight light runs inside mesquite
barreling across dusty purple sagebrush
grinning / head weaving / 90 mph;
my hands leave the steering wheel
at every chord change of the magical Hohner!

As patch-eyed Jordan stomps his electronic pedals
my foot gets heavier
barreling inside the river midnight light mesquite vein
illuminating this silver highway halfway to Del Rio.

This illumination is carried by the "King" of accordions
propelled by the enigmatic energy
conjuntos lift their wings
along this midnight light mesquite vein river
running at the moon
music to spirits who peel away the night emitting
auras commingle jade / lapis / purplesage / energy
light conjuntos music (mightier than gunpowder) pounding
drums, the accordion cries and the guitar
plays snake-eyes sure bet to ever flowing Rio Grande bass lines.

I arrive with the midnight sun
timeless inside this quilted multilayered quicksand
bubbling fresh piñons and thick coffee and
drink what I remember of the journey
running inside mesquite midnight light river vein

running at the moon
grinning / head weaving / 90 mph before takeoff
with Steve Jordan conjunto gypsy spirit
commingle jade / lapis / purplesagebrush / against this
orange midnight sunrise;
timeless I arrive
ready to ride the cliffs at Amistad Reservoir
listening to conjunto
listening to Steve Jordan.
I awake in a rocky arroyo
surrounded by rattlesnakes
whose tongues hiss like a stinging guitar
whose tails rattle like a Hohner's buttons
coiled, yet ready to pound like a drum
I walk off alone with the ever flowing
Rio Grande bass lines.

30

Conjunto at Night

✧

FRANCES YTURRI

1992

Stars bob on the blue-gray surface of
near night, above treetops that
struggle to stir hot darkness.
Dry leaves scuttle across the
moonlit asphalt, pushed by a
breeze that carries the swell . . . of music.

Above the rustle of leaves
suddenly comes
a steady crash and thump of drums,
sweet wheeze of the accordion,
syncopated strumming of guitars
as the musical wind of Conjunto
quenches burning moonlight.

From far away rises
the rich voice of the border,
conjuring pictures in two tongues
of a carnival-bright marketplace
between two lands;
breathing life into the stillness
of night.

31
El Baile Grande

✧

JOSÉ FLORES PEREGRINO

1992

for Manuel Peña and his conjuntos

There must have been a thousand people there
and one legend on the stage
serious fingers on la 'cordeón
firo fi, firo fa
the rastri-rastri of feet
and feet to the bajo sexto's
clanging, clanging
and brown on brown cachetes
sweating by.

There were a thousand people there
and chants muffled in the dust
y a o ra paraque si gan bai lando
bailando
bailando
bailando
in the air
till feet and floor and dust and sound
hum the hum
of five hours going that way
and circle people dancing
counterclockwise
killing time.

32

Body by Fisher

✧

JOE SALDÍVAR

1985

One bright and sunny summer morning, Chicho leaned against a rumpled pack of Camels. He was admiring a throng of young Chicanos as they crossed *la calle* Brazos to reach *la 21*, an elementary school. He stood at the intersection of Brazos and Guadalupe Streets on the West Side of San Antonio. Most of the pedestrians were residents of the nearby housing projects, the Alazán-Apache Homes. The Homes were built in the 1930s, and though numerous and similar housing developments had cropped up around the city in recent years, these were known simply as Los Courts.

Chicho smiled as he exposed himself to the pleasant sunlight near the entrance steps to a *panadería*. He considered his good fortune. He loved watching the early morning bustle of the crowds despite the many dangers involved. Chicho was a gregarious individual and this particular intersection became a beehive of activity half an hour before the first bell of *la 21* began to peal, or as soon as the Casa Blanca Mexican Restaurant or the Progreso Drug Store opened for business.

Chicho was drawn to this intersection like a cockroach to a bread crumb. The *panadería* was a favorite of Chicho's because it drew many customers from the surrounding neighborhood. Chicho would observe the steady stream of students, construction workers, painters, carpenters, and other early-morning risers as they plunked their nickels and quarters on the counter of Doña Mechela's Panadería in exchange for *marranitas, buñuelos, donas,* and other freshly baked *pan dulce*.

Chicho had epicurean reasons for being there. The aromas were exhilarating and Chicho's nostrils would flare as they were mercilessly assaulted on all sides by the intermingling smells of *huevos rancheros, tacos, menudo, repostería,* and many other delicacies from the restaurant and *panadería*. Chicho was already contemplating, with *gusto,* the feast he would treat himself to in the next few minutes. He turned his head and noticed the garbage can in the driveway of the restaurant rapidly filling up with leftovers. Chicho was a shameless glutton when it came to eating Mexican food.

Chicho loved Chicanos. He not only loved their ingenious invention, hot *tamales,* he also embraced the Chicano culture as a whole. The language of Chicanos was music to his ears. Chicho and his gang spent countless hours each day just listening to older Chicanos as they conversed in their distinct style of watered-down Castilian Spanish. The younger members of *la raza* preferred their Spanish even more diluted. These young people used a mixture of the Spanish and English languages to produce a colorful slang in communication which had permeated throughout Chicano society and which was called *caló*.

Moments earlier, Chicho overheard and was impressed by a brief florid exchange between Doña Borcelana and Doña Liendres, two *comadres* who lived nearby on Veracruz.

"Buenos días, señora Liendres. ¿Cómo amaneció?" greeted Doña Borcelana.

"Con salud, gracias, Chana. ¿Y usted, comadre?" answered Señora Liendres affectionately, adding, "No deje de invitarme a la boda de su hija."

"Seguro que sí," assured Doña Borcelana, formally, with a touch of pride. "El enlace se llevará a cabo el próximo domingo."

Earlier that morning, Chicho had also observed two young Chicanos, obviously students at *la 21,* meet and greet one another.

"¿Qué pasó, ese? You going to school ora?"

"Chale, carnal," answered the other. "Me voy a maderiar at the Progreso. I'm gonna wachar que 'ta pasando por allí."

Since moving to this barrio, Chicho and his gang had not only adopted Chicano names but had become almost fluent in the language. Greeting each other in the morning with "buenos días" was becoming second nature to them. They could also spew out "chingada madres" as smoothly as the most profane of the *batos locos*. Yet they were still learning the meanings and experiencing the effects of new words every day. Just last Tuesday Chicho overheard a couple of dope fiends, Ratón and Chango, severely cut down a fellow *tecato*.

"Ese, Chango. ¿No has visto al Vampiro?" asked Ratón.

"Sí, I saw him yesterday," answered Chango. "Pero olvídate de ese bato porque ya no trae nada. Andaba todo mechudo y bien mugroso. He had not one penny on him y me pidió pa'l wine. ¡Es puro cucaracho!"

Chicho had been outraged upon hearing the dialogue. He had been flabbergasted. Not that he was taking up for the unfortunate Vampiro, whoever he might be, but the language these guys used. Obviously Chicho's interpretation of the word *cucaracho* had been all wrong. At least, as it was currently in use by *tecatos*. He had shuddered at the connotation. The implication. This revelation had hit him like a slap in the face. Apparently, in *tecato* jargon, *cucaracho* meant a down-and-out person, a hobo, or a wino, even. This wasn't only ironic, it was utterly disgusting!

Chicho was a real *cucaracho!* A real, live, genuine, 100 percent Blattarian cockroach! The dictionary defined Chicho and his ilk as "flat-bodied, brownish insects, common as household pests."

Chicho was proud of his insectitude. As far as he knew, *cucarachos* were one of, if not the, cleanest creatures on the face of the earth. He was sure he had read something to this effect recently in some magazine.

"We go back a long time, carnal," Chicho had grumbled angrily to himself that Tuesday. "So what if we are called pests? And, what if we are flat-bodied? Nobody's perfect! That's a misnomer if I ever heard one!"

Then, a bit more stoically, he had concluded, "Bueno, ¿qué espera uno de la gente?"

But, that had been last Tuesday and Chicho had since gotten over his initial indignation. *Cucarachos* soon got over indignation. This type of personal affront was just another of the many psychological and social, not to mention physical, and other difficulties he had learned to overcome in his life of living in the gutter.

He still loved these interesting humans, despite their many shortcomings. Chicho was particularly fond of these proud brown people who laid claim to being the number-one race on earth by calling themselves La Raza. Los Chicanos.

Already he had mastered the art of standing and walking on his hind legs, as was the custom among humans. He and the gang had readily adopted the cool, insolent, swaggering strut of the *batos locos*. Indeed, Chicho had taken to wearing a tiny piece of red cloth wound around his head in imitation of the sweat bands and colorful bandannas worn by the *barrio* lowriders. He hadn't yet learned to smoke the thin, brown, roll-your-own favored by the lowriders and he hadn't been able to grow a mustache, yet, but he was working on it. Eventually, he might even be able to get a tattoo. A Virgen de Guadalupe on his back.

Chicho loved the Chicanos' music as much as he loved their food and language. In particular, he loved *los bailes* and *las polcas,* though he had not yet been to such a dance.

¡Chingado! thought Chicho, I would gladly give my right antenna just to be able to dance una polquita with one of the chavalonas de Los Courts. These chavalonas, Chicho had noticed, were good dancers and as foxy as can be.

Indeed, Chicho, daydreaming of just such an encounter, listened dreamily to the harmony of Los Pavos Reales on Doña Mechela's radio. All Chicano music lovers tuned in to San Anto's Radio Jalapeño, and Doña Mechela was never too busy or too tired to listen as Güero Polkas or Relámpago provoked laughter over the radio waves between selections of the latest hits. El Pavo Grande, Óscar, and Frank could sing the shit out of "Chiquitita, chiquitita," thought Chicho.

"¡Ajúa!" howled Chicho, beside himself, as he attempted a *grito al estilo mexicano.*

Chicho was knee-deep into a daydream. He placed his right foreleg on his stomach. He extended his left one outward, slightly bent at the elbow, and danced away from the pack of Camels smoothly to the tune of "Chiquitita, chiquitita."

Chicho was so engrossed in his daydream and the shuffling dance routine that he almost failed to see Doña Mechela's broom as she swept the rumpled pack of Camels he had been leaning against just a moment before. Chicho heard the swoosh of the giant broom just in time to duck and avoid the fatal sweep. He crouched and scampered off rapidly on all six to a crevice in the wall of the *panadería* where he and his *cucaracho* friends had taken up residence.

"¡Hijo de la chingada!" gasped Chicho to the other *cucarachos.* "That was a close call!" Chicho wiped the dust from his brow with a feeler and then wiped that feeler with another feeler. He was still shaking. He had forgotten the accordion music and wasn't even paying attention now as Tierra crooned its heart out with "Memories" on KEDA.

"The floors and sidewalks are full of hazards," Chicho stated to his *camaradas* as he began to pace the surface of their cozy crevice home. His *camaradas* were standing or sitting here and there around Chicho as he continued to pace back and forth, his forelegs clutched behind his back in the manner of a lecturing professor.

"We will have to be more careful," Chicho continued, raising an antenna up in the air as if to make a point. "When we venture out into the jungle of the sidewalks, or onto the floors of the houses around here, we have to be more careful because it is very easy to be swept away like so many bread crumbs, or to be squashed into the woodwork by the humans."

"What wisdom, y ¡qué sabiduría!" interjected Trucha, loudly and sarcastically. Trucha was sitting regally in a corner on an easy chair that had been carved out of a large pinto bean especially for him. This old, crusty, and wise *cucaracho* knew that Chicho simply never practiced what he preached.

"Life isn't easy when one is only so many centimeters tall," Chicho persisted, undaunted by the criticism.

"¡Bravo, bravo!" said Trucha.

"Hey, Chicho, you almost got wasted, ese," said a young *cucaracho* with genuine concern. This was none other than the recently baptized Chicharrón. He was lying on a tiny pile of folded rags in the corner of the abode, resting on an elbow. Chicharrón was wise for his age and he had some experience on which to base his opinions.

"You sure take a lot of chances, ese," said Chicharrón. "You know better than to be messing around too close to the humans. Polkas and the pursuit of the good things in life are fine, but mingling too close to the humans, even if they are Raza, is not for us. You better watch out, ese, because one of these days you won't be around to complain about it."

"Bien dicho, Chicharrón," offered the wise Trucha in his hoarse and commanding voice. "Have I not personally taught you all about the Golden Mean?"

"That's right, ese," continued Chicharrón, waving his antennae excitedly and now feeling more confident with the encouragement he had received from the influential Trucha. "You have to live in moderation," he said, and then put in what he considered to be a brilliant analogy. "Take tortillas, for example. They taste damn good,

¿no? Everybody likes tortillas, but if you eat too many, te puedes empachar, ¿no?"

"Hey, hey, alright, carnales, I hear you!" Chicho snapped. He had stopped his pacing and was standing by the entrance to the crevice in deep thought, his hands on his hips. He didn't even notice the Oldsmobile passing on *la calle* Brazos. The gang was right, he thought.

The *cucarachos* had to live by their wits every single moment of the day. It didn't take but a well-aimed swat with a rolled-up page from the *San Antonio News* to render any one of them into a gooey splotch on a wall. A well-placed footstep by a human, in fact, even an ill-placed footstep, could spread any one of them into an indistinguishable smear on a concrete sidewalk or wooden floor.

Cucarachos are an admirable breed that has evolved successfully for ages. Chicho liked to boast in the presence of any other insect who would listen that *cucarachos* were the most durable and intelligent, not to mention clean, creatures on the face of the earth. Any biologist worth his microscope could tell you that.

Still, thought Chicho, we can't afford to take any chances with these fragile bodies where humans are concerned. Exoskeleton bodies were definitely not built by Fisher.

Time passed uneventfully the rest of that day, and the next sunrise caught Chicho inside of a half-opened Diamond matchbox munching away on a breakfast of tortilla crumbs and *chile pitín*. Around seven-thirty that Saturday, Chicho heard Bosho calling his name. Chicho quickly shifted a tortilla crumb to one feeler and raised the other one up stiffly over the edge of the matchbox like a periscope scanning the horizon.

"¡Ese, Chicho, Chicho!" Bosho called out excitedly. He cupped his feelers around his mouth to throw his voice off as far as possible.

"Blow it out, carnal," Chicho punned with a grin from inside the box. "I'm all antennas."

"Did you check out the poster they just tacked up en el poste de la esquina?"

"Can't say that I did," Chicho mimicked in imitation of W. C. Fields. Growing curious, he became serious. "What's it say, Bosho?"

"Pues, trae un retra de Mingo y los Cuatro Espadas, Los Paisanos y Henry Zimmerle. Dice que mañana those bands will play en una boda aquí en el barrio."

"¡Hijo de la chingada, Bosho! ¡Allí estamos!" howled Chicho, elated. Immediately, he clambered over the edge of the matchbox and raced Bosho back to the crevice to share the happy news with the other *cucarachos*.

When they got there, Chicho noticed the entire gang had already gathered and were all chattering noisily discussing the coming event. According to the poster, a dance was scheduled to celebrate the wedding of Doña Borcelana's daughter, Tomasa, to a young truck driver named Simplicio. Reports from the other *cucarachos* indicated the dance was to be held that Sunday at the old Progreso Theater on *la calle* Guadalupe. The old Progreso Theater had ceased to be a movie house many years before, and after a few years as a recreation center, had finally been converted into a nut house—that is, a pecan-shelling business.

As reported by the widely travelled Chismes, a rather cosmopolitan *cucaracho* who had a yen for gossip and adventure, the Progreso Theater had been undergoing repairs and remodeling during the past few months. The management planned its grand opening by staging the Simplicio-Tomasa wedding. It was now to be the Progreso Ballroom.

"No wonder," exclaimed Chicho. "That accounts for so many carpenters and pintores around the intersection."

"¡Qué suerte de perro!" Chicho said to the others. "El Progreso is just around the corner and we can get there in a couple of hours if we take the route behind Doña Mechela's backyard."

Most of the *cucarachos* agreed except for an as-yet-undecided Chicharrón and a quiet Trucha who sat on the pinto bean in the corner and who slowly shook his head. All of a sudden, everyone had forgotten the admonishment of the day before.

The home of the *cucarachos* thus turned into a den of chatter as soon as the news of the *boda* broke out. The den sounded more like a *gallinero* under attack by a pack of *coyotes* than the dignified home of a *cucaracho* clan. Every single member of the gang was present. In addition to Chicho, Chicharrón, Pachorras, Bosho, Trucha, and Chismes, other members of the gang included Chícharo, "the Pea," as he was known on the North Side, and Frito, who was engaged to the other female member of the gang, Papas.

Chícharo was a young, tough, streetwise *cucaracho* whom the gang had met and had recruited on the spot one day as he was crawling out of a discarded can of Campbell's Pea Soup. The gang had been impressed when they observed how Chícharo had rolled the can of soup single-handedly under a porch and how he had then crawled inside and proceeded to lick the entire remains in leisure and safety.

Chícharo was a connoisseur of fine food and drink, and he loved peas. The gang had grown very fond of him because his antennae were especially sensitive to leftover canned goods. He was very useful in the gang's constant foraging for meals. Chícharo's popularity among the gang was further enhanced by the faint but unmistakable odor of peas issuing from his body when he became excited.

Rounding out the gang were Frito and Papas. This male-and-female duo had much in common. They shared many tastes in the things of the human world. The two were sitting in a corner of the crevice discussing the coming event. Frito had his arm around Papas. She was sitting, legs crossed, emulating Farrah Fawcett, gleaming with joy at the prospect of a dance with live conjunto music. Next to Fritos and potato chips, these two loved dancing. Last Sunday they had been overwhelmed to see Manuel Guerrero, Oro de Tejas, and Los Aguilares on the Johnny Canales show on Doña Mechela's TV set. Frito and Papas were elegant dancers. Their expertly patterned movements were a thing to see, and the *cucarachos* loved watching Papas cling tightly to Frito as they glided swiftly backward, cheek to cheek, as Flaco Jiménez sang his version of "Soy troquero." Papas would wiggle her behind rhythmically and sensually in time with each pluck of the bass guitar, trying to look sexy and succeeding. When these two got up to dance, even the impervious Trucha would find himself eyeing the couple, wistfully tapping his toes to the beat of Rubén Valle's bass playing. While Frito and Papas glowed in the spotlight, the shy and unobtrusive Pachorras would hunker in a corner quietly nursing a nascent envy of the uninhibited and vivacious Papas. Pachorras longed for Chicho to pay her more attention. She was forever admiring the handsome *cucaracho* and, through the course of several weeks, had fallen hopelessly in love. She would indulge in fancies, picturing themselves in blissful wedlock, enjoying a quiet evening in the comfort of their own crevice listening to the pitter-patter of little feet. Tomorrow night she would unfold her scheme to win the heart of the unwary Chicho.

The day of the wedding arrived. Toward eight in the evening the crevice home was the scene of much activity as the *cucarachos* scurried around the abode grooming themselves for the occasion. Pachorras took great pains to make herself attractive. She applied the essence of several foodstuffs to her body and converted a piece of blue material into a shawl. She hoped the blue shawl would catch the attention of the up-to-now indifferent Chicho.

Just as Pachorras was adding the final touches to the shawl, Chícharo burst into the crevice and boomed, "¡Órale, cucarachos, vámonos! The dance is almost due to start and we have to cross Doña Mechela's backyard!"

"¡Allá estamos!" responded Chicho, who was already halfway to the entrance, and howled, "¡Ajúa!"

The rest of the *cucarachos* filed out of the entrance behind Chicho and Chícharo as a troubled Trucha, and Chicharrón, who remained home out of respect for his ill health, bade them farewell.

As soon as the partygoers were gone, Trucha retreated to the pinto bean chair, where he sat quietly and pensively.

"¿Qué pasó, viejito?" Chicharrón asked. "You look worried."

"Sí," answered Trucha, and explained, "Estos cucarachos locos se atreven a hacer cosas que no son buenas. They're too wild."

"Estás bien, Trucha," agreed Chicharrón, and added, "Pero ¿qué se puede hacer? You can't deny them an occasional night of fun."

"Claro," said Trucha, and explained, "But these cucarachos want to party every night. No podemos esperar que la vida sea una gran noche de baile. I just have this terrible feeling."

After a few moments in silence, Trucha raised himself from the pinto bean, slowly moved to the entrance, and stood on the threshold to consider the stars.

Presently, he observed, "La vida de un cucaracho es muy corta. Too short and too unpredictable and we are but inconsequential beings roaming about blindly like gallinas descabezadas. One can be snuffed out in an instant and your entire life will have affected the cosmos no more than it is affected by a sigh in the wind."

Completely awed by the depth of such a novel and somber conception, Chicharrón retired to his corner. After mulling over what Trucha had told him, he finally turned over in his bed of rags and immediately fell into the clutches of deep and troubled slumber.

Meanwhile, the other *cucarachos* had crossed the weed beds that marked the boundaries of Doña Mechela's backyard and had marched, safari-like, down a winding route along the base of the towering carpet grass, zigzagging here and there to avoid the obstacles they encountered along the way. They crossed the yard and the alley without incident and as they approached another weeded area they walked and ran and sometimes hopped and crawled nimbly and hastily over pebbles, papers, rags, twigs, and leaves and around stones, broken bottles, beer cans, and numerous other objects discarded by the humans, who, evidently, were oblivious to the theme of Keep America Beautiful. Finally, they reached and easily walked under a cyclone fence. At this point they climbed up a concrete curb and ran along its top until they reached the Progreso Ballroom.

Chicho couldn't contain his excitement. "¡Órale, camaradas!" he exclaimed loudly. "Hurry up, the dance has already started." Chicho was right. Apparently, the wedding march had already been staged. Los Cuatro Espadas were playing their opening number: "Sácate las pulgas, Chencha," a polka.

"Vamos a subirnos en una ventana," said Papas. "We can watch from there and dance on the windowsill."

The *cucarachos* crawled up the wall of the Progreso Ballroom in a mad, scrambling rush. They appeared not unlike a herd of tiny buffalo stampeding up a vertical plain. As each would attain the edge of the windowsill, they would race to the window and press their faces to the pane, their little faces contorting comically with the pressure.

Through the panes emerged a sensational scene. Humans were everywhere. Under ten rows of brightly glowing chandeliers, the dance floor was a mass of dancing couples who shuffled around glued to each other in step to the brisk pace of a polka. On three sides of the dance floor, a multitude of celebrants sat around long banquet tables upon which were cluttered scores of ashtrays, paper cups, and cigarette packs, in addition to hundreds of beer cans and an assortment of liquor bottles with labels bearing such names as José Cuervo, Bacardí, and Club 45, and an occasional gallon of Gallo. The band was singing the last verse of "Secreto amor."

At one end of the ballroom, bride and groom were proudly receiving congratulations and blessings from their relatives, friends, and neighbors, in addition to the usual unspoken curses from envious old maids and spurned would-be lovers. As the band played the soft melody of a lover's waltz, a line of men formed near the Simplicio-Tomasa table to await their turns to whirl around the floor for a few moments with the radiant bride, according to custom. Meanwhile, the women would forgo the traditional waltz with the groom because Simplicio was nodding on a chair with the black bow tie of his rented tuxedo drooping from his opened neck, thoroughly plastered.

Suddenly, the *cucarachos*' attention was drawn to the bandstand as Los Cuatro Espadas abruptly broke into the opening lyrics of "Tú sentida y yo sentido." At mid stage, inches away from a microphone, Mingo was squeezing and pulling and running his fingers in rapid succession over the buttons of a sparkling red accordion which was strapped to his chest. Mingo was bursting with moves as he kicked to the right and then to the left to the beat of the polka, while Chivo and Óscar crowded each other on mike number two and accompanied Mingo in the three-part harmony. The crowd of Chicanos responded with rounds of ecstatic *gritos* and applause. In moments they were pairing off to shuffle along the floor in double time.

Overwhelmed by the titillating sounds, Chicho and Frito snatched up Pachorras and Papas. Pairing off, they stomped around wildly on the windowsill in time to the lively rhythms. The other *cucarachos* soon joined them as the musicians dipped into their extensive repertoire. As the evening progressed, the *cucarachos* took turns dancing *polcas, valses, boleros,* and *cumbias* with the two *cucarachas,* showing off their stuff.

Unable to corner the wayward Chicho long enough to broach the subject foremost in her mind, Pachorras wondered whether he was worth the trouble. He had not even noticed her shawl. He was thoroughly engrossed with the performance on the bandstand and it appeared her plans had been for naught. She brightened up considerably, however, nearing the end of the dance as Chicho finally sidled up to her.

"Say, Pachorritas," Chicho said with a mischievous gleam in his eye. "Let's go dance on the bandstand."

"¿Qué tienes?" Pachorras replied, fully startled. "We can't go up there!"

"Yo voy contigo, Chicho," volunteered Papas, as Frito looked on, mildly amused.

Before anyone could object, Chicho grabbed the giggling Papas, virtually dragging her to the edge of the sill, where they disappeared around the jamb. Speeding along the wall of the building, they reached a window near the bandstand and slipped inside.

The ambiance of the windowsill altered dramatically. Pachorras sat down and quietly brooded.

"You should have tried to stop them, Frito," Pachorras complained sadly.

"I'm sorry, Pachorras, but you know how crazy Chicho and Papas can be."

The *cucarachos* became increasingly concerned when at the end of several numbers Chicho and Papas failed to return. Pachorras grew even more despondent when Juan García mounted the stage to sing the haunting verses of "Qué casualidad" in a voice reminiscent of a long-gone Mexican idol, a number the band usually played next to last on their list of selections. Soon the band was playing *la despedida* and Chícharo and Frito crawled to the window near the bandstand to see if they could locate Chicho and Papas. When they returned alone, the music had come to an end. The ballroom was nearly empty as the crowd headed for the exits. In an attempt to assuage the fears of the others, Chícharo lightly suggested they retreat to the cyclone fence so they would not miss Chicho and Papas when the two decided to return to the crevice.

"Vamos a esperarlos en la cerca," suggested Frito, casually but without conviction. "They'll be along soon and they have to pass through the fence."

The *cucarachos* descended the wall in silence. Reaching the cyclone fence, they sat down to wait for Chicho and Papas.

An hour later the members of the band were preparing to leave. As the musicians were gathering up their instruments and other equipment which made up their sound system, Eddie, the drummer, suddenly gasped as he moved a speaker away from the back wall of the bandstand. Two cockroaches were squashed on the wall. The cockroaches were in an upright position, stuck to the wall on the strength of their own messy goo. Eddie was struck by the tiny but spectacular discovery, for, incredibly, the cockroaches appeared to be embracing each other. Eddie was extremely amused and he called Mingo over.

"Wacha, jefe," Eddie said, pointing at the cockroaches and chuckling. "Parece que andaban bailando, ¿no?"

Will you look at that, thought Mingo, they certainly did appear to have been dancing.

"¡Hey, cúrate, Óscar!" Mingo called to the *bajista* excitedly.

As Óscar approached them and saw the cockroaches, he smiled and joked, "Escríbeles un corrido, compadre," and they all had a good laugh at the suggestion that Mingo compose them a ballad.

Outside, on the now quiet and deserted sidewalk of *la calle* Guadalupe, under the dimmed marquee of the Progreso Ballroom, was parked a late-model flashy Olds that belonged to the emcee of the night's entertainment, an enterprising promoter known as Canelo. It was two in the morning. Canelo was preparing to leave. Traffic had come to a standstill and Canelo had the front door of the immaculate Olds ajar. His right foot was resting on the edge of the running board and he was stooped over, wiping the toes of his Florsheims with a piece of cloth. As he was facing downwards, he noticed a smudge on the running board. He ran the cloth over the smudge revealing a metal plaque bearing the legend: BODY BY FISHER. Canelo then boarded his car, slammed the door shut, and switched on the ignition and the silence was broken by the powerful roar of internal combustion. Canelo swerved the solid machine of iron and steel into *la calle* Guadalupe and thundered down the dark, deserted street under gathering clouds.

The billowing clouds lumbered along, portending a rainstorm. As a cloud broke away from another, allowing a streak of moonlight to descend to the earth, a tiny figure was exposed in a dark, lonely alley. A piece of blue material was clasped to its breast. As the clouds surged along, a beam of moonlight fell on the face of Pachorras, revealing the tiny gleam of a teardrop trickling down her cheek.

33

Conjunto Memories

✧

SUSANA NEVÁREZ MORTON

1992

I was wild. I was innocent. I was young.
Music was a fever in my soul. At thirteen, I became a professional teenager. I carried the push-button transistor radio that Uncle Amador had given me for my birthday from room to room. Mamá, still lovely in her single motherhood, tolerated my new, noisy appendage with saintly patience. I was blessed with youth, but cursed with legs too long and ungainly for the rest of me.

"Teach me to dance, Mamá, please?" I implored my mother. "Mrs. Corder lets us dance in P.E. when it's raining and we can't go outside. All the girls know how, except me! Please, Mamá, will you teach me?"

My mother rarely denied me. We shared a closeness that only a single parent and her daughter can share.

She pursed her lips for a second, and nodded.

"I'll teach you how to dance the right way."

I didn't like the way she said "the right way." It was like putting a red detour flag on the smooth, heretofore untravelled road I had chosen for my dancing feet. At the same time, "the right way" implied there was a wrong way. I certainly did not want to be ostracized by my friends for dancing in an unseemly fashion—unless, of course, my friends danced the wrong way to begin with. If only I danced in this right way, I might be doomed to spend my teenage years alone, without friends.

Setting aside my apprehensions, I followed Mamá into the kitchen. I helped tuck the comfortable, yellow padded chairs under the big, formica tabletop that had the shiny chrome trim on the edges.

"Put Uncle Amador's radio there," she said, pointing to the center of the table.

"Mamá, when will you stop calling it 'Uncle Amador's radio'? He gave it to me for my birthday, and that was two months ago."

I obeyed as Mamá pushed the big, rectangular table flush against the wall. The hot-water heater stood in a corner. Along the opposite wall, the gleaming white refrigerator, sink, cabinets, and stove were lined up like attentive soldiers waiting to be called to duty.

"Change the station to something in Spanish," Mamá said, frowning at the radio, as if it were a muddy footprint on her clean linoleum.

"Mamá," I protested vehemently, "I want to learn to dance rock and roll."

She looked at me blankly. "I can't dance to music in English."

"It's the same as dancing to music in Spanish, Mamá," I blurted out before I could stop myself. This wasn't going to work. I had argued myself into a corner, but all was not lost. I could try a reverse tactic. "Mamá, if you can't dance in English, how can I dance in Spanish?"

"*Hija mía,*" she replied, passionately, "it's in your blood!"

Rolling my eyes heavenward, as only a teenager can do, I turned the knob on Uncle Amador's radio until I heard a thick-sounding melody similar to one I had heard on the merry-go-round at Playland Park. I had one final defense.

"Won't all those old Spanish songs make you sad, Mamá?" I asked.

"Sad? Music is for singing and dancing and laughing," she said, looking at me curiously. "Why should it make me sad?"

"It might remind you of things," I replied, smartly.

She flashed a hot, knowing look at me. "Things?" she asked. "What kind of things?"

"Oh, just things," I said, not wanting to go any further.

As young as I was, I had heard rumors of my father's sins from the conversations of various relatives. He was a Romeo who had left my mother with a young child, me. Mamá had sent him away as a punishment. He had never come back. Not once. That the punishment had fallen on the intended shoulders was questionable since I had never seen Mamá dance, or sing, or even laugh very much. According to her, these were the things one did when one was not sad.

I remembered my childhood and how she talked of my father. How they had danced together, *boleros, valses,* and *redovas.* As I got older, she stopped speaking of him. I thought she had forgotten him and that she wanted me to forget about him, as well. I had never known him. The only thing I could forget was my vague, imaginary picture of him. It was a picture without a face, for it was the picture of a man I had never seen.

The old kitchen, where I had once watched my Aunt Nolberta twist off a chicken's head before plucking it and cooking it for supper, was big enough to serve as a dance floor.

Mamá led.

"Put your left arm here," she said. "Give me your other hand. Pretend I'm the boy."

I looked up into her face and giggled with teenage embarrassment.

The disc jockey gabbled in Spanish while the oompah of the accordion music raced away with a fast beat in double time. It was a *polca,* but it reminded me of the organ grinder and the monkey I had seen at Brackenridge Park two months earlier when Uncle Amador had come for my birthday.

"Loosen up and follow my feet," my mother instructed.

"I'm not used to this music, Mamá," I told her, not very warmly.

"This is conjunto music," she said, almost reverently. Then, she tried to twist me around. "You're too stiff," she observed.

When she went one way, I went the other way. She shuffled her feet in time to the music, but my steps couldn't keep up with hers. My knees bumped into her legs and my feet seemed to be trying to climb up her ankles.

"I'm trying, Mamá," I said, as a fast-paced *ranchera* began to play. The accordion flourishes came in between anguished pleadings. Mamá started moving in a whole new direction, which I did not think possible. The accordion punctuated each quatrain like delicate, little hands patting *tortillas.*

"It's too much, too soon, Mamá," I wailed in harmony with the singer's words.

Next came a lively *cumbia.* "You have to move everything for this one," she explained, making every part of her body wiggle. Her hands and arms moved independently of each other, seeming to be apart from her shoulders. Her feet claimed independence from her legs. Her hips knew no sovereign. She turned her head from side to side and seemed to be having a great deal of fun. Finally, I just stood there and watched her having a party for one, smiling all the while.

"Follow behind me," she said, "like a little train."

This might work, I thought, with renewed hope. The bunny hop was very popular at school. I tried moving my feet as she moved hers, but my arms insisted on hanging stiffly down my sides like planks of wood. I couldn't turn my head from side to side as Mamá did because I had to look down to watch her feet and try to make mine do the same thing.

By the time the *cumbia*'s rhythms finally infected my feet, the disc jockey was announcing the next song. This *ranchera* was slower than the first. It reminded me of proud, erect *charros,* with big hats, singing of their *dolor.* Somehow, I just couldn't see any of the bands that played at our school dances belting out songs that sounded like this one, . . . *si acaso quisieras volver* . . .

We sat out the next one so Mamá could catch her breath and pour herself a glass of iced tea. It was a *huapango,* which reminded me of an accordion concerto, but with lively dancers kicking up their heels in time to the spirited rhythm. It sounded like the kind of Mexican folk music my pretty cousin Belinda danced to at Cinco de Mayo festivals.

If this radio station was any gauge, polkas were clearly the listening audience's favorites. Mamá pulled me up to my feet again when the polka's strong *bajo sexto* beat beckoned once more.

"It's too fast," I told her. "Maybe we should look for a nice slow song on one of the English stations," I suggested, adding, "I can barely understand this one. I don't even know what a *gorrión* is."

"You understand it," Mamá insisted. "A *gorrión* is a little bird. A sparrow. I spoke to you in Spanish before you even knew how to walk. Listen, here's a slow one. *Un vals.* A waltz. One-two-three. One-two-three. One-two-three."

Once I untangled my feet from hers, they followed on their own the slow, pronounced tempo of the conjunto waltz. The melody played on the accordion still sounded like pure organ-grinder music to my young, rock-and-roll ears.

I looked up into my mother's eyes and began to express my displeasure, but I held my tongue. Her gaze had travelled far away from our warm, linoleum-floor kitchen. No longer was I the dancer in her arms. A pang of long-ago-forgotten yearning pinched my tender heart.

Suddenly, I ached to see clearly the partner who held her. When the accordion mourned its last note and the *vals* ended, Mamá pulled me to her and hugged me tightly. She pushed me back gently and with saddened eyes searched my face for someone who was not I, but who was there with me, who was there in me, an integral part of me. I knew, from the talk of assorted relatives, that I bore an uncanny resemblance to my father, a tall, thin *güero* with hazel eyes. My dimpled smile was his smile, as my dark brows and light-colored eyes were his eyes.

"He loved conjunto," my mother said at last.

The words of the song in my mother's language became clearer to me. Love stood side by side with pain and anguish and they embraced each other. It was there that I first saw my father—in my mother's eyes when she danced.

About the Contributors

Authors

RAMIRO BURR is a *San Antonio Express-News* reporter covering rock, pop, and country music. He is also a *Billboard* correspondent and a freelance writer published by *Pulse, Cashbox,* and *New Country Music* magazines and several Texas newspapers. Since 1986, Burr has specialized in Spanish-language music. His weekly *Express-News* column is syndicated as "Ramiro Burr's Latin Music." Burr's *Billboard Guide to Tejano and Regional Mexican Music,* published by Billboard Books in 1999, is the first reference work on the subject.

JOSÉ B. CUÉLLAR, originally from San Antonio, is a scholar, activist, and musician. He is a professor of La Raza studies and director of the César E. Chávez Institute of Public Policy at San Francisco State University. He has received a number of fellowships, including a 1997 Gateways Humanities Fellowship from the Guadalupe Cultural Arts Center to study the development and diffusion of the Tex-Mex saxophone. A saxophonist and singer, Cuéllar performs with Dr. Loco's Rockin' Jalapeño Band and Amorindio.

ISMAEL DOVALINA was born in Laredo, Texas, and raised in San Antonio. He obtained bachelor's and master's degrees in psychology from Columbia University and the University of Michigan, respectively. Currently he is an associate professor of psychology at Palo Alto Community College in San Antonio. He studied both accordion and guitar under the auspices of the Xicano Music Program of the Guadalupe Cultural Arts Center.

JOSÉ FLORES PEREGRINO is originally from Laredo, Texas. He is a musician, songwriter, poet, and teacher, and *jefe* of Xinachtli, a traditional, ceremonial Aztec *conchero* dance group based in Austin. A longtime Austin resident, Flores is currently an English professor at Austin Community College, where he teaches literature and creative writing. He also plays the *bajo sexto* and sings with Conjunto Aztlan. A book of his poetry, *Mesquitierra*, was published by Pajarito Publications in 1977.

CARLOS JESÚS GÓMEZ FLORES, a native of Monterrey, Nuevo León, is a writer and arts administrator. He received bachelor's degrees in economics and political science from the Universidad Autónoma de Nuevo León, in Monterrey, and a master's degree in business administration from the Universidad Regiomontana, also in Monterrey. Gómez Flores has been a producer of radio and television programs and a singer with *norteño* groups. Currently he is director of Acción Cívica y Cultural of the state of Nuevo León.

CARLOS GUERRA, who was born in Robstown, Texas, graduated from Texas A&I University (now Texas A&M University–Kingsville). During the 1960s and 1970s he was active in the Chicano civil-rights movement in South Texas, and helped found the Mexican American Youth Organization and the Raza Unida Party. In 1991, Guerra became a columnist for the *San Antonio Light*. After the *Light* closed he joined the *San Antonio Express-News*, where he writes a weekly political column that is syndicated in other Texas newspapers.

LONGINOS (LONNIE) GUERRERO was a singer and prolific songwriter who was inducted into the Tejano Music Hall of Fame in 1983. Born and raised in Austin, he served in the U.S. Air Force during World War II. For most of his life Guerrero worked as a janitor in Austin, employed by the Austin Independent School District, the Internal Revenue Service, and other public-sector institutions. He passed away on January 10, 1994, at the age of seventy-six.

JEFFREY A. HALLEY is an associate professor of sociology at the University of Texas at San Antonio. He earned a master's degree at the New School for Social Research and a Ph.D. at the Graduate School of the City University of New York. Halley focuses his research primarily on avant-garde movements in culture and art. In collaboration with Avelardo Valdez, he also examines issues of gender and identity in conjunto music.

RAMÓN HERNÁNDEZ, JR., is currently the entertainment editor at *La Prensa,* San Antonio's bilingual newspaper. A photographer and journalist specializing in Tejano music, Hernández has published his work in numerous newspapers and magazines, including the *San Antonio Express-News, Billboard, Hispanic,* and various Tejano-music publications. He is also the publisher of the *National Hispanic Entertainment Directory.*

JOSÉ E. LIMÓN is a professor of English and anthropology and the director of the Center for Mexican American Studies at the University of Texas at Austin. A native of Laredo, Texas, he obtained his M.A. in English and his Ph.D. in cultural anthropology from UT Austin. His most recent books are *American Encounters: Greater Mexico, the United States, and the Erotics of Culture* (Beacon Press, 1998) and *Dancing with the Devil: Society and Cultural Poetics in Mexican-American South Texas* (University of Wisconsin Press, 1994).

CARMEN LUÉVANOS, originally from San Antonio, now lives in Austin, where she holds a job with the state of Texas. She researched the Tejano Conjunto Festival for a course in cultural anthropology with Américo Paredes, at the University of Texas at Austin. A graduate student in the LBJ School of Public Affairs at the time, Luévanos earned her master's degree in 1994. She received her undergraduate degree from Trinity University in broadcast journalism.

MAX MARTÍNEZ was born and raised in Gonzales County, east of San Antonio. After serving nine years in the U.S. Navy he enrolled at St. Mary's University in San Antonio, where he received a B.A. in English. He later earned a master's degree in comparative literature from East Texas State University, Commerce (now Texas A&M University–Commerce). Martínez, a longtime San Antonio resident, is the author of five books of fiction, all published by Arte Público Press: two collections of stories and three novels—*Schoolland* (1988), *White Leg* (1996), and *Layover* (1997).

SUSANA NEVÁREZ MORTON is a first-generation Mexican American and a native of San Antonio. Born and raised in that city's South Side, she spent her teenage years in a small house adjacent to her aunt and uncle's mom-and-pop store on historic Mission Road. In 1992, at the time of her story's publication in *Tonantzin,* she was employed at Kelly Air Force Base in San Antonio.

MANUEL PEÑA, originally from the Lower Rio Grande Valley of Texas, has a Ph.D. in anthropology from the University of Texas at Austin. Currently a professor of music at California State University, Fresno, he has also taught anthropology at UT Austin. Peña is the foremost scholar of Mexican American music, with three works on the subject: *The Texas-Mexican Conjunto* (University of Texas Press, 1985), *The Mexican American Orquesta* (University of Texas Press, 1999), and *Música Tejana* (Texas A&M University Press, 1999).

CATHY RAGLAND, a native of San Antonio, is an ethnomusicologist and folklorist. She has worked with Texas Folklife Resources in Austin and Northwest Folklife in Seattle, and has also been a popular-music critic and features writer with various newspapers. Currently, Ragland is coordinator of special projects for the Center for Traditional Music and Dance in New York City. She is also working on a book, "Reclaiming Texas: The Tejano-Music Explosion," to be published by Smithsonian Institution Press.

JOSÉ R. REYNA is a professor of Spanish at California State University, Bakersfield, where he teaches Chicano literature and folklore. He has published widely on Chicano humor, and has also written liner notes for several of Rounder's conjunto albums. Reyna, who earned his M.A. and Ph.D. at the University of California, Los Angeles, has served on folk arts and music panels of the California Arts Council, the National Endowment for the Arts, and the Grammy Awards (Latin Music Category).

JOE "FLACO" SALDÍVAR, a self-taught writer and painter, was born in San Antonio. Traveling with his family to work on farms in Texas and other states, he attended a number of different elementary schools before dropping out in the eighth grade. After being convicted of several burglaries he was sentenced to life imprisonment in the Texas Department of Corrections. While in prison he has obtained his G.E.D. and completed various college courses. Saldívar is also active in the prison-reform movement.

CLAYTON T. SHORKEY is a professor of social work and director of the Social Work Learning Resource Center at the University of Texas at Austin. He has published extensively in the areas of behavior therapy, child abuse, medical social work, alcohol and drug abuse, and culturally sensitive social-work practice. Shorkey, who is the founder and president of the Texas Music Museum, has been researching folk music in Texas and photographing musicians since the early 1980s.

About the Contributors ✧ 413

JUAN TEJEDA is a musician, songwriter, arts administrator, and teacher. From 1980 to 1998, he served as director of the Xicano Music Program of the Guadalupe Cultural Arts Center, where he founded the Tejano Conjunto Festival and directed it for seventeen years. Currently, Tejeda is producing the first International Accordion Festival in San Antonio as well as teaching in the Division of Bicultural-Bilingual Studies at the University of Texas at San Antonio. He also plays the button accordion and sings with Conjunto Aztlan.

EDÉN TORRES was raised primarily in Mercedes, in the Lower Rio Grande Valley of Texas. She earned a Ph.D. in American studies from the University of Minnesota–Twin Cities, where she is now an assistant professor in the departments of Chicano Studies and Women's Studies. Torres teaches a wide range of courses, including the folklore of Greater Mexico, Mexican American feminism, Mexican American cultural studies, and Mexican American history.

JERRY TUMLINSON is a native Houstonian who currently lives in Kunsan, South Korea. A professor of English at Howon University, he also owns and operates a small press, Third Ear Books. Tumlinson received a B.A. from the University of Houston–Downtown and an M.F.A. from the Naropa Institute's Jack Kerouac School of Disembodied Poetics, in Boulder, Colorado. He has three books of poetry to his credit: *Flattened Fifths* (Backporch Press, 1998), *Grey* (Dristal Press, 1998), and *Broken Balance* (Erastus St. Publishers, 1999).

AVELARDO VALDEZ is a professor of sociology and director of the Center for Drug and Social Policy Research at the University of Texas at San Antonio. He researches issues related to violence, substance use, culture, and gender in the Mexican American population. Valdez, who has a Ph.D. from the University of California, Los Angeles, has also written on topics in conjunto music. Since 1982 he has served on the board of directors of the Guadalupe Cultural Arts Center—as member, from 1982 to 1988; chair, from 1989 to 1990; and advisor, from 1991 to the present.

RON YOUNG, originally from San Antonio, has been a popular-music critic for the *San Antonio Light* and a freelance writer for the *San Antonio Express-News*. Young currently resides in Nashville, where he is pursuing a career as a songwriter. He is also a regular contributor to *Music Row* magazine, a national biweekly out of Nashville that is geared toward the country-music industry.

FRANCES YTURRI, who was born and raised in San Antonio, was a high-school student at the time of her poem's publication in *Tonantzin*. In 1997 she obtained a bachelor's degree in education from the University of Texas at Austin, graduating with highest honors. Yturri is currently a third-year student at the UT School of Law, where she is an associate editor for the *Review of Litigation*. She continues writing poetry.

Poster Artists

JESSE ALMAZÁN, a San Antonio native, has been an artist for more than forty years. He studied in several private art schools, and also honed his skills by airbrushing movie stars' portraits on San Antonio theater facades. Since the age of twenty-one he has been employed as a civilian graphic-arts designer with the U.S. Air Force. Almazán has participated in many exhibitions, and his paintings and posters have won numerous awards, including the Texas Watercolor Society's top award in 1986.

JAMES COBB is a longtime resident of San Antonio. Involved in the visual arts since high school, he began painting in the mid 1980s. He has received several major awards, including an NEA visual-arts fellowship, and has shown his work in solo and group exhibitions throughout the West and Southwest. His paintings have been collected by the Blanton Museum of Art at the University of Texas at Austin and the San Antonio Museum of Art, among others. Recently Cobb has concentrated on creating digital imagery and making music.

JOSÉ ESQUIVEL has pursued a career in graphics and fine art for more than thirty-five years. After studying at the Warren Hunter School of Art in the 1950s, he worked for San Antonio's City Public Service for twenty-nine years, retiring in 1986 as supervisor of the art department. Esquivel has participated in numerous art shows. The most recent include the 1999 *La Virgen de Guadalupe* exhibition at the Centro Cultural Aztlán in San Antonio, and the 1998 *Bucking the Texas Myth* exhibition at the Dougherty Arts Center in Austin.

ROGER GARCÍA, who was raised in San Antonio, earned an associate's degree in advertising art at San Antonio College in 1979. After serving in the U.S. Navy for four years, he returned to San Antonio, and in 1991 obtained a bachelor's degree in accounting from the University of Texas at San Antonio. Currently employed as a computer programmer for a Texas state agency, García resides in San Antonio and continues making art.

About the Contributors

JESÚS DAVID GONZÁLEZ was born in Nueva Rosita, Coahuila, and raised on the southeast side of San Antonio. He studied art at the University of Texas at San Antonio. Currently he is a freelance artist working in murals, portraiture, mosaic, and graphic design. In recent years he has won several national and statewide art competitions, among them "El Arte Que Nos Mueve," a national contest sponsored by the Chrysler Corporation.

JACINTO GUEVARA is a musician and self-taught artist. Originally from Los Angeles, he earned a B.A. at California State University, Northridge. Since 1986 he has focused on painting "urbanscapes" of Los Angeles, and subsequently of San Antonio. Adept on a variety of instruments, he has also played with a number of bands, including his own group, Jacinto y su Conjunto. Guevara currently works as a carpenter and as a substitute teacher in the Edgewood school district of San Antonio.

CLEMENTE F. GUZMÁN III, who was raised in San Antonio, has been drawing since the third grade. As a child, he migrated with his family to Minnesota every summer to work in the fields. He subsequently obtained a scholarship to that state's Mankato Technical Institute, and earned an associate's degree in commercial art. Since 1988 he has been an artist with Texas Parks and Wildlife in Austin. There he has gained recognition for his colorful wildlife illustrations, receiving the Izaak Walton League Award in 1996 as well as three Austin Addys.

RICK HUNTER is a self-taught photographer who started his career as an army photojournalist. After working freelance in New York City, he returned to his native Texas in 1991. Since then he has been a staff photographer for the *San Antonio Express-News*. Hunter has exhibited his photography throughout Texas as well as in New Mexico and New York City. His work appears regularly in national publications and has been honored by numerous organizations, including the National Press Photographers Association.

DOUGLAS JASSO was born in San Antonio and raised in Edinburg, in the Rio Grande Valley. He moved to Kansas City in 1977 to attend the Kansas City Art Institute, and has remained in that city ever since. For many years Jasso worked as a freelance illustrator, publishing his work in the *Kansas City Star* and various trade magazines; he also devoted himself to printmaking and painting. He is currently employed by Open Options–United Cerebral Palsy, working with adults who have developmental disabilities.

BEN MATA is an artist based in San Antonio. Born and raised in that city, he is completing a B.F.A. at Southwest Texas State University, in San Marcos. Through the Juntos en Arte program, which is sponsored by the Guadalupe Cultural Arts Center, he works with Bexar County Jail inmates as an artist in residence. Mata also teaches art to at-risk elementary-school children through the program Urban Smarts.

PRISCILLA REYNA-OVALLE was born in the West Side of San Antonio about a mile from the historic Guadalupe Theater. She became interested in art at a very young age, when her mother introduced her to Picasso's work. Reyna-Ovalle has exhibited her art regionally and has also written dramatic sketches that have been produced by the Jump-Start Performance Company. She is currently devoting herself to caring for her two children, Miguel Adrián and Crista Eliana.

ROBERTO B. SOSA, a native of San Antonio, graduated from Burbank High School in 1980. The following year, he and Robert Sosa (no relation) started the agency Robert Sosa Advertising Concepts & Design. In 1985 he joined forces with Robert's brother Lionel, a pioneer in Hispanic advertising, and worked for six years as his art director. Sosa now lives in California, where he is the creative director for Ad Américas, a Los Angeles–based agency that creates advertising for the U.S. Latino population.

THOMAS VÁSQUEZ earned a B.F.A. in advertising art from the University of North Texas in 1990 (after twice winning the Tejano Conjunto Festival poster contest). He subsequently worked for various design firms, and also taught design at UNT. From 1997 to 1999 he was the senior art director for a Dallas advertising agency. Now living in New York City, Vásquez is an associate creative director at Ogilvy & Mather. His work has been featured in numerous graphic-arts books and annuals, among them *Graphis Design 97: The International Annual of Design and Illustration* (Graphis Press, 1996).

MARCELINO F. VILLANUEVA, JR., began his career in advertising, design, and illustration in 1979, after completing a two-year course in advertising at San Antonio College. A San Antonio native, he is currently a graphic artist with the *San Antonio Express-News*. Villanueva has received several awards for his graphic work. He is also known for the three large murals he painted at San Juan de los Lagos Church in San Antonio's West Side.

Photographer

AL RENDÓN, born and raised in San Antonio, is a commercial freelance photographer and owner of Foto Real, an art gallery. He has served as the official photographer for the Guadalupe Cultural Arts Center, the San Antonio Fiesta Commission, and *Images* (the former Sunday magazine of the *San Antonio Express-News*). Rendón's work has appeared in many magazines and newspapers, including *Newsweek, USA Today, People, Hispanic,* and *Texas Monthly*. His portraiture includes Selena, Flaco Jiménez, Henry Cisneros, and numerous other celebrities.

Index

Note: The interviews (part 6) are indexed only in their English translations.

Ábrego, Eugenio, *161*
  death of, 373
  mentions of, 75–78, 346
  musical style, 343
accordion
  attractions of, 74, 123–125
  chromatic accordion, 41, 101, 117, 119
  classes in playing, 232, 357
  in conjunto ensembles, 6–7, 20, 23, 76–78, 97–98, 202, 336
  as cultural symbol, 208–209, 213–214, 219, 225
  economics and use of, 4, 118
  future of, 224, 337, 340, 342, 345, 348
  history of, 76, 116–117
  image of, 115, 116, 120, 121
  as instrument for men, 231
  introduction into border area, 4, 14, 73–74, 97
  loss of interest in, 217
  manufacture of, 116–117, 119–120
  musical characteristics of, 4–5, 116–118, 124–125
  musical experimentation, 224
  in nonconjunto music, 109, 122
  popularization of, 74–76, 118, 122, 197, 222
  Rockordeon, 118–119, 122
  styles of playing, 6, 19–20, 21, 22, 41, 74, 77, 79, 100–101
  synthesizer contrasted with, 120, 124
  in Tejano music (progressive conjunto), 208
  tuning, 4–5, 7–8, 98, 117–118, 119, 287, 347
  types of, 117, 119, 120, 344
  vocals and, 336
  women accordionists, 91–93, 232, 234–235, 360
Accordion Abuse Fest, 356
Accordion Discs, 93
"Accordions That Shook the World" (record series), 122
Aceves Mejía, Miguel, 87
acordeón. See accordion
Acosta, Miguel Orta, 127
  on playing the *bajo sexto*, 128
Acuña, Tomás, 310, 312

419

Acuña y Leal, 75
Adán y Eva y su Conjunto, 90
"La Adelita," 312, 355
"El aguacero," 269, 271
Aguilera, Sal, 146
Aguirre Rocha, Esteban, 138
Aguirre Rocha, Víctor, 138
Agustín y sus Chicanos, 203
Alanís, Juan, 138
Los Alegres de Terán, 161
   mentions of, 63, 76, 107, 140, 315, 333, 335, 339, 349
   norteño music and, 73, 74
   recordings by, 75
   vocal duo, 21–22
All American Jazz Orchestra, 137
Allegato, Joe, 203
Almaguer, Fidencio, 137
Almazán, Jesse (poster by), *171*
Almeida, Santiago, xix, 16, 36, 63, 81–82, 127
   as *bajo sexto* player, 129, 132
   Narciso Martínez and, 82
   on playing the *bajo sexto*, 128
Alurista, 365
Amor Bonito, 50–51
Andrade, José Daniel, 76
Anglo American social classes. *See* Chicano social classes
Apodaca, Manuel, 291
Applen, Tudor, 137
Arcaraz, Luis, 195, 337
Arhoolie Records, 93, 151, 197, 218, 223, 274
Armendáriz, Armando, 346
Armendáriz, Wally, 144, 147
Arredondo, Alvino, 293
Arredondo, Julián Garza, 76
Arredondo, Miguel, 140
Arturo Aldaré y Machismo, 145
Los Astronautas, 203
"Atotonilco," xiii, 151
audience characteristics. *See also* performance venues
   Chicano culture and, 206

conjunto music, 108–109, 110, 111, 143, 200, 203, 208–209, 214, 217, 223, 224
   at dances, 242
   Narciso Martínez on, 337
   orquesta tejana, 200, 207, 217
   by performance venues, 203–206
   Tejano music, 208–209, 218
   Tejano radio, 221
awards and honors in Tejano music. *See also* Grammy Awards
   Conjunto Female Vocalist of the Year, 90
   Conjunto Music Hall of Fame, 81–84
   Pura Vida Hispanic Music Awards, 150
   Tejano Music Awards, 93, 149
   Tejano Music Hall of Fame, 88
   Texas Women Hall of Fame, 88
   West Texas Awards, 90
Ay Te Dejo en San Antonio, 121
Ayala, Mario, 335
Ayala, Pedro
   career, 14, 19, 62, 139, 197, 343
   collaborations, 143
   death of, 373
   inducted into Conjunto Music Hall of Fame, 370
   on Narciso Martínez, 36
   Narciso Martínez, relationship with, 62
   mentions of, 74, 107, 220, 335, 340, 346
   musical style, 19, 37, 77, 97, 349
Ayala, Ramiro, 335
Ayala, Ramón
   Los Bravos del Norte, 63, 108
   mentions of, 77, 204, 276, 294, 339, 346

bajo quinto, 129
bajo sexto. *See also* Macías, Martín
   in conjunto ensemble, 5, 8, 20, 37, 63

craft of making, 127, 128, 132–134
description of, xv, 127–128
evolution of *bajo quinto* from, 129
origins of, 127, 131
players of, 81–84, 127, 358
role in Conjunto Bernal, 22
tuning, 128, 129, 132
use in ensembles, 128–129
bandolón. See bajo sexto
Barrera, Reynaldo, xix, 81–83
"El barrilito," 290, 355
bass (electric bass guitar), 8, 20
Beausoleil, 122
"Beer Barrel Polka." *See* "El barrilito"
Bego Records, 103, 192
Beltrán Ruiz, Pablo, 195
Berlanga, Andrés, 127
Bernal, Eloy
　mentions of, xix, 65, 82
　as musician, 40–41, 81, 83–84, 99, 103
　personal background, 83–84, 99
Bernal, Max, 144
Bernal, Paulino, *180*
　career, 40–42, 99–103, 344
　chromatic accordion and, 101, 344
　conjunto gospel music, 103
　on conjunto style, 325–327, 343–345
　mentions of, 82, 220, 299, 336
　musical education, 99
　musical style, 21–22, 40, 64, 100–101, 338, 344
　as musician, 104–105, 346, 350
　personal background, 40, 98–99
　at Tejano Conjunto Festival, *180*, 371
　vocals in musical style, 338, 341, 344, 350
Bernardo Martínez y sus Compadres, 341
Betancourt, Paco, and Beto Villa, 44, 143
Beto Villa y su Orquesta, 87

Bluebird Records (RCA)
　and Narciso Martínez, 336
　mentions of, 35, 87
bolero. See also dance types
　chord variations and, 23
　integration into conjunto music, 38–39, 64, 102
　mention of, 191
Bone, Ponty, 122
Borjas, Cuco, 341
Borjas, Gil, 341
Brave Combo, 108, 122, 124
Bravo, Joe, 52, 207
Los Bravos del Norte, 42, 63
Bronco (group), 74
Los Broncos de Reynosa, 78
Brown Express, 91
Buckwheat Dural, 122
Buena Suerte Records, 192
Bugarín, Pedro, 144
Burr, Ramiro, xix, xxiv
Buschmann, Friedrich, xix
Bustos, Louie, 146, 371

Caballero, Lorenzo, 63
Cáceres, David, 153
Cáceres, Ernie, 153
Los Cachorros de Juan Villarreal, 339
Cadena, Chano, 350
Los Cadetes de Linares, 76, 246, 248
Cajun music, 109, 110, 122
Camacho, Ray, 146
Los Caminantes, *175*
Canales, Johnny, 356
Canales, Laura, xix, 229
　career, 93–94
　on conjunto music, 94, 95
Los Canarios, 140
Canasta (label), 90
canción ranchera
　chord progression in, 52
　in conjunto music, 18–19, 22, 38, 42, 191, 221, 225
　defined, 9

canción ranchera (continued)
  Valerio Longoria popularizes, 64
  in *orquesta tejana,* 206
  in Tejano music (early/classic), 191
  in Tejano music (progressive conjunto), 217
cantinas. See performance venues
Cantú, Laura. *See* Carmen y Laura
Cantú, Timoteo, 75
Capitol Records, 93–94, 149, 208
Los Cardenales, 140
Carlos y José, 73, 76, 78, 340
Carmen y Laura
  career, 88–89
  mentions of, xix, 75, 83
Carozza, Alex, 115, 120
La Carpa Monsiváis, 83
carpas. See performance venues
Carrasco, Joe "King," 122
Carrillo, Tacho, 140
CASA, 365
Casiano, Jesús "El Gallito," 61, 290
Catacalos, David, 358
Cavazos, Lolo
  musical style, 36, 61
  recordings, 15, 17
CBS Records, 192, 197, 208
Centro Cultural del Pueblo, 368
Los Chachos, 103
Los Chamacos, 348
Charles, Ray, 350
Chavarría, Al "Chato," 90
Chavarría, Alfonso, 75
Chavarría, Martín, 75
Chavela (Isabel Salaiza)
  career, 91–92, 235
  death of, 373
  mentions of, xix, 299
  on women in conjunto, 91–92
Chavela y su Grupo Express, 235
Chávez, Cathy, 93
Chávez, Luis, 147
Chenier, Clifton, 122
chicanismo and names of ensembles, 195

Chicano Art Students Association. *See* CASA
Chicano culture. *See also* Chicano Movement; Chicano social classes; Tejano culture
  accordion and, 358
  audience characteristics and, 206
  collective narrative, 247–248
  cultural resistance, 251
  dances and, 241–242
  gender roles, 229–230, 238, 251
  Hispanic Generation, 201–202
  leadership and gender, 235–237
  music and, 206, 369–370
  musicians as bearer-communicators of, 200
  segregation by gender, 231
  social norms, 244–246
  transmission of, 367
  view of dances, 251–252
  women in, 85–86, 94, 229
Chicano Movement. *See also* Chicano culture
  Little Joe's repertoire and, 207
  relationship to *orquesta* music, 207–208
  Tejano music and, 195–196
  views of, 364–367
Chicano music. *See also* conjunto music; *orquesta tejana;* Tejano music (early/classic); Tejano music (progressive conjunto)
  audience characteristics, 199
  defined, 202
  hybridization of, 200–201, 205, 209
Chicano music industry. *See also* music industry; Tejano music industry
  development of, 5–6
  radio programming affected by, 192–193
Chicano Renaissance, 366
Chicano social classes
  attitudes of divided classes, 54–55

development of conjunto music
and, 24–27, 55–56, 65–67, 102,
199, 206
development of *orquesta* music
and, 43, 56–58, 118, 207
economic differentiation and, 4,
54, 201
evolution of, 24–25, 66, 201
expressions of in *música tejana*,
31–32, 39
middle-class characteristics, 201–
202
music and upward mobility of, 50,
66
music preferences and, 5, 200
performance venues and, 203–206
working-class characteristics, 201
Los Chicanos, 195
Chicanos Artistas Sirviendo a
Aztlan. *See* CASA
"La chicharronera," 15, 16, 78
Chicho y Chencho, 75
Chicken Skin Music, 217
Chief Recording Studios, 356
chord variations, 52, 146, 148, 224
chotís (schottische). *See* dance types
"El chubasco," 73, 91
Los Chukos, 104
Chulas Fronteras (film), 197
"Cielito Polka," 291, 373
Cisneros, Henry, 107
Cobb, James (poster by), 165
Colorado, Juan, 78, 144
Columbia Records, 62, 89, 273, 292
Cometa Records, 90, 91
Compeán, Chuy, 144, 151
La Conexión Mexicana, 195
Conjunto Aztlan, 366, 369, 370
musical style, 377
Conjunto Bernal, xix, 97–105. *See
also* Bernal, Paulino; Los Herma-
nitos Bernal
as conjunto gospel group, 103
decline of, 103
formation of, 99

innovations in conjunto music, 21–
22, 23, 40–42, 64
musical style, 22, 99–103
popular songs of, 104
recordings, 83
at Tejano Conjunto Festival, 371
trío style in, 338
vocals and vocalists in, 41, 83,
101, 102, 338, 350
El Conjunto de Bennie Medina, 87
El Conjunto de Lupita Rodela, 92
conjunto ensembles. *See also* accordion; conjunto music; performance venues; women in conjunto music; *specific instruments;
specific musicians; specific names
of conjuntos*
amplification in, 202
conjunto duos, 89
gender and, 230, 235–238
instrumentation, xv, 5, 6, 7–8, 14,
15, 33–34, 39, 97, 98, 369–370,
374
leadership of, 235–237
saxophone in, 14, 23, 141–153
sexual tension in, 237–238
traditional, 20, 39, 65, 82, 129,
191, 202, 217, 229, 341
traditional instrumentation, 224
Conjunto Estrella de Miguel Allende,
140
Conjunto Falcón, 163
conjunto music. *See also* audience
characteristics; Chicano music;
conjunto ensembles; Conjunto
Music Hall of Fame; musical
style; performance venues; Tejano
Conjunto Festival; Tejano music;
women in conjunto music; *specific conjuntos; specific musicians*
as Chicano music, 369–370
Chicano social classes and emergence of, 24–27, 55–56, 65–67
chord variations, 52, 146, 148,
224

conjunto music *(continued)*
  commercial distribution of, 17, 28–29
  community role of, 224, 356
  compared with *orquesta*, 26, 275
  complexity in, 225, 287, 344
  conjunto gospel music, 103
  conservative turn in development, 42, 59, 65–66
  contrasted with pop music, 67–68
  convergence with *norteño*, 79–80, 153
  convergence with *orquesta*, 23, 27–28, 34, 39, 45, 208–209, 375
  creativity versus continuity, 68–69
  cross-genre appeal, 199
  cross-genre experimentation, 207, 208–209, 218–219, 224
  cultural influence of, 208–209, 214, 215–217, 219, 223–224, 229, 230
  cultural influences on, 78–80, 225–226
  cumbia, xv, 191, 336, 340
  as dance music, 3–4, 6–7, 9, 18–19, 38, 88–89, *185*, 191, 242, 337
  defined, xiv–xv
  development as genre, 5–7, 14–23, 34–42, 61–69, 97–98, 191, 224, 225–226, 375
  economics of as profession, 17, 22, 93, 94, 95, 203, 288–289, 291
  economics of the market, 193, 208, 218, 220, 223–224
  elements of, 100–101, 369–370
  ethnicity and, 27–29
  future of, 294, 337, 340, 342, 345, 348, 350–351
  historical synopses, 131, 333–334
  image of, 85–86, 88, 94–95, 194, 369
  music industry and, 5–6, 17–18, 74–76, 220–221, 223–224
  musical taste, 108, 342, 349
  norteño music affected by, 193–194
  origins of, 4–5, 229
  popularity of, 3, 15–16, 18, 28–29, 62–63, 219, 225, 344
  popularization of, xv–xvi
  radio broadcast of, 211–213, 221
  relation to other musical styles, 109
  relation to Tejano music, 208–209, 223–224
  relationship to *norteño* music, 13–14, 347
  relationship to *orquesta*, 32, 58–59
  rhythm, 9, 219
  scholarship in, xvii, 287, 372
  singers, 87–91, 233–234, 236
  stylistic development, 17–18, 19–23, 27, 38–39, 77, 334
  Tejano compared to Mexican conjunto, 345
  Tejano music industry's effect on, 223–224
  tempo, 6–7, 16, 19, 27, 341–342, 348–349
  vocals in, 38, 87–89, 98, 100, 101
Conjunto Music Hall of Fame, xvi, 370, 373
  award statue for, *159*, 372
  bajo sexto players, 81–84
  Valerio Longoria inducted into, 288
  Lydia Mendoza accepting award, *159*
  Bruno Villarreal inducted into, 309
conjunto musicians. *See also specific musicians*
  characteristics of, 35
contrabajo. *See tololoche*
contrabass (upright bass). *See tololoche*
Cooder, Ry
  on accordions, 117
  collaboration with Flaco Jiménez, 217–218

mentions of, 121, 197
musicians worked with, 145, 151, 217–218
Cornelio Reyna y su Conjunto, 78
Corona (label), 37, 273, 292
Corrales, Carlos, 89
corridos, 225
  Américo Paredes on, 215
  in Tejano music, 207, 217
Costello, Elvis, 121
Los Costeños, 75
"El Cotulla," 271, 358
Count Basie, 350
Cruz, Alfredo, 366
El Cuarteto Carta Blanca, 87
Cuéllar, José, xx
cultural identity. See also cultural symbols; Tejano culture
  conjunto music and, 215–217, 219, 230
  heroes, 220
  music and, 207, 214, 222, 225
cultural symbols. See also accordion; conjunto music; cultural identity; *lo ranchero*
  campesino, 46, 85
  charro, 46
  lo moderno, 47–48
  music as, 224–225
cumbia. See dance types in conjunto music
Czech culture, 141–142

La Dama del Acordeón. See Chavela
dance styles (polka)
  serruchito, xiv, 7, 348
  tacuachito, xiv, 6–7, 20–21, 27, 63, 335, 348
  tiezo, 7, 348
dance types, 241, 276
  Aztec traditional dance, 367
  effect of musical style on, 20–21
  German influence, 268, 276–277
  huapango, 276
  in *orquesta* music, 48, 206
  Paul Jones, 277
  in Tejano music, 221
  waltz, 276
dance types in conjunto music, 3–4, 6–7, 9, 18–19, 38, 88–89, 185, 191, 242
  cumbia, xv, 276, 336, 340
    Tony de la Rosa on, 341
  huapango, 38, 276
  polka, xv, 18–19, 64, 344
  waltz, 337
dances (events), xiii–xiv, 6, 241–242, 289–290
  audience characteristics, 242
  bailes de negocio, 308
  bailes de patio, 357
  bailes de regalo, 251–252
  changes in, 250, 251–252
  devil figure and, xxi, 247–252
  early versions, 268
  economics of, 86, 288–289
  gender roles at, 251
dancing
  at *bailes,* xiv
  class and, 5
  description of, 241
  at Tejano Conjunto Festival, 185
la danza azteca, 367
  philosophy, 376–377
David Lee Garza y los Musicales, 135, 150, 222, 375
Dávila, Albert, 94–95
Dávila family, 193, 269
Dávila, Rick "Güero Polkas," 212
  promotion of conjunto music and, 211–213, 214–215, 225
"De China a Bravo," 75, 78
de la Rosa, Adán, 90
de la Rosa, Eva, 90
de la Rosa, Tony, 162
  on Paulino Bernal, 104
  career, 39–40, 42, 64
  collaborations, 143, 152
  compared to other musicians, 212
  conjunto ensemble of, 19–20

de la Rosa, Tony *(continued)*
  on conjunto music and musicians, xiii
  on conjunto style, 322–325, 340–343
  heart attack, 373–374
  inducted into Conjunto Music Hall of Fame, 370
  influences on, 340, 342
  instrumentation, 217
  instrumentation with saxophone, 151–152
  Flaco Jiménez on, 346
  mentions of, 22, 74, 77, 78, 83, 107, 144, 204, 218, 220, 336, 349, 350
  on musical cycles, 342
  musical style, xiii, 20, 39, 40, 64, 98, 143, 343
  musicians worked with, 151
  personal background, 39
  recordings by, 20, 40, 88, 151–152, 293
  tempo and, 338, 341–342
de León, Arnoldo, 216
de Monteclaro, Lorenzo, 141
Decca, 270, 273
Degollado, Johnny, 107
Delgado, Roosevelt, 140
"Las delicias," 44, 142
Demian, Cyril, xix, 76
devil figure
  in collective narrative, 244, 247–248
  reasons for appearance, 249–250
  in Tejano Conjunto Festival poster, xxi
  variation in views of, 243, 245, 249–251
Los Diamantes del Norte, 204
"Dices pescao," 17, 269
La Diferenzia, 153, 375
Dina (label), 90
Los Dinámicos
  recordings, 140–141

Los Diositos
  instrumentation, 73
Discos Bernal, 90
Discos Falcón. *See* Falcón Records
Discos Fama, 91
Discos Ideal. *See* Ideal Records
Discos Joey. *See* Joey Records
DLB Records, 88, 89, 91
Los Donneños, 63, 77, 78, 335
Los Dos Gilbertos, 90, 108, 293, 347
Los Dos Rancheros, 77
Dovalina, Ismael, xxii, 355, 356–358
drums
  in Conjunto Bernal, 22
  in conjunto ensembles, 8, 20, 39, 64, 129
  players of, 358, 362
Dueto Carta Blanca de George y Mague (Orozco), 90–91

E., Santiago, 75
Eduardo Martínez Orchestra, 88
Edward, Jimmy (Jimmy Edward Treviño)
  colleagues of, 146
  diversity of sound types, 52, 59
Elizondo, Pablo, 74, 77
Ely, Joe, 122
Emilio Navaira y Río, 135, 148, 149, 150. *See also* Navaira, Emilio
Encanto, 93
Escobar, Linda, 90
Escobedo, Gibby, 147, 149, 150
Espinoza, Benito, 340
Esquivel, José (poster by), 174
Esteban Jordán y su Río Jordán, 371
ethnicity. *See also* Chicano culture; Chicano Movement
  cultural resistance and, 72
  relationship between *orquesta* and conjunto and, 28, 33–34
Eva de la Rosa y su Conjunto, 90
Eva Ybarra y Sistema, 93
"La Evangelina," 75, 78

Falcón Records, 192
  musicians recording with, 88, 89, 139, 291–292
La Familia Fama, 299
Fandango USA, 222
Farías family, 231–232
Father of Conjunto Music. *See* Martínez, Narciso
Fernández, Rosita "San Antonio's First Lady of Song," 88
Festival Estudiantil Chicano de Arte y Literatura, 365–366
Finch, Carl, 124
Firma (label), 293
Flaco's Amigos, 151
Flores, Amadeo, 83
Flores, Ángel, 74, 77, 223, 349
Flores, Jimmy, 91, 146
Flores Peregrino, José, xxii
  joins Conjunto Aztlan, 366
Floricantos, 366
Fonovisa (recording company), 92
Four Star (label), 88
Frank Alonzo y sus Rancheros, 144
Freddie Records, 90, 192

Gabriel, Peter, 124
Gaitán y Cantú, 83
Los Gallardos, 360
Gaona, Marcelo, 174
Garcés, Daniel, 83, *158*, 346
García, Elsa, 229, 375
García, Gilberto, 347
García, Lalo, 74, 76, 77, 140
García, Richard, 216
García, Roger (poster by), *172*
García, Salvador, 339
García Tijerina, Abelardo, 141
García Torres, Salvador, 346
Garnica Ascencio sisters, 75
Garza, Álvaro, 140
Garza, David Lee
  awards, 149
  mentions of, 135, 148
  musical style, 152, 222, 375

Garza, Mike, *175*
Garza, Rubén, *184*
Garza Guajardo, Gustavo, 136–137
Gasca, Louie, 344
Gato Negro, 356
Los Gatos, xvi, 153
Gaytán, Juan, 75, 88
gender issues. *See* Chicano culture; conjunto ensembles; women in conjunto music
German-style accordions, 117–118
Globe Style Records, 122
Gloria, Lencho, 137
Gómez, Al, 371
Gómez, Frank, 146
Gómez Flores, Carlos, xix
Gonzales, Corky, 192
Gonzales, Ismael
  inducted into Conjunto Music Hall of Fame, 373
González, Balde, 67, 144, 337
  musical style of, 48–49
González, Carlos, 56
González, Jesús David (poster by), *178*
González, Pepe, 139
González, Tommy, 151
Los Gorriones del Topo Chico, 78, 139, 140, 147
Graceland, 121, 124
Grammy Awards, 121–122, 124. *See also* awards and honors in Tejano music
Gramsci, Antonio, 199–200
El Grupo Express, 91
El Grupo Mayo, 90
Los Guadalupanos de Joey López, 90, 91
Guadalupe Cultural Arts Center. *See also* Tejano Conjunto Festival en San Antonio
  activities and programs of, xvi, 197
  mentions of, 107, 222
  mission of, xv

Guadalupe Cultural Arts Center
  (*continued*)
  music education, 232, 356–357, 370, 376
  origins of, 368
  Tejano Conjunto Festival as program of, xv–xvi, 196, 369
Guadalupe Theater, 369
Güero Polkas. *See* Dávila, Rick
Guerra, Carlos, xviii, xix
Guerra, Manuel (Manny), 152
Guerra, Rudy, 152
Guerrero, Lalo "El Piporro," 140
Guerrero, Lonnie, xxii
Guerrero, Manuel, 107, 370
  death of, 373
  mentions of, 93, 341, 346
Guerrero, Tony, 50–51, 65
Guevara, Jacinto (poster by), 175
Gurst, Art, 123
Gutiérrez, Eugenio, 19, 23, 144
Gutiérrez, Rogelio, 140–141
  mention of, 78
Gutiérrez, Salomé
  mention of, 152
  on musical ensembles, 86
  on women in conjunto music, 89
Guzmán, Carlos, 194
Guzmán, Clemente F. III (posters by), 173, 176

Hacienda Records, 192, 223
Halley, Jeffrey, xxi
harmonica, 116
La Herencia, 195
Las Hermanas Degollado, 89
Las Hermanas Góngora, 89
Los Hermanitos Bernal, 83, 99. *See also* Conjunto Bernal
Los Hermanos Ayala, 83
Los Hermanos Cadena, 90
Los Hermanos de la Rosa, 90
Los Hermanos Farías. *See* La Tropa F
Los Hermanos Prado, 78, 139
Los Hermanos Villarreal, 290

Hernández, Anselmo, 78
Hernández, Carlos, 146
Hernández, Eduardo, 92
Hernández, Joe "Little Joe." *See also* Little Joe and the Latinaires; Little Joe y la Familia
  career, 50–51
  musical style, 49–50, 207, 375
  as musician, 221
Hernández, Óscar
  Conjunto Bernal and, 41, 101, 103
  mentions of, 21, 74, 83, 93, 299, 341, 373
  musical style, 23, 77, 103–104, 335, 338
Hernández, Ramón, xix
Hernández, Rodolfo (Fito), 139–140
Herrera, Richard, 175
Hidalgo, David, 123
Hobbs, Gary, 147
Hohner (accordion manufacturer)
  harmonicas of, 355
  promotion of accordions, 119–120
  Rockordeon, 197
Hohner, Matthias, 116–117
Holly, Buddy, 212
Hooters (group), 121, 124
La Hora Anáhuac, 269
La Hora de Alice, 193
La Hora de Domingo Peña, 193
La Hora de Elpidio Barrera, 193
Hornsby, Bruce, 121
huapango. See dance types
Hunter, Rick (poster by), 179
El Huracán del Valle. *See* Martínez, Narciso
Los Huracanes del Norte, 135
Hyman, Rob
  on accordions versus synthesizers, 124

"I Am Joaquín" (poem), 192
Ideal Records, 44–45, 192, 373
  musicians recording with, 38, 40, 83, 88, 90, 291–292

Iglesias, Julio, 69
Las Incomparable Hermanas Ortiz, 91
Infante, Pedro, 87
In Lak' Ech (group), 366
instrumentation
  geographical roots of, 72–74
  song lyrics and, 73–74
Los Invasores de Nuevo León, 77
Irene y Fidel, 89

Jasso, Douglas (poster by), *169*
Jay, George, 152
jazz, 191
Jiménez, Braulio, 152
Jiménez, Chacha, 102, 103
Jiménez, Chago. *See* Jiménez, Santiago Jr.
Jiménez, David, *161*
Jiménez, Flaco, *161*, *175*
  on Paulino Bernal, 328
  career, 111, 121, 346
  collaboration with Pancho Villarreal, 151
  collaboration with Ry Cooder, 217–218
  collaboration with Texas Tornados, 218
  on conjunto styles, 327–330, 346–348
  diffusion of conjunto and, 205, 223
  instrumentation with saxophone, 151
  mentions of, 107, 205, 220, 272, 315, 333, 341
  musical style, 148, 205, 217–219, 344
  musicians worked with, 145, 218, 371
  popularization of accordion and, 222
  recordings, 151, 217, 218, 274–275
  at Tejano Conjunto Festival, *161*, 204, 370, 371

Jiménez, José Alfredo, 87
Jiménez, Leonardo. *See* Jiménez, Flaco
Jiménez, Patricio, 267–268, 269, 277
Jiménez, Santiago Jr., *184*
  mentions of, 107, 122, 205, 220, 272, 369
  as musician, 356, 357, 358
  relationship with Tejeda family, 362
  as teacher, 232, 356–357, 361–362
  at Tejano Conjunto Festival, 204, 371
Jiménez, Santiago Sr., *166*
  on accordion music, 275–276
  career, 17, 18, 37, 62, 269–273
  compared to other musicians, 212
  death of, 373
  inducted into Conjunto Music Hall of Fame, 370
  instrumentation, 270, 273
  on Patricio Jiménez (father) as musician, 267–268
  mentions of, 107, 122, 220, 223, 340, 346, 361, 368, 372
  musical style, 17, 97, 335, 349
  as musician, 346, 347
  musicians worked with, 151, 274, 371
  performance style, 273–274
  personal background, 17, 36, 268–69, 270–271, 271–272, 277–278
  recordings, 17, 62, 269, 270–271, 273, 274
  at Tejano Conjunto Festival, 371
Joe "King" Carrasco y las Nuevas Coronas, 108–109
Joe Patek Orchestra, 142
Joey Records, 223, 274, 293
Jordán, Esteban, *181*
  on accordions versus synthesizers, 120, 124

Jordán, Esteban *(continued)*
  on Paulino Bernal, 104–105
  on conjunto styles, 330–332, 342, 348–351
  inducted into Conjunto Music Hall of Fame, 370
  influences on, 349–350
  mentions of, 21, 23, 68, 102, 107, 108, 122, 205, 315, 333, 341, 358
  musical style, 205, 293–294, 335, 338, 341, 343–344, 346
  musicians worked with, 372
  performances, 115, 120
  at Tejano Conjunto Festival, *181*, 371
Jordan, Steve. *See* Jordán, Esteban
José Ángel Reyes y los Norteños de China, 78
Juan Ramos y los Príncipes de Nuevo Laredo, 204

KCOR (radio station), 358
KEDA-AM "Radio Jalapeño"
  format evolution, 212–213
  mentions of, 220, 225, 358
  promotion of conjunto music, 211–212, 222–223, 224
  Santiago Jiménez, Sr., and, 269
  support of Tejano Conjunto Festival, 369
KINE (radio station), 193
King, Ben, 368–369
KOPY (radio station), 193
KRIO-FM, 221
KVAR "La Fiera" (radio station), 358
KXTN-FM, 221

Lalo García y su Conjunto, 78, 140
language
  in Chicano music, 202
  cultural bias and, 192–193
Lara, Agustín, 87
Lares, Shelly, 93, 229

Latin American Theatrical Association, 368
Latin Breed, 52, 148, 152, 195, 222
Latin Playerz, 153
Laureano, "Tío," 145
"Los laureles," 58, 362
Le Grand, Jeanne, 93, 229
leadership in groups, 235–237, 373
League of United Chicano Artists, 365
Liberty Band, 222
Límite, 74
Limón, José, xxi, xxiv
  background, 243
  mentions of, 216, 372
Little Joe and the Latinaires. *See also* Hernández, Joe; Little Joe y la Familia
  musical style of, 49–50
  the *ranchero* sound and, 50–51
  recordings of, 50–51
  renamed "y la Familia," 53, 195
Little Joe y la Familia. *See also* Hernández, Joe; Little Joe and the Latinaires
  mention of, 146
  as prototypic *orquesta tejana*, 207
  repertoire, 207
Llamas, Beatriz
  career, 89–90
  mention of, 83
Los Lobos, 108, *181*, 218
  Grammy award, 121
  musical style, 197, 339
  roots music and, 123
  at Tejano Conjunto Festival, *181*, 371
Lomas, Adán
  Conjunto Bernal and, 40, 83
Longoria, Valerio, *157*, *182*
  accordion modifications and, 119
  awards, 197
  on Paulino Bernal, 104
  career, 37–39, 64, 98, 288–289, 292–293
  collaborations, 151

compared to other musicians, 212
on conjunto styles, 293–294, 320–322, 338–340
in Germany, 290
inducted into Conjunto Music Hall of Fame, 370
instrumentation, 288–289
instrumentation with saxophone, 151
mentions of, 20, 88, 107, 127, 204, 218, 220, 315, 333, 335, 340, 346, 358, 372
musical background, 288
musical style, 343, 349
payment for performances, 288–289, 291
performance venues, 288–289, 290–291, 369
personal background, 292–293
on recording process, 292
as teacher, 182, 232, 370
Juan Tejeda visits, 373
tuning, 119, 287
vocals in musical style, 38, 339, 341, 343
López, Bob, 146
López, Isidro
career, 49, 144, 145
development of *orquesta,* 375
mentions of, 83, 88
musical style, 49, 152, 207
López, Joe, 151
López, Joey, 90, 91
López, Juan, 74, 77, 78
López, Lupe, 83
LUChA. *See* League of United Chicano Artists
Luévanos, Carmen, xix, xxiii
Luis y Julián (duo), 76
Lydia Mendoza y Familia, 75

Machito, 350
El Macho, 350
Macías, Alberto, 127, 129, 132–134
Macías, Gilberto, 127, 129

Macías, Luis, 132–134
Macías, Martín
bajo sexto made by, *183*
as craftsman, 127, 132–134, 371
death of, 373
inducted into Conjunto Music Hall of Fame, 371
Los Madrugadores, 78
La Mafia, 149, 208, 356
instrumentation, 151
Los Magníficos, 203
Maltos, Valentín, 150–151
Mancini, Henry, 350
mariachi groups, 86, 192, 194
Mariachi Project, 368, 369
market for conjunto music. *See* audience characteristics
market for Tejano music. *See* audience characteristics
Marroquín, Armando
Conjunto Bernal and, 40
death of, 373
Ideal Records and, 88
mention of, 82
recordings, 83, 142–143
on Beto Villa, 44, 47
Marroquín, Carmen. *See* Carmen y Laura
Martha, Manuel, 137
Martin (label), 142
Martínez, Bernardo, 341
Martínez, Cookie, 358
Martínez, Freddie, 52, 194
Martínez, Jesús, 138
Martínez, Jet, 93
Martínez, Lupe, 75
Martínez, Marc, 150
Martínez, Max, xix
Martínez, Mencho, 77
Martínez, Narciso, 21, *157, 158*
accordion in conjunto of, 336
career, 14, 17, 18, 35–36, 62–63, 122, 337
collaboration with Beto Villa, 45, 143

Martínez, Narciso *(continued)*
  compared to other musicians, 212
  conjunto development and, 315–316, 333–334
  on conjunto ensemble, 82
  on conjunto versus *orquesta*, 26, 27–28
  on conjunto styles, 317–319, 334–337
  emergence of conjunto music and, 15–16, 287, 288
  inducted into Conjunto Music Hall of Fame, 370
  influenced by José Rodríguez, 61–62
  influences on, 335
  interviewed by Juan Tejeda, 373
  mentions of, 74, 75, 76, 78, 88, 107, 132, 218, 220, 346
  musical style, 16–17, 36, 62–63, 77, 97, 343, 349
  personal background, 16, 35
  recordings, 16, 36, 61, 82, 336
  relationship with Santiago Almeida, 82
  relationship with Pedro Ayala, 62
  saxophone in ensemble, 153
  vocal music and, 21–22, 336
Martínez, Rudy, 308
Mata, Ben (poster by), 177
Matamoros, Tony, 146
MAYO. *See* Mexican American Youth Organization
Mazz, 135, 208, 222, 356
  instrumentation, 151
  musical style, 375
Mellencamp, John Cougar, 121
Mendoza, Danny, 366
Mendoza, Juanita, 75
Mendoza, Leonora, 75
Mendoza, Lydia, *159*
  awards and honors, 88, *159*
  career, 87–88, 234
  mentions of, xix, 75
  personal background, 87–88
  recordings, 87–88
  on *La Voz Latina*, 87
Mendoza, Manuel, 75
Mendoza, María, 75
Mercury Records, 273
Mexican American. *See* Chicano
Mexican American Youth Organization (MAYO), 365
Mexican Revolution (group), 195, 355
Meyers, Augie, 108, *181*, 371
  mention of, 122
"Mi único camino," 22, 338
Mission County Park, 204, 370
Molina, Tony, 151
Monje, Jesús (Chucho), 75
Los Montañeses del Álamo, 73, 78
  recordings by, 137
  saxophone in ensemble, 137–138
Montejano, David, 216
Montemayor, Óscar, 150
"Monterrey," 139, 143, 144
Montes, Mario, 74, 77
Morales, Joe, 151
Morales, Rocky, 371
Morton, Susana Nevárez, xxii–xxiii
"Mujer paseada," 99
Muñiz, Ramsey, 365
music education
  accordion classes, 232
  barriers to women, 230–232
  mentor system, 321–232
music industry (major labels). *See also* Chicano music industry; Tejano music industry
  competition and, 62
  conjunto music and, 5–6, 17–18, 28–29, 35
  Tejano music (progressive conjunto) in, 224
música tejana. *See* Tejano music
música tropical, 207
musical experimentation, 224. *See also* chord variations; tempo; tuning

musical style. *See also specific musicians*
  chord variations, 52, 146, 148, 224
  complexity in, 52, 225, 344
  in conjunto music, 8–9, 97–98, 152, 191, 202, 214, 215, 347
  creativity and, 339
  cross-genre adaptations, 224
  cycles in, 342
  defined, 33
  Kineño style, 350
  music education's effect on, 194–195
  in *orquesta tejana*, 51–53, 191, 206–209, 207
  as response to sociocultural environment, 33, 344–345
  saxophone, 137, 145–146, 148, 149, 152
  singers and, 350
  success and, 342, 343
  tempo and, 338, 339, 341–342, 348–349
  traditional instruments, 73, 98
  tuning, 98, 347
musicians. *See also specific musicians*
  lifestyle of active, 233
  musical education, 230–231
  as organic intellectuals, 200
  skill development, 230–231

Nacel, Miguel, 358
Los Nacionales de Linares, 140
NACS. *See* National Association for Chicano Studies
Nagata, Ichiro, 153
Naranjo, Bobby, 103, 104, 341
Naranjo, Rubén, 76, 340, 350
National Association for Chicano Studies (NACS), 366
Navaira, Emilio
  mentions of, 93, 122, 208
  musical style, 152, 222, 375
  as musician, 147, 149
  musicians worked with, 148, 149
Navarro, Robert, 146
Nezahualcoyotl, 359
nightclubs. *See* performance venues
Niño, Arturo, 63
norteño music
  accordions and accordionists, 76–78
  chord variations, 146
  conjunto's effect on, 193–194
  convergence with conjunto, 79–80, 153
  cultural influences on, 78–80
  ensemble instruments, 14, 73
  musical style, 148
  relationship to conjunto, 13–14, 77–80
Los Norteños de Nuevo Laredo, 140–141

Olivares, Fito, 140
Olivares, Víctor, 291
la onda chicana, 53, 93
La Onda Chicana (group), 195
organic intellectual
  defined, 200
Orozco, George and Mague, 90–91
Orquesta Falcón, 87
orquesta tejana. *See also* Chicano music; conjunto ensembles; conjunto music; musical style; Tejano music (early/classic); Tejano music (progressive conjunto)
  convergence with conjunto music, 19, 23, 27–28, 34, 51, 375
  dance music and, 18, 48, 191
  at dances, 242
  description, 374–375
  development as genre, 42–53, 191, 206–209, 375
  economics of style and, 52–53, 207
  the "high class" (*jaitón*) versus *ranchero* sound in, 51–52

Index ✧ 433

orquesta tejana (continued)
   instrumentation, 14, 33–34, 118, 120, 202
   music education's effect on, 194–195
   musical influences on, 28, 217
   relationship to conjunto music, 26, 32, 58–59
   social class and, 42–43, 51–53, 56–58, 206
   stylistic variation within and among *orquestas*, 48, 51–52
   Tejano Music Awards and, 197
orquesta típica
   class and, 5, 118
   instrumentation, 4, 6, 118
   popularity of, 337
Ortiz, Tomás, 161
Óscar G. y Grupo Sol, 376
Owens, Buck, 197
Ozuna, Sunny
   career, 51
   in films, 194
   mentions of, 93, 207
   musical style, 49–50, 52, 207

Padilla, Margarita, 75
Padilla, María, 75
Los Paisanos de Chalito Johnson, 104, 107, 369, 370
Palafox, Manuel, 146
Panchito Villarreal y su Conjunto, 145
Para la Gente, 53
Paredes, Américo
   on *corridos*, 215
   ethnographic transcriptions by, xxiv
   on festivals, 107
   Tejano cultural development, 213
Partners, 151
La Patria, 195
Los Pavos Reales, 339, 346
"La pecosita," 139, 143
Peña, Armando, 41
Peña, Devon, 366

Peña, Manuel, xviii, xxiv
   on conjunto musical style, 214, 225–226
   on cultural symbols, 213
   mention of, 372
Perales, Jesse, 151
Pérez, Danny, 146
Pérez, Darío, 144
Pérez, Gilberto, 350
Pérez, Jay, 135
   colleagues of, 147
   as musician, 150, 152, 222
   recordings, 149, 151
Pérez, Joey, 146
Pérez, Louie, 123
Pérez, Rubén "La Pulga," 350
   Conjunto Bernal and, 41, 83, 102, 338
Performance Artists Nucleus, Inc., 368, 369
   becomes Guadalupe Cultural Arts Center, 369
performance venues. *See also* audience characteristics; Tejano Conjunto Festival
   Arneson River Theater, 369
   avant-garde conjunto venues, 205–206
   bailes de negocio, 308
   Brackenridge Park, 369
   cantinas, 203
   citywide and regional clubs, 204
   dance halls, 290, 360
   dance platforms, 289
   large festivals, 204–205
   neighborhood venues, 202
   norteño neighborhood venues, 203–204
   parks and local festivals, 87, 204
   range of, 86, 87, 362, 366
   Tejano music, 192
"La Piedrera," 62, 271, 335, 361
Pineda, Delia, 56
Pineda, Moy
   on class and music, 56, 58

La Pistola y el Corazón, 121, 123
plataformas. See performance venues
polkas. *See also* dance styles
  in conjunto music, xv, 18–19, 64, 344
  in *orquesta* music, 48
Polygram, 208
Los Populares de China, 139, 140
"Por qué te ríes," 44, 142
El Porvenir Jazz Group, 137
Posada, Joe
  career, 149–150
  colleagues of, 147
  as musician, 146
Prado, Julio, 140
Prado, Valentín, 140
Presley, Elvis, 212
Primavera, 135
Los Príncipes de Raymundo Valero, 145
Profono (label), 92
Puente, Tito, 350
Pulido, Joel "El Gordo," 152
Pulido, Raúl "El Flaco," 152
Pulido, Roberto, 188. *See also* Roberto Pulido y los Clásicos
  conjunto and *orquesta* synthesis and, 23, 59, 65, 152, 188, 375
  mention of, 337
  as musician, 222
  at Tejano Conjunto Festival, *188,* 204

Queen Ida and the Bon Temps Zydeco Band, 122, *181*
Queen of Tejano Music. *See* Canales, Laura
Quezada, Guadalupe, 138, 139
Quezada, Salomón, 104
Quintanilla, Sunny, 93
Quintanilla Pérez, Selena. *See* Selena

radio
  audience characteristics and, 221
  conjunto music on, 193, 221, 224, 230, 269
  cultural identity and, 214, 221, 224
  economics of programming, 193, 208
  influence on musical styles, 74–76, 78–80, 212–213, 214
  Tejano culture and, 192–193
  Tejano music on, 192, 221
Radio Jalapeño. *See* KEDA-AM
Rafael Silva y su Conjunto, 78
Ragland, Cathy, xxi
Ramírez, Agustín, 52, 146
Ramírez, Bobby, 366
Ramírez, Daniel, 75
Ramírez, Janie C., 93
Ramírez, Kiko, 366
Ramírez, Santos, 140
Ramón Ayala y los Bravos del Norte, 108, 161
Ramos, Alfonso, 146
Ramos, Joe, 103
Ramos, Rubén, 146
Los Rancheritos del Topo Chico, 139, 147
lo ranchero. See also canción ranchera; cultural symbols
  Conjunto Bernal and *ranchero* sound, 41
  cultural concept described, 45–46
  as link between *orquesta* and conjunto, 44
  orquesta following *ranchero* sound, 52
  orquesta tejana and, 27
  separation of classes and musics and, 24–25
Randolph, Boots, 152
Rangel and Company, 291
Rangel, Cecilia (artist), 372
Rangel, Mr., 291
La Raza (group), 195
Raza Unida Party, 196, 365
RCA Victor, 62, 197, 292
  musicians recording with, 89, 273
redovas. See dance types

Reforma o . . . Revolución (group), 366
regional festivals, 205
regional (Mexican). *See* norteño music
regional (Tejano). *See* conjunto music
Los Regionales de Linares, 139
Los Relámpagos del Norte, 42, 63
Rendón, Al, xvii
Reyes, Gerardo, 41, 102
Reyes, José Ángel, 75
Reyes, Laura, 93
Reyna, Cornelio, 78, 194, 349
Reyna, José, xxi, 372
Reyna-Ovalle, Priscilla (poster by), 167
rhythm
  in conjunto music, 219
  European rhythms in border music, 71
  Santiago Jiménez, Sr., on, 275
Rich, Adrienne
  on the arts, 358
Rich, Buddy, 350
Los Rieleros, 135
Rifón, Joseph, 146
Ríos, Javier
  on accordionists, 77
  on *norteño* versus conjunto, 77–78
Rivas, George, 145
Rizardi, Aldo, 93
Roberto Pulido y los Clásicos, 208
  mentions of, 108, 135
  musical style, 59, 104, 152, 188, 375
Rocha, Pedro, 75
rock music, 191
Rockin' Ravens, 152
Rockin' Sidney, 122
Rockordeon, 118–119, 197
Rodela, Lupita, xix, *187*
  career, 92
  Flaco Jiménez and, 92, 234
  mention of, 299
  music education, 232
  as musician, 234
  on women in conjunto music, 95

Rodeo (group), 149
Rodríguez, José, 36, 61–62
Rodríguez, R., 75
Rodríguez, Tito, 350
Rogelio Gutiérrez y su Conjunto, 78
Rolling Stone (magazine), 121
Ronstadt, Linda, 218
roots music, 123, 124
  conjunto music as, 219
Rosedale Park, 204, 370
"Rosita vals," 19, 45, 143
Rosita y Laura, 88. *See also* Cantú, Laura
Rositas, Roy, 146
Rounder Records, 197, 218, 223, 234
Royal Jesters, 146, 149, 152
Rubén Naranjo y los Gamblers, 107–108, 204
Rubén Vela y su Conjunto, *158*
La Rubia y la Morena, 349
Rubin, Mark, 358

Sáenz, Rubén, 83
Sahm, Doug, 108, *181*, 371
Salaiza, Isabel. *See* Chavela
Saldívar, Joe, xxii, xxiv
Saldívar, Mingo, *186*
  mentions of, xxiv, 223, 224, 372
Salinas, Beto, 103, 341
salones de baile. *See* performance venues
salsa, 191
San Antonio Consortium for the Hispanic Arts, 368
San Antonio Express-News, 368–369
Sánchez, Cuco, 87
Santiago Jiménez Jr. y su Conjunto, 362, 369. *See also* Jiménez, Santiago Jr.
Santiago Jiménez y sus Valedores, 335
Sax, Adolphe, 135

saxophone
  in conjunto ensemble, 14, 23, 141–153
  introduction into northeastern Mexico, 136–137, 153
  introduction into Texas, 141–142, 153
  keyboard substitute for, 147
  in *norteño* music, 136–141, 146
  styles of playing, 145–146, 148, 149, 152
  in Tejano music, 375
schottische. *See* dance types
Segura, Andrés, 367
Selena, 93, 221, 229, 234
el serruchito. *See* dance styles
Sifuentes, Juan, 350
  Conjunto Bernal and, 102
  writing with Eloy Bernal, 83
Silva, Chelo, xix, 89
Simon, Paul, 121, 124, 197
singers, 229, 233–234, 236. *See also* vocal music; *specific musicians*
  trío in conjunto music, 338, 341, 344, 350
Smith, Jimmy, 350
social classes. *See* Anglo American social classes; Chicano social classes
social environment
  of active musicians, 233–235
  conjunto-music style and, 19–21, 55, 68, 88, 98, 118
  conservative turn in conjunto and, 42
  cultural assimilation of *tejano* society, 54
  at dances, 245–246
  emergence of conjunto music and, 24–27, 31–32, 85–86
  orquesta styles and, 49–53, 118, 207–208
  sexual tensions in bands, 237–238
  vocal music and, 38
  work and, 71–72

Solís, Jimmy, 146
Solís, Manuel
  Conjunto Bernal and, 41, 83, 102
Sombrero (label), 90
The Sonny Boys, 43–45
Sosa, Roberto B. (posters by), 164, 166
Southside Kid, 203
Steve Jordan Tex-Mex Rockordeon. *See* Jordán, Esteban; Rockordeon
Stills, Stephen, 218
Strachwitz, Chris, 197
  on Bruno Villarreal, 308
  on Eva Ybarra, 93
Sueño (group), 145
Sunglows (group), 152
Sunny (Ozuna) and the Sunliners, 93, 146
  caters to middle-class audience, 51, 52
  as musician, 222
  orquesta development and, 375
Supremo (label), 90
synthesizer
  accordion contrasted with, 120, 124
  in *orquesta*, 65
  in Tejano music, 375

'Ta cincho (book), 366
taco circuit, 40, 64
el tacuachito. *See* dance styles
Talking Heads, 121, 197
Los Tall Boys, 145, 148
taloneros
  defined, 86 (*See also* conjunto ensembles)
tambora de rancho, 5, 14–15
Los Tamborileros de Linares, 78
Tanguma Guajardo, Antonio, 75–76, 77
tardeadas. *See* dances (events)
La Tejanita. *See* KEDA-AM
Tejano bands. *See orquesta tejana*

Tejano Conjunto Festival en San Antonio. *See also* Guadalupe Cultural Arts Center; *Tonantzin* (magazine); *specific musicians*
  accordion students' recital, 376
  audience characteristics, xvi, 108–109, 110, 111, 204–205
  beginnings of, 368–369
  The Best of the Eighth Annual Tejano Conjunto Festival, 152, 372
  The Best of the Eleventh Annual Tejano Conjunto Festival, 372
  Cajun/zydeco and, 109, 110
  "Conjunto Meets Cajun/Zydeco," *181,* 372
  cycle of musical styles in, 110–111
  first festival, xiii–xiv, 370–371
  founding of, xv, 369–370
  goals of, 370, 374
  highlights of, 107–111, 370–374, 376
  mentions of, 61, 122, 220, 232
  musicians appearing at, xiii, 103, 149, 150, 204, 234, 371, 372–373
  "New Directions in Conjunto Music," 108–110, *181,* 371
  posters for, xvi, xvii–xviii, xx–xxi, 370
  recognition for, 196
  response to, 108, 115
  San Antonio Express-News and, 368–369
  supporting conjunto music, xv–xvi, 222
  themes, xvi, 108, 110, 372
Tejano culture. *See also* Chicano culture
  versus Anglo American culture, 32
  conjunto music influenced by, 78–80
  development of, 213, 225–226
  heroes, 220
  identity development in, 222, 223
  interaction with Czech culture, 141–142
  mention of, 219
  music's role in developing, 207, 215, 225
  names of *orquestas* and conjuntos and, 195
  performance venues and, 203
  research on, 215–216
  support for conjunto music, 224
Tejano music (early/classic). *See also* Chicano music; conjunto music; musical style; *orquesta tejana;* Tejano music (progressive conjunto)
  crossing Mexican border, 193–194
  defined, xiv–xv
  development as genre, 191–198, 375
  as folk music, 197–198
Tejano music (progressive conjunto, *conjunto orquestal*). *See also* Chicano music
  chord variations, 148
  commercialization of, 208
  cross-genre experimentation, 218–219, 224
  cultural identity and, 214, 216, 222–223
  dance styles in, 221
  defined, 213, 221–222, 374–375
  development of, 153–154, 375
  hybridization in, 209
  instrumentation, 151
  integration of conjunto and *orquesta* into, 59, 208–209, 375
  musical style, 217, 275
  popularity of, 208, 209, 220–221, 223
  relation to conjunto music, 223–224
  singers, 229
Tejano Music Awards, 197
Tejano Music Hall of Fame inductees, 88

Tejano music industry, 5–6, 220–221, 223–224. *See also* music industry
  cultural identity and, 223
  economics and, 194
  radio programming and, 192–193
Tejeda, Armando, 377
Tejeda, Bobby, 362
Tejeda, Francisco Mariano, 360
Tejeda, José Antonio, 360
Tejeda, Juan, xv, xxii, xxiii
  as activist, 365
  la danza azteca and, 367, 376–377
  education, 361, 363–366
  Guadalupe Cultural Arts Center and, xv, 368
  Mariachi Project and, 368
  mention of, 107
  musical education, 271, 361–362
  musicians worked with, 373, 377
  plays with Santiago Jiménez, Jr., 362
Tejeda, Lillie Cisneros, 360
Tejeda, Rogelio, 360, 362
Tejeda, Santa Martínez, 360
Tejeda, Tony, 362
Tejidos (magazine), 366
tempo
  conjunto music, 6–7, 16, 20, 64, 348–349
  Tony de la Rosa on conjunto music, 340, 341–342
  Valerio Longoria on conjunto tempo, 338
  Valerio Longoria's use of, 343
Test Tube Babes, 109, 372
Texas Revolution, 146, 152
Texas Talent Musicians Association, 197
Texas Tornados, 218, 358
Texas Women Hall of Fame, 88
theaters. *See* performance venues
They Might Be Giants, 121
TH-Rodven Records, 91
Tierranegra, Carlos, 76

el tiezo. *See* dance styles
Los Tigres del Norte
  mentions of, 74, 92, 135, 148
Tijerina, Lupe, 76, 77
Tirado, Estevan, 140
tololoche
  Santiago Jiménez includes in ensemble, 17, 37
  players of, 358
  use in recording, 37
  and Juan Viesca, 160
Tonantzin (magazine). *See also* Tejano Conjunto Festival
  biographies in, 371–372
  coverage, xvi, 370, 372
Tonka y Libre, 104
Torres, Eddie (Lalo)
  mentions of, 87, 89, 204
Torres, Edén, xxii
Torres, Juan, 76–78
Torres, Patsy, 93
Torres, Toby, 91, 92, *182*, *183*, 358
  description of *bajo sexto*, 127–128
  mention of, 107
  as teacher, 183
  Tejano Conjunto Festival and, 373
Tortilla Factory, 65, 146, 195
Trece Aliens (book), 366
Trejo, Xavier, 376
Los Tremendos Gavilanes, 77
Los Tres Reyes, 63, 102, 344, 346
Treviño, Adrián, 94
Treviño, Jimmy Edward. *See* Edward, Jimmy
Treviño, Manuel, 139, 140
Treviño, Ramón, 103, 104
Treviño, Reymundo, 88
Trío Garnica Ascencio, 75
Trío los Conquistadores, 88
Trío los Panchos, 102, 344
Trío San Miguel, 88
tríos in conjunto music. *See* vocal music
La Tropa F, 222, 231, 370
Tumlinson, Jerry, xxii

"La tuna," 141, 269
tuning
  accordion, 4–5, 7–8, 98, 117–118, 119, 287, 347
  bajo quinto, 129
  bajo sexto, 8, 128, 132
two-tone accordions, 118

Los Únicos, 196
upright bass (contrabass). *See* tololoche

V., Linda, 93
Valdez, Avelardo, xv, xxi
Valerio Longoria y su Conjunto. *See also* Longoria, Valerio
  performances, 369
vals. See dance types
Vásquez, Thomas (posters by), 168, 170
Vela, Rubén, 184
  mentions of, 25, 63, 74, 77, 78, 204, 220, 315, 333
  musical style, 350
  tempo and, 338
Vienna-style accordions, 117, 118
Viesca, Juan, 160, 274
  death of, 160, 373
  lighting *tololoche*, 160
Vigil y Robles, E., 75
Villa, Beto
  career, 43–45, 142–144
  development of *orquesta*, 375
  Narciso Martínez and, 153
  mentions of, 23, 82, 83, 87, 88, 152, 337
  musical style, 147, 152
  musical-style changes, 45, 207
  the *ranchero* sound and, 44, 47
  recordings, 44–45, 139, 142–143
Villanueva, Marcelino F. Jr. (poster by), 163
Villarreal, Bruno "El Azote del Valle"
  on accordions, 310–311
  death of, 373
  mentions of, 220, 346
  music education, 311
  on musical style, 312–313
  performance venues, 314
  personal background, 308–309
  recordings, 15, 61, 97, 308, 310, 311–312
Villarreal, Frank (Panchito)
  career, 147–149
  musicians worked with, 145
Villarreal, Javier, 145
Villarreal, Juan, 76–77
Villarreal, Nick
  mentions of, 204, 223, 224, 315, 333, 372
  musical style, 205, 349
Villarreal, Pancho
  career, 145
  collaboration with Flaco Jiménez, 151
  influences on, 147
  musical style, 145–146
  personal background, 144–145
Villarreal, Ruco, 144–145
"Viva Seguín," 62, 271, 335, 361
vocal music. *See also* women in conjunto music
  accordion and, 336
  Los Alegres de Terán, 21–22
  Conjunto Bernal, 41, 83, 101, 102, 338
  Conjunto Female Vocalist of the Year, 90
  in conjunto music, 38, 98, 100, 101, 144, 350
  in *norteño* tradition, 137
  singers, 87–91, 229, 233–234, 236
  trío in conjunto music, 338, 341, 344, 350
Volcán (label), 293

Warner Brothers, 208, 218
Welk, Lawrence, 121

Westside Horns, 108, *181*, 371
Williams, Hank, 212
Wills, Bob, 212
women in conjunto music, 85–95, *159, 187*. *See also* Chicano culture; *specific conjuntos; specific musicians*
   accordionists, 91–93, 232, 234–235, 360, 373
   career barriers, 85–86, 94–95, 233–235, 238
   family support for, 232–235, 360
   instruments and, 231–232
   leadership and, 235–237, 373
   reasons for low numbers of, 94–95, 229–238
   sexual tension in bands, 237–238
   as singers, 87–91, 229, 233–234, 236
   women conjunto leaders, 92–93, 187

XETKR (radio station), 78
Xicano Music Program, xv
   beginnings, 369
   mention of, 107

Xinachtli, 367. *See also la danza azteca*
X-Men y Presente Band, 376

Ybarra, Eva, xix, *187*
   career, 92–93, 234–235, 299, 300
   mentions of, 223, 224, 372
   music education, 298
   musical style, 299
   personal background, 298
   on women accordionists, 299
Ybarra, Pedro, 93, 145, 299
Ybarra, Santos, 137–139
Yoakam, Dwight, 121, 218
Young, Ron, xx
Yturri, Frances, xxii

Zamen, 90
Zarape Records, 50, 192
Zimmerle, Fred, *158*
   as teacher, 232, 376
Zimmerle, Henry, *175*
   mention of, 107, 204
Zúñiga, Agapito, 145
zydeco, 109, 110, 122

CMAS BOOKS

✧

Puro Conjunto, An Album in Words and Pictures: Writings, Posters, and Photographs from the Tejano Conjunto Festival en San Antonio, 1982–1998 was designed by Jace Graf and Víctor Guerra. The text was composed primarily in Sabon, with Nueva used for display. The book was printed and bound by Thomson-Shore, Inc., of Dexter, Michigan. The color section was printed by the Whitley Company, of Austin, Texas.